FULL METAL PANIC OVERLOAD! 2

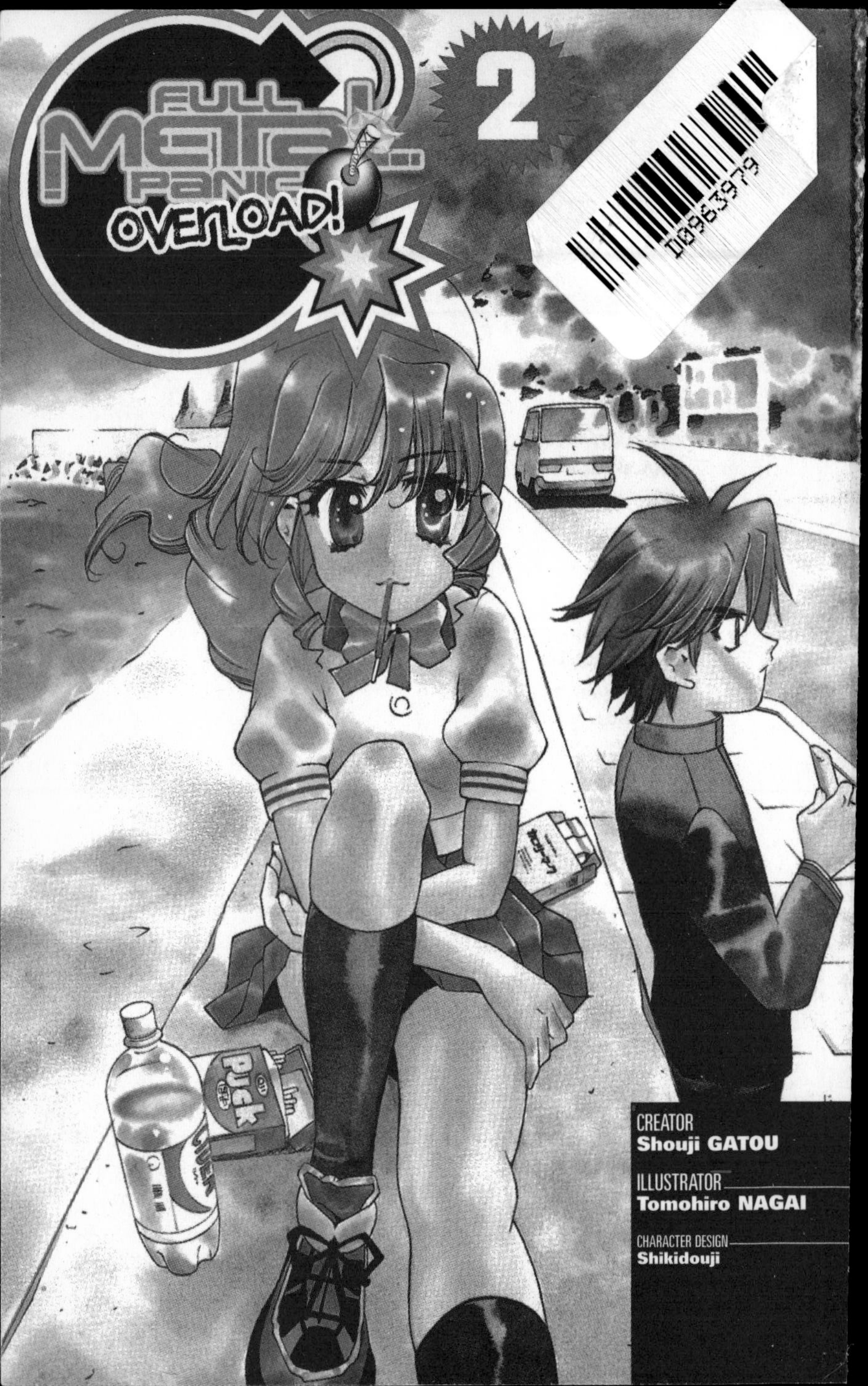

CREATOR
Shouji GATOU

ILLUSTRATOR
Tomohiro NAGAI

CHARACTER DESIGN
Shikidouji

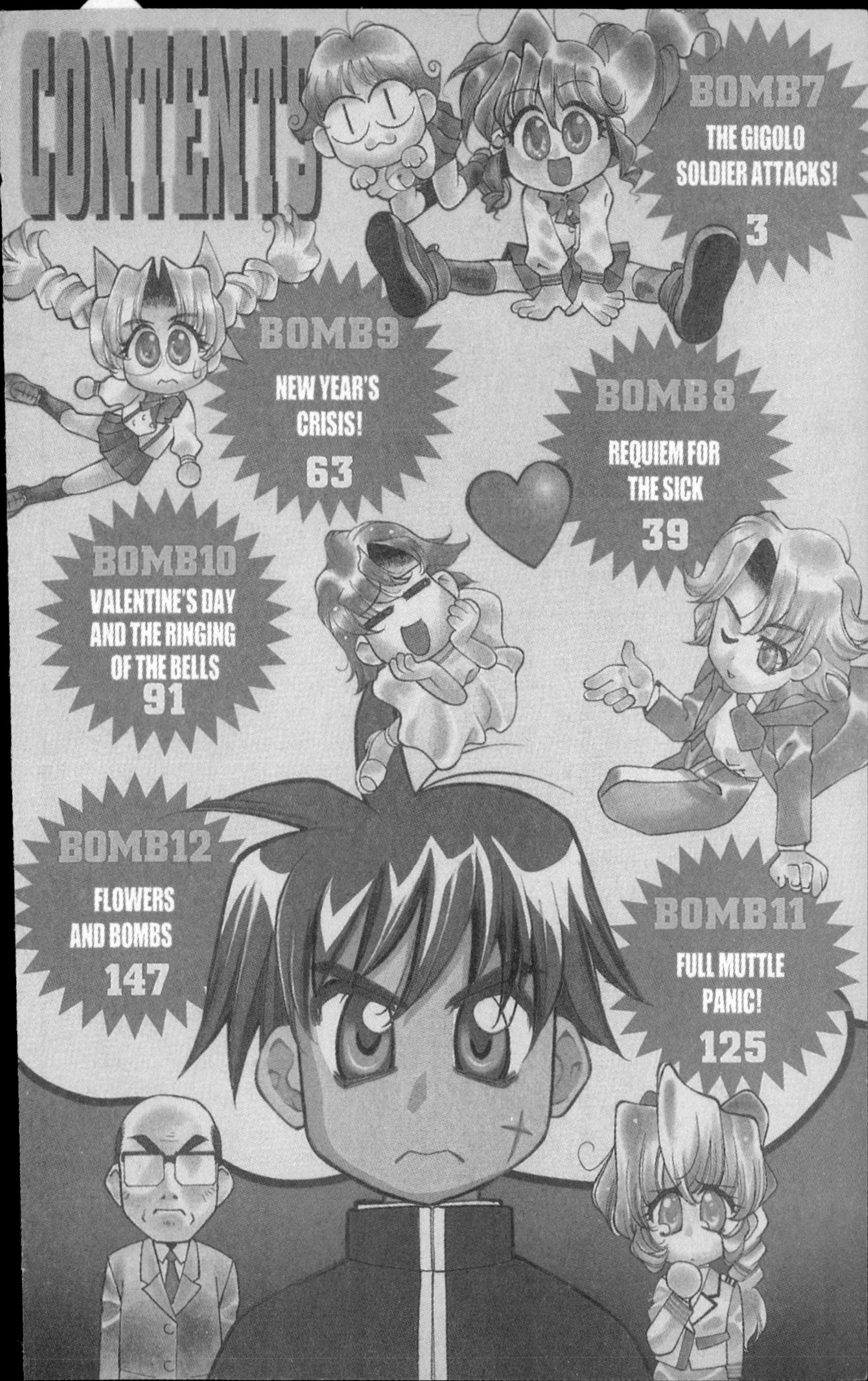

CONTENTS

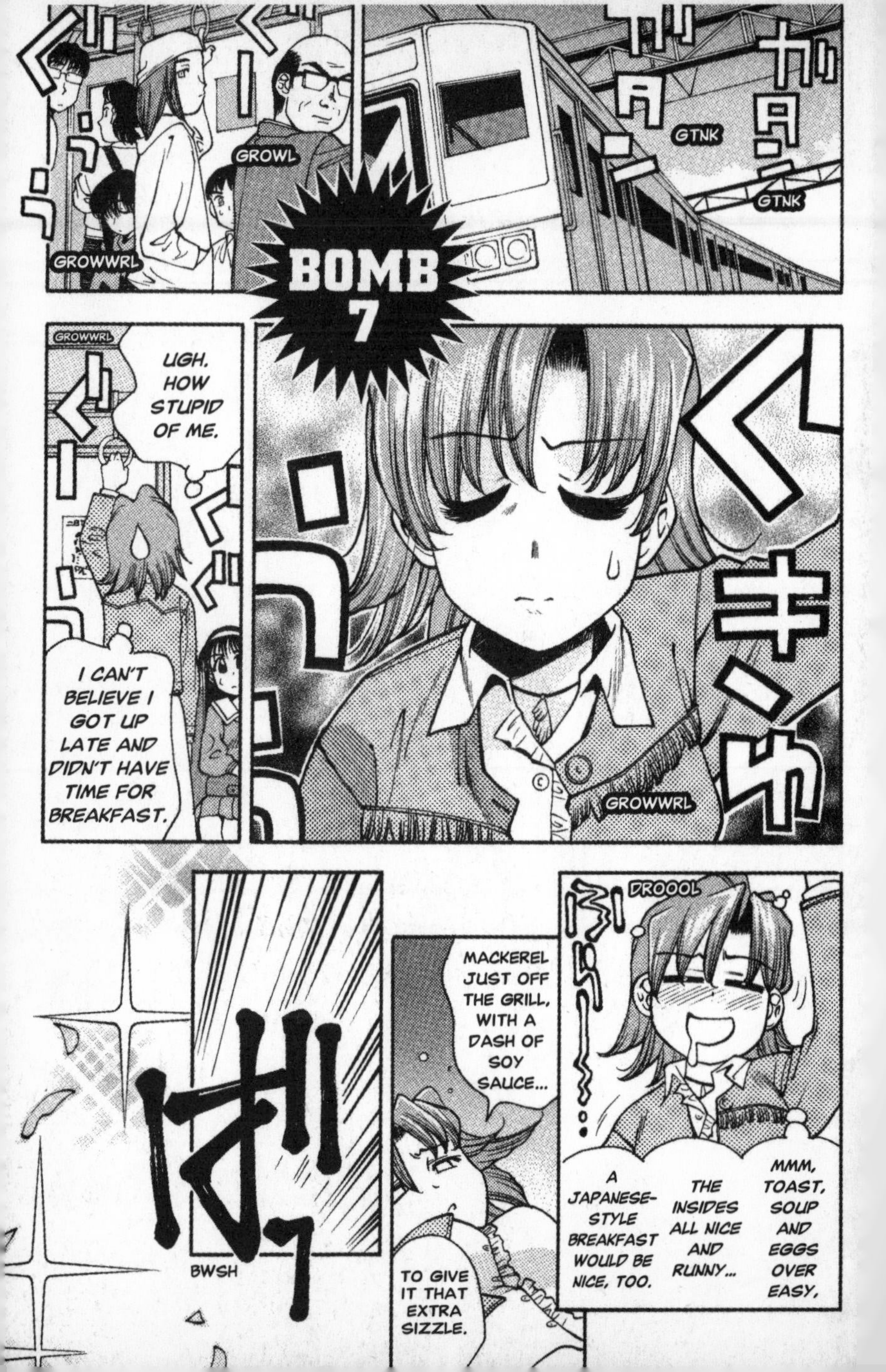

GTNK
GTNK
GROWL
GROWWRL
BOMB 7
GROWWRL
UGH. HOW STUPID OF ME.
I CAN'T BELIEVE I GOT UP LATE AND DIDN'T HAVE TIME FOR BREAKFAST.
GROWWRL
DROOOL
MMM, TOAST, SOUP AND EGGS OVER EASY,
THE INSIDES ALL NICE AND RUNNY...
A JAPANESE-STYLE BREAKFAST WOULD BE NICE, TOO.
MACKEREL JUST OFF THE GRILL, WITH A DASH OF SOY SAUCE...
TO GIVE IT THAT EXTRA SIZZLE.
BWSH

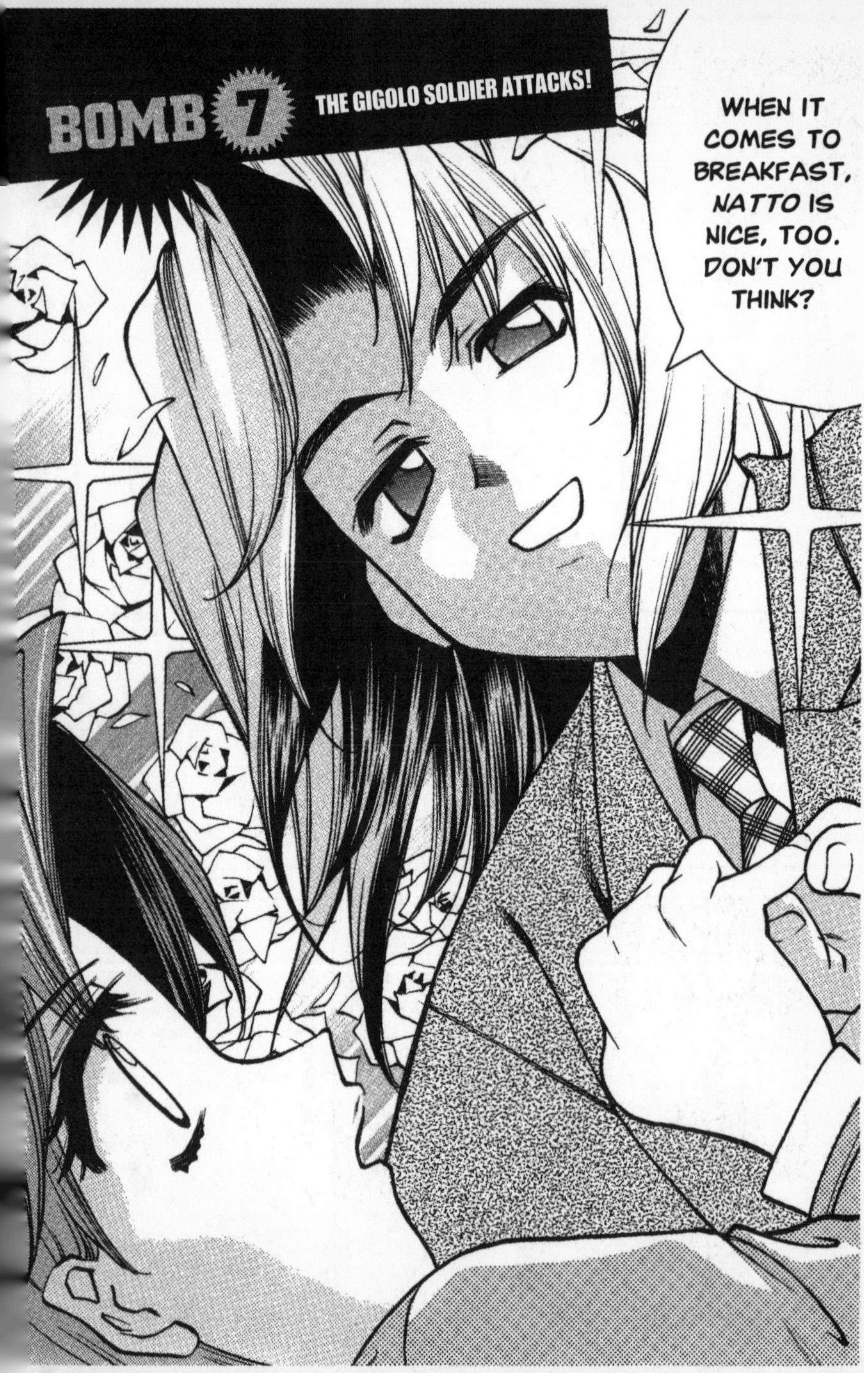
BOMB 7
THE GIGOLO SOLDIER ATTACKS!
WHEN IT COMES TO BREAKFAST, NATTO IS NICE, TOO. DON'T YOU THINK?

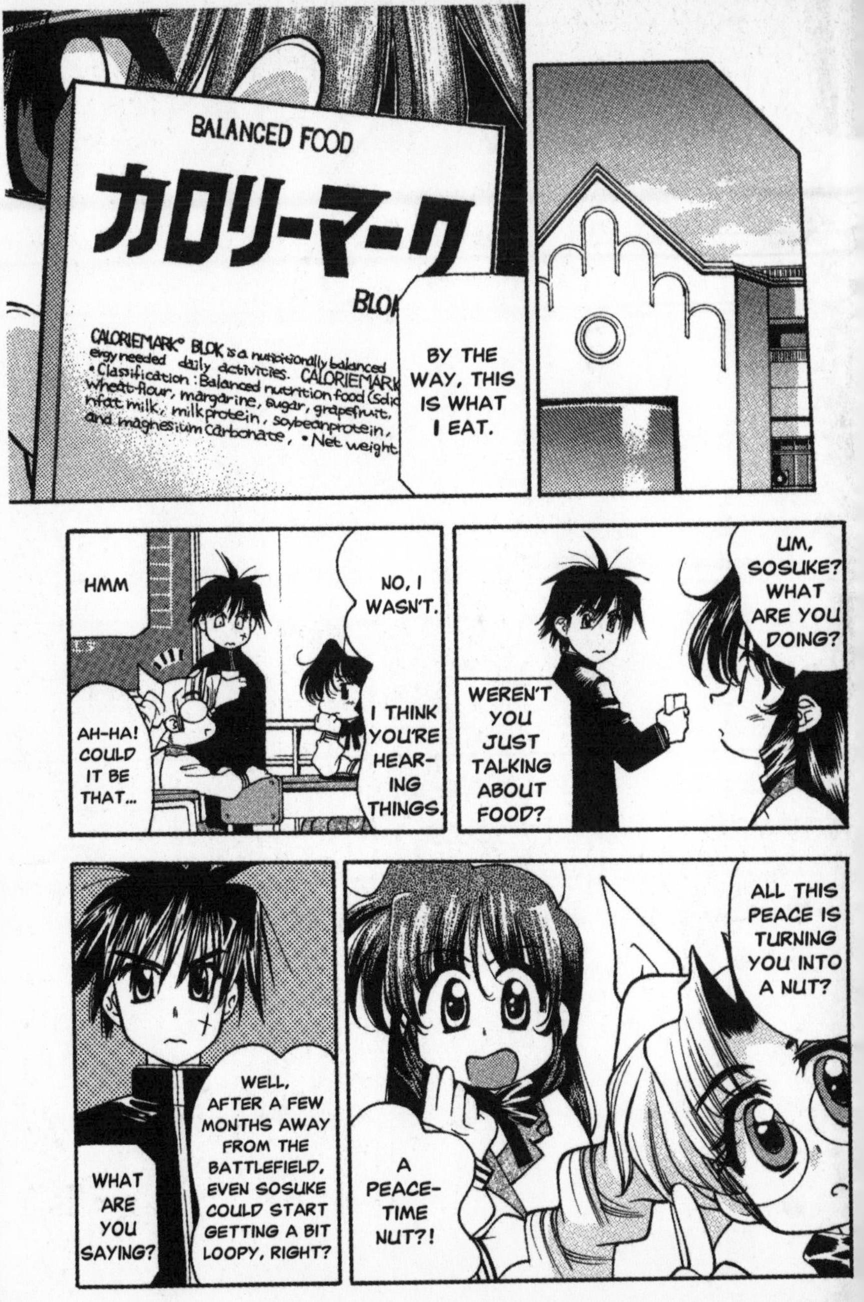
BALANCED FOOD
カロリーマーク
BLOK
CALORIEMARK® BLOK is a nutritionally balanced
ergy needed daily activities. CALORIEMARK
• Classification : Balanced nutrition food (Solid
wheat flour, margarine, sugar, grapefruit,
nfat milk, milk protein, soybean protein,
and magnesium carbonate, • Net weight
BY THE WAY, THIS IS WHAT I EAT.
UM, SOSUKE? WHAT ARE YOU DOING?
WEREN'T YOU JUST TALKING ABOUT FOOD?
NO, I WASN'T.
I THINK YOU'RE HEAR-ING THINGS.
HMM
AH-HA! COULD IT BE THAT...
ALL THIS PEACE IS TURNING YOU INTO A NUT?
A PEACE-TIME NUT?!
WELL, AFTER A FEW MONTHS AWAY FROM THE BATTLEFIELD, EVEN SOSUKE COULD START GETTING A BIT LOOPY, RIGHT?
WHAT ARE YOU SAYING?

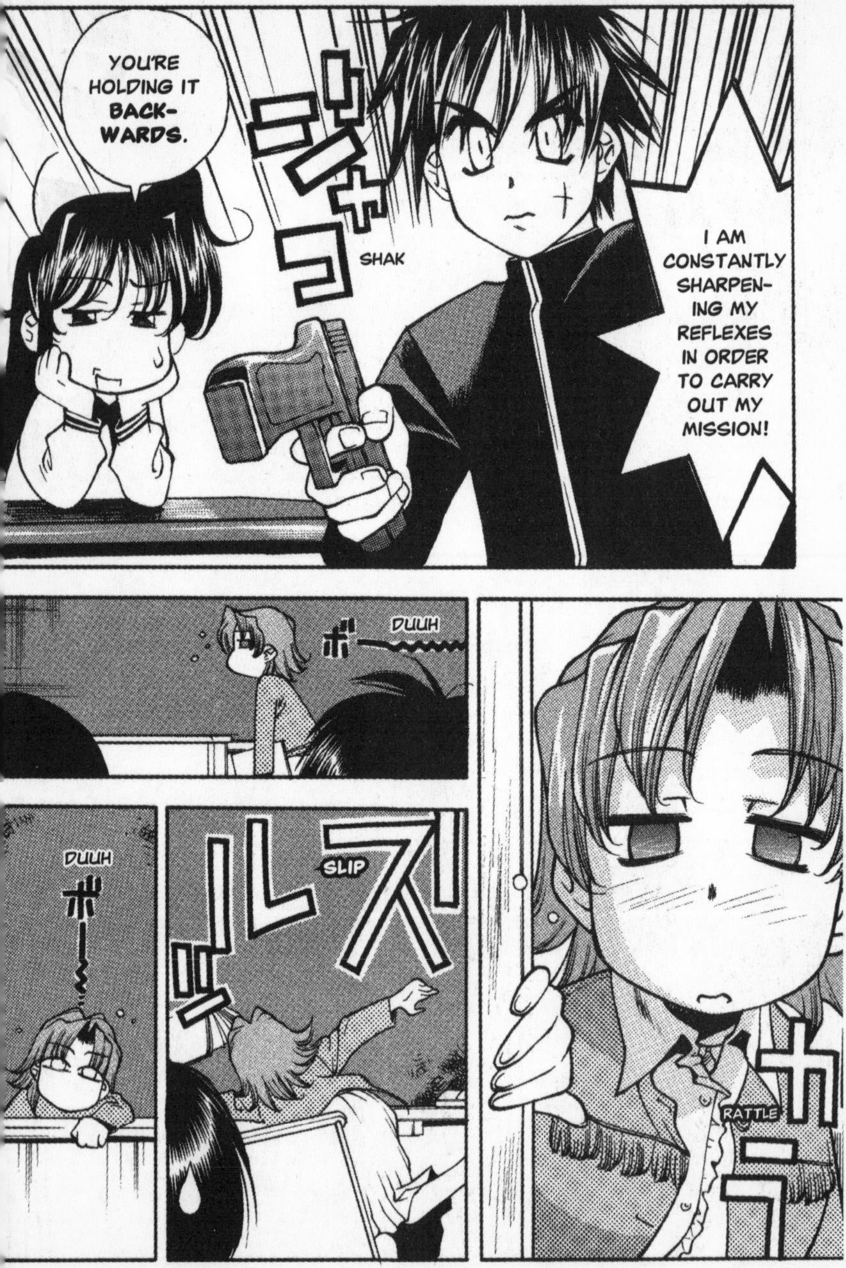
I AM CONSTANTLY SHARPEN-ING MY REFLEXES IN ORDER TO CARRY OUT MY MISSION!
SHAK
YOU'RE HOLDING IT BACK-WARDS.
RATTLE
DUUH
DUUH
SLIP

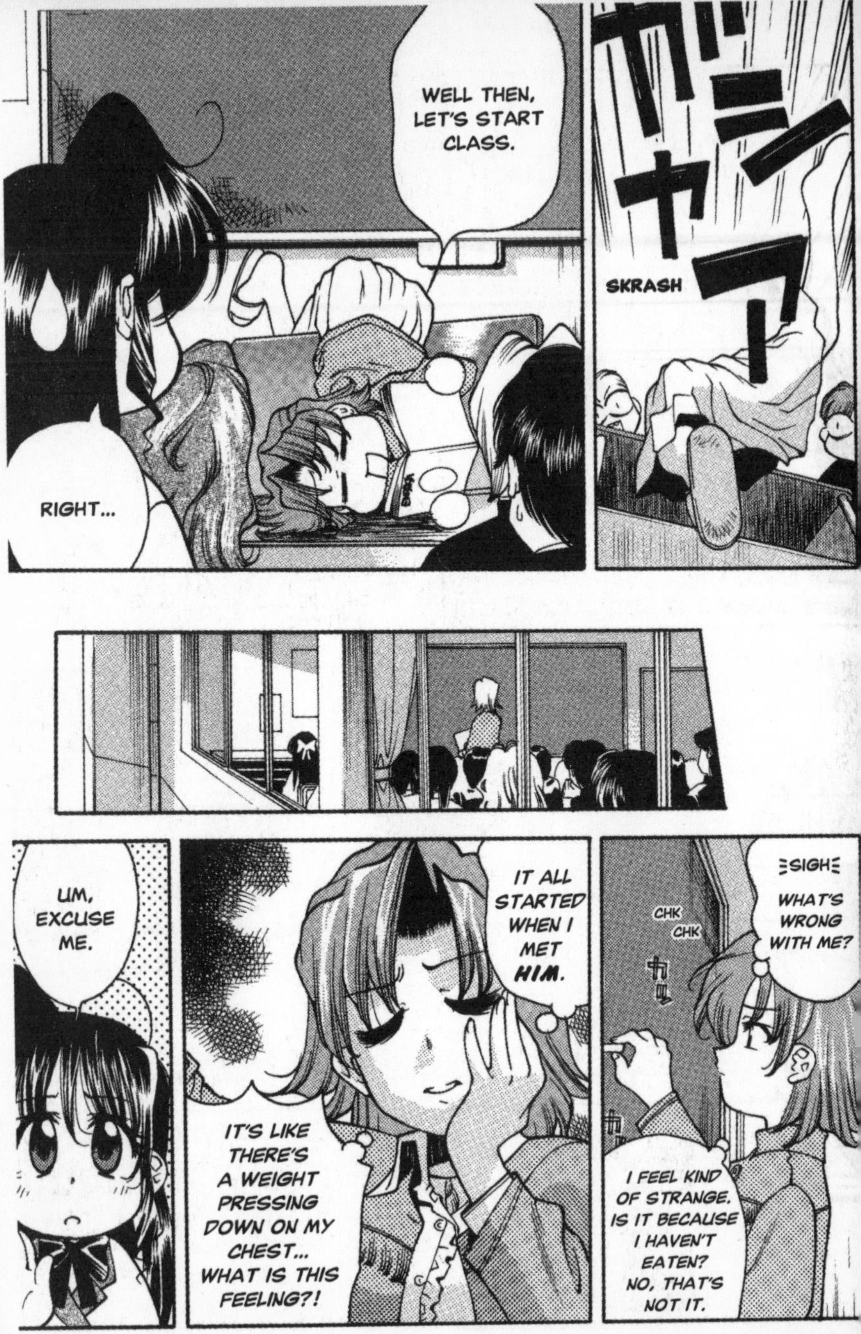
SKRASH
WELL THEN, LET'S START CLASS.
RIGHT...
ΞSIGHΞ WHAT'S WRONG WITH ME?
CHK CHK
I FEEL KIND OF STRANGE. IS IT BECAUSE I HAVEN'T EATEN? NO, THAT'S NOT IT.
IT ALL STARTED WHEN I MET HIM.
IT'S LIKE THERE'S A WEIGHT PRESSING DOWN ON MY CHEST... WHAT IS THIS FEELING?!
UM, EXCUSE ME.

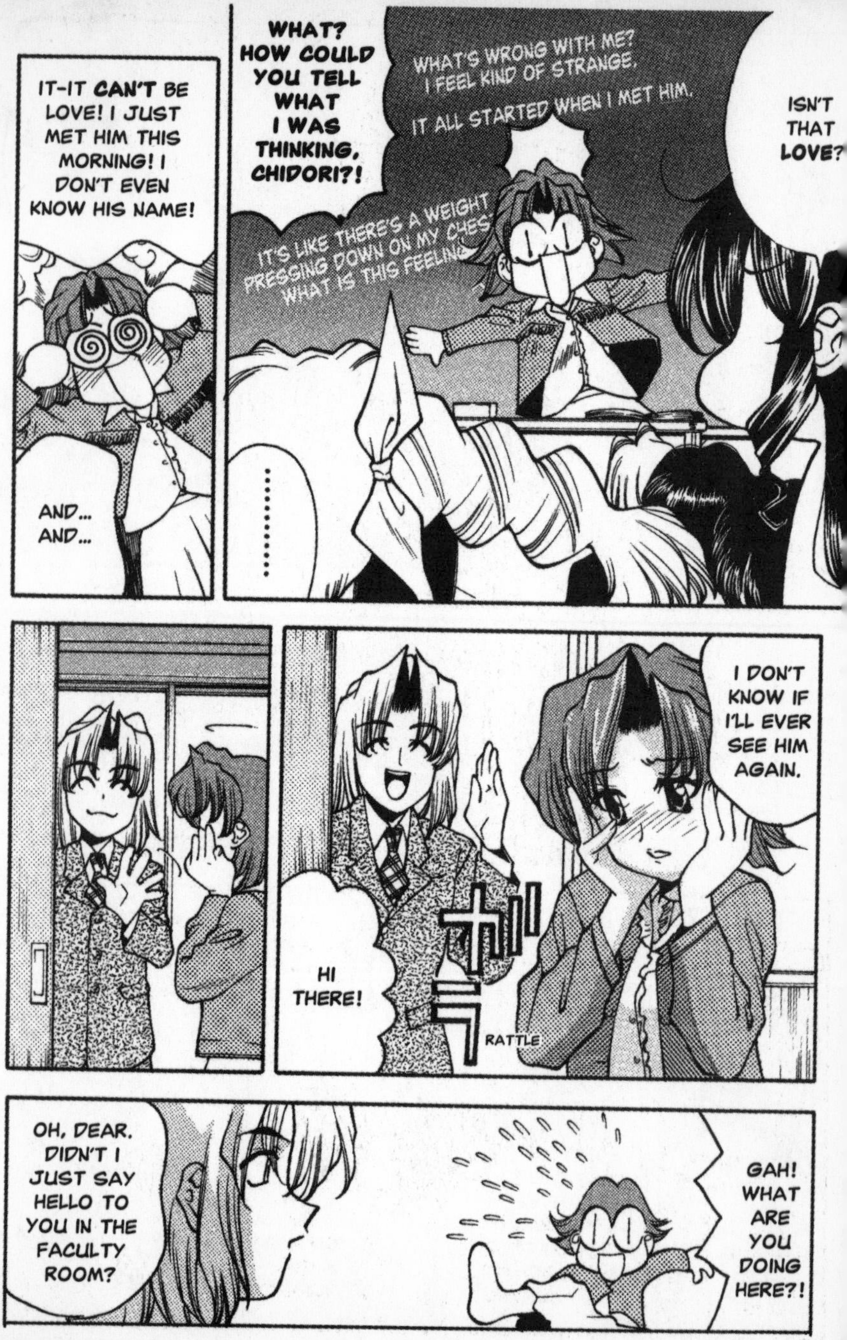
ISN'T THAT **LOVE**?
WHAT'S WRONG WITH ME? I FEEL KIND OF STRANGE.
IT ALL STARTED WHEN I MET HIM.
IT'S LIKE THERE'S A WEIGHT PRESSING DOWN ON MY CHES WHAT IS THIS FEELIN
WHAT? HOW COULD YOU TELL WHAT I WAS THINKING, CHIDORI?!
....
IT-IT **CAN'T** BE LOVE! I JUST MET HIM THIS MORNING! I DON'T EVEN KNOW HIS NAME!
AND... AND...
I DON'T KNOW IF I'LL EVER SEE HIM AGAIN.
RATTLE
HI THERE!
GAH! WHAT ARE YOU DOING HERE?!
OH, DEAR. DIDN'T I JUST SAY HELLO TO YOU IN THE FACULTY ROOM?

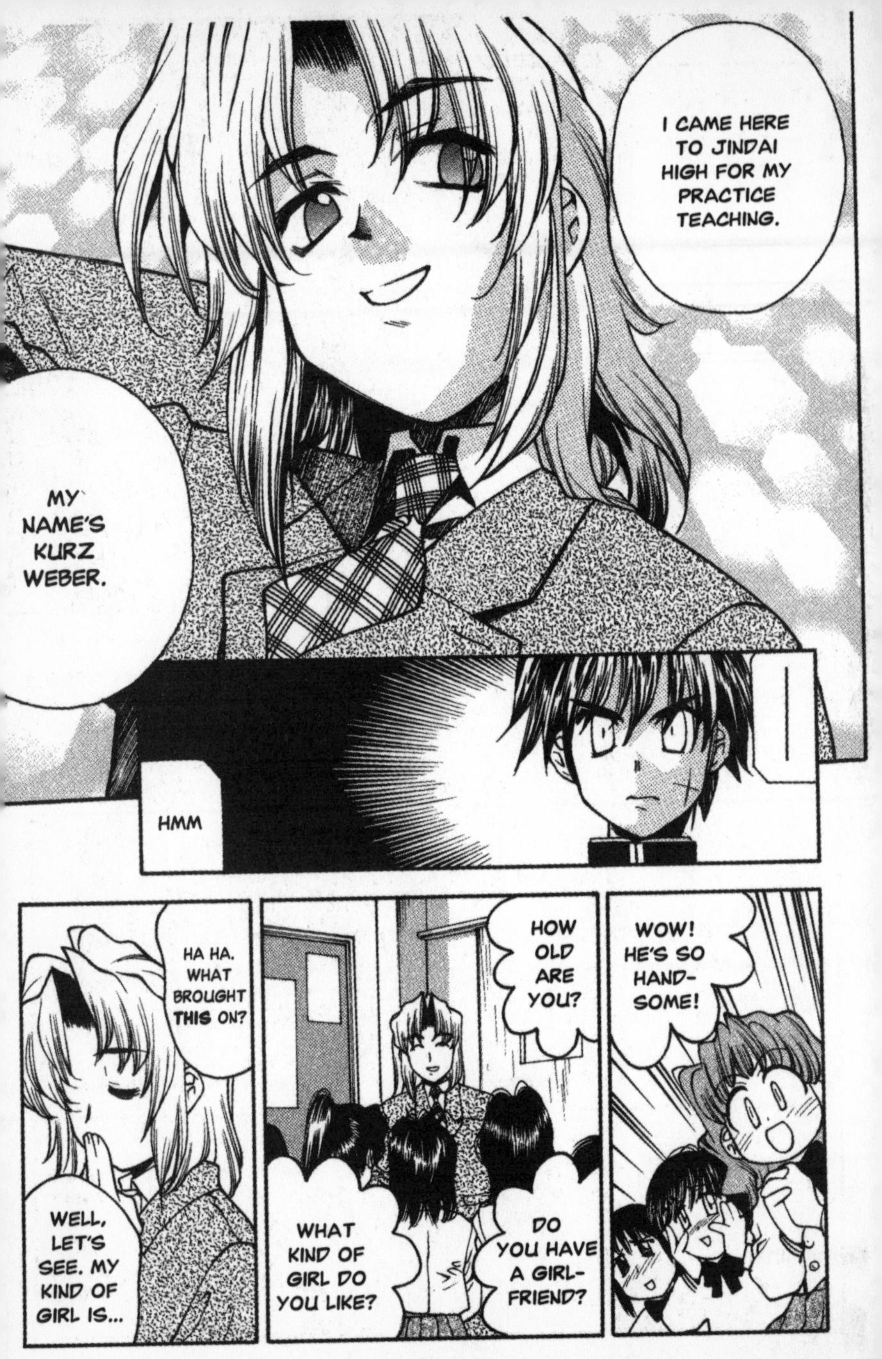
I CAME HERE TO JINDAI HIGH FOR MY PRACTICE TEACHING.
MY NAME'S KURZ WEBER.
HMM
WOW! HE'S SO HAND-SOME!
HOW OLD ARE YOU?
DO YOU HAVE A GIRL-FRIEND?
WHAT KIND OF GIRL DO YOU LIKE?
HA HA. WHAT BROUGHT **THIS** ON?
WELL, LET'S SEE. MY KIND OF GIRL IS...

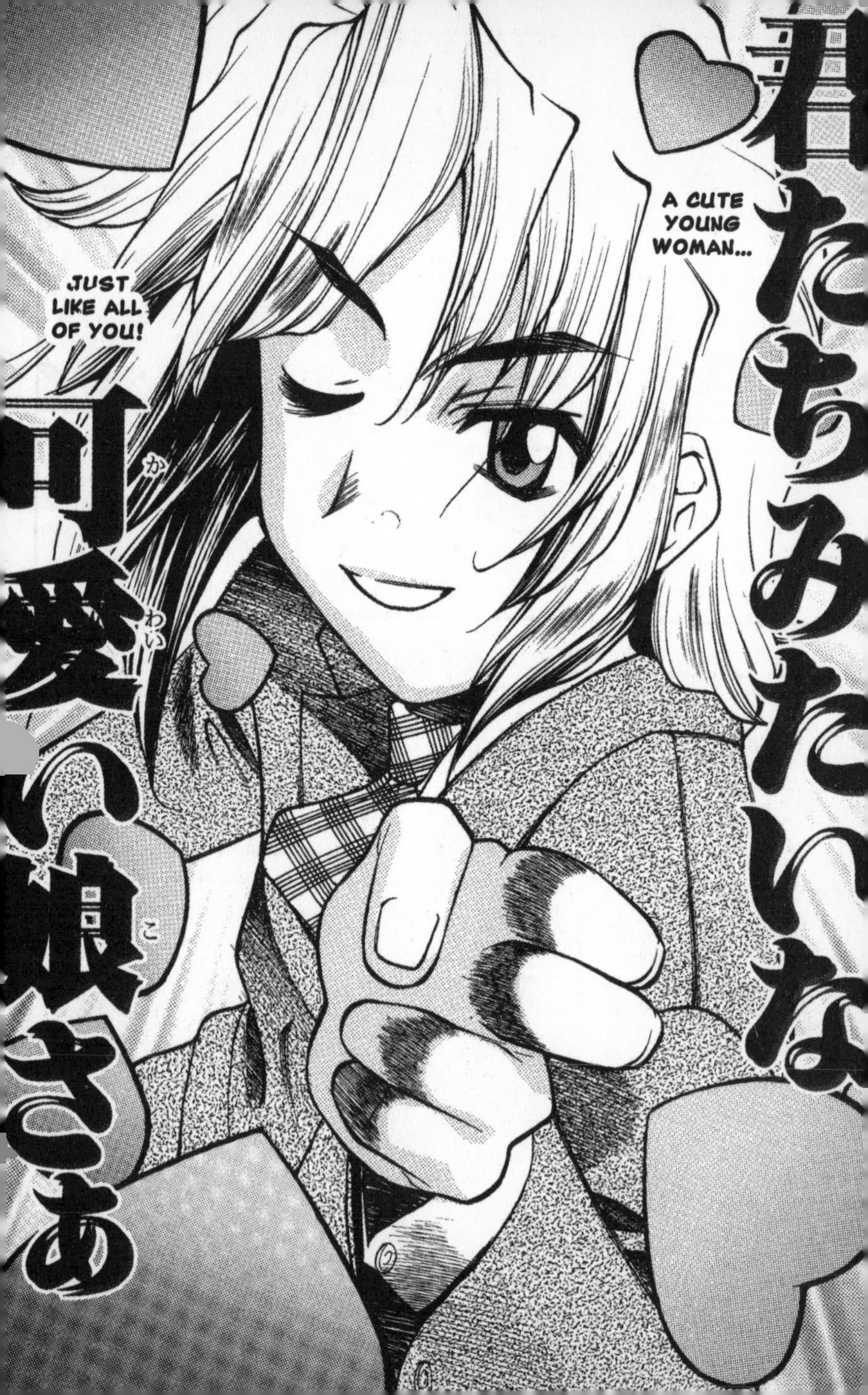
君たちみたいな
A CUTE YOUNG WOMAN...
可愛い娘さぁ
JUST LIKE ALL OF YOU!

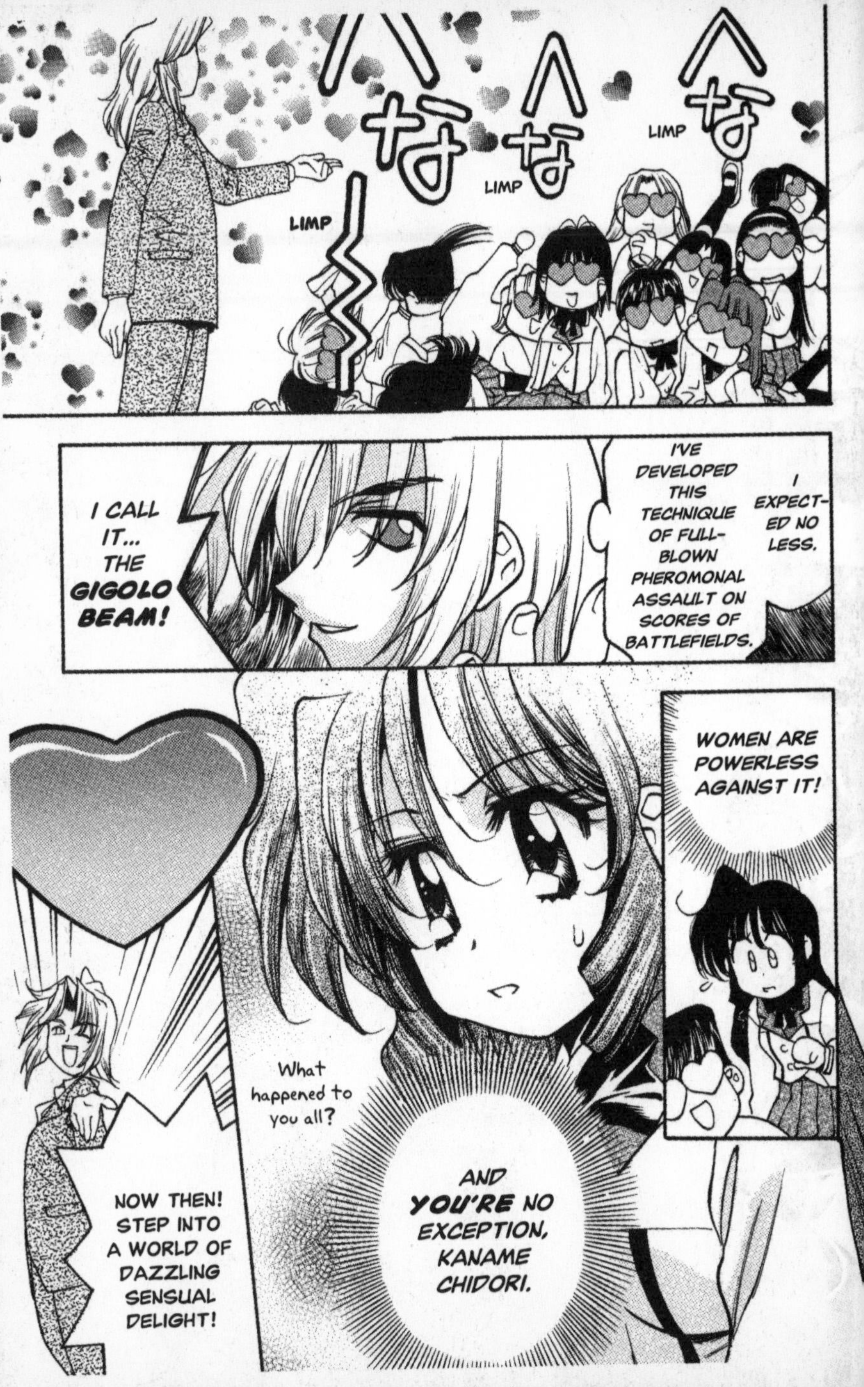
へなへなへな
LIMP
LIMP
LIMP
I EXPECTED NO LESS.
I'VE DEVELOPED THIS TECHNIQUE OF FULL-BLOWN PHEROMONAL ASSAULT ON SCORES OF BATTLEFIELDS.
I CALL IT... THE GIGOLO BEAM!
WOMEN ARE POWERLESS AGAINST IT!
AND YOU'RE NO EXCEPTION, KANAME CHIDORI.
What happened to you all?
NOW THEN! STEP INTO A WORLD OF DAZZLING SENSUAL DELIGHT!

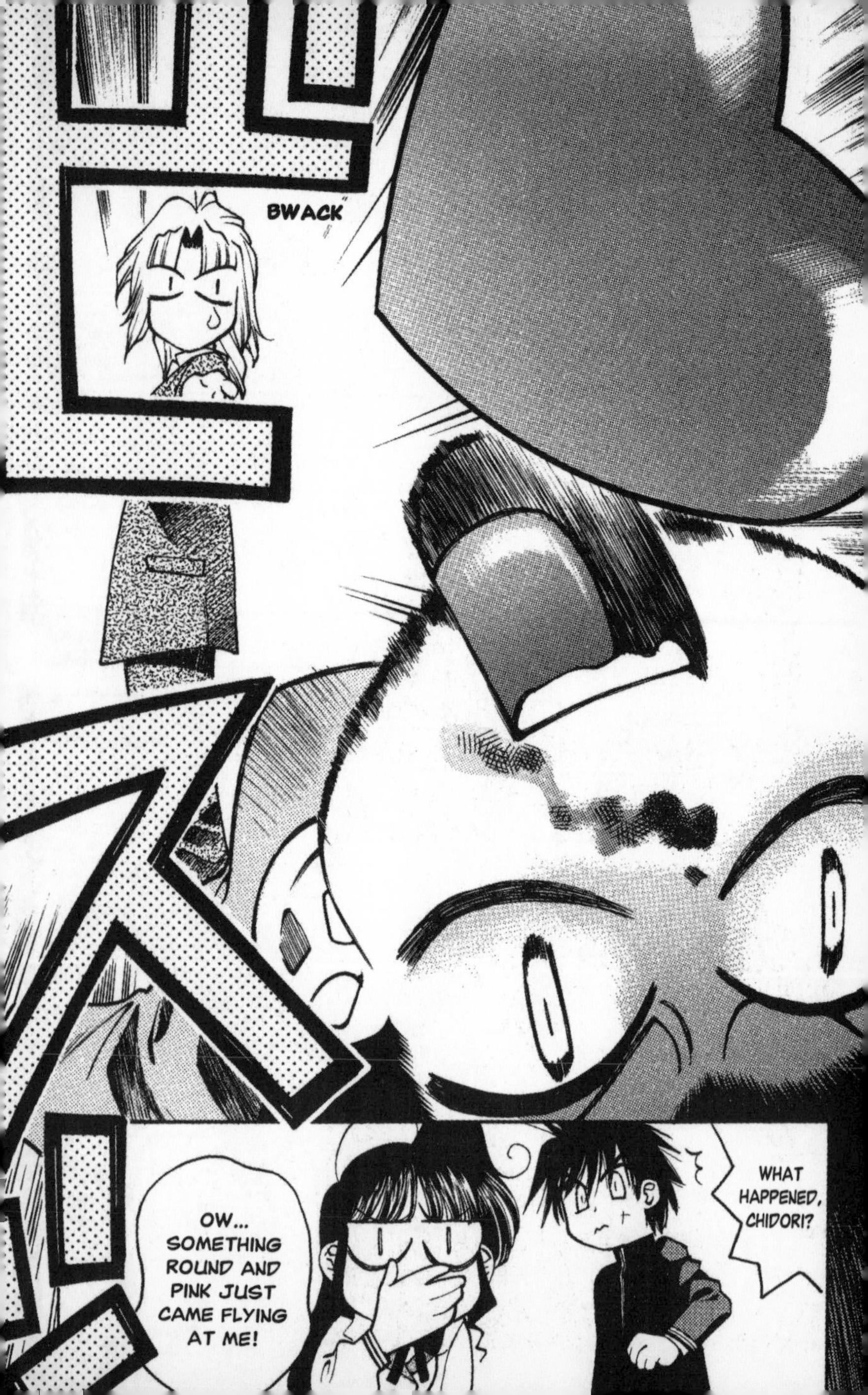
BWACK
WHAT HAPPENED, CHIDORI?
OW... SOMETHING ROUND AND PINK JUST CAME FLYING AT ME!

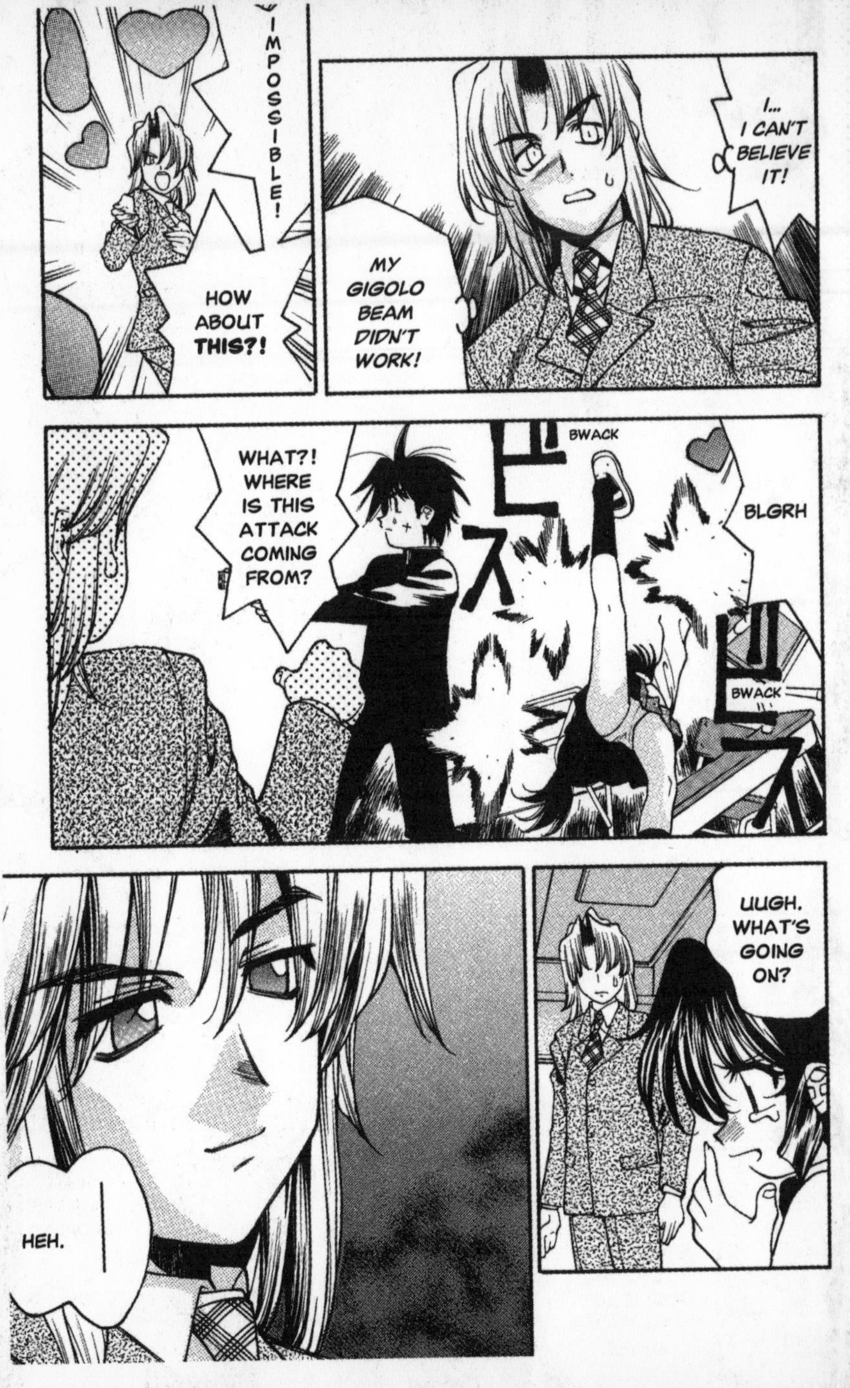
I... I CAN'T BELIEVE IT!
MY GIGOLO BEAM DIDN'T WORK!
IMPOSSIBLE!
HOW ABOUT THIS?!
BWACK
BLGRH
BWACK
WHAT?! WHERE IS THIS ATTACK COMING FROM?
UUGH. WHAT'S GOING ON?
HEH.

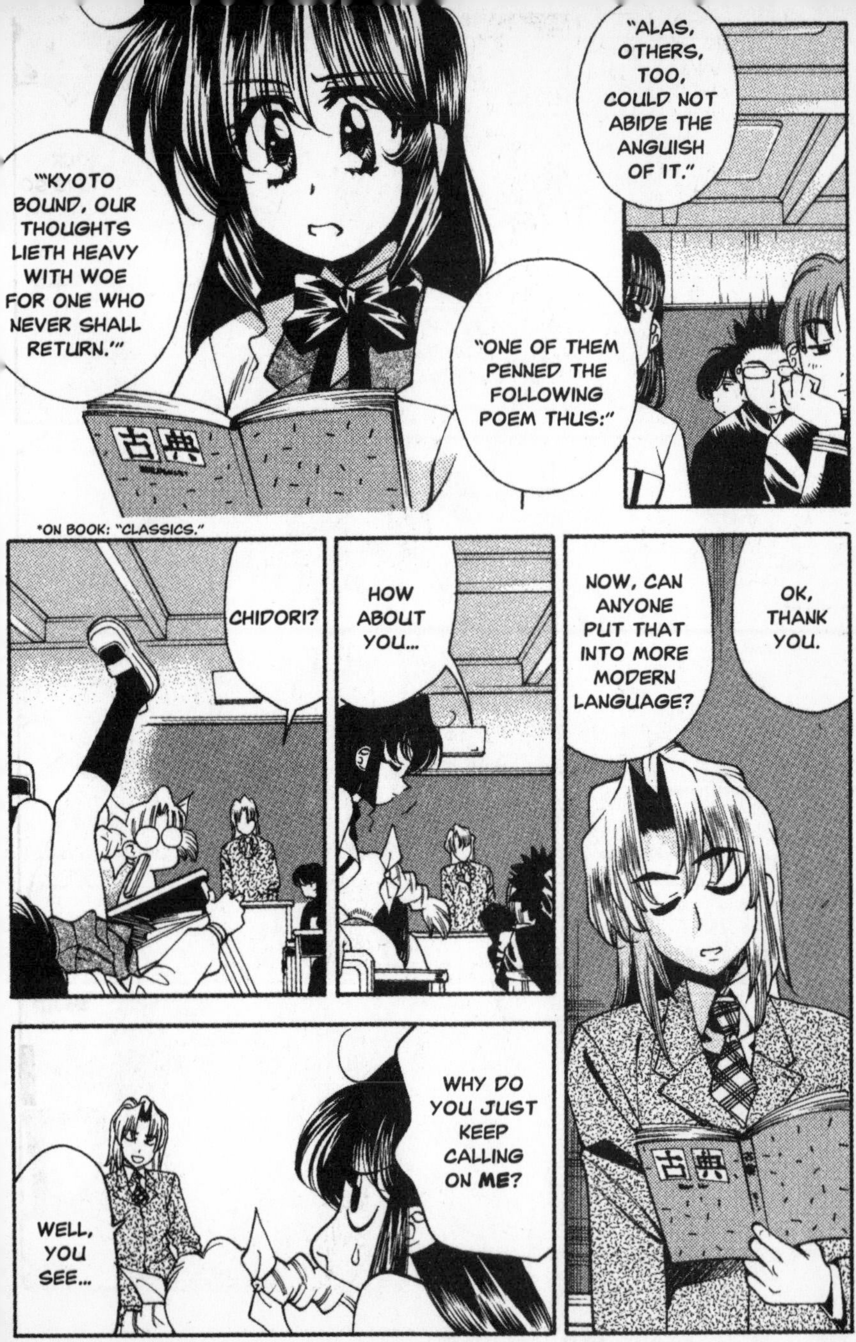

"ALAS, OTHERS, TOO, COULD NOT ABIDE THE ANGUISH OF IT."
"ONE OF THEM PENNED THE FOLLOWING POEM THUS:"
"'KYOTO BOUND, OUR THOUGHTS LIETH HEAVY WITH WOE FOR ONE WHO NEVER SHALL RETURN.'"
*ON BOOK: "CLASSICS."
OK, THANK YOU.
NOW, CAN ANYONE PUT THAT INTO MORE MODERN LANGUAGE?
HOW ABOUT YOU...
CHIDORI?
WHY DO YOU JUST KEEP CALLING ON ME?
WELL, YOU SEE...

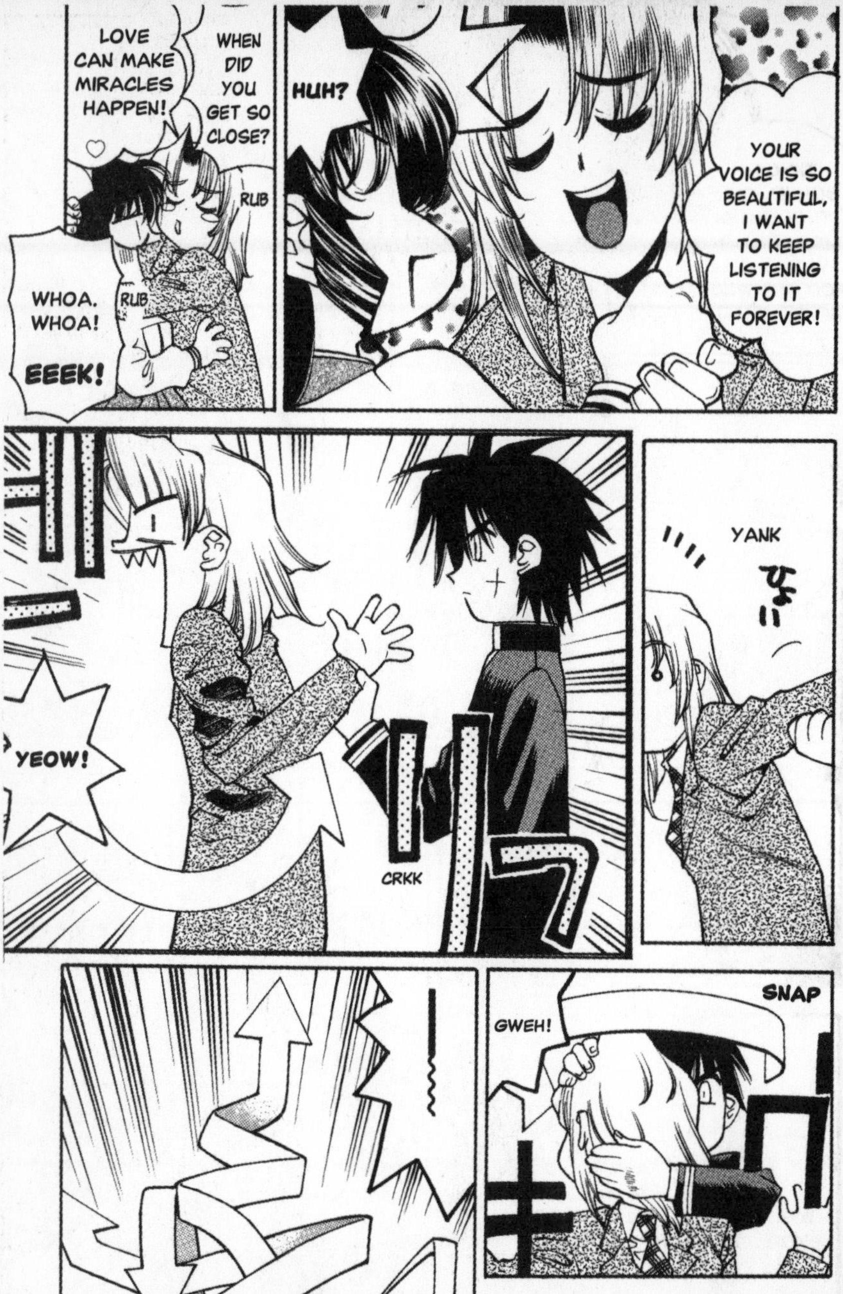
YOUR VOICE IS SO BEAUTIFUL, I WANT TO KEEP LISTENING TO IT FOREVER!
HUH?
WHEN DID YOU GET SO CLOSE?
LOVE CAN MAKE MIRACLES HAPPEN!
RUB
RUB
WHOA. WHOA!
EEEK!
YANK
YEOW!
CRKK
SNAP
GWEH!

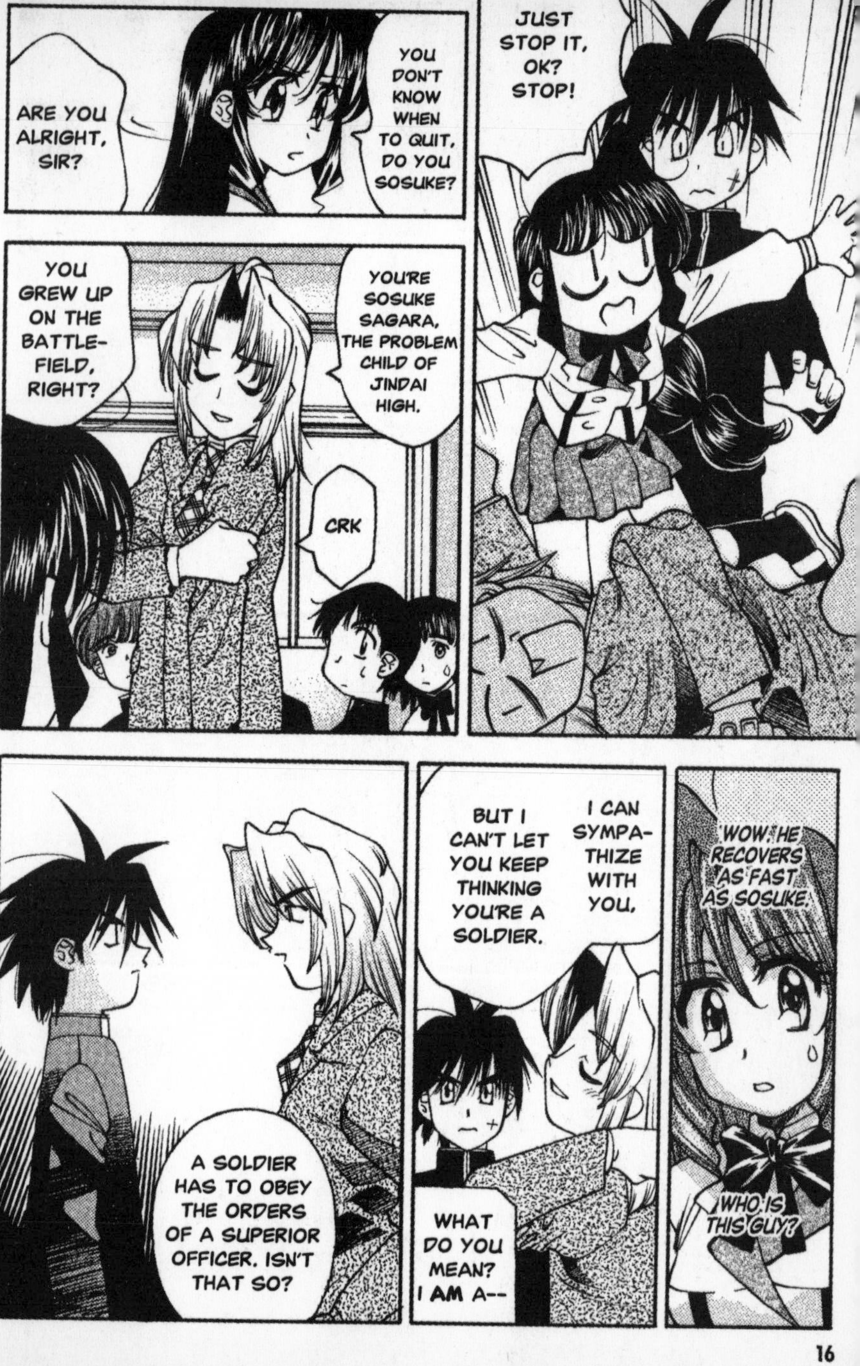
JUST STOP IT, OK? STOP!
YOU DON'T KNOW WHEN TO QUIT, DO YOU SOSUKE?
ARE YOU ALRIGHT, SIR?
YOU'RE SOSUKE SAGARA, THE PROBLEM CHILD OF JINDAI HIGH.
YOU GREW UP ON THE BATTLE-FIELD, RIGHT?
CRK
WOW! HE RECOVERS AS FAST AS SOSUKE.
WHO IS THIS GUY?
I CAN SYMPATHIZE WITH YOU,
BUT I CAN'T LET YOU KEEP THINKING YOU'RE A SOLDIER.
WHAT DO YOU MEAN? I AM A--
A SOLDIER HAS TO OBEY THE ORDERS OF A SUPERIOR OFFICER. ISN'T THAT SO?

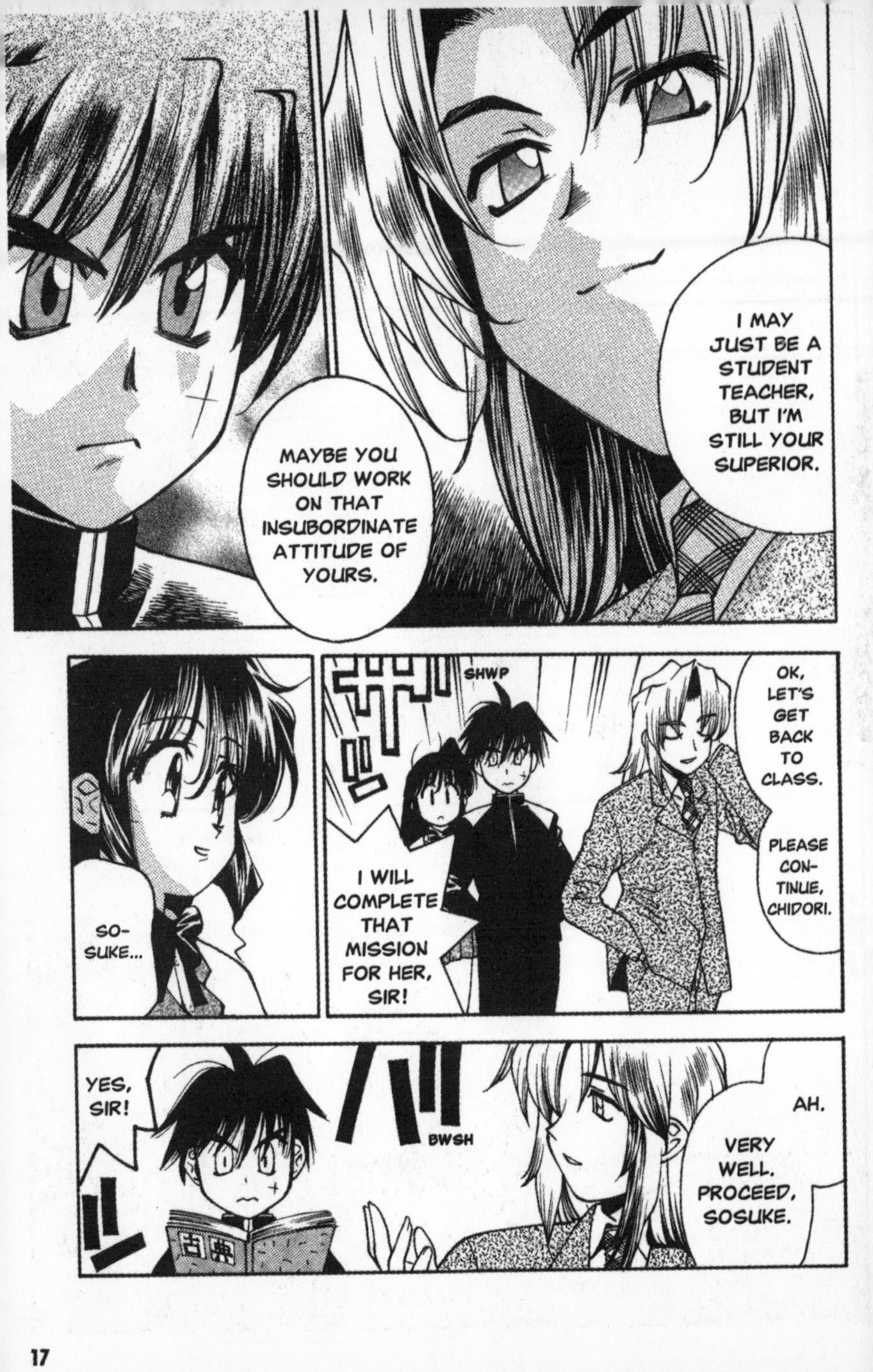
I MAY JUST BE A STUDENT TEACHER, BUT I'M STILL YOUR SUPERIOR.
MAYBE YOU SHOULD WORK ON THAT INSUBORDINATE ATTITUDE OF YOURS.
OK, LET'S GET BACK TO CLASS.
PLEASE CON-TINUE, CHIDORI.
SHWP
I WILL COMPLETE THAT MISSION FOR HER, SIR!
SO-SUKE...
AH.
VERY WELL. PROCEED, SOSUKE.
BWSH
YES, SIR!
古典

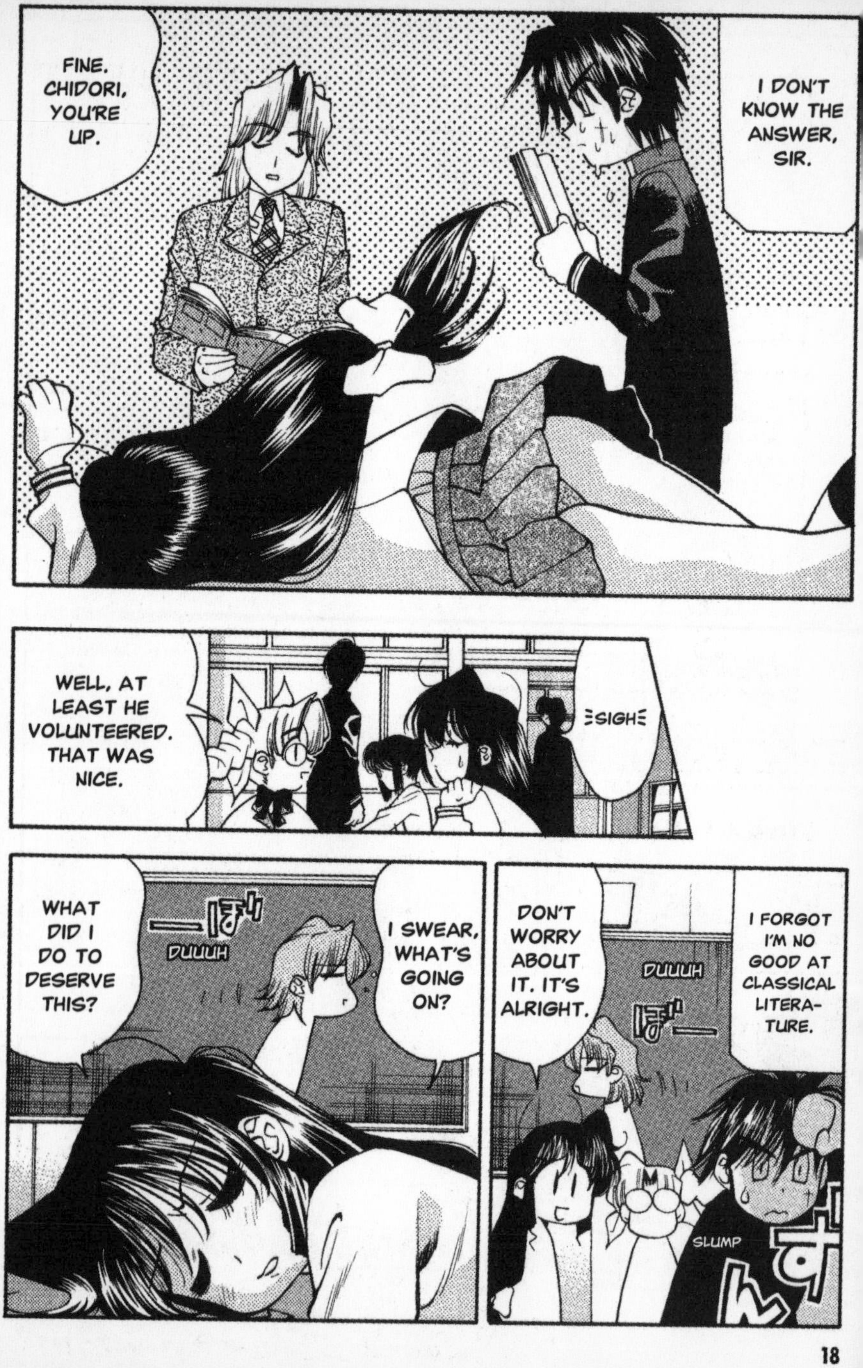
I DON'T KNOW THE ANSWER, SIR.
FINE. CHIDORI, YOU'RE UP.
SIGH
WELL, AT LEAST HE VOLUNTEERED. THAT WAS NICE.
I FORGOT I'M NO GOOD AT CLASSICAL LITERA-TURE.
DUUUH
DON'T WORRY ABOUT IT. IT'S ALRIGHT.
SLUMP
I SWEAR, WHAT'S GOING ON?
DUUUH
WHAT DID I DO TO DESERVE THIS?

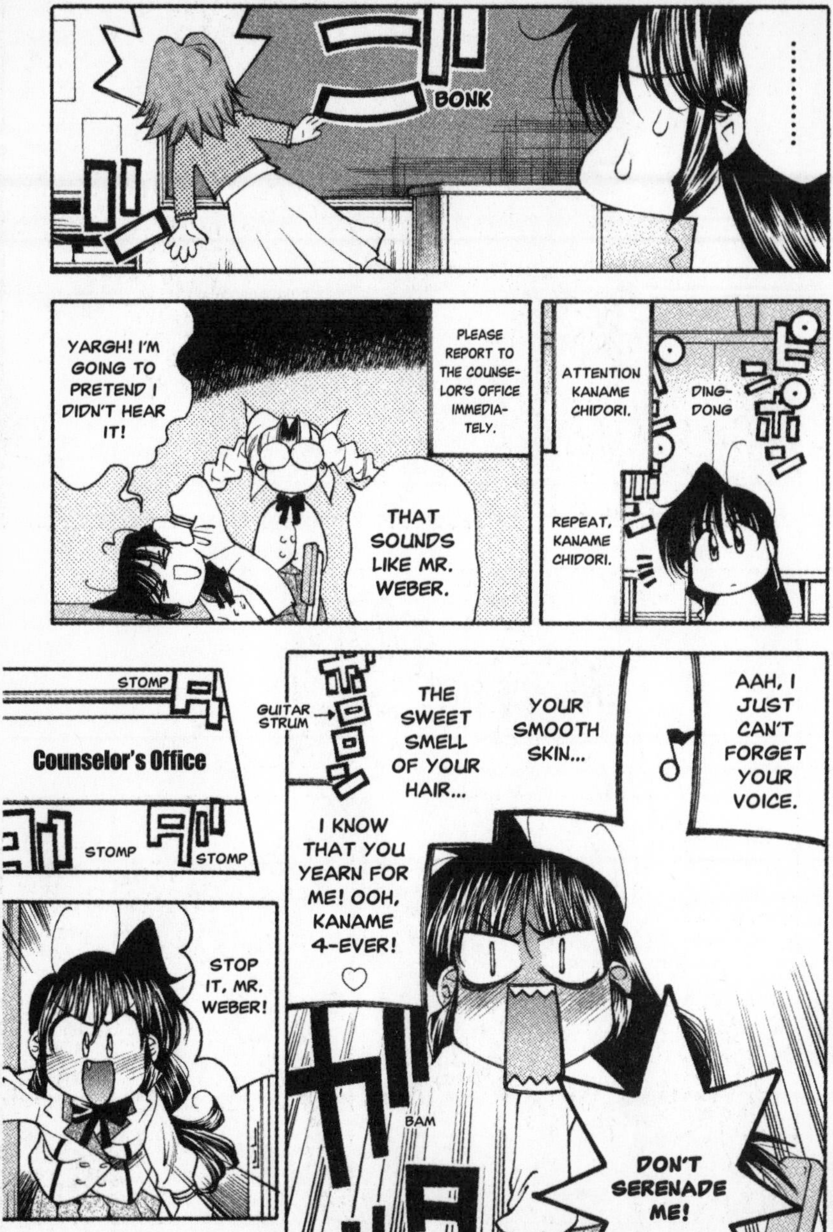
BONK
......
ATTENTION KANAME CHIDORI.
DING-DONG
REPEAT, KANAME CHIDORI.
PLEASE REPORT TO THE COUNSELOR'S OFFICE IMMEDIATELY.
YARGH! I'M GOING TO PRETEND I DIDN'T HEAR IT!
THAT SOUNDS LIKE MR. WEBER.
STOMP
Counselor's Office
STOMP
STOMP
AAH, I JUST CAN'T FORGET YOUR VOICE.
YOUR SMOOTH SKIN...
THE SWEET SMELL OF YOUR HAIR...
GUITAR STRUM
I KNOW THAT YOU YEARN FOR ME! OOH, KANAME 4-EVER!
STOP IT, MR. WEBER!
BAM
DON'T SERENADE ME!

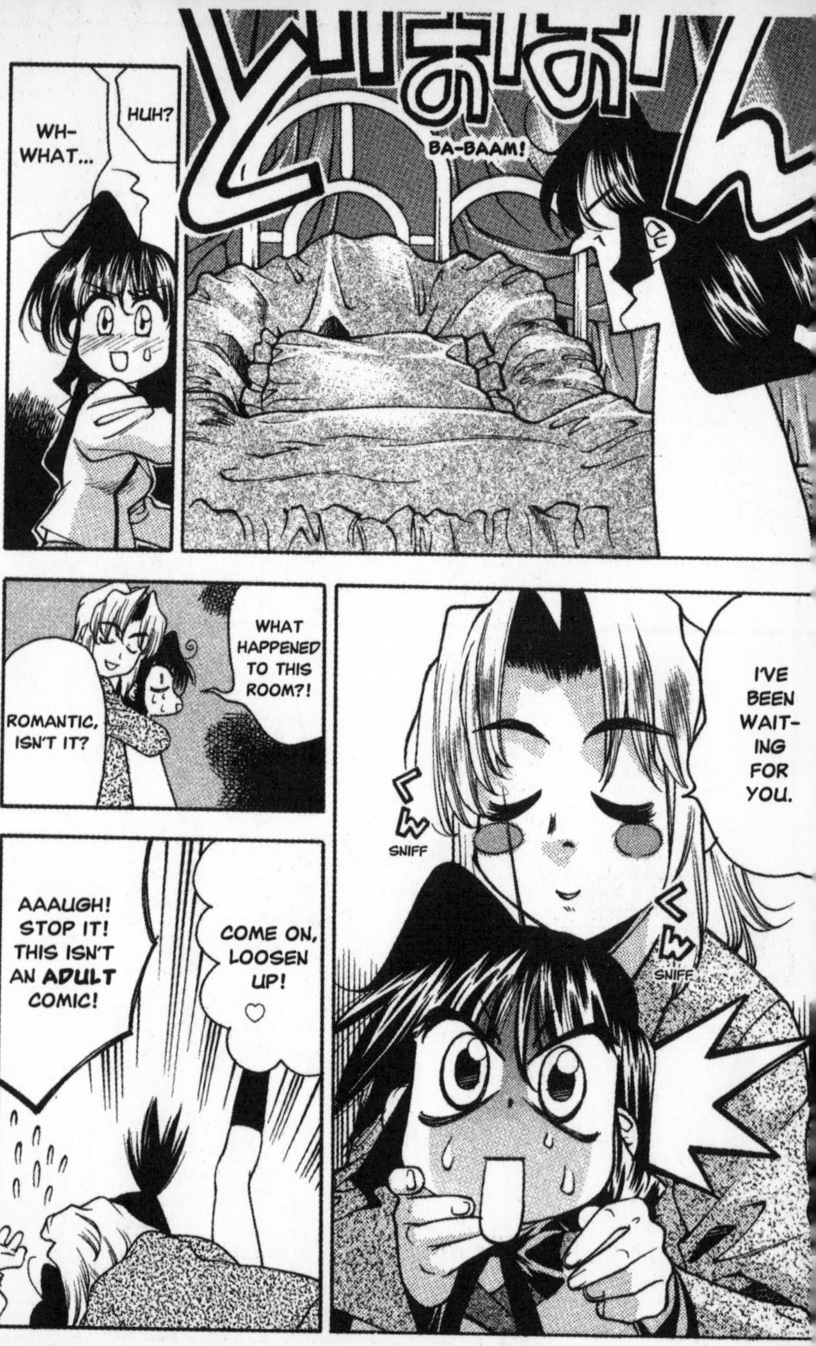
BA-BAAM!
HUH?
WH-WHAT...
I'VE BEEN WAIT-ING FOR YOU.
SNIFF
SNIFF
WHAT HAPPENED TO THIS ROOM?!
ROMANTIC, ISN'T IT?
COME ON, LOOSEN UP!
AAAUGH! STOP IT! THIS ISN'T AN **ADULT** COMIC!

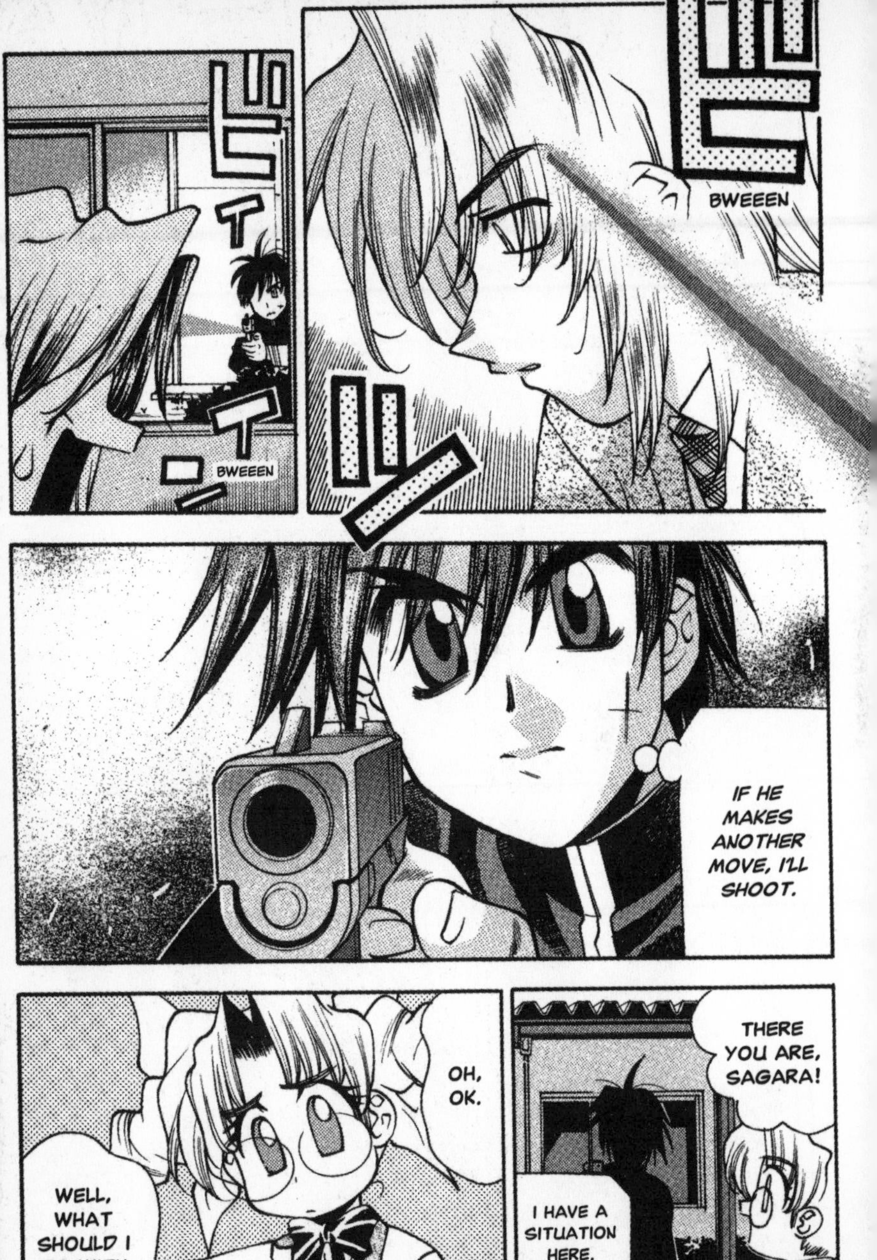
BWEEEN
BWEEEN
IF HE MAKES ANOTHER MOVE, I'LL SHOOT.
THERE YOU ARE, SAGARA!
I HAVE A SITUATION HERE. WE'LL TALK LATER.
OH, OK.
WELL, WHAT SHOULD I DO WITH THIS?

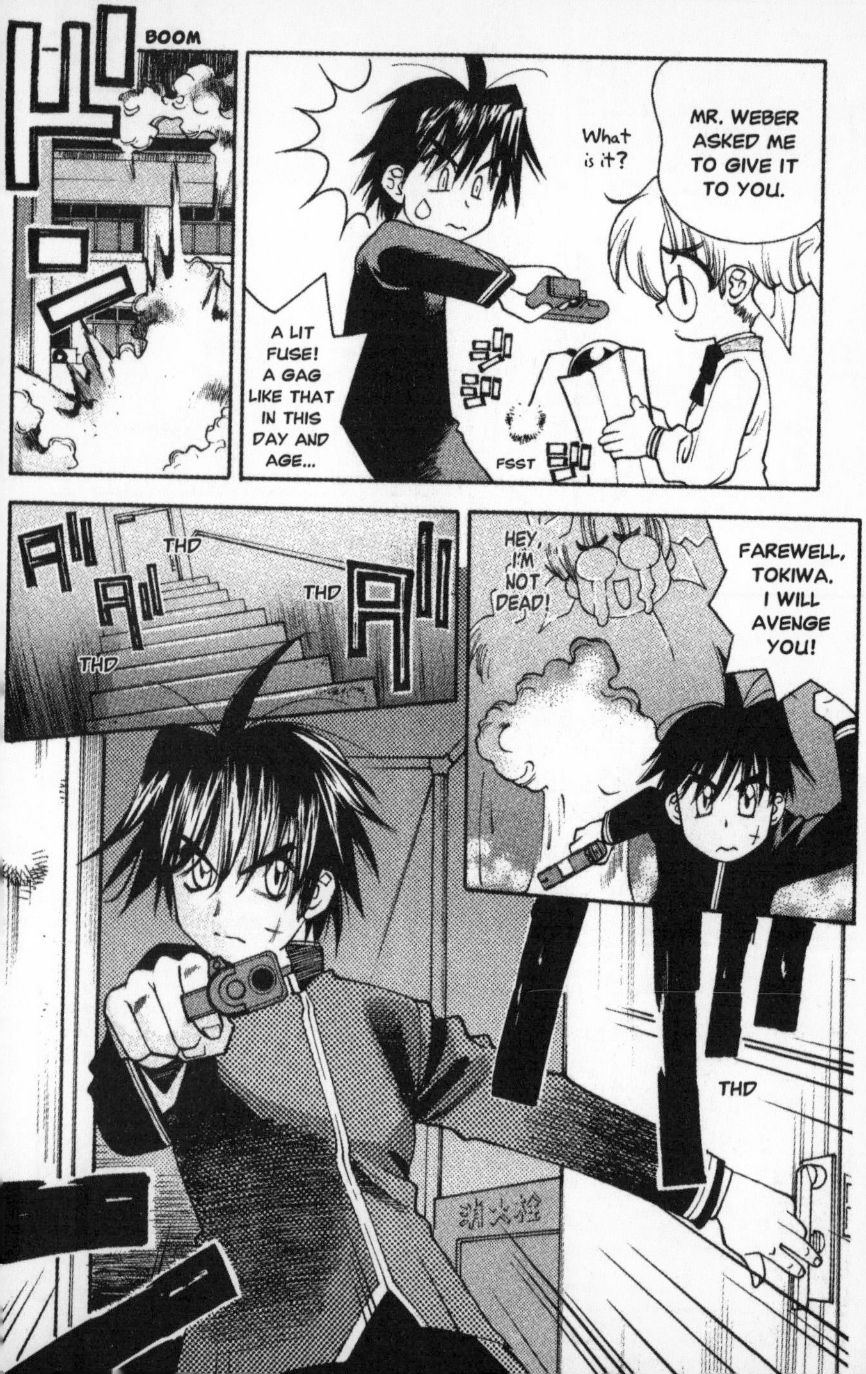
BOOM
MR. WEBER ASKED ME TO GIVE IT TO YOU.
What is it?
A LIT FUSE! A GAG LIKE THAT IN THIS DAY AND AGE...
FSST
FAREWELL, TOKIWA. I WILL AVENGE YOU!
HEY, I'M NOT DEAD!
THD
THD
THD
THD

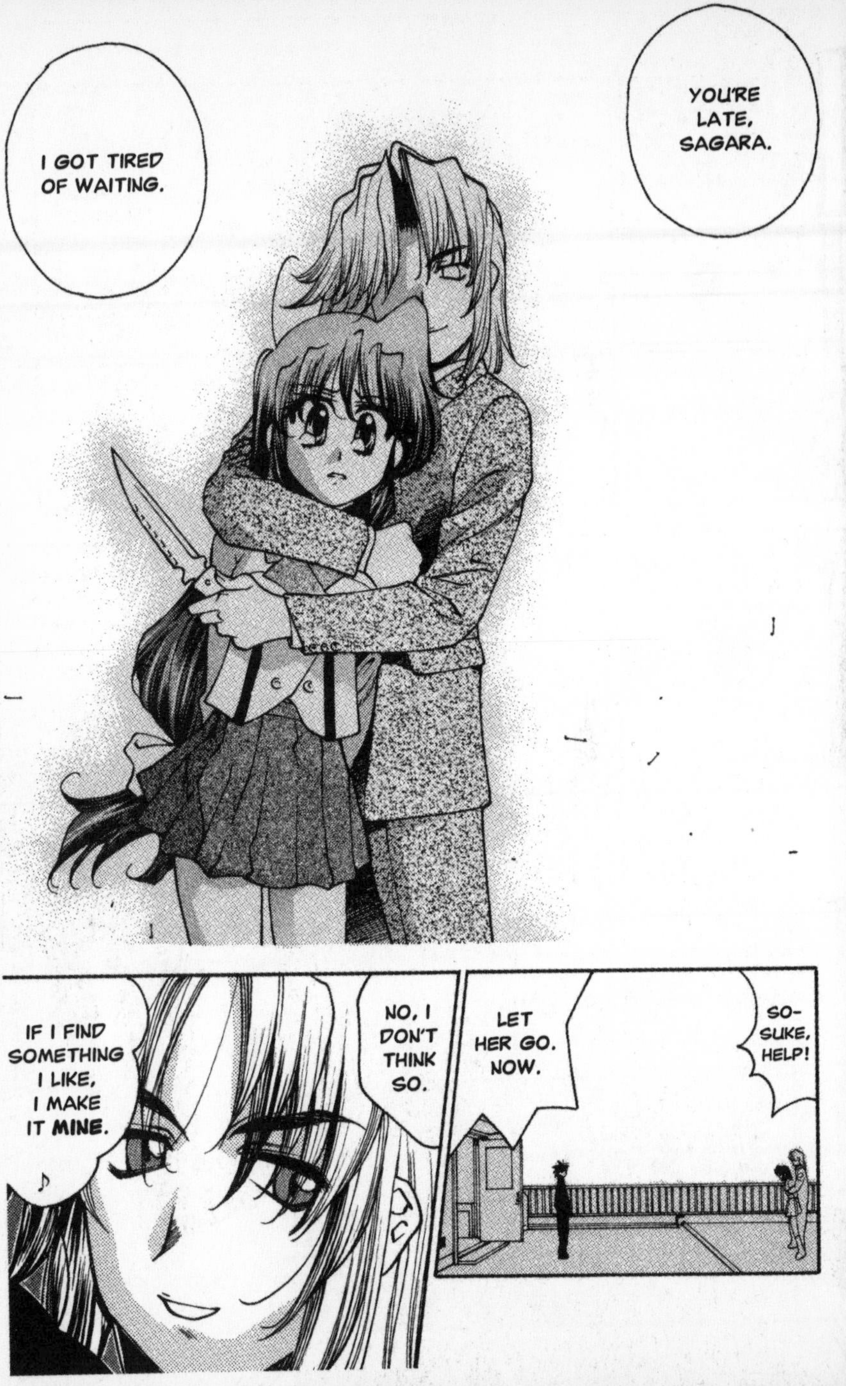
YOU'RE LATE, SAGARA.
I GOT TIRED OF WAITING.
SO-SUKE, HELP!
LET HER GO. NOW.
NO, I DON'T THINK SO.
IF I FIND SOMETHING I LIKE, I MAKE IT MINE. ♪

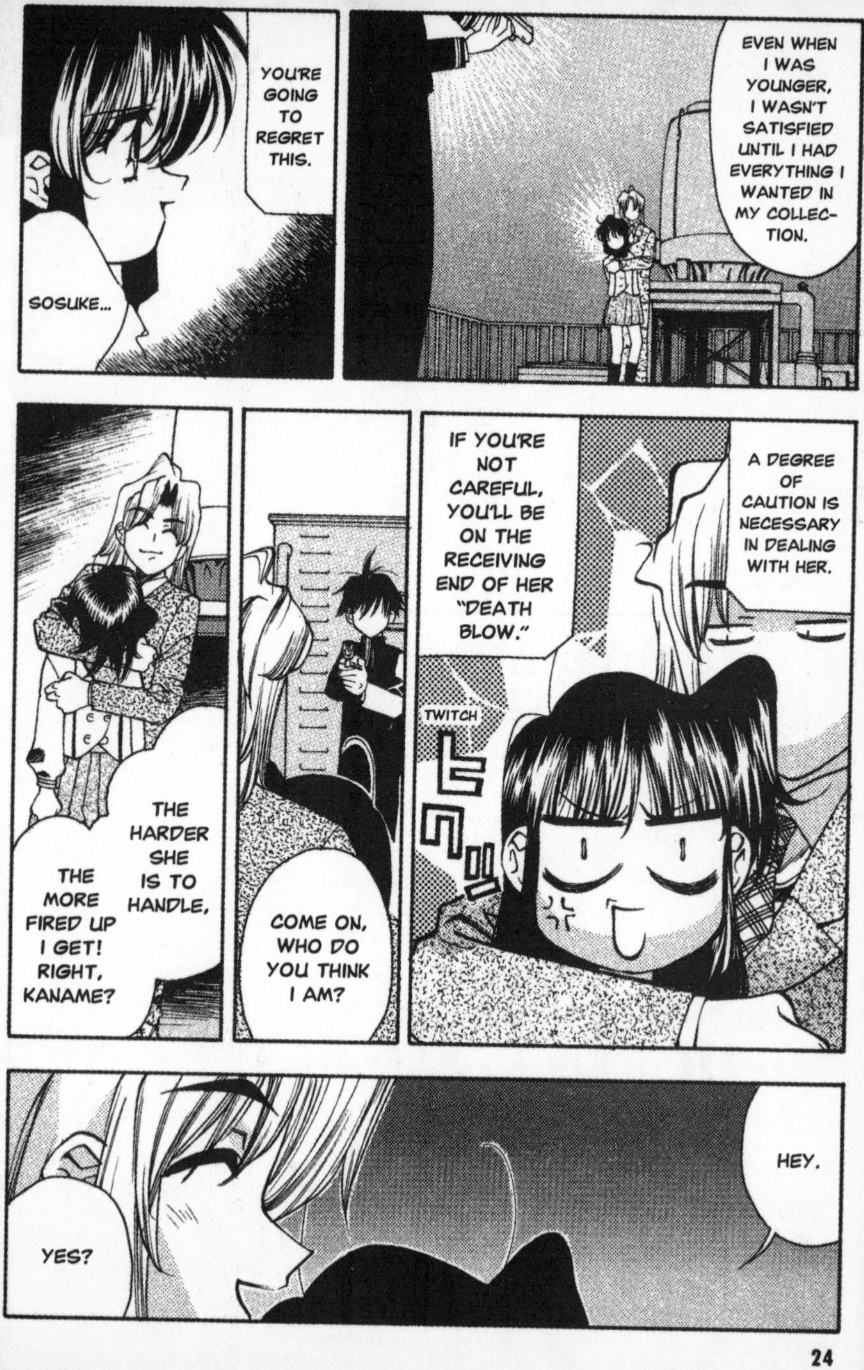
EVEN WHEN I WAS YOUNGER, I WASN'T SATISFIED UNTIL I HAD EVERYTHING I WANTED IN MY COLLEC-TION.
YOU'RE GOING TO REGRET THIS.
SOSUKE...
A DEGREE OF CAUTION IS NECESSARY IN DEALING WITH HER.
IF YOU'RE NOT CAREFUL, YOU'LL BE ON THE RECEIVING END OF HER "DEATH BLOW."
TWITCH
COME ON, WHO DO YOU THINK I AM?
THE HARDER SHE IS TO HANDLE,
THE MORE FIRED UP I GET! RIGHT, KANAME?
HEY.
YES?

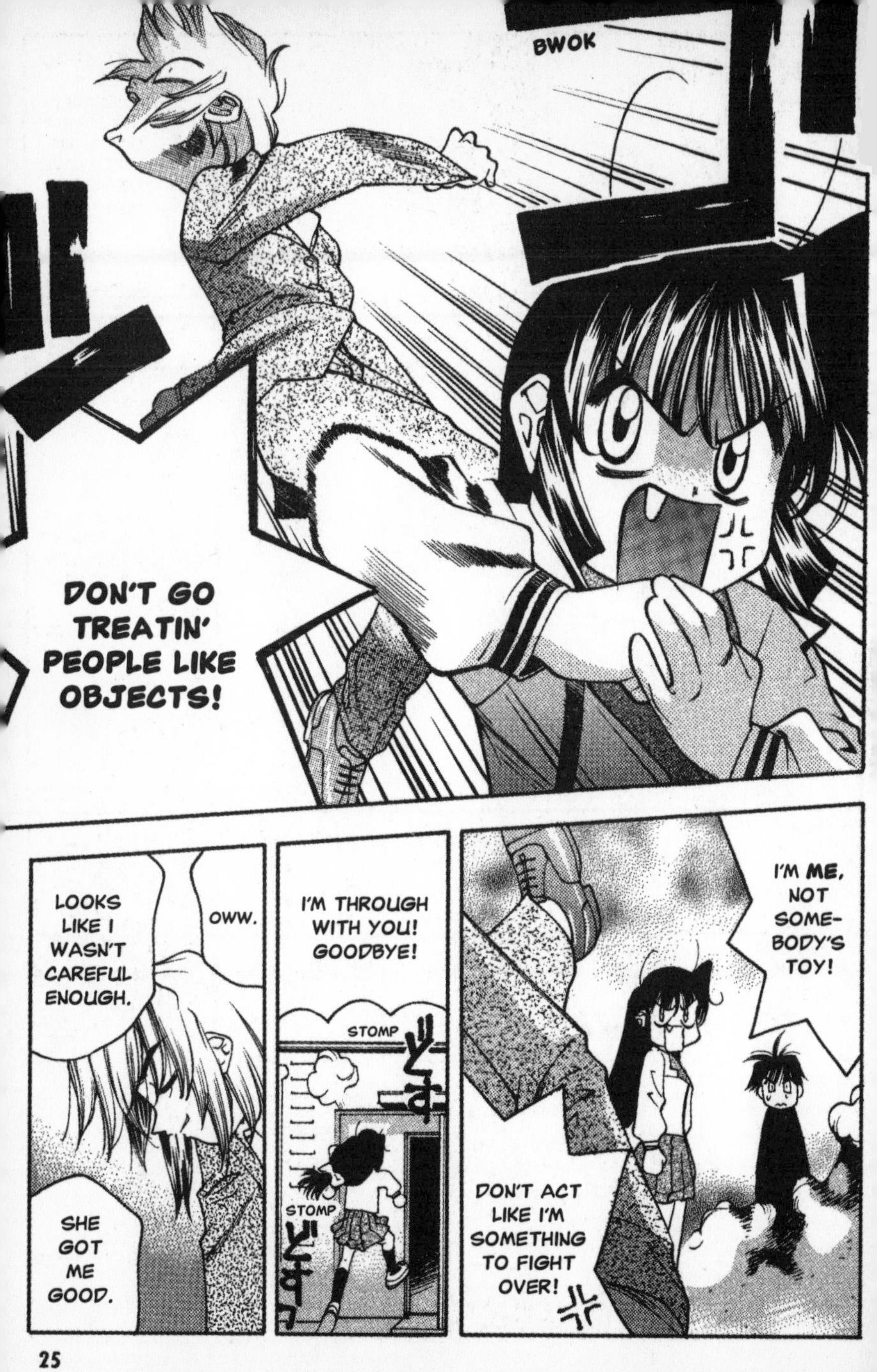
BWOK
DON'T GO TREATIN' PEOPLE LIKE OBJECTS!
I'M ME, NOT SOMEBODY'S TOY!
DON'T ACT LIKE I'M SOMETHING TO FIGHT OVER!
I'M THROUGH WITH YOU! GOODBYE!
STOMP
STOMP
OWW.
LOOKS LIKE I WASN'T CAREFUL ENOUGH.
SHE GOT ME GOOD.

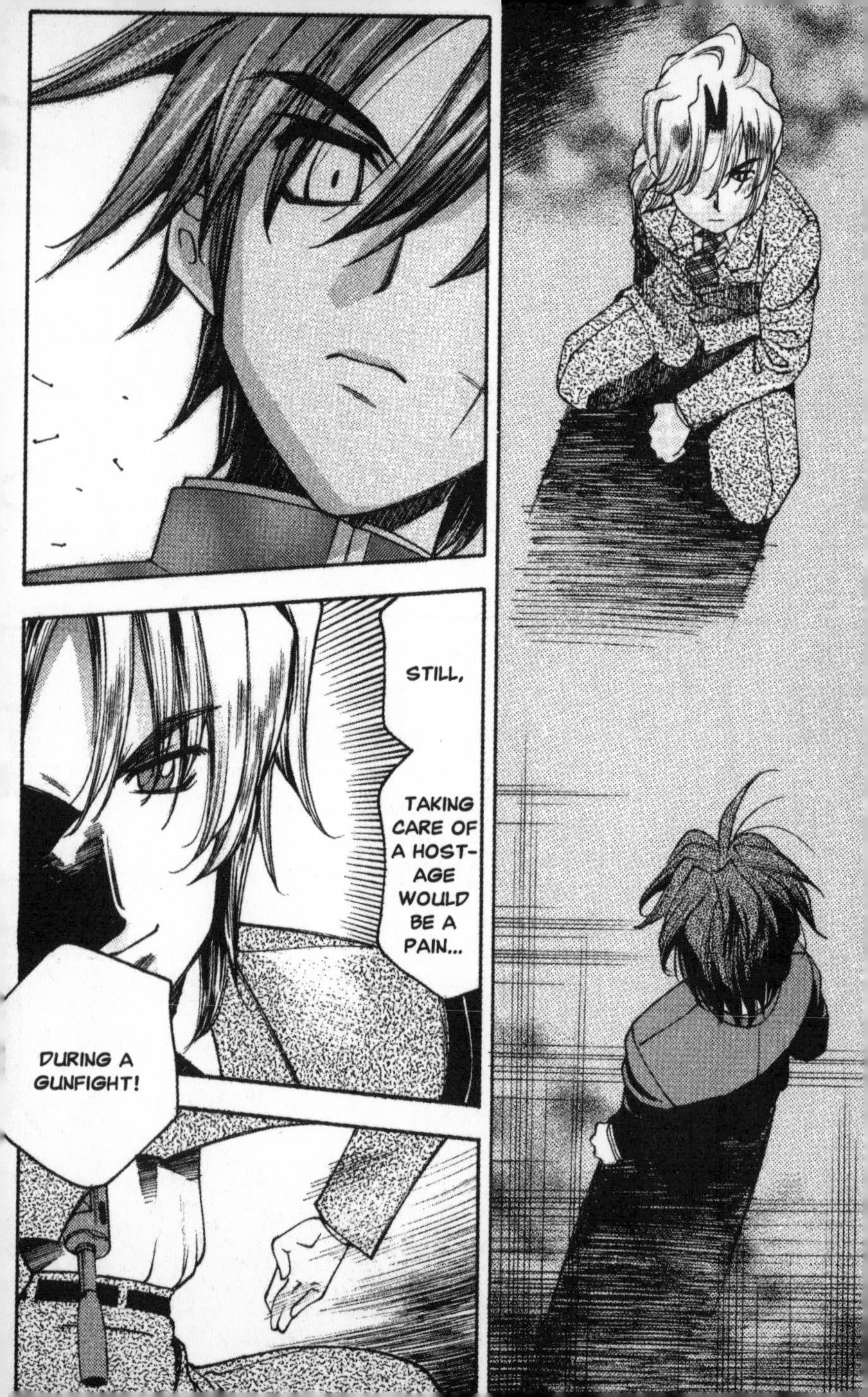
STILL,
TAKING CARE OF A HOST-AGE WOULD BE A PAIN...
DURING A GUNFIGHT!

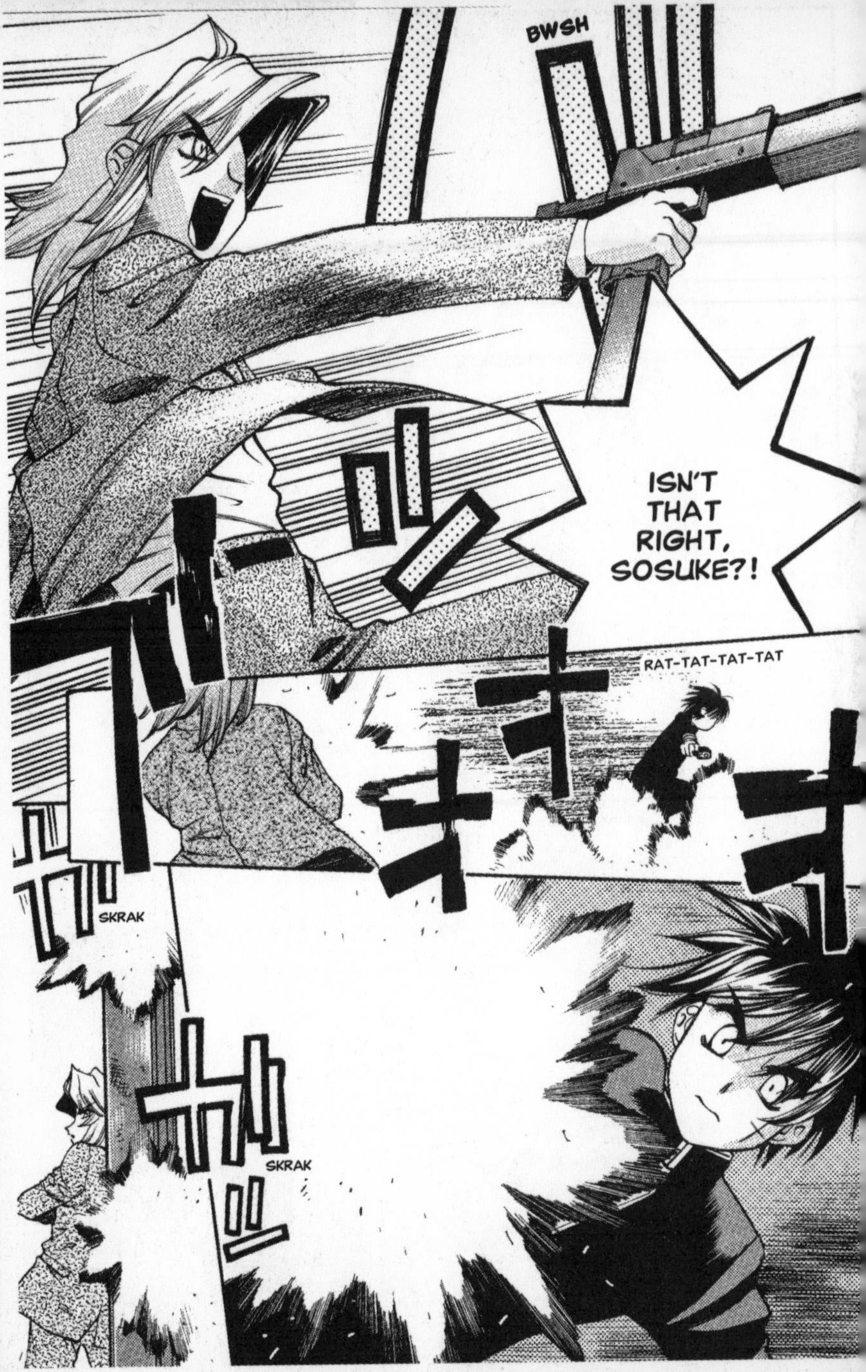
BWSH
ISN'T THAT RIGHT, SOSUKE?!
RAT-TAT-TAT-TAT
SKRAK
SKRAK

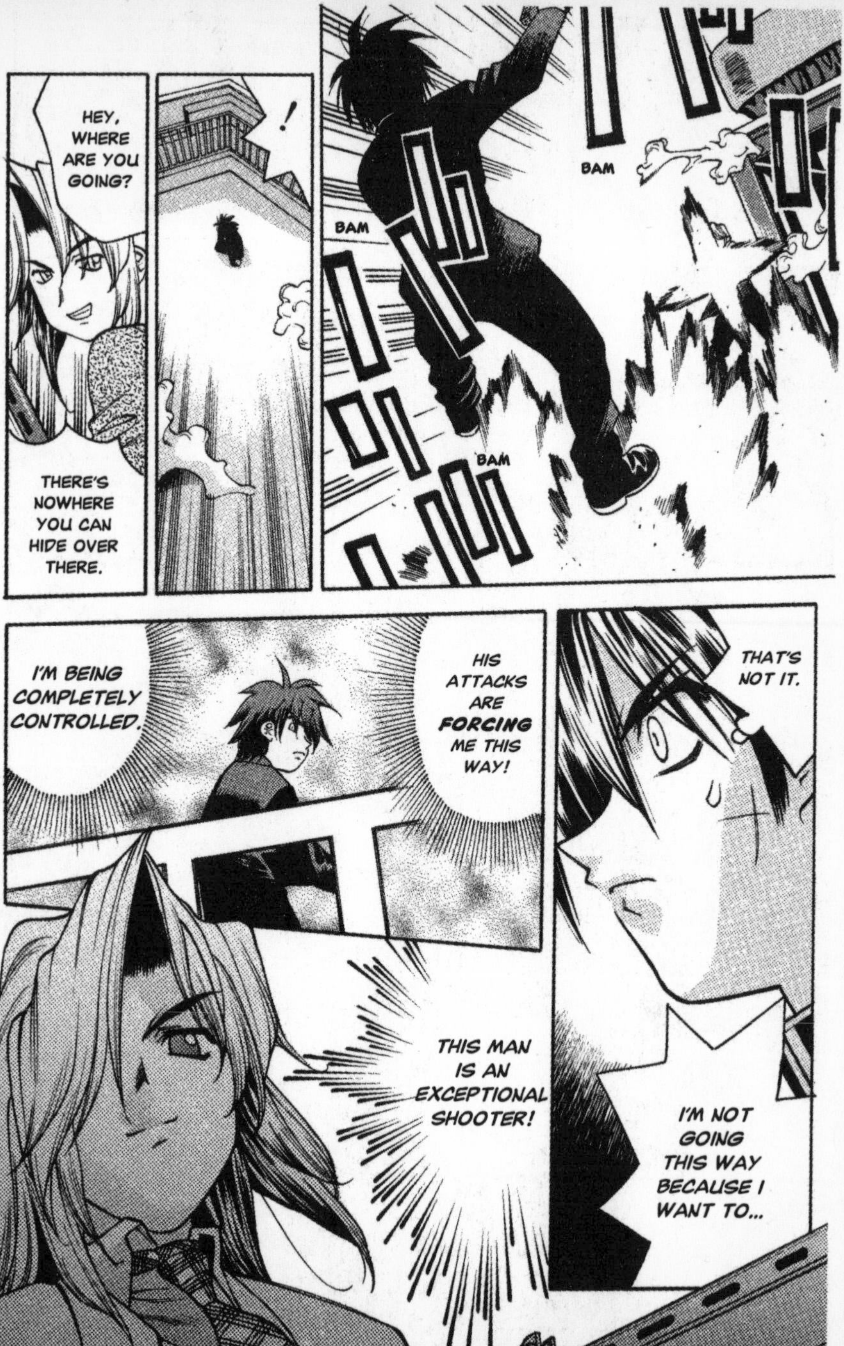
BAM
BAM
BAM
!
HEY, WHERE ARE YOU GOING?
THERE'S NOWHERE YOU CAN HIDE OVER THERE.
I'M BEING COMPLETELY CONTROLLED.
HIS ATTACKS ARE FORCING ME THIS WAY!
THAT'S NOT IT.
I'M NOT GOING THIS WAY BECAUSE I WANT TO...
THIS MAN IS AN EXCEPTIONAL SHOOTER!

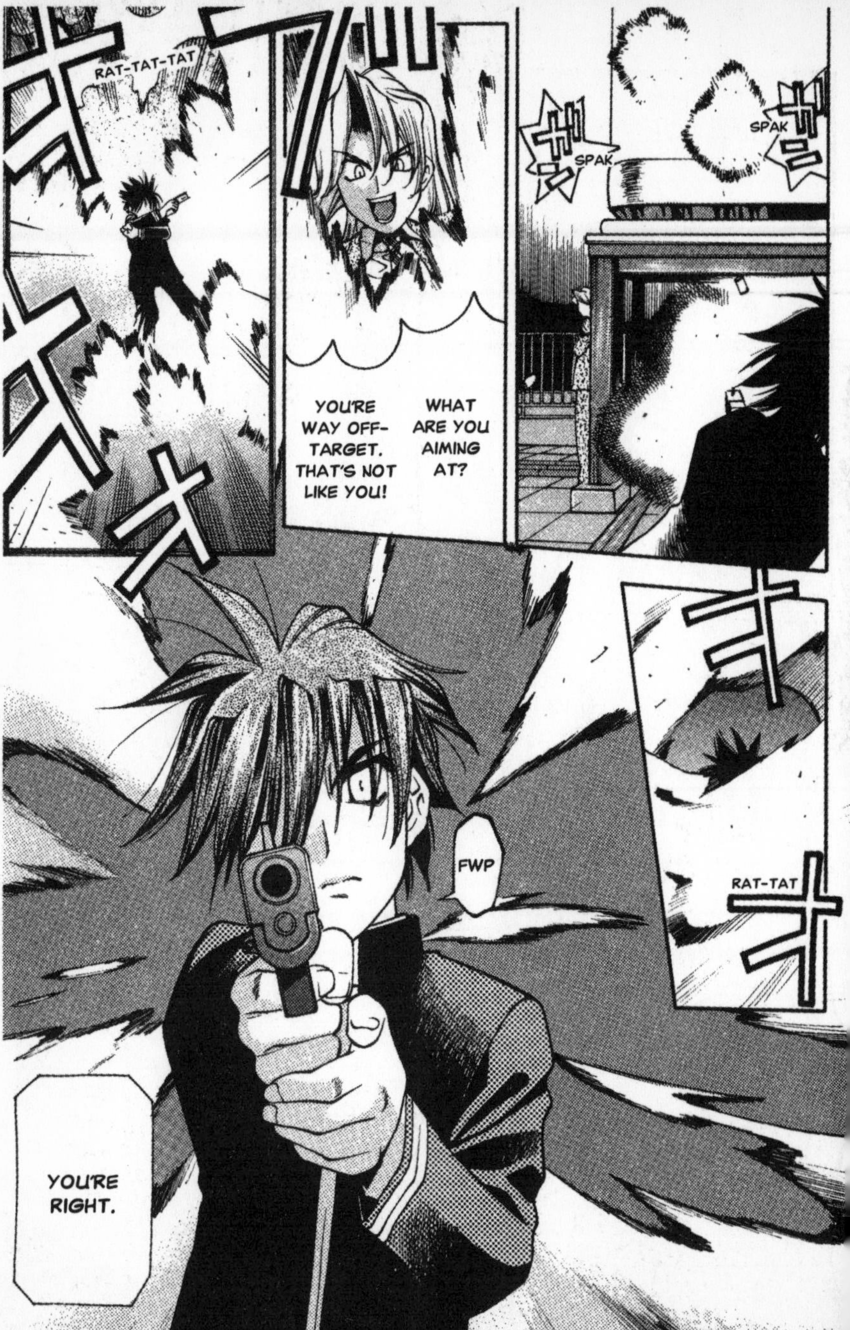
RAT-TAT-TAT
WHAT ARE YOU AIMING AT?
YOU'RE WAY OFF-TARGET. THAT'S NOT LIKE YOU!
SPAK
SPAK
RAT-TAT
FWP
YOU'RE RIGHT.

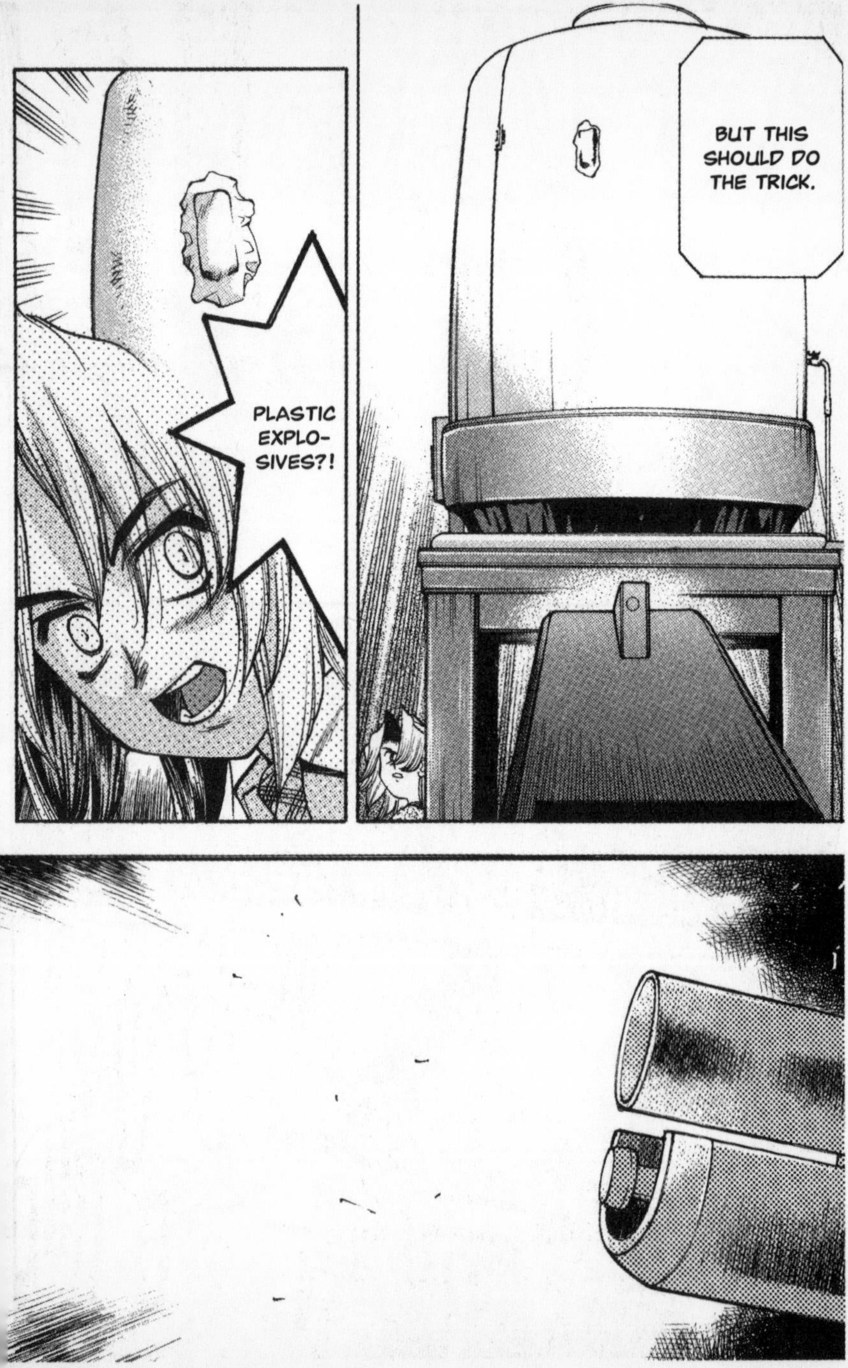
BUT THIS SHOULD DO THE TRICK.
PLASTIC EXPLO-SIVES?!

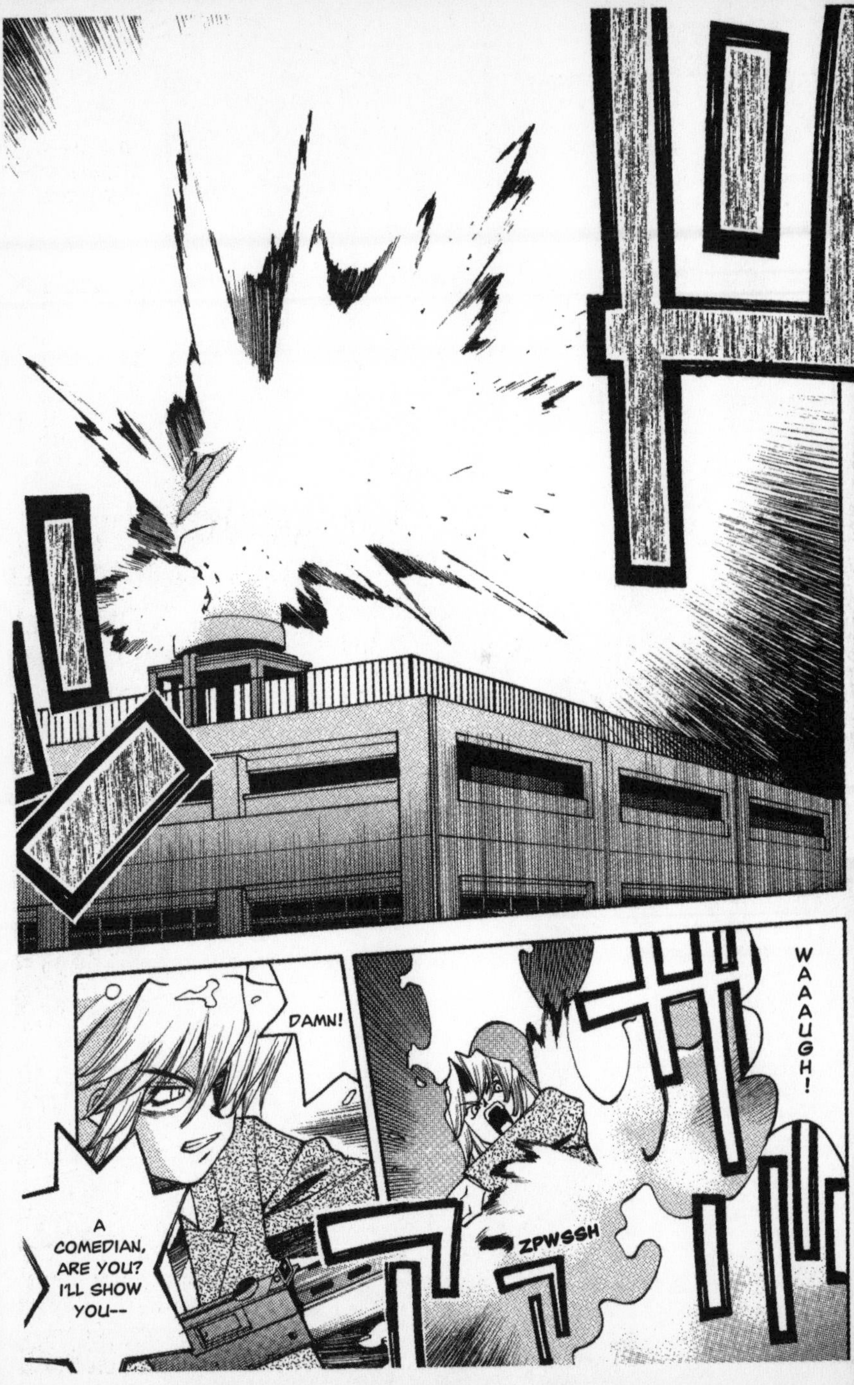
WAAAUGH!
DAMN!
A COMEDIAN, ARE YOU? I'LL SHOW YOU--
ZPWSSH

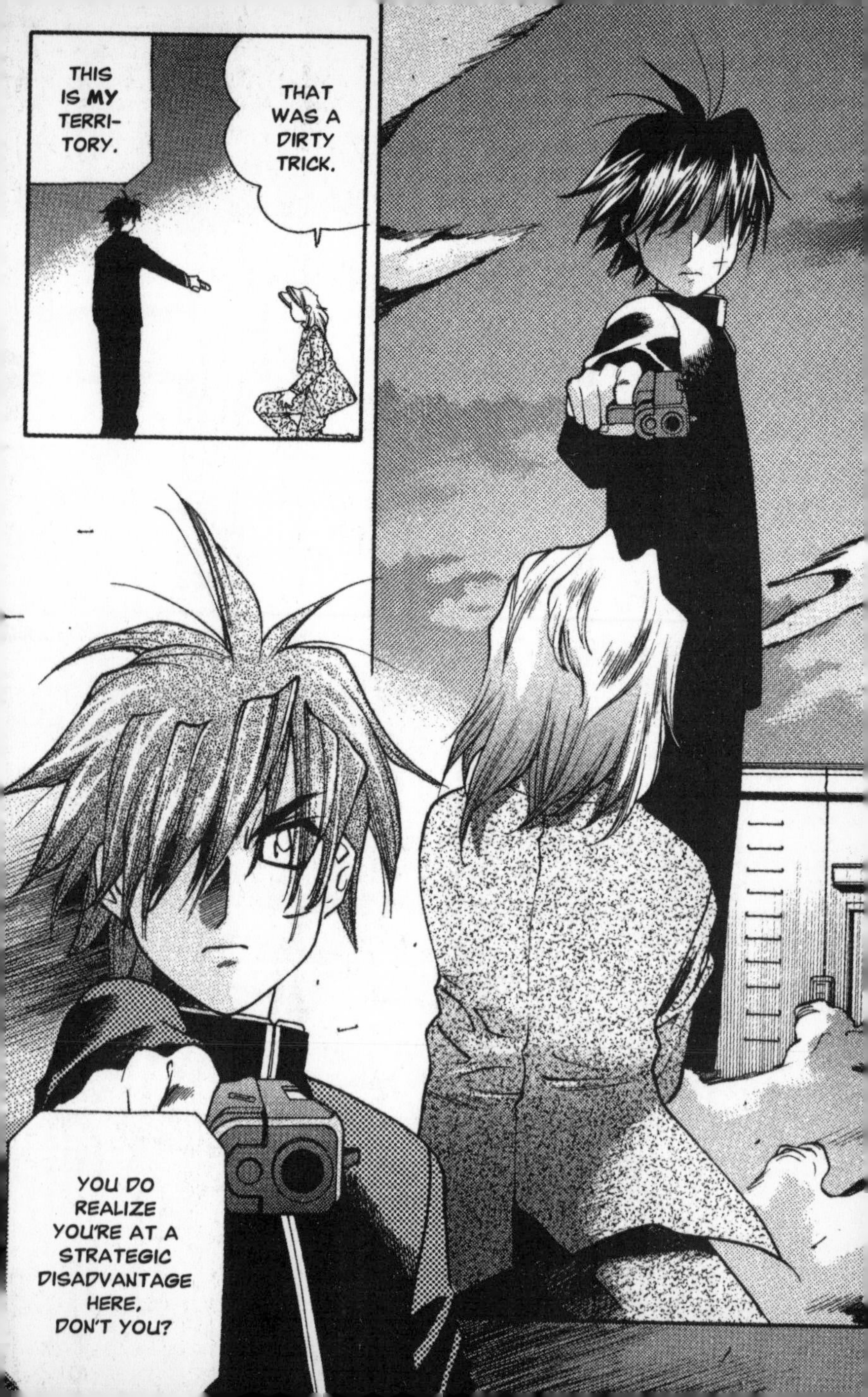

THAT WAS A DIRTY TRICK.
THIS IS MY TERRI-TORY.
YOU DO REALIZE YOU'RE AT A STRATEGIC DISADVANTAGE HERE, DON'T YOU?

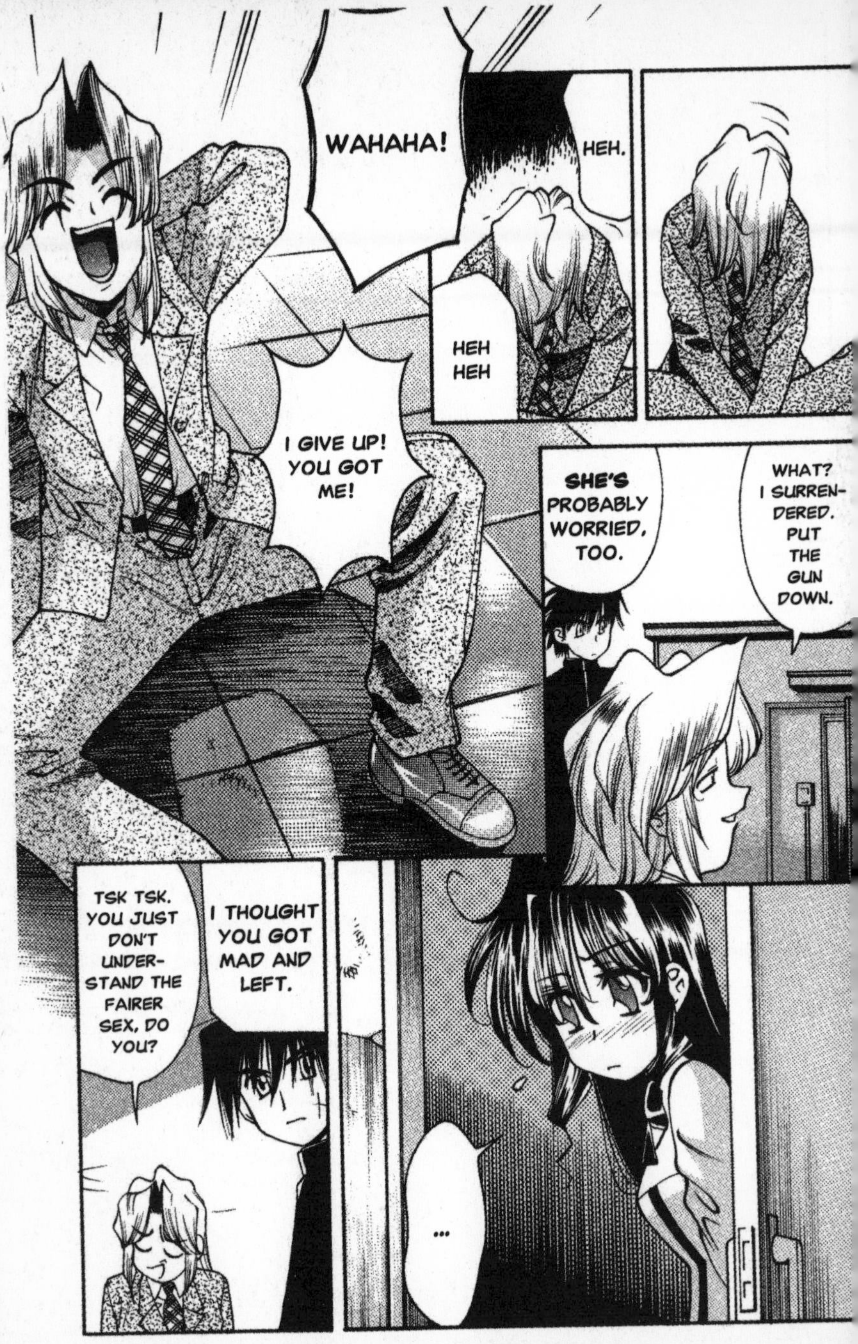
HEH.
HEH HEH
WAHAHA!
I GIVE UP! YOU GOT ME!
WHAT? I SURRENDERED. PUT THE GUN DOWN.
SHE'S PROBABLY WORRIED, TOO.
...
I THOUGHT YOU GOT MAD AND LEFT.
TSK TSK. YOU JUST DON'T UNDERSTAND THE FAIRER SEX, DO YOU?

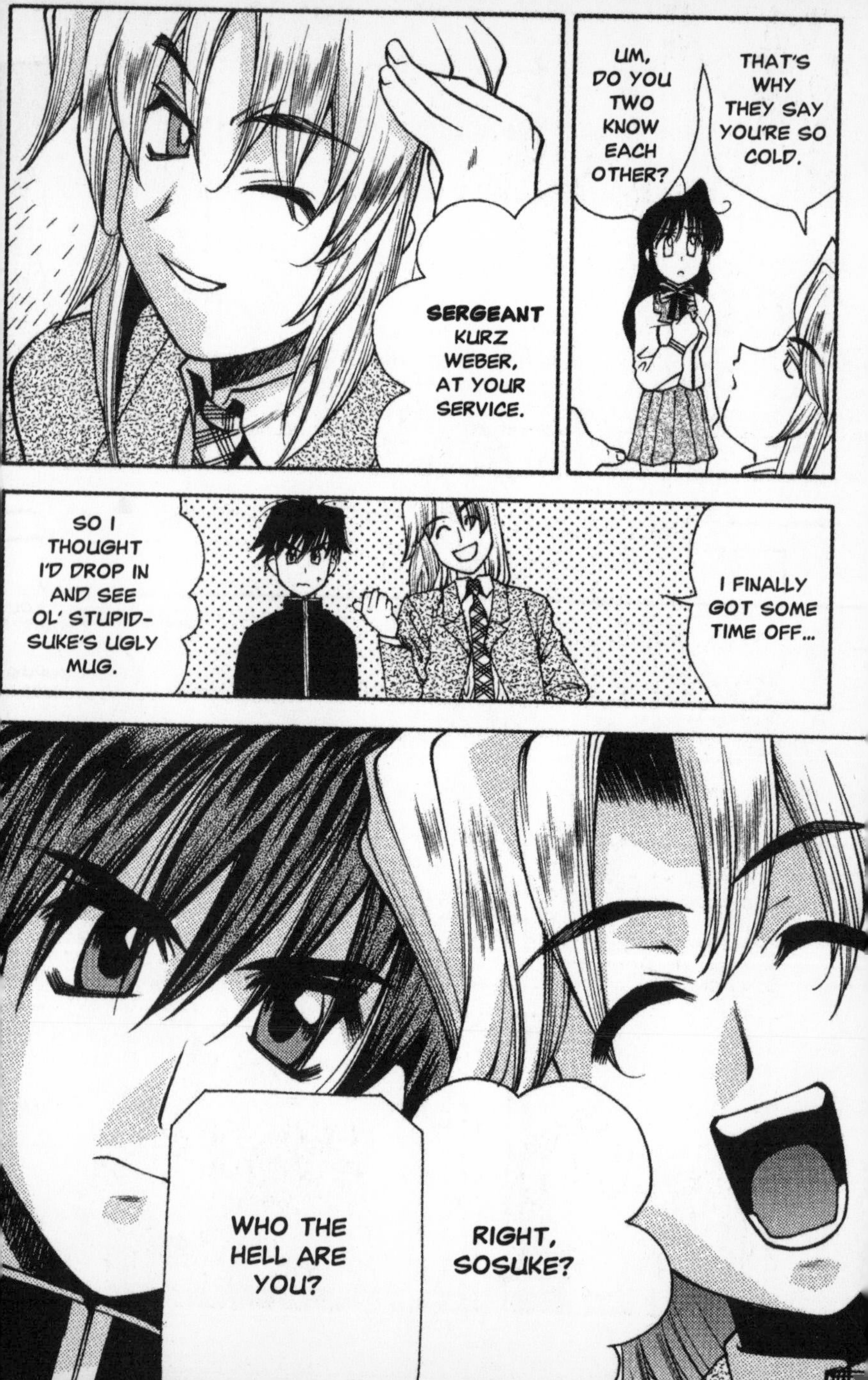
THAT'S WHY THEY SAY YOU'RE SO COLD.
UM, DO YOU TWO KNOW EACH OTHER?
SERGEANT KURZ WEBER, AT YOUR SERVICE.
I FINALLY GOT SOME TIME OFF...
SO I THOUGHT I'D DROP IN AND SEE OL' STUPID-SUKE'S UGLY MUG.
RIGHT, SOSUKE?
WHO THE HELL ARE YOU?

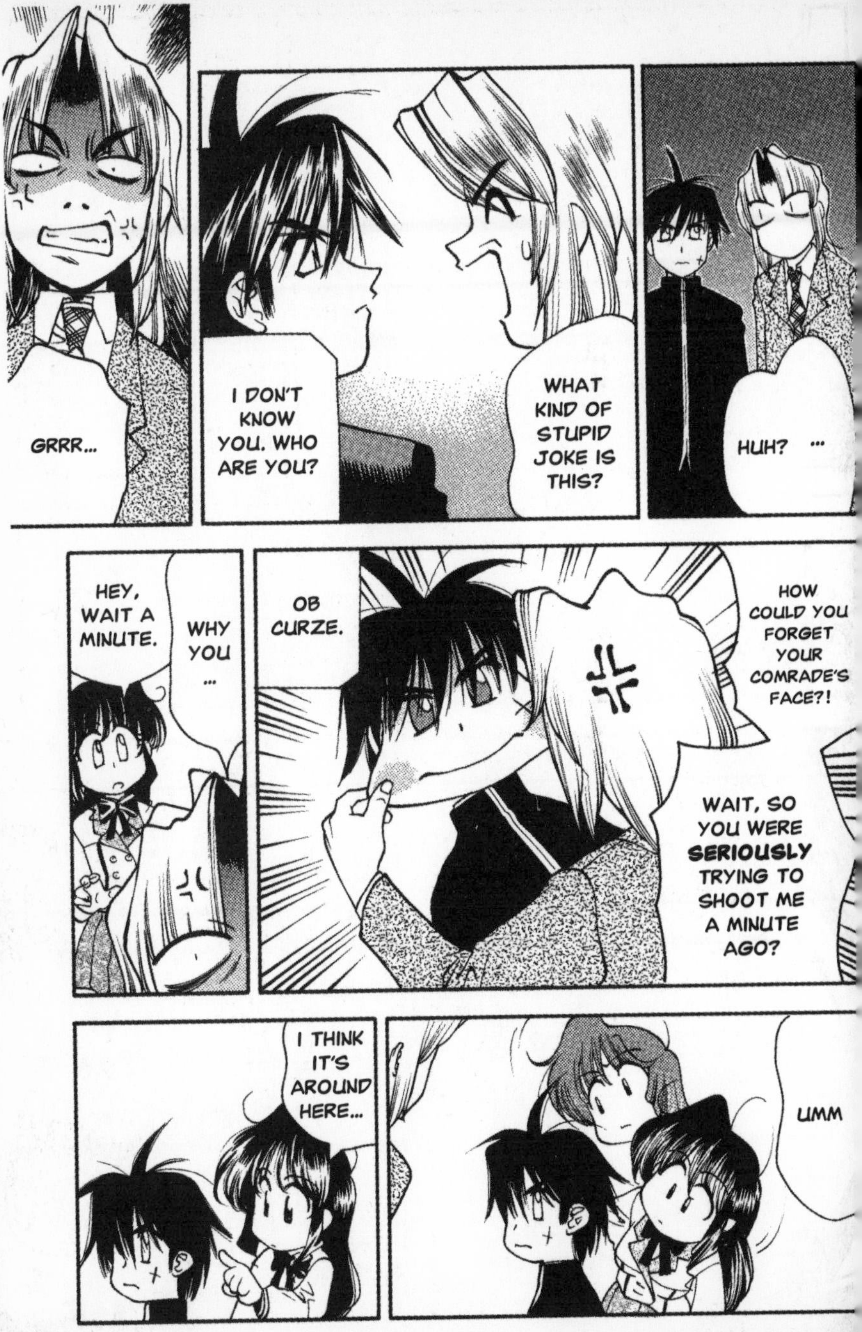
HUH? ...
WHAT KIND OF STUPID JOKE IS THIS?
I DON'T KNOW YOU. WHO ARE YOU?
GRRR...
HOW COULD YOU FORGET YOUR COMRADE'S FACE?!
OB CURZE.
WAIT, SO YOU WERE **SERIOUSLY** TRYING TO SHOOT ME A MINUTE AGO?
WHY YOU ...
HEY, WAIT A MINUTE.
UMM
I THINK IT'S AROUND HERE...

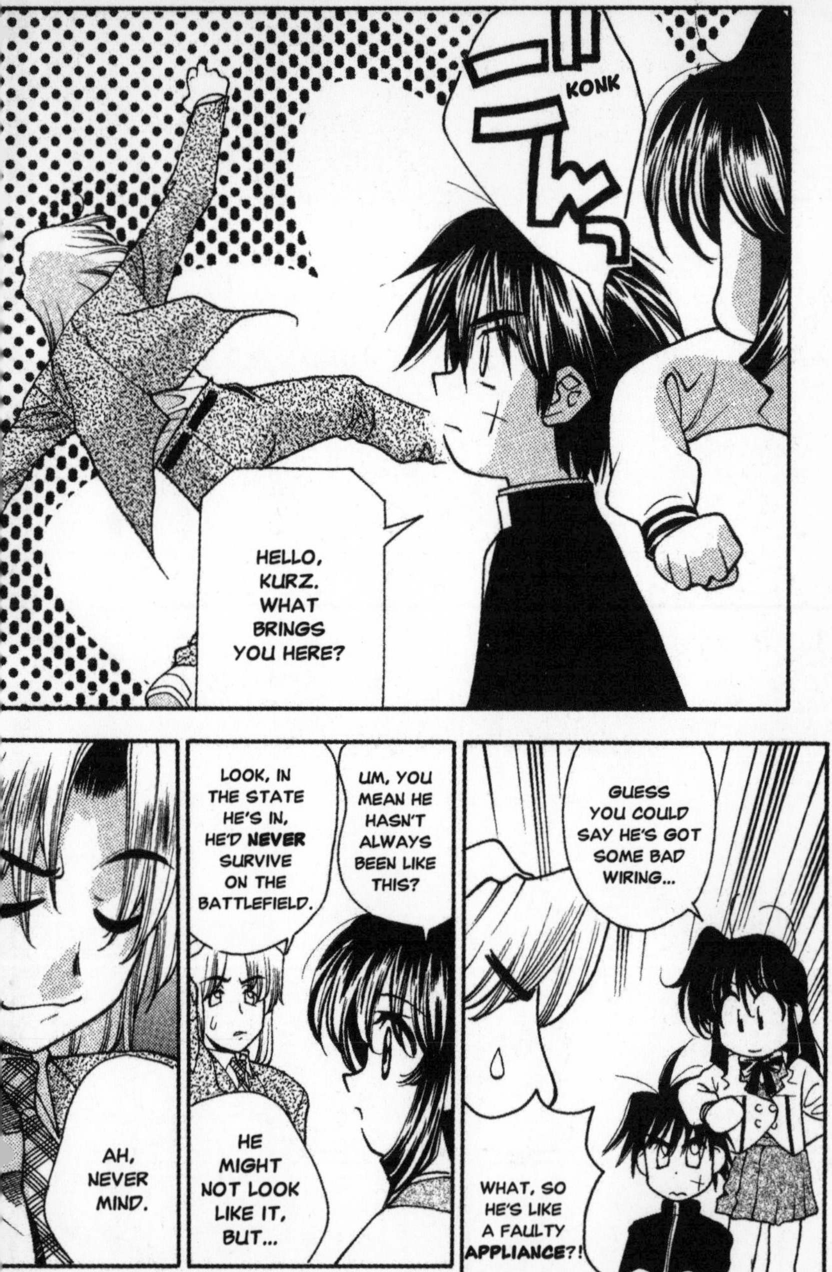
KONK
HELLO, KURZ. WHAT BRINGS YOU HERE?
GUESS YOU COULD SAY HE'S GOT SOME BAD WIRING...
WHAT, SO HE'S LIKE A FAULTY APPLIANCE?!
UM, YOU MEAN HE HASN'T ALWAYS BEEN LIKE THIS?
LOOK, IN THE STATE HE'S IN, HE'D NEVER SURVIVE ON THE BATTLEFIELD.
HE MIGHT NOT LOOK LIKE IT, BUT...
AH, NEVER MIND.

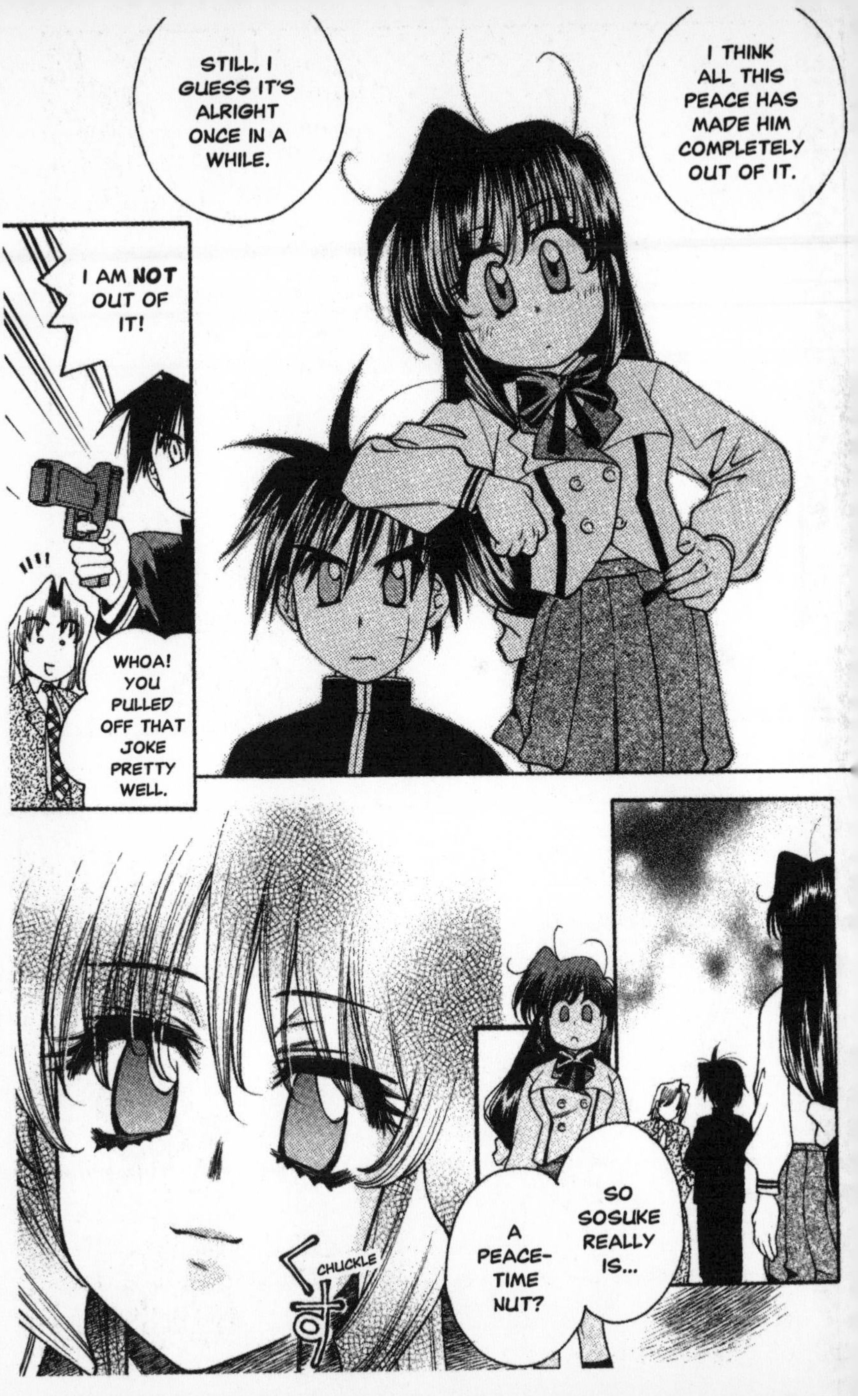
I THINK ALL THIS PEACE HAS MADE HIM COMPLETELY OUT OF IT.
STILL, I GUESS IT'S ALRIGHT ONCE IN A WHILE.
I AM NOT OUT OF IT!
WHOA! YOU PULLED OFF THAT JOKE PRETTY WELL.
SO SOSUKE REALLY IS...
A PEACE-TIME NUT?
CHUCKLE

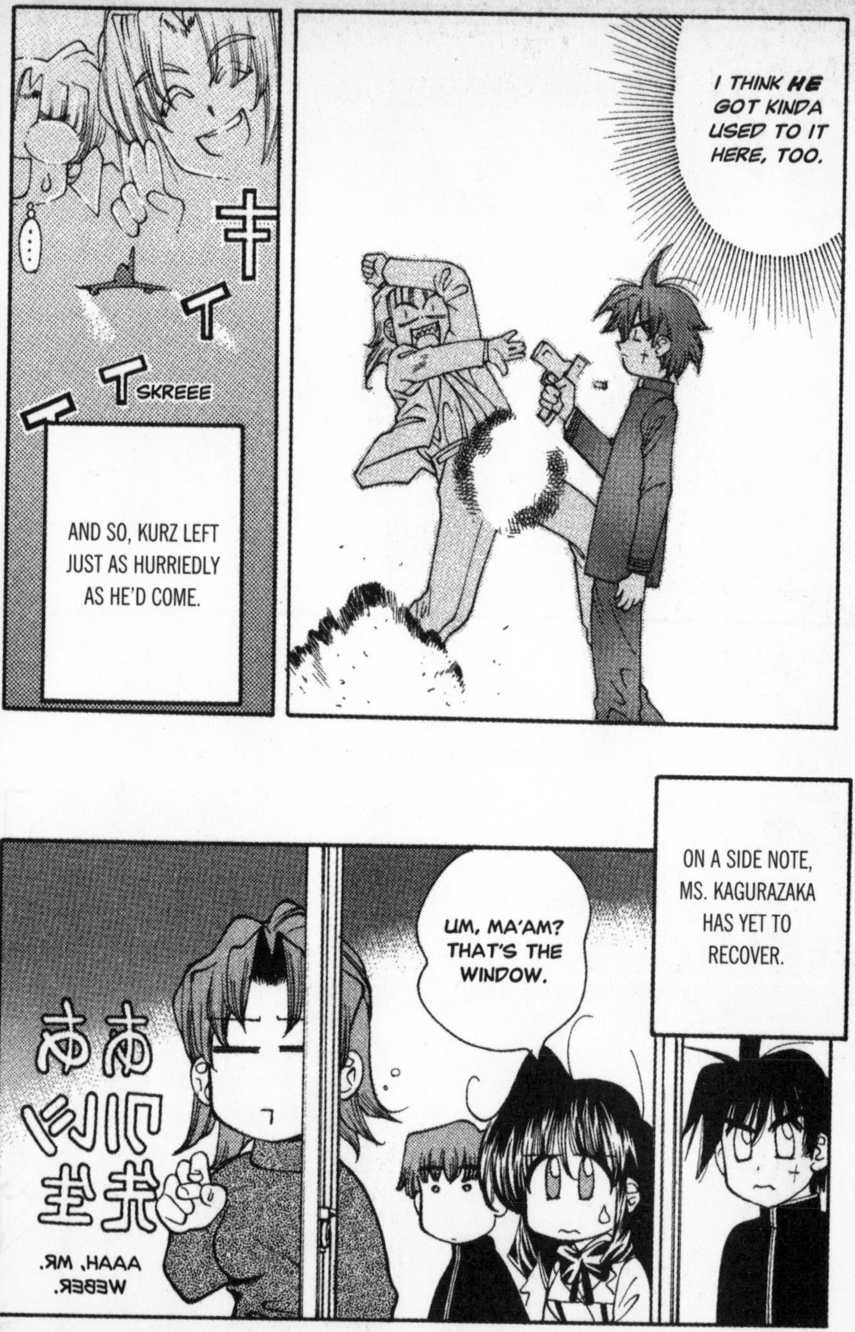
I THINK **HE** GOT KINDA USED TO IT HERE, TOO.
SKREEE
AND SO, KURZ LEFT JUST AS HURRIEDLY AS HE'D COME.
ON A SIDE NOTE, MS. KAGURAZAKA HAS YET TO RECOVER.
UM, MA'AM? THAT'S THE WINDOW.
AAAH, MR. WEBER.

BOMB 8 REQUIEM FOR THE SICK

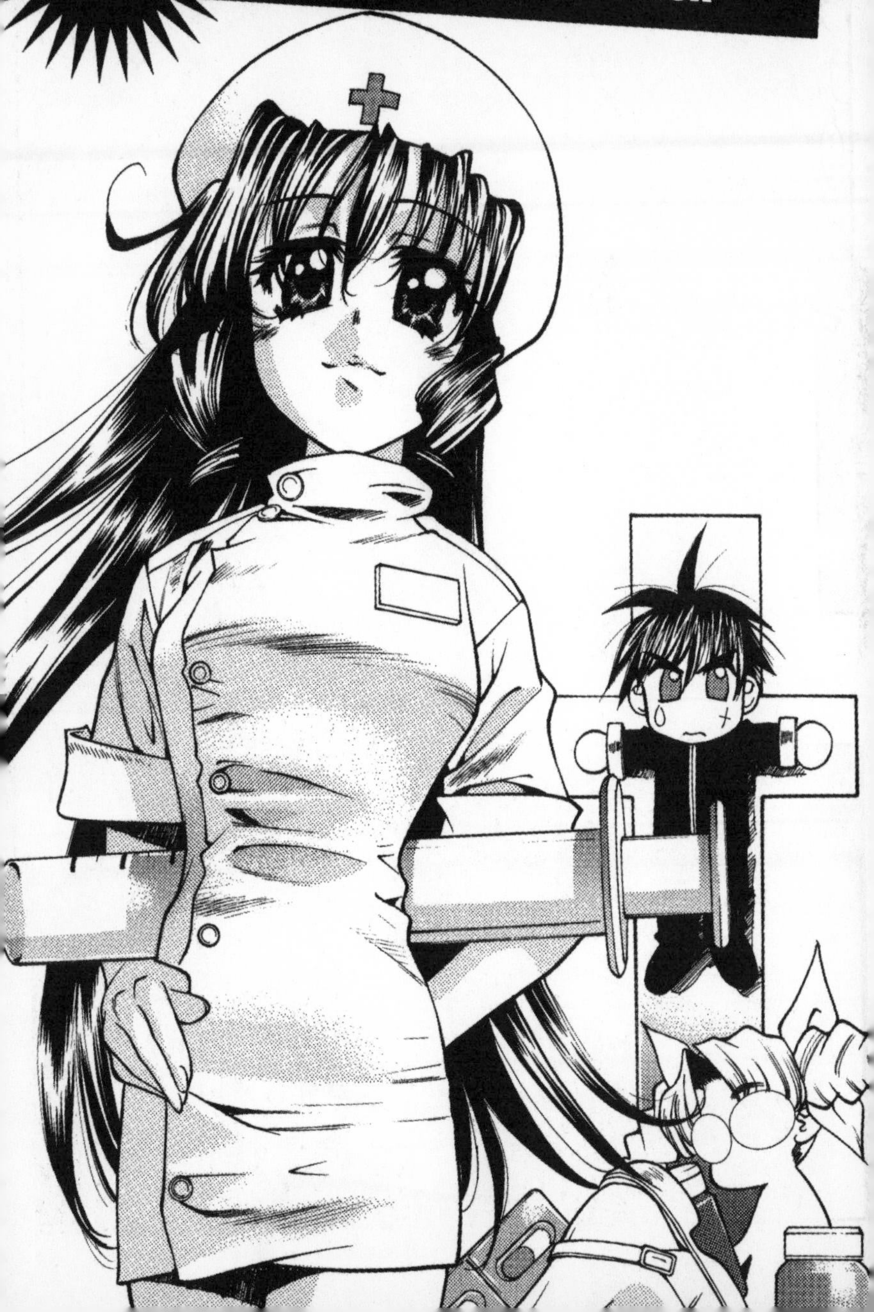

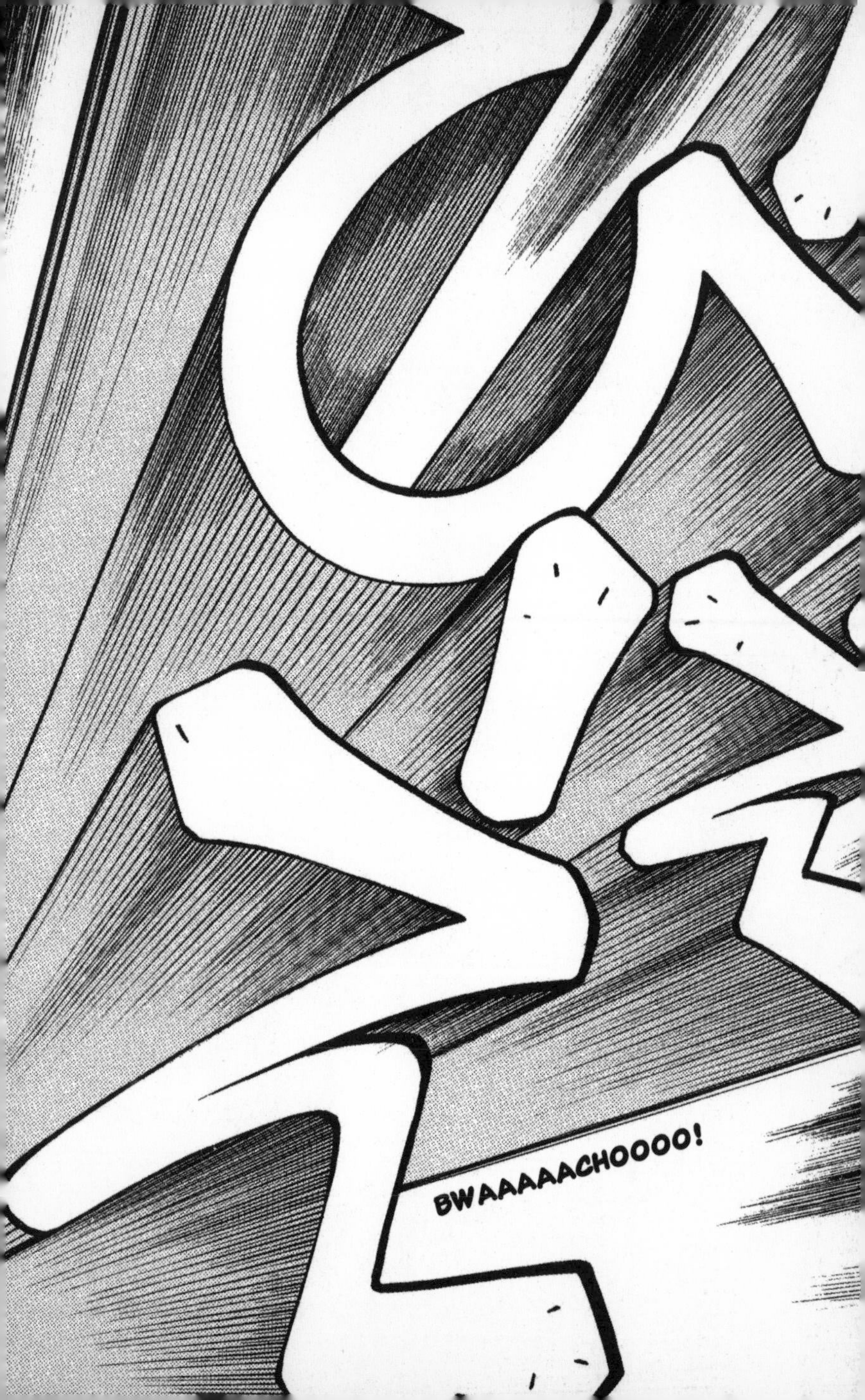
BWAAAAACHOOOO!

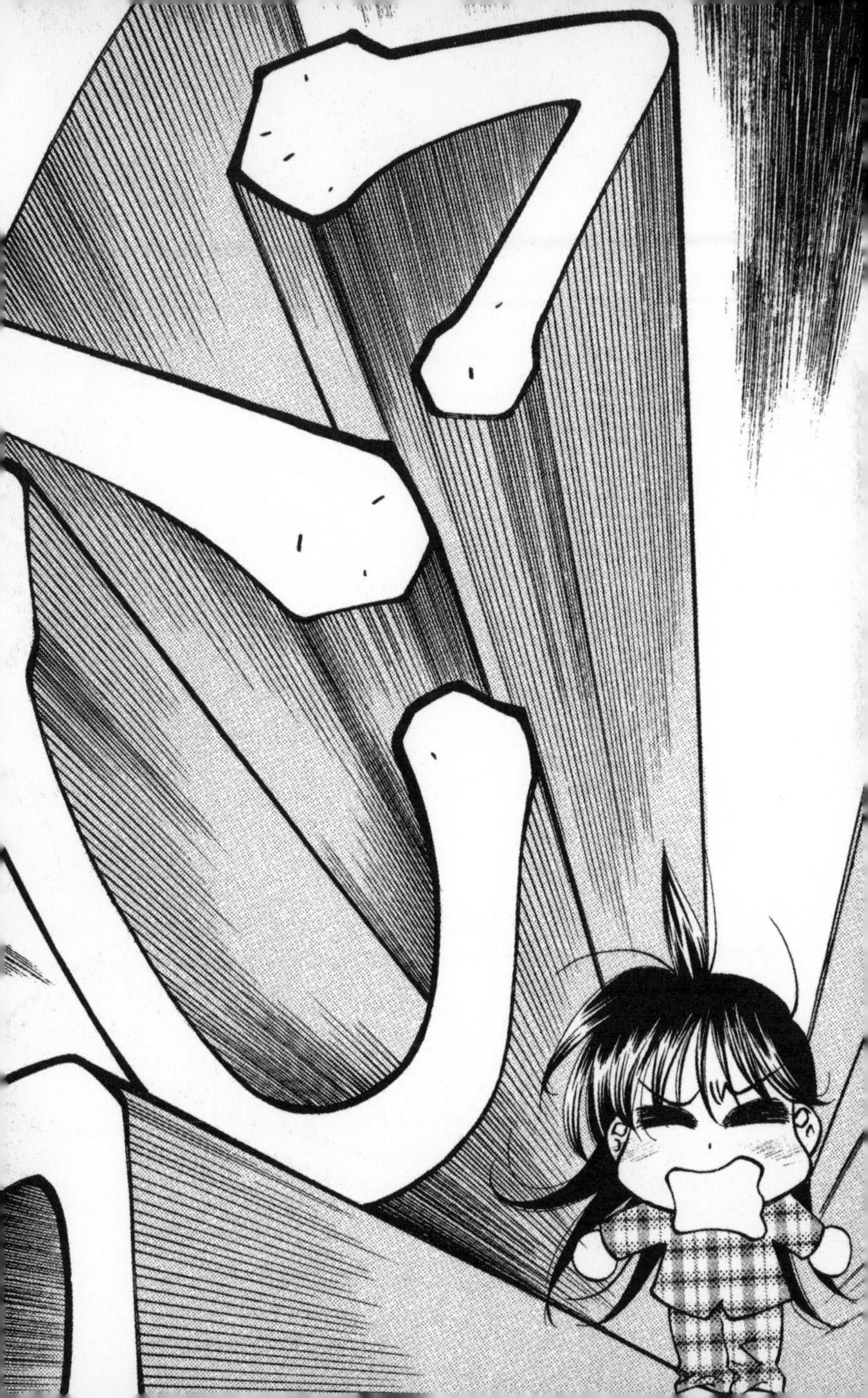

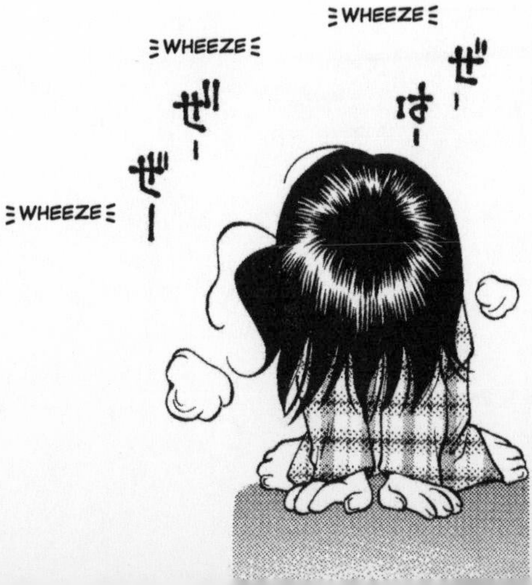
WHEEZE
ぜー
はー
WHEEZE
ぜー
ぜー
WHEEZE

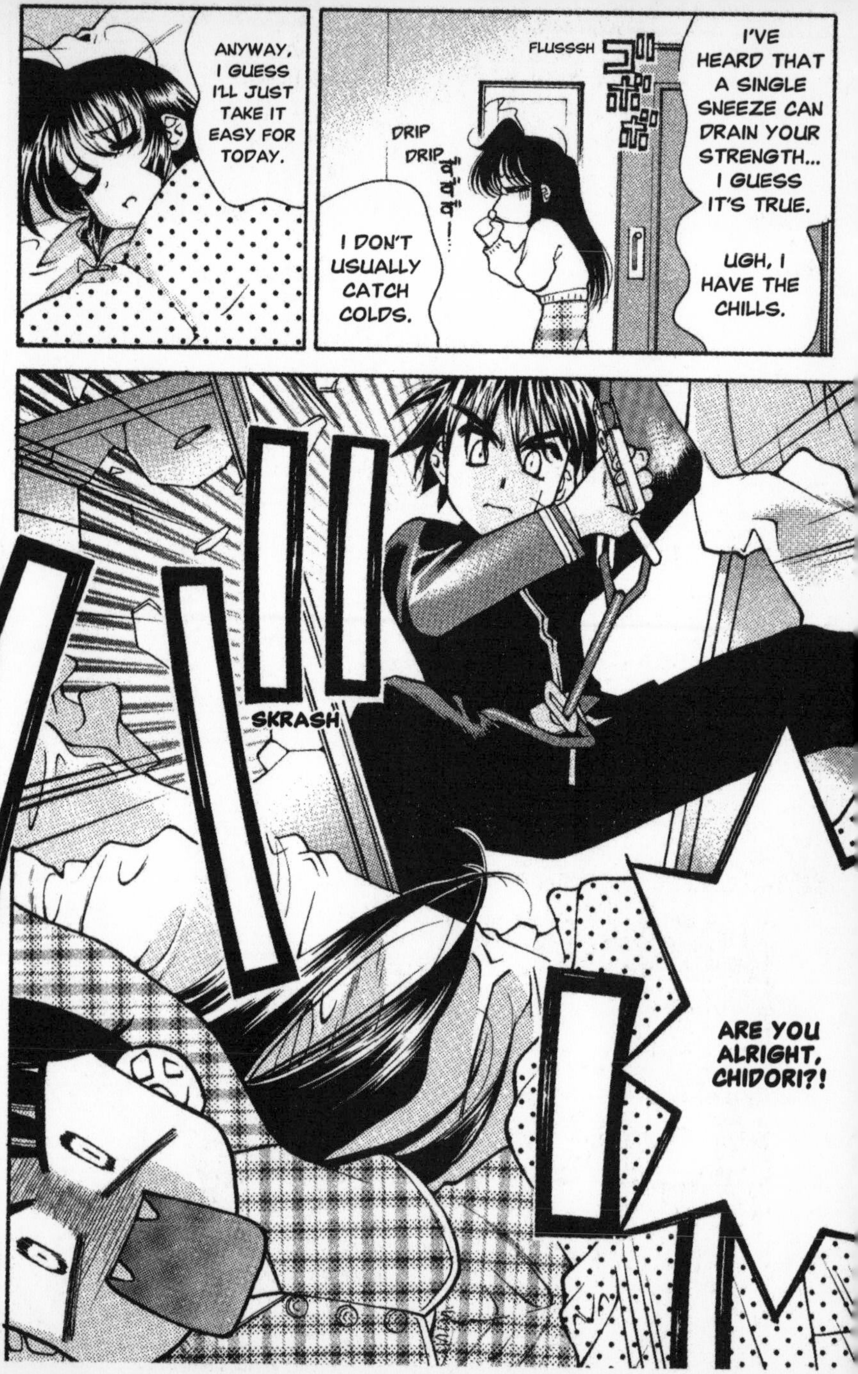
FLUSSSH
I'VE HEARD THAT A SINGLE SNEEZE CAN DRAIN YOUR STRENGTH... I GUESS IT'S TRUE.
UGH, I HAVE THE CHILLS.
DRIP DRIP
I DON'T USUALLY CATCH COLDS.
ANYWAY, I GUESS I'LL JUST TAKE IT EASY FOR TODAY.
SKRASH
ARE YOU ALRIGHT, CHIDORI?!

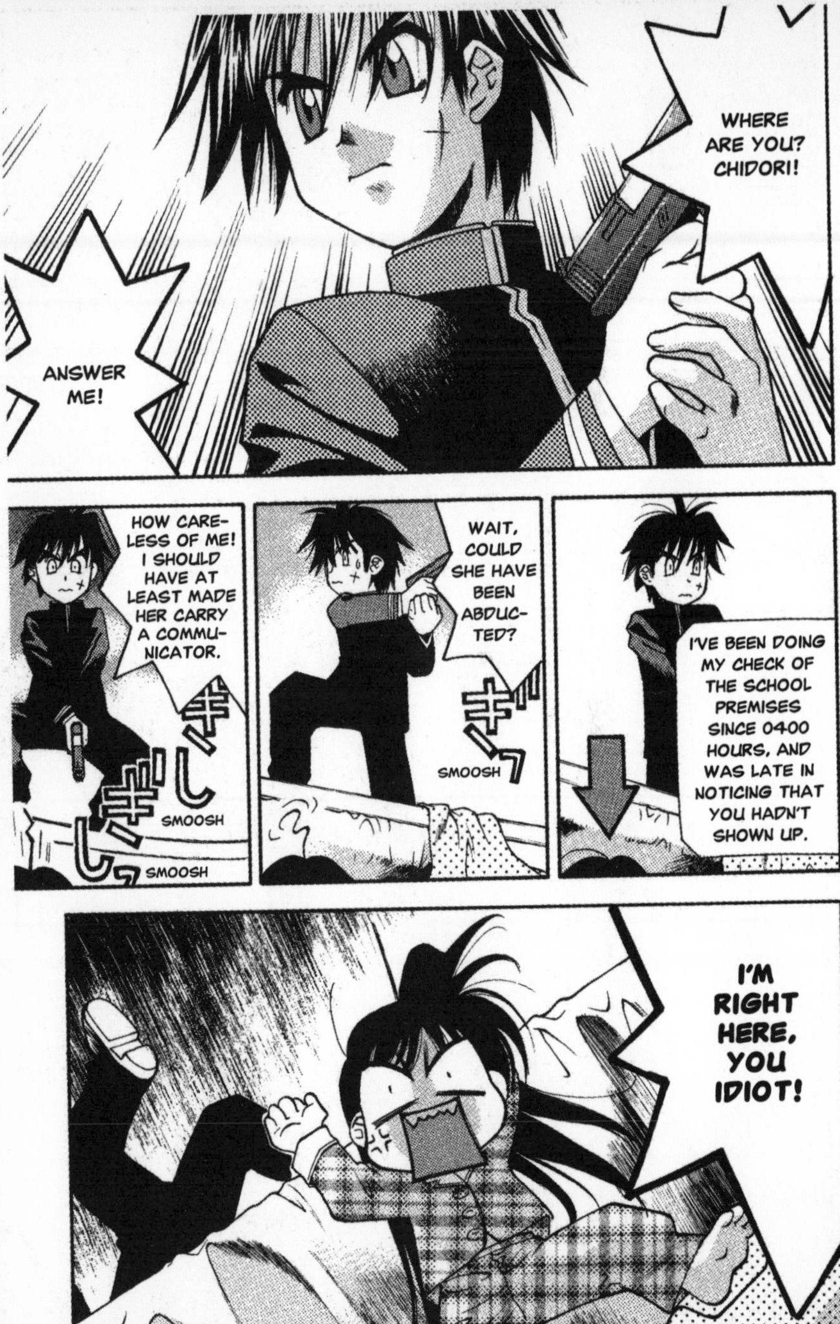
WHERE ARE YOU? CHIDORI!
ANSWER ME!
I'VE BEEN DOING MY CHECK OF THE SCHOOL PREMISES SINCE 0400 HOURS, AND WAS LATE IN NOTICING THAT YOU HADN'T SHOWN UP.
WAIT, COULD SHE HAVE BEEN ABDUCTED?
SMOOSH
HOW CARELESS OF ME! I SHOULD HAVE AT LEAST MADE HER CARRY A COMMUNICATOR.
SMOOSH
SMOOSH
I'M RIGHT HERE, YOU IDIOT!

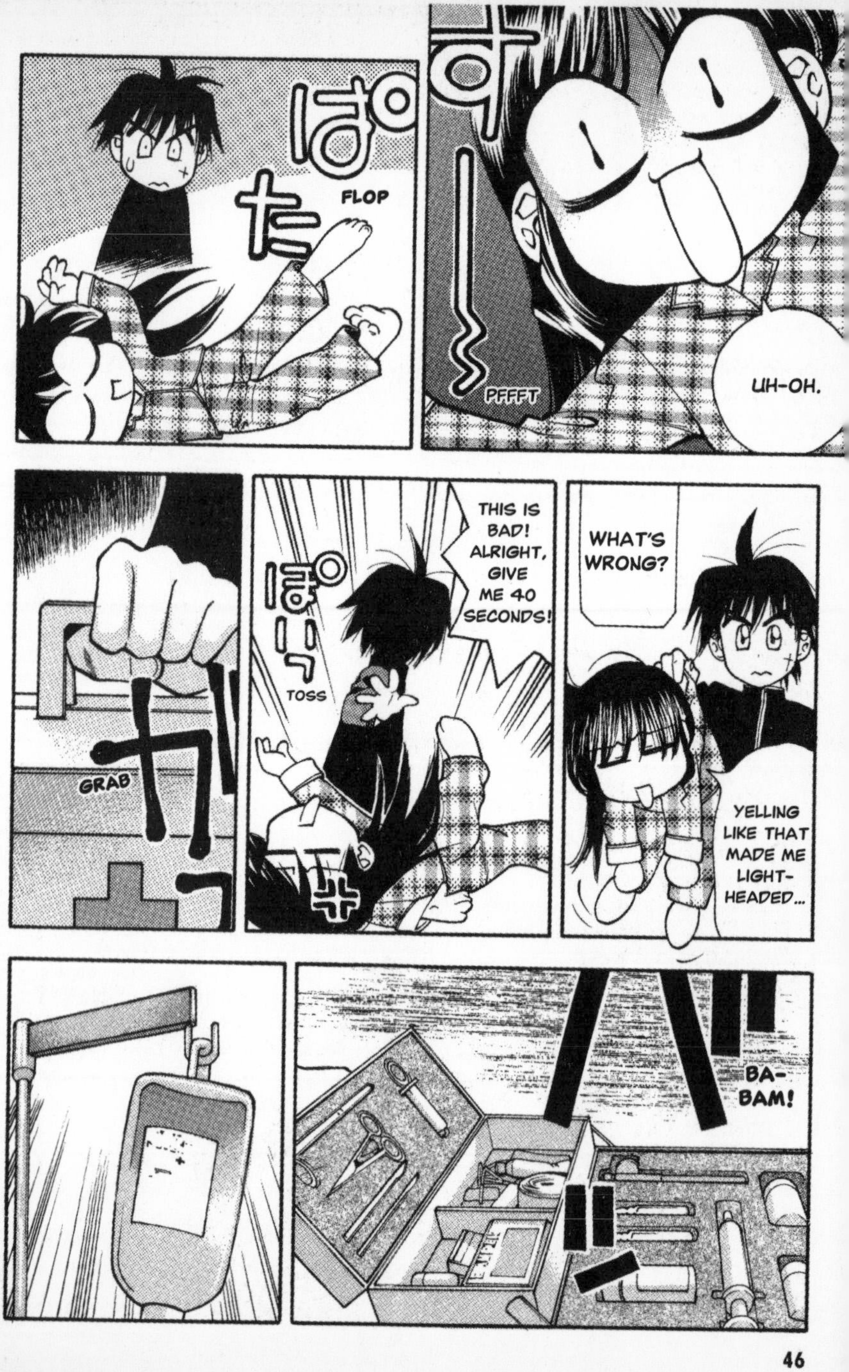
すー
PFFFT
UH-OH.
ぱた
FLOP
WHAT'S WRONG?
YELLING LIKE THAT MADE ME LIGHT-HEADED...
THIS IS BAD! ALRIGHT, GIVE ME 40 SECONDS!
ぽいっ
TOSS
ガッ
GRAB
BA-BAM!

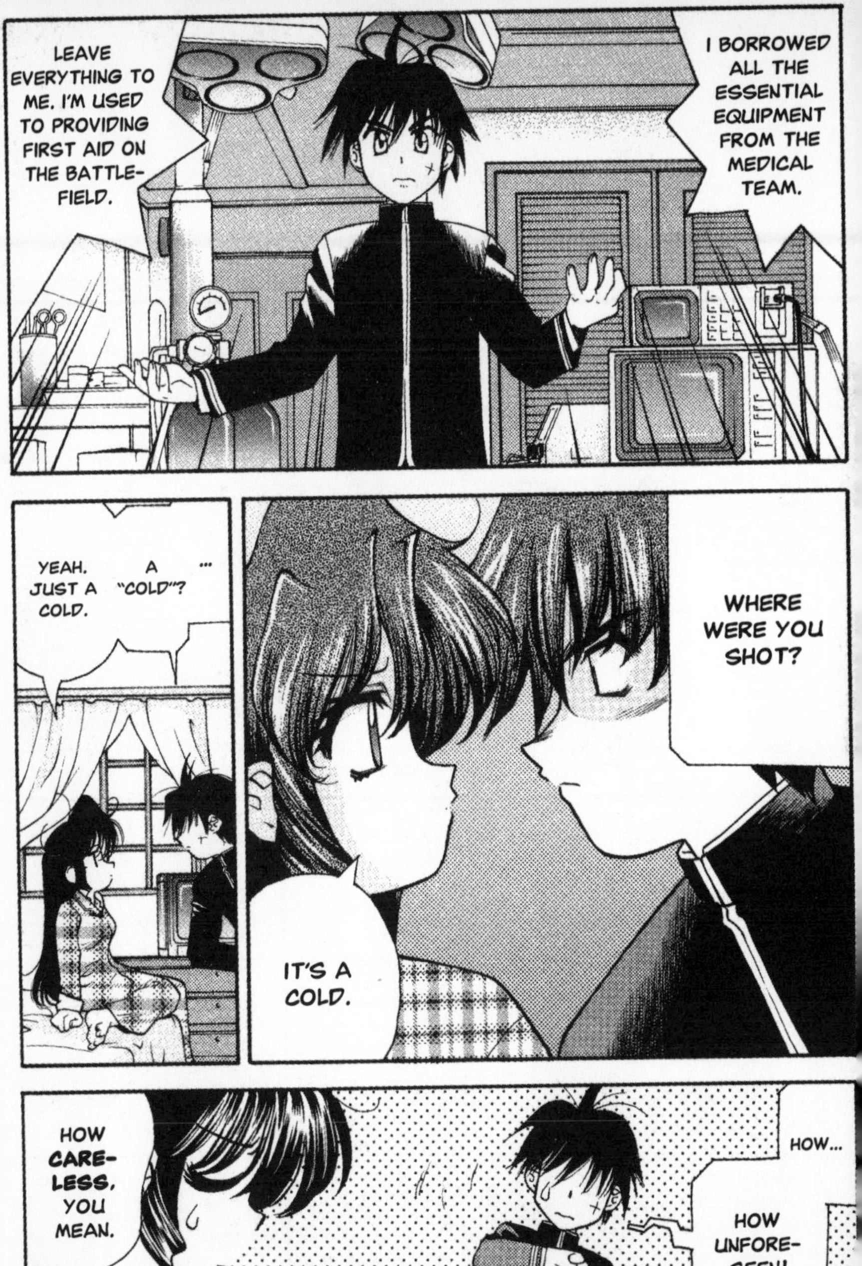

I BORROWED ALL THE ESSENTIAL EQUIPMENT FROM THE MEDICAL TEAM.
LEAVE EVERYTHING TO ME. I'M USED TO PROVIDING FIRST AID ON THE BATTLE-FIELD.
WHERE WERE YOU SHOT?
IT'S A COLD.
...
A "COLD"?
YEAH. JUST A COLD.
HOW...
HOW UNFORE-SEEN!
HOW CARE-LESS, YOU MEAN.

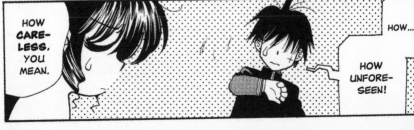

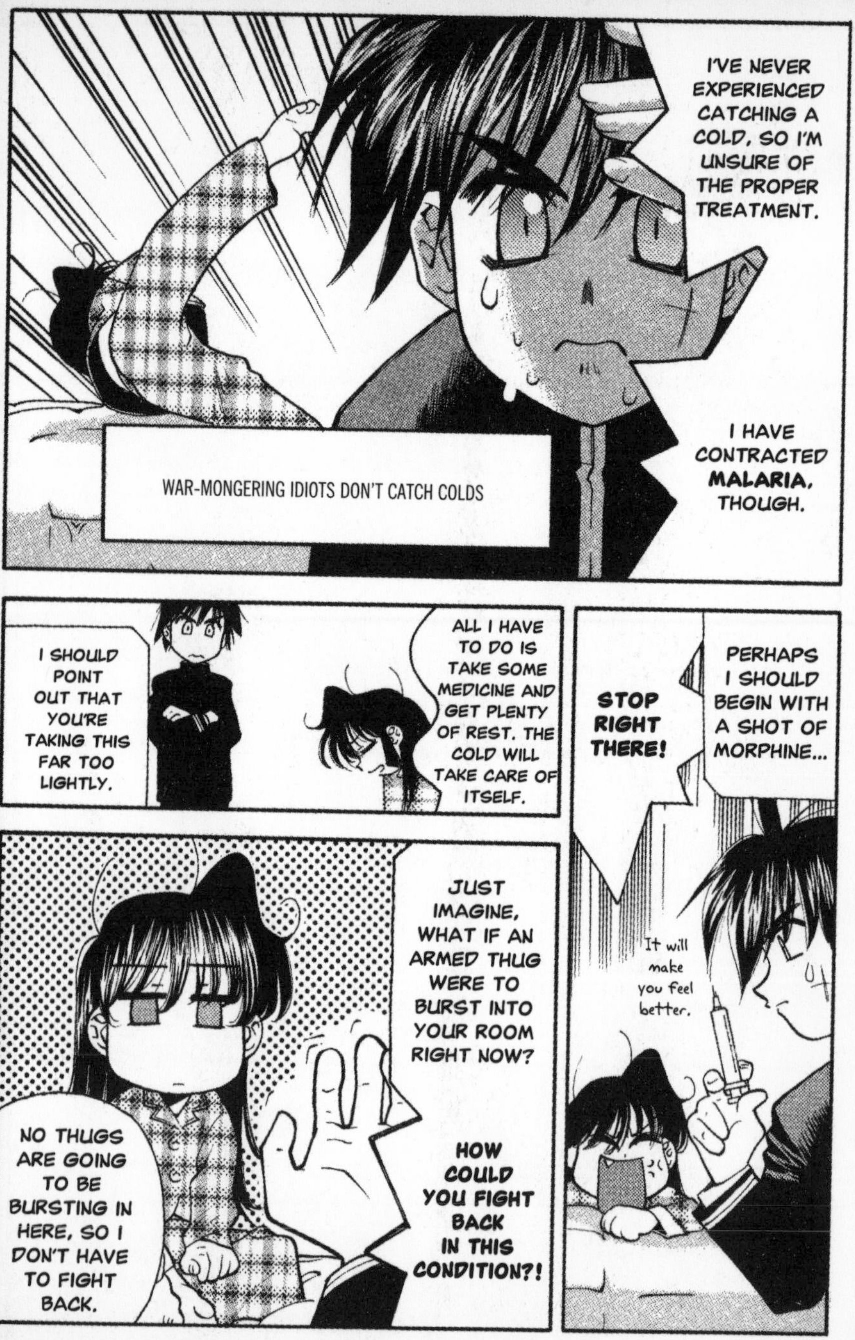
I'VE NEVER EXPERIENCED CATCHING A COLD, SO I'M UNSURE OF THE PROPER TREATMENT.
I HAVE CONTRACTED **MALARIA**, THOUGH.
WAR-MONGERING IDIOTS DON'T CATCH COLDS
ALL I HAVE TO DO IS TAKE SOME MEDICINE AND GET PLENTY OF REST. THE COLD WILL TAKE CARE OF ITSELF.
I SHOULD POINT OUT THAT YOU'RE TAKING THIS FAR TOO LIGHTLY.
JUST IMAGINE, WHAT IF AN ARMED THUG WERE TO BURST INTO YOUR ROOM RIGHT NOW?
HOW COULD YOU FIGHT BACK IN THIS CONDITION?!
NO THUGS ARE GOING TO BE BURSTING IN HERE, SO I DON'T HAVE TO FIGHT BACK.
PERHAPS I SHOULD BEGIN WITH A SHOT OF MORPHINE...
It will make you feel better.
STOP RIGHT THERE!

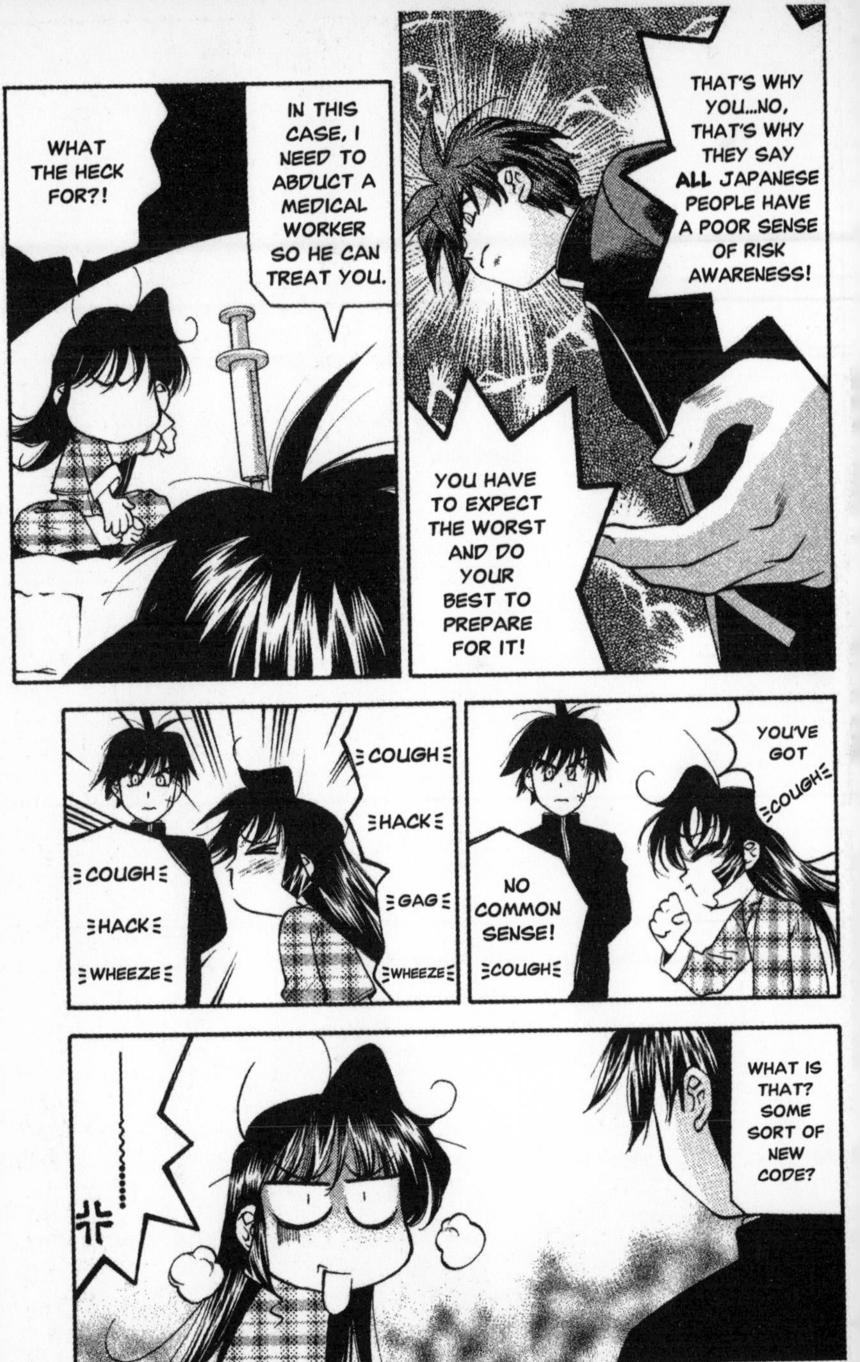

THAT'S WHY YOU...NO, THAT'S WHY THEY SAY **ALL** JAPANESE PEOPLE HAVE A POOR SENSE OF RISK AWARENESS!
YOU HAVE TO EXPECT THE WORST AND DO YOUR BEST TO PREPARE FOR IT!
IN THIS CASE, I NEED TO ABDUCT A MEDICAL WORKER SO HE CAN TREAT YOU.
WHAT THE HECK FOR?!
YOU'VE GOT
COUGH
NO COMMON SENSE!
COUGH
COUGH
HACK
GAG
WHEEZE
COUGH
HACK
WHEEZE
WHAT IS THAT? SOME SORT OF NEW CODE?

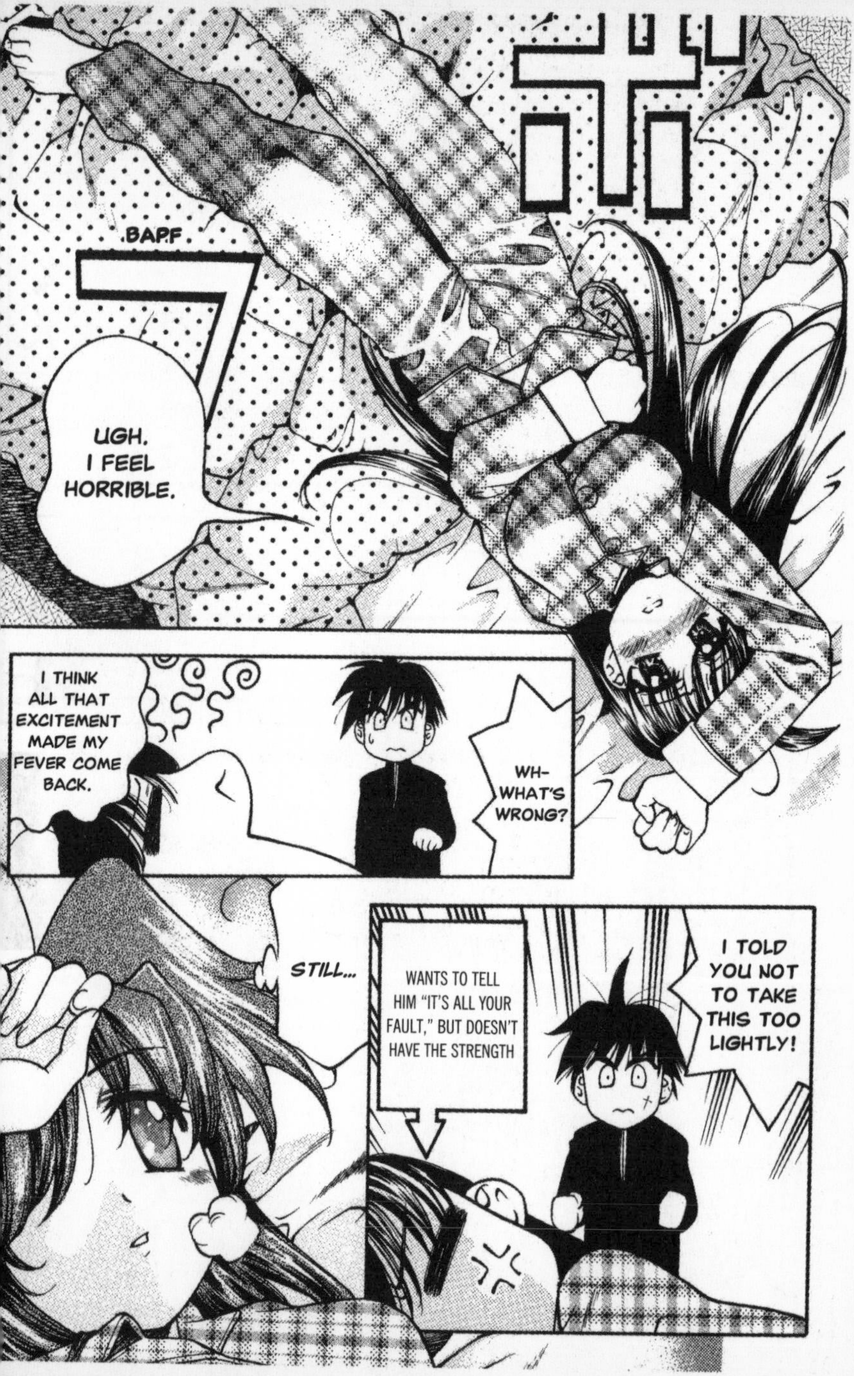
BAP.F
UGH. I FEEL HORRIBLE.
WH-WHAT'S WRONG?
I THINK ALL THAT EXCITEMENT MADE MY FEVER COME BACK.
I TOLD YOU NOT TO TAKE THIS TOO LIGHTLY!
WANTS TO TELL HIM "IT'S ALL YOUR FAULT," BUT DOESN'T HAVE THE STRENGTH
STILL...

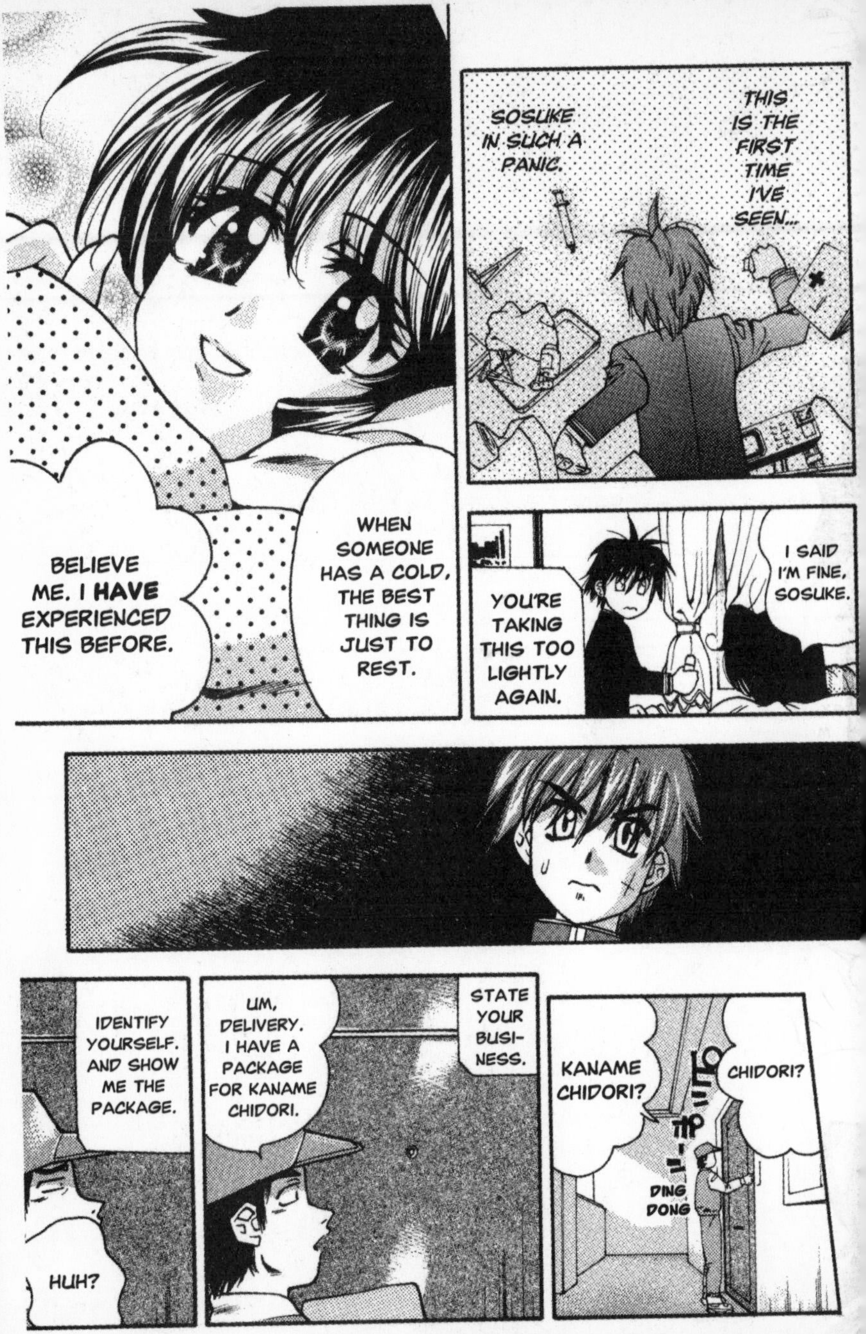
THIS IS THE FIRST TIME I'VE SEEN...
SOSUKE IN SUCH A PANIC.
I SAID I'M FINE, SOSUKE.
YOU'RE TAKING THIS TOO LIGHTLY AGAIN.
WHEN SOMEONE HAS A COLD, THE BEST THING IS JUST TO REST.
BELIEVE ME. I HAVE EXPERIENCED THIS BEFORE.
CHIDORI?
DING DONG
KANAME CHIDORI?
STATE YOUR BUSI-NESS.
UM, DELIVERY. I HAVE A PACKAGE FOR KANAME CHIDORI.
IDENTIFY YOURSELF. AND SHOW ME THE PACKAGE.
HUH?

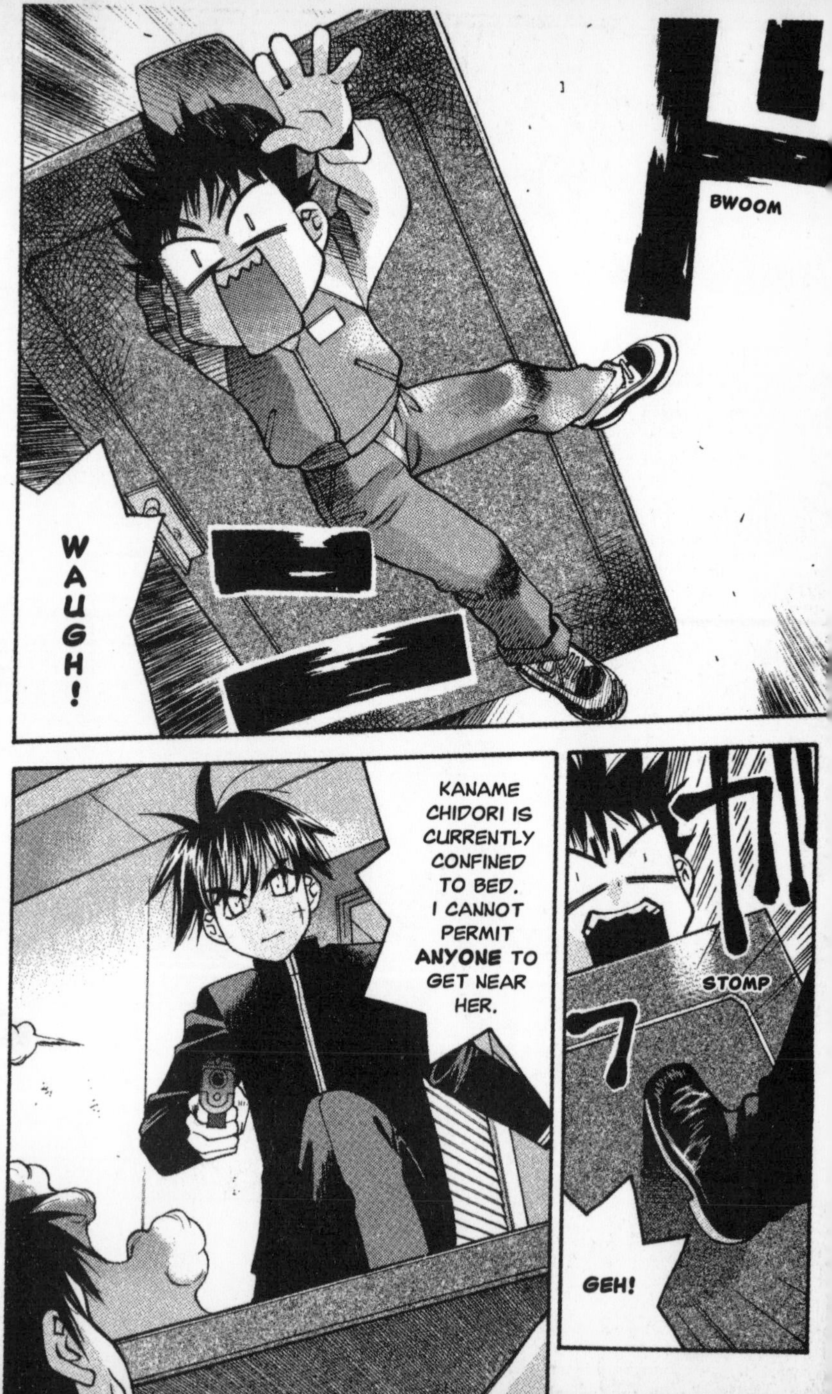
BWOOM
WAUGH!
STOMP
GEH!
KANAME CHIDORI IS CURRENTLY CONFINED TO BED. I CANNOT PERMIT ANYONE TO GET NEAR HER.

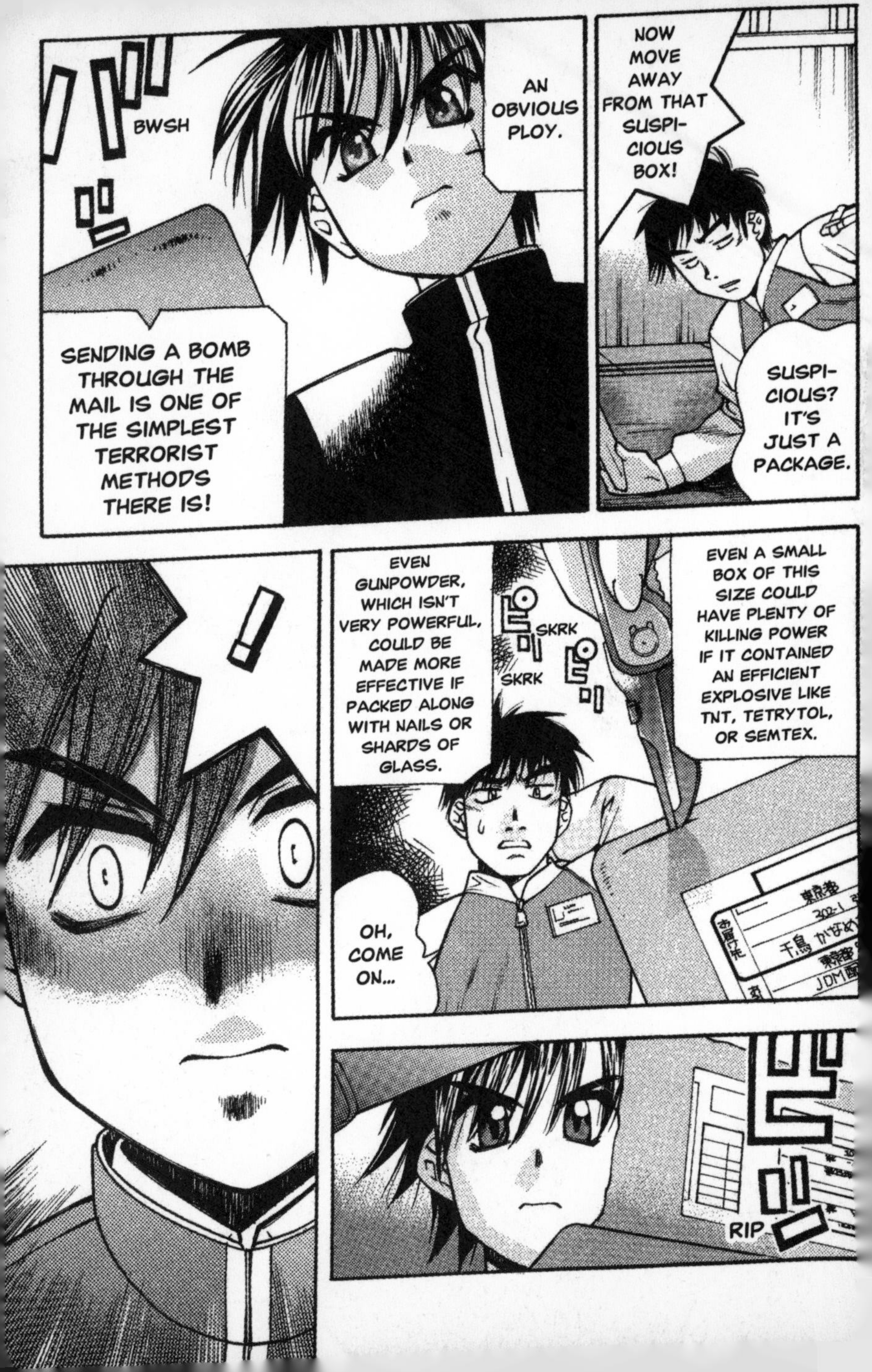

NOW MOVE AWAY FROM THAT SUSPI-CIOUS BOX!
SUSPI-CIOUS? IT'S JUST A PACKAGE.
AN OBVIOUS PLOY.
BWSH
SENDING A BOMB THROUGH THE MAIL IS ONE OF THE SIMPLEST TERRORIST METHODS THERE IS!
EVEN A SMALL BOX OF THIS SIZE COULD HAVE PLENTY OF KILLING POWER IF IT CONTAINED AN EFFICIENT EXPLOSIVE LIKE TNT, TETRYTOL, OR SEMTEX.
EVEN GUNPOWDER, WHICH ISN'T VERY POWERFUL, COULD BE MADE MORE EFFECTIVE IF PACKED ALONG WITH NAILS OR SHARDS OF GLASS.
SKRK
SKRK
OH, COME ON...
RIP

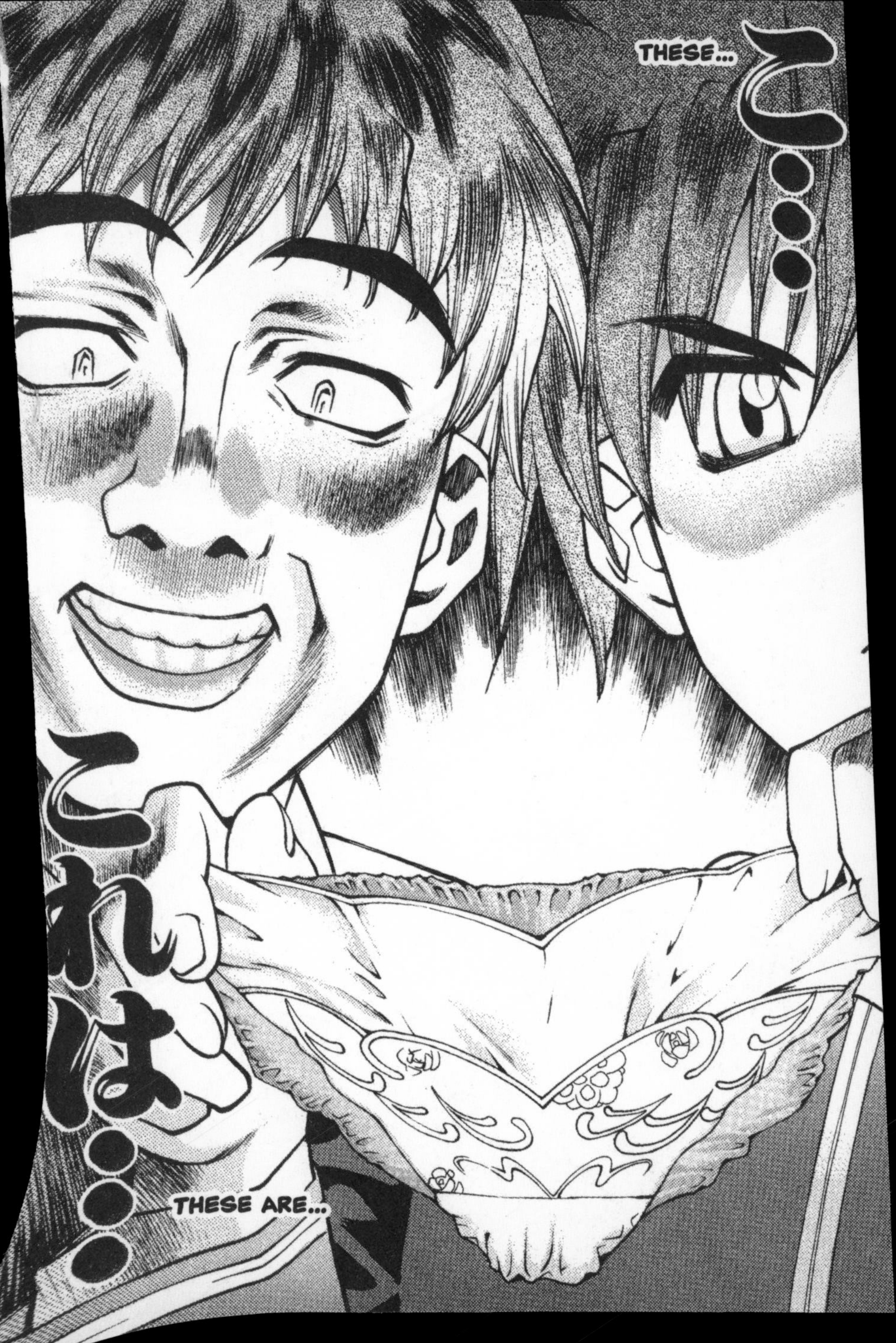

こ…
THESE...
これは…
THESE ARE...

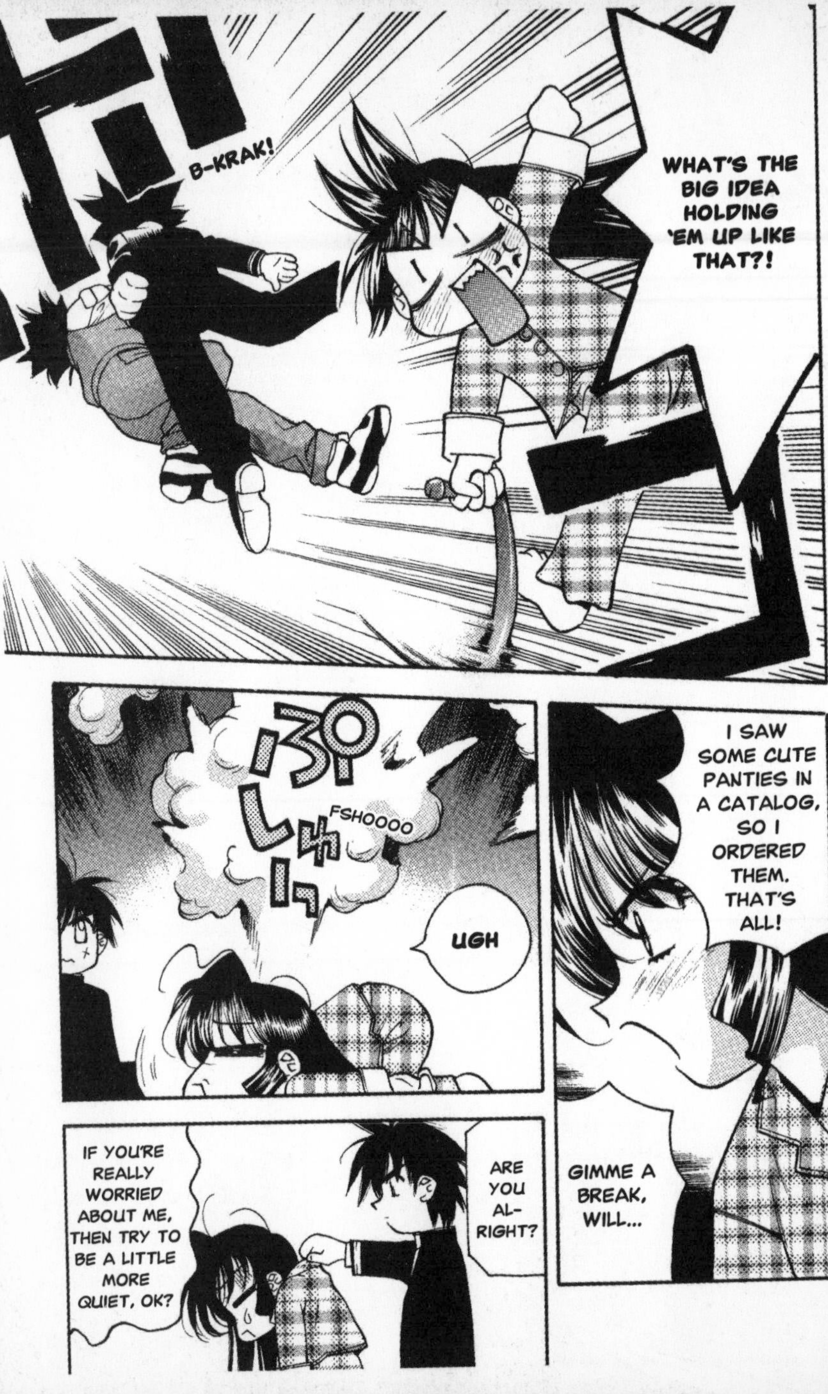
WHAT'S THE BIG IDEA HOLDING 'EM UP LIKE THAT?!
B-KRAK!
I SAW SOME CUTE PANTIES IN A CATALOG, SO I ORDERED THEM. THAT'S ALL!
GIMME A BREAK, WILL...
FSHOOOO
UGH
ARE YOU AL-RIGHT?
IF YOU'RE REALLY WORRIED ABOUT ME, THEN TRY TO BE A LITTLE MORE QUIET, OK?

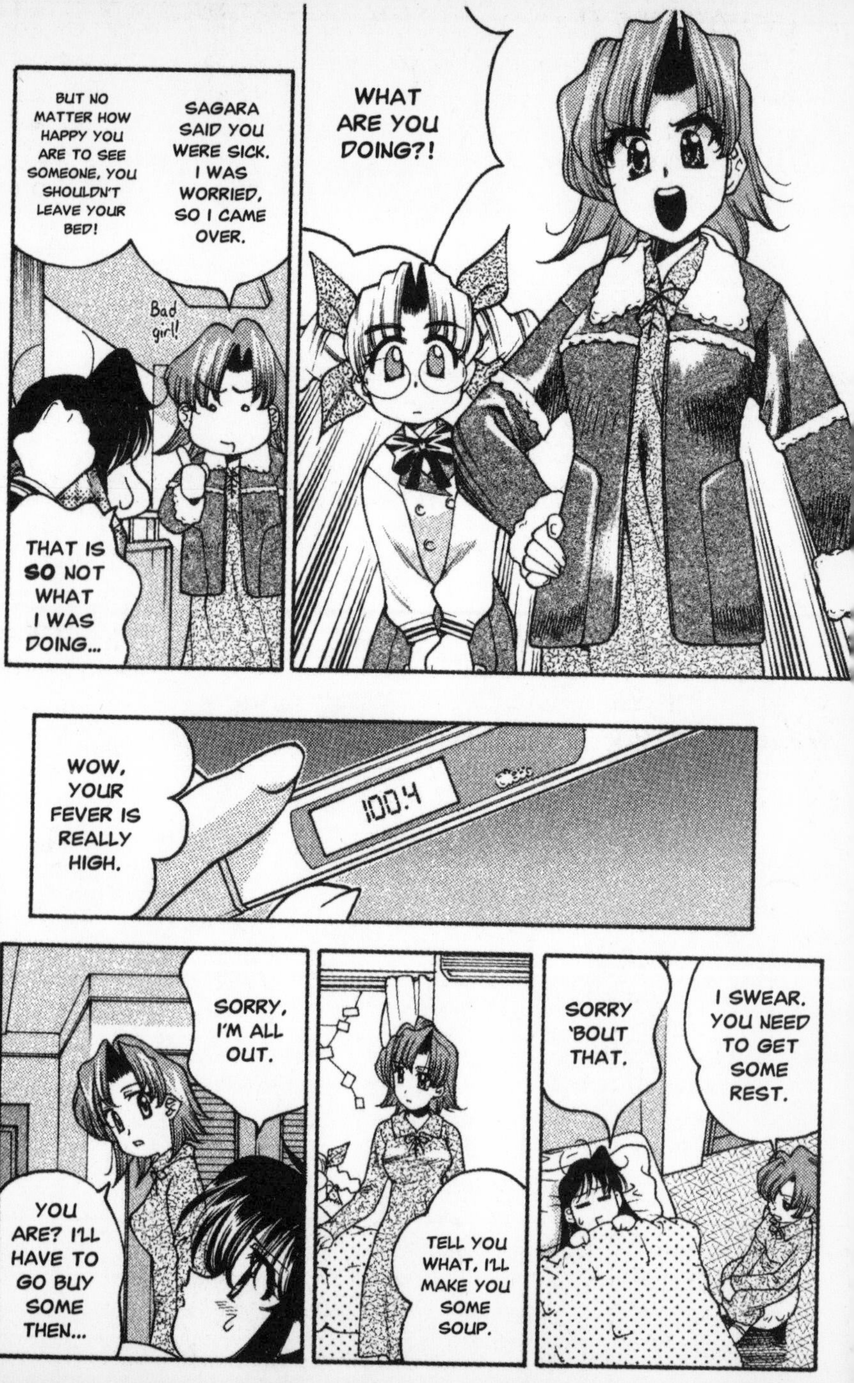
WHAT ARE YOU DOING?!
SAGARA SAID YOU WERE SICK. I WAS WORRIED, SO I CAME OVER.
BUT NO MATTER HOW HAPPY YOU ARE TO SEE SOMEONE, YOU SHOULDN'T LEAVE YOUR BED!
Bad girl!
THAT IS **SO** NOT WHAT I WAS DOING...
WOW, YOUR FEVER IS REALLY HIGH.
100.4
I SWEAR. YOU NEED TO GET SOME REST.
SORRY 'BOUT THAT.
TELL YOU WHAT, I'LL MAKE YOU SOME SOUP.
SORRY, I'M ALL OUT.
YOU ARE? I'LL HAVE TO GO BUY SOME THEN...

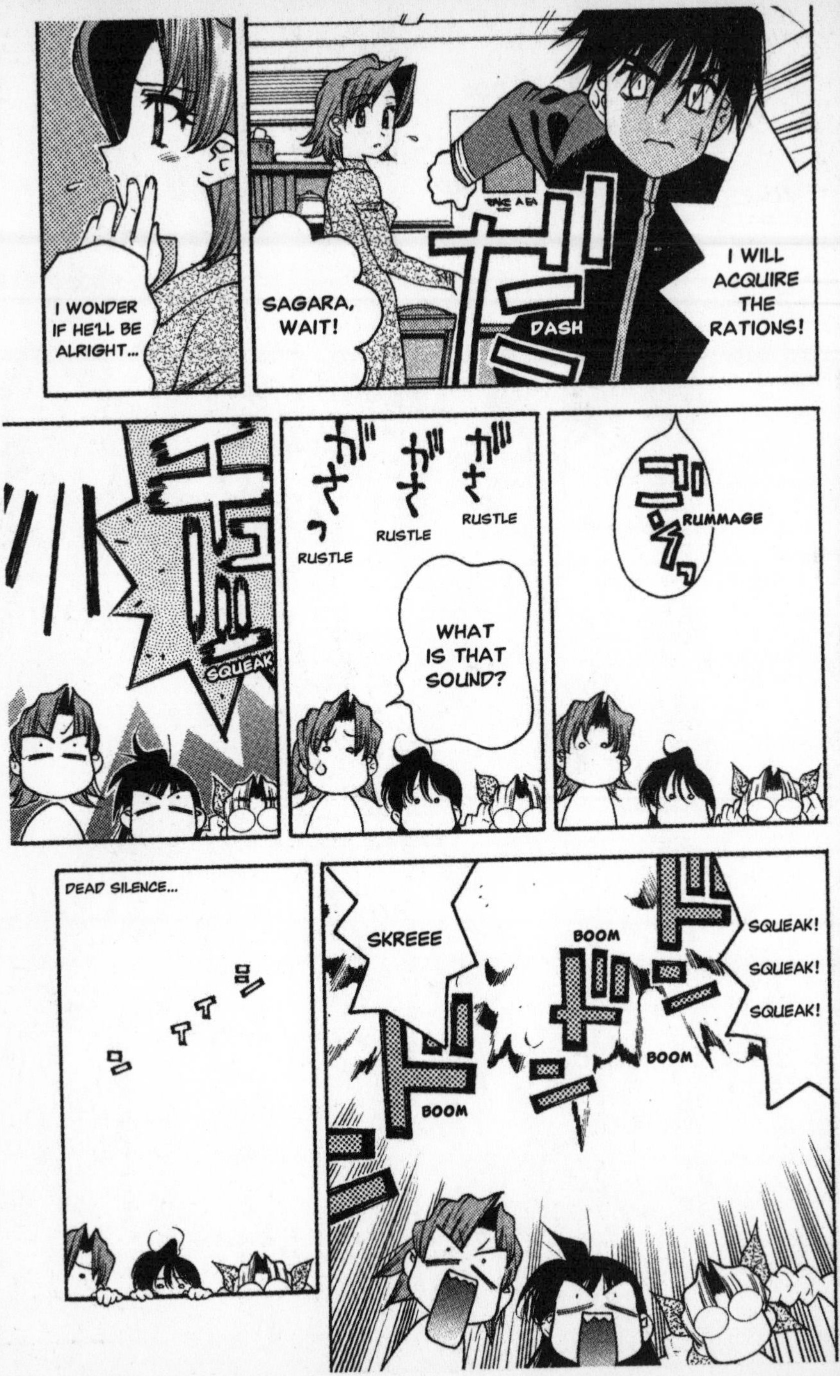

I WILL ACQUIRE THE RATIONS!
DASH
SAGARA, WAIT!
I WONDER IF HE'LL BE ALRIGHT...
RUMMAGE
RUSTLE
RUSTLE
RUSTLE
WHAT IS THAT SOUND?
SQUEAK
SQUEAK!
SQUEAK!
SQUEAK!
BOOM
BOOM
SKREEE
BOOM
DEAD SILENCE...

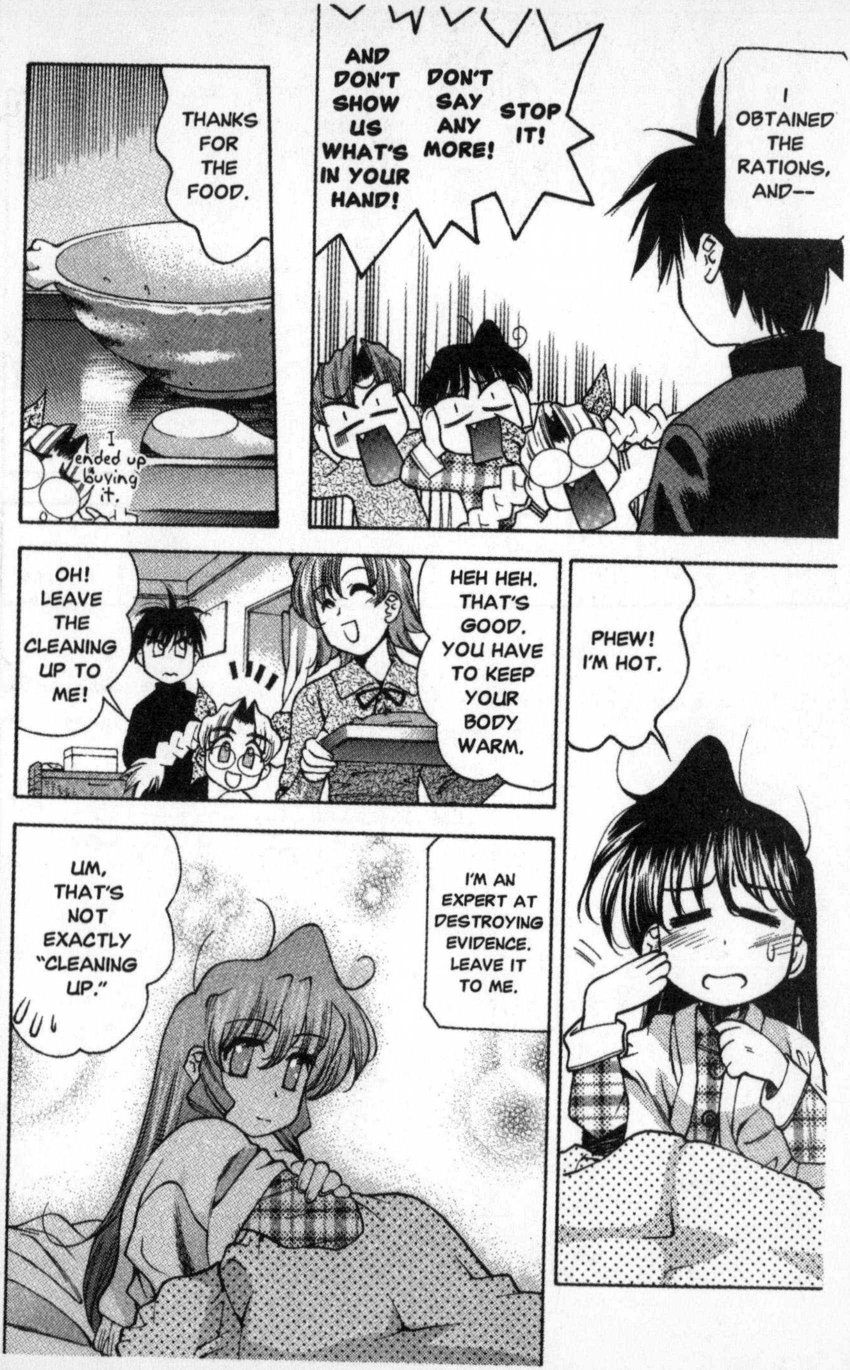
I OBTAINED THE RATIONS, AND--
STOP IT!
DON'T SAY ANY MORE!
AND DON'T SHOW US WHAT'S IN YOUR HAND!
THANKS FOR THE FOOD.
I ended up buying it.
PHEW! I'M HOT.
HEH HEH. THAT'S GOOD. YOU HAVE TO KEEP YOUR BODY WARM.
OH! LEAVE THE CLEANING UP TO ME!
I'M AN EXPERT AT DESTROYING EVIDENCE. LEAVE IT TO ME.
UM, THAT'S NOT EXACTLY "CLEANING UP."

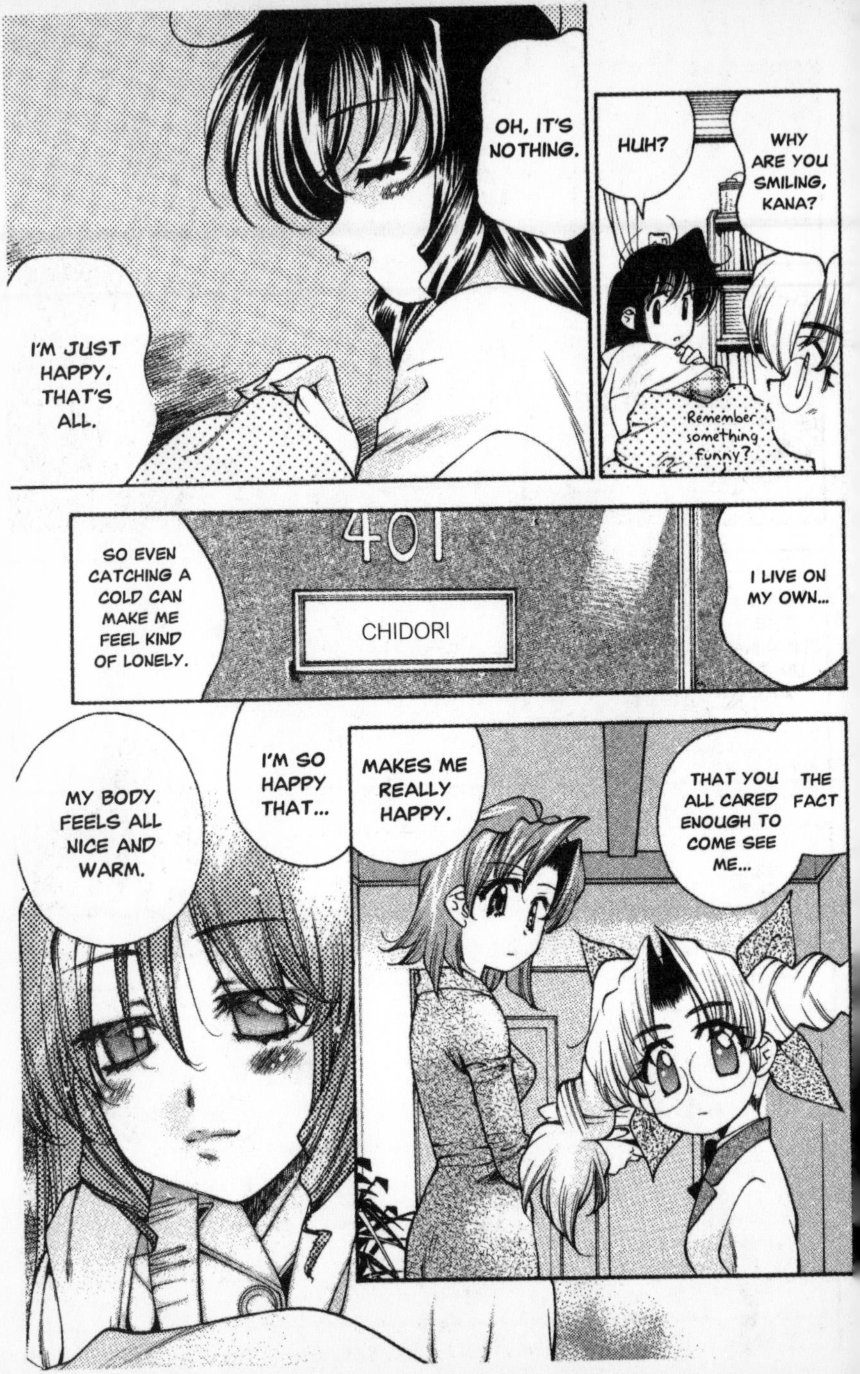
WHY ARE YOU SMILING, KANA?
HUH?
Remember something funny?
OH, IT'S NOTHING.
I'M JUST HAPPY, THAT'S ALL.
I LIVE ON MY OWN...
401
CHIDORI
SO EVEN CATCHING A COLD CAN MAKE ME FEEL KIND OF LONELY.
THE FACT
THAT YOU ALL CARED ENOUGH TO COME SEE ME...
MAKES ME REALLY HAPPY.
I'M SO HAPPY THAT...
MY BODY FEELS ALL NICE AND WARM.

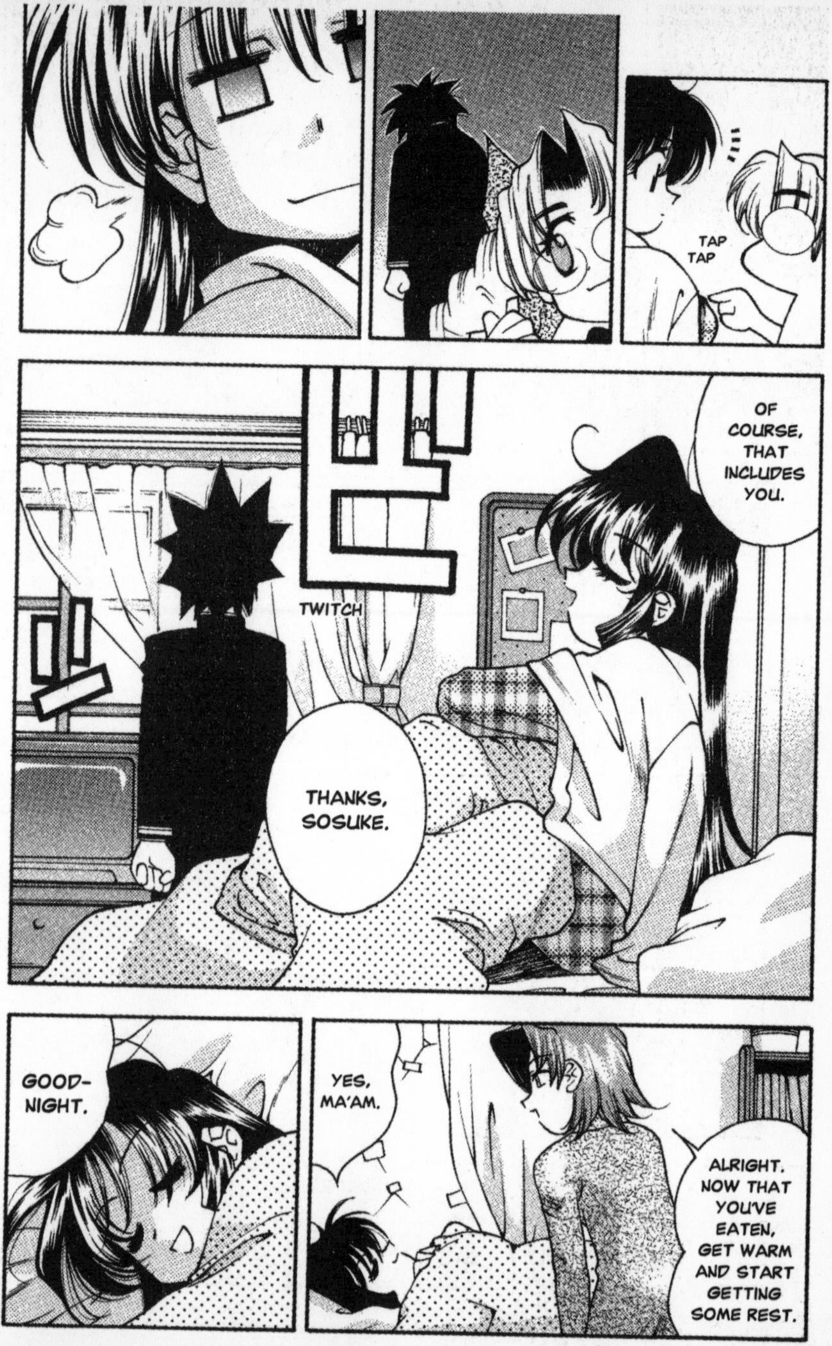
TAP TAP
OF COURSE, THAT INCLUDES YOU.
TWITCH
THANKS, SOSUKE.
ALRIGHT. NOW THAT YOU'VE EATEN, GET WARM AND START GETTING SOME REST.
YES, MA'AM.
GOOD-NIGHT.

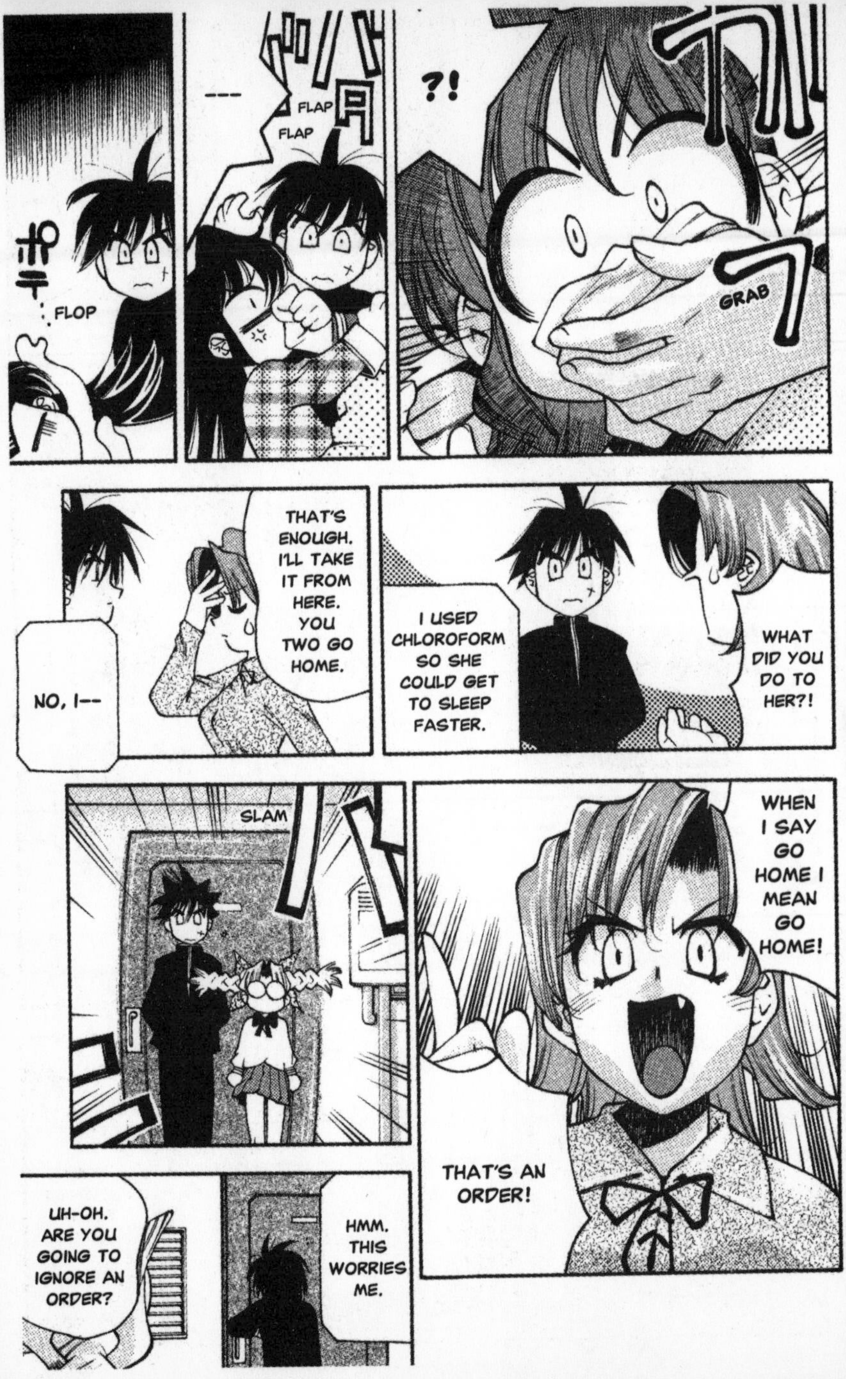
?!
GRAB

FLAP
FLAP
FLOP
WHAT DID YOU DO TO HER?!
I USED CHLOROFORM SO SHE COULD GET TO SLEEP FASTER.
THAT'S ENOUGH. I'LL TAKE IT FROM HERE. YOU TWO GO HOME.
NO, I--
WHEN I SAY GO HOME I MEAN GO HOME!
THAT'S AN ORDER!
SLAM
HMM. THIS WORRIES ME.
UH-OH. ARE YOU GOING TO IGNORE AN ORDER?

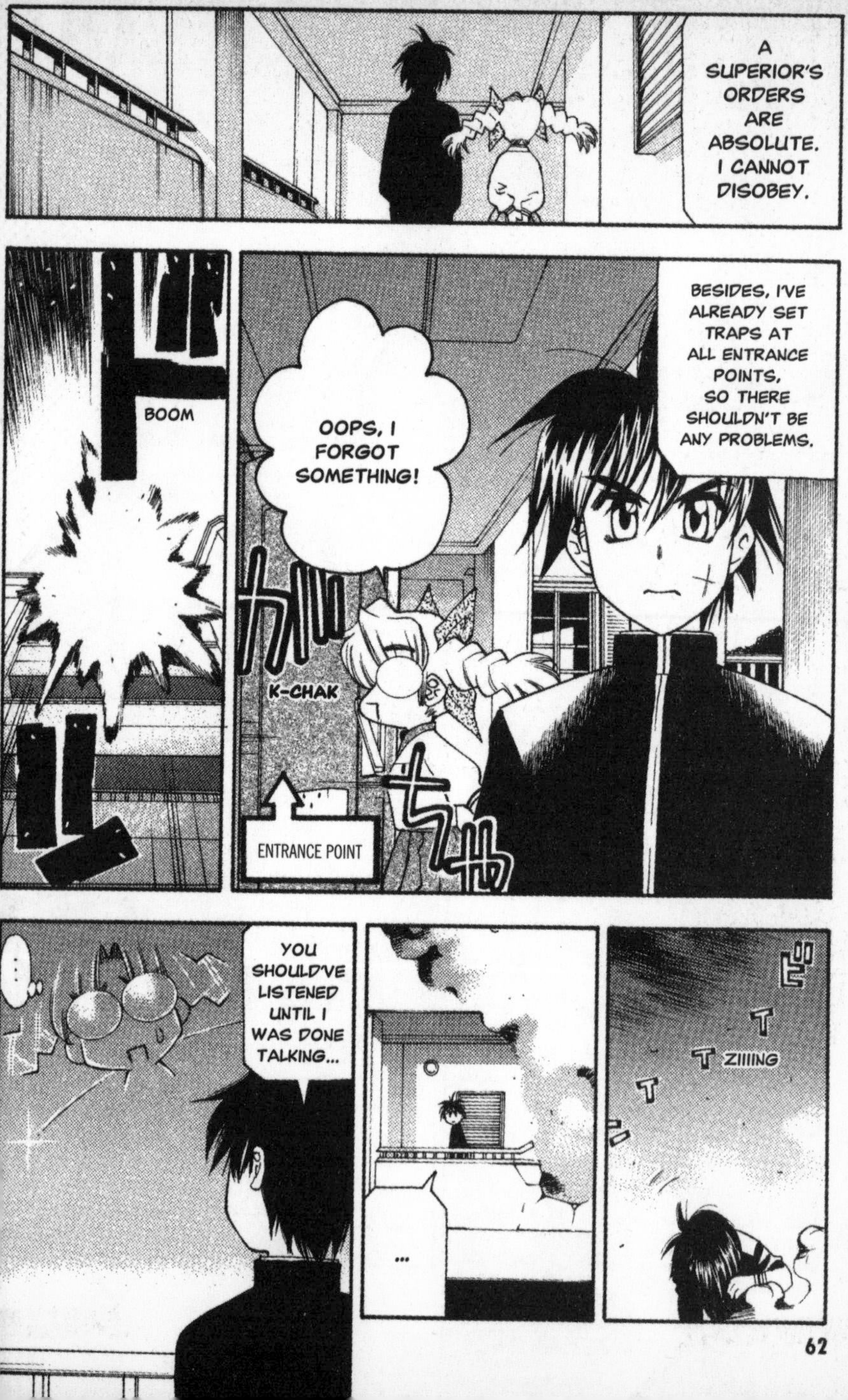
A SUPERIOR'S ORDERS ARE ABSOLUTE. I CANNOT DISOBEY.
BESIDES, I'VE ALREADY SET TRAPS AT ALL ENTRANCE POINTS, SO THERE SHOULDN'T BE ANY PROBLEMS.
OOPS, I FORGOT SOMETHING!
K-CHAK
ENTRANCE POINT
BOOM
ZIIING
...
YOU SHOULD'VE LISTENED UNTIL I WAS DONE TALKING...
...

BOMB 3 NEW YEAR'S CRISIS!

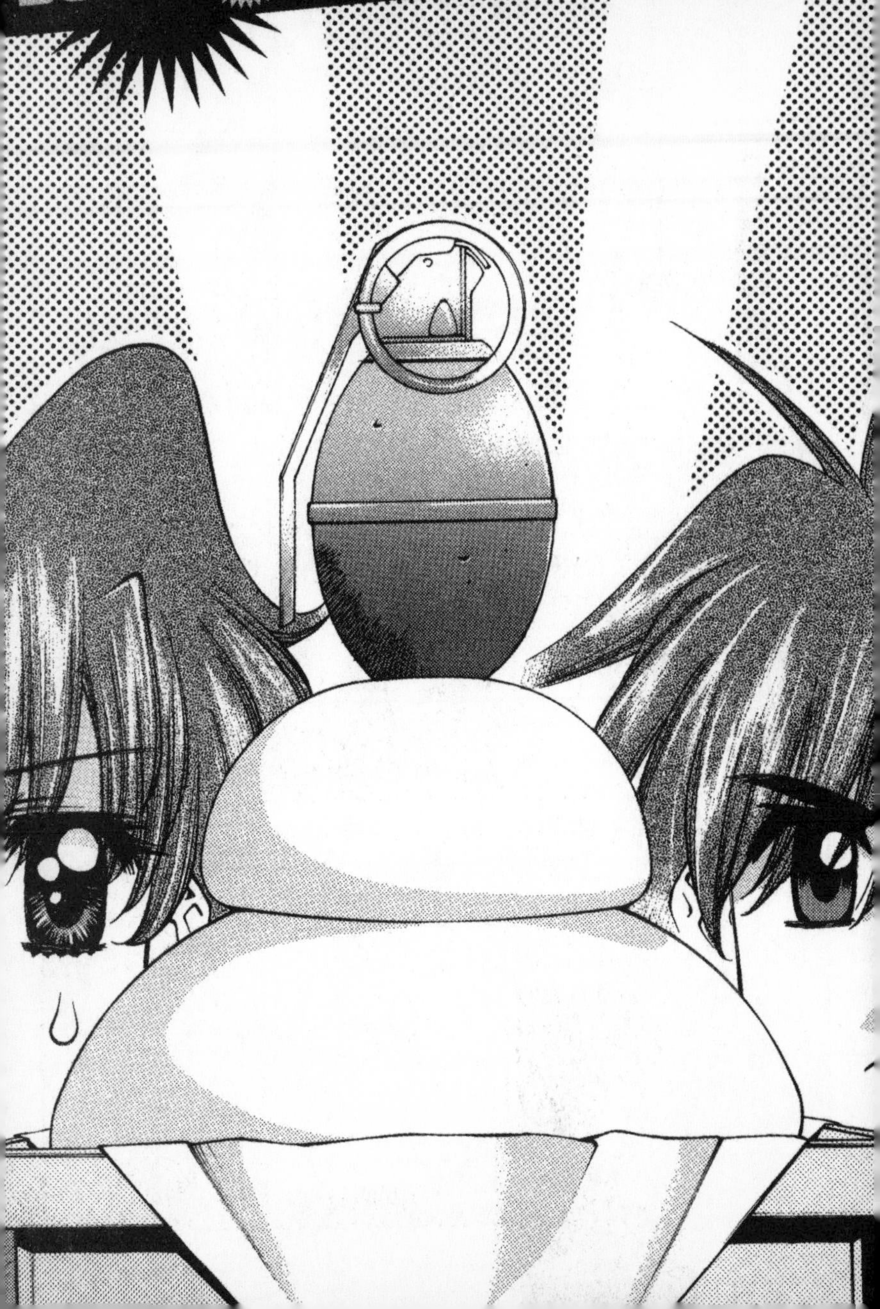

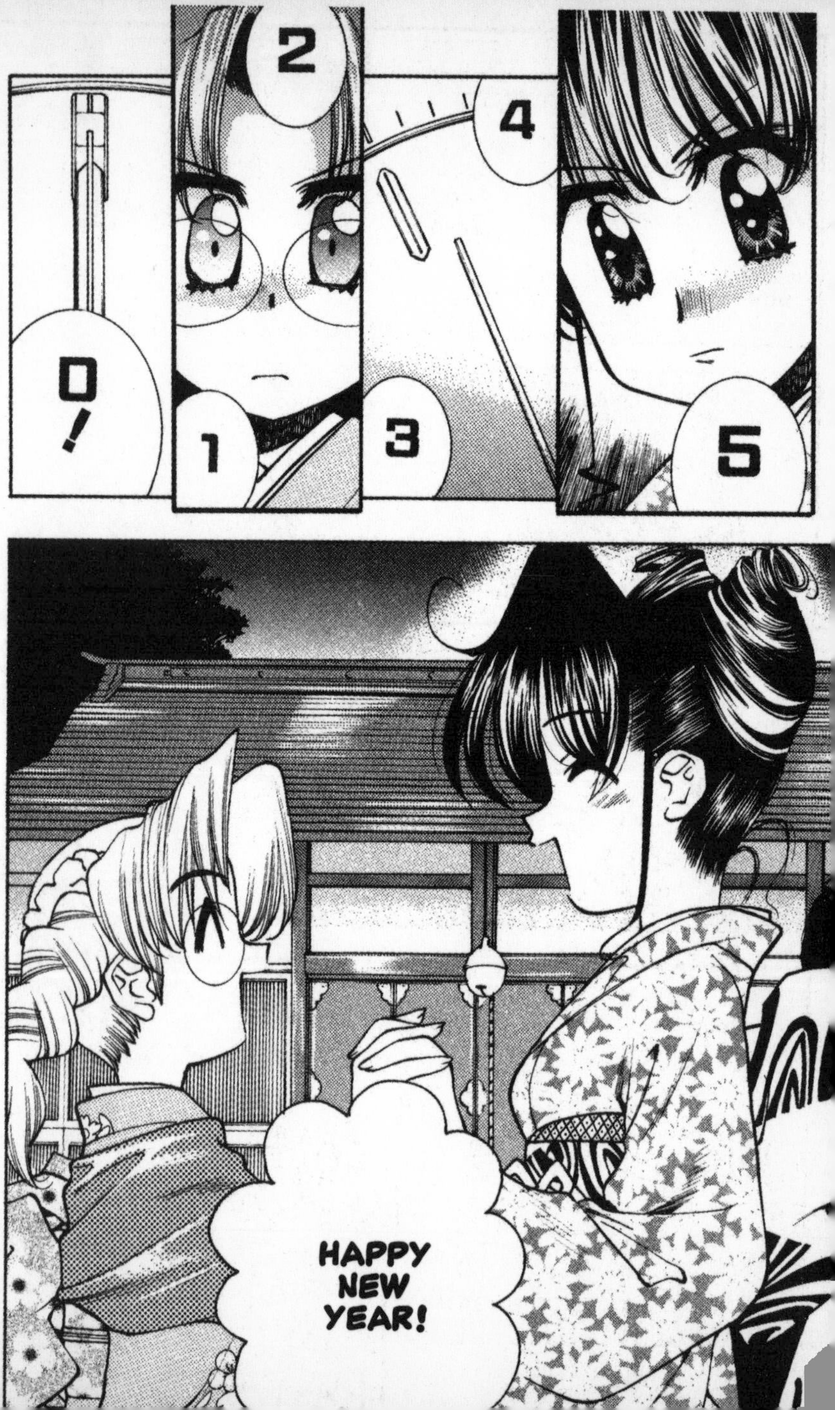
5
4
3
2
1
0!
HAPPY NEW YEAR!

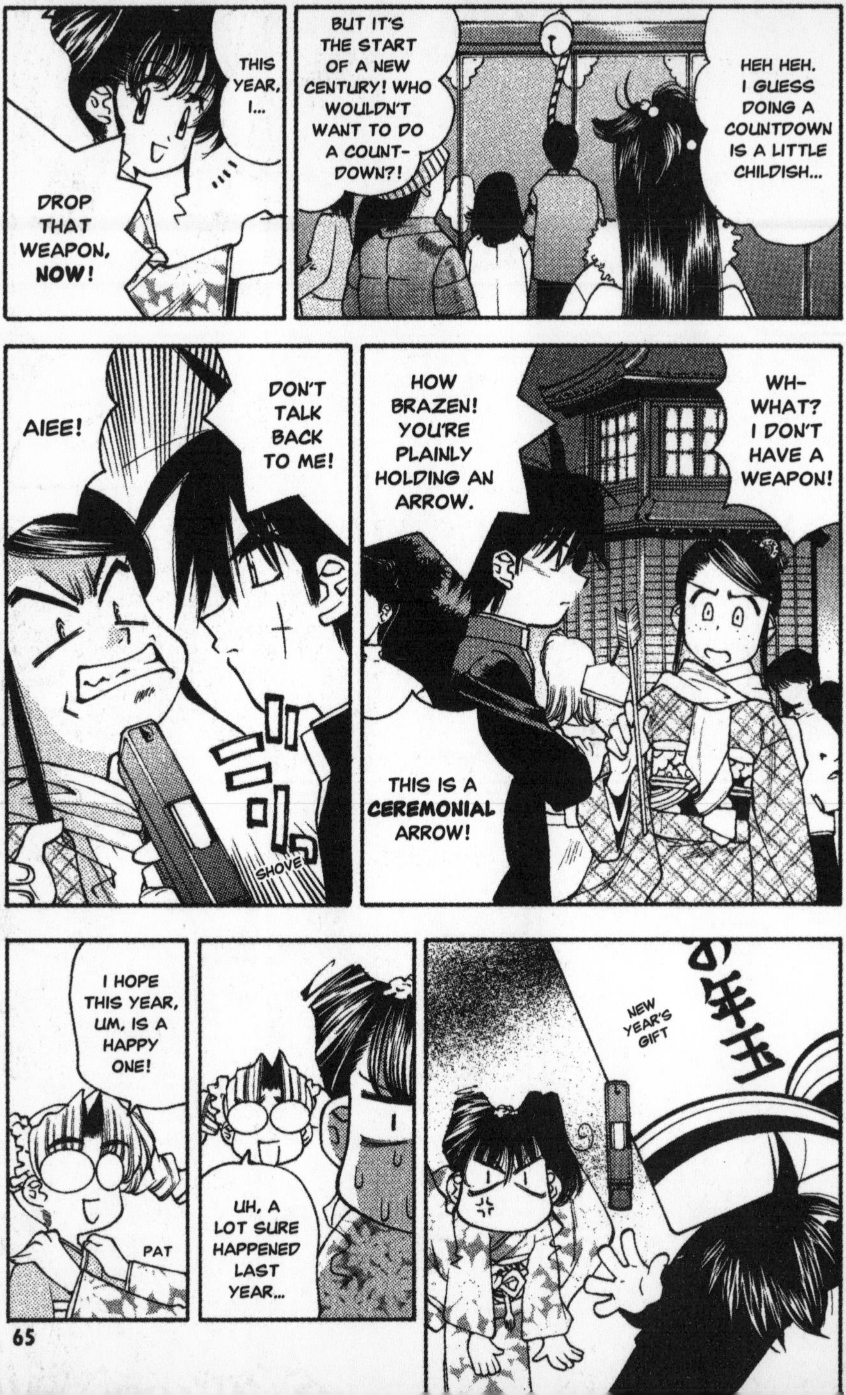
HEH HEH. I GUESS DOING A COUNTDOWN IS A LITTLE CHILDISH...
BUT IT'S THE START OF A NEW CENTURY! WHO WOULDN'T WANT TO DO A COUNT-DOWN?!
THIS YEAR, I...
DROP THAT WEAPON, NOW!
WH-WHAT? I DON'T HAVE A WEAPON!
HOW BRAZEN! YOU'RE PLAINLY HOLDING AN ARROW.
THIS IS A CEREMONIAL ARROW!
DON'T TALK BACK TO ME!
AIEE!
SHOVE
お年玉
NEW YEAR'S GIFT
UH, A LOT SURE HAPPENED LAST YEAR...
I HOPE THIS YEAR, UM, IS A HAPPY ONE!
PAT

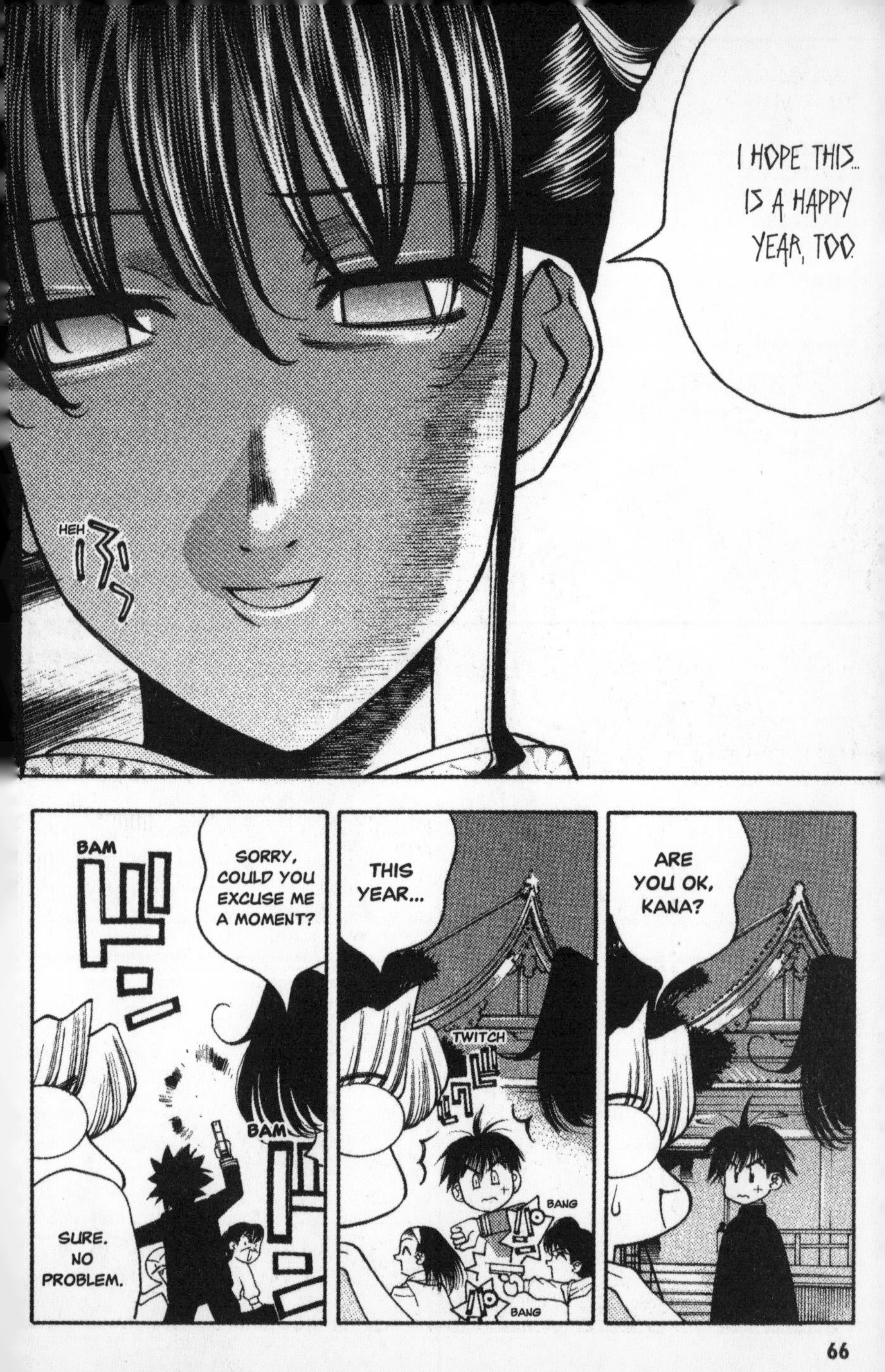
I HOPE THIS...
IS A HAPPY YEAR, TOO.
HEH
ARE YOU OK, KANA?
THIS YEAR...
TWITCH
BANG
BANG
SORRY, COULD YOU EXCUSE ME A MOMENT?
BAM
BAM
SURE. NO PROBLEM.

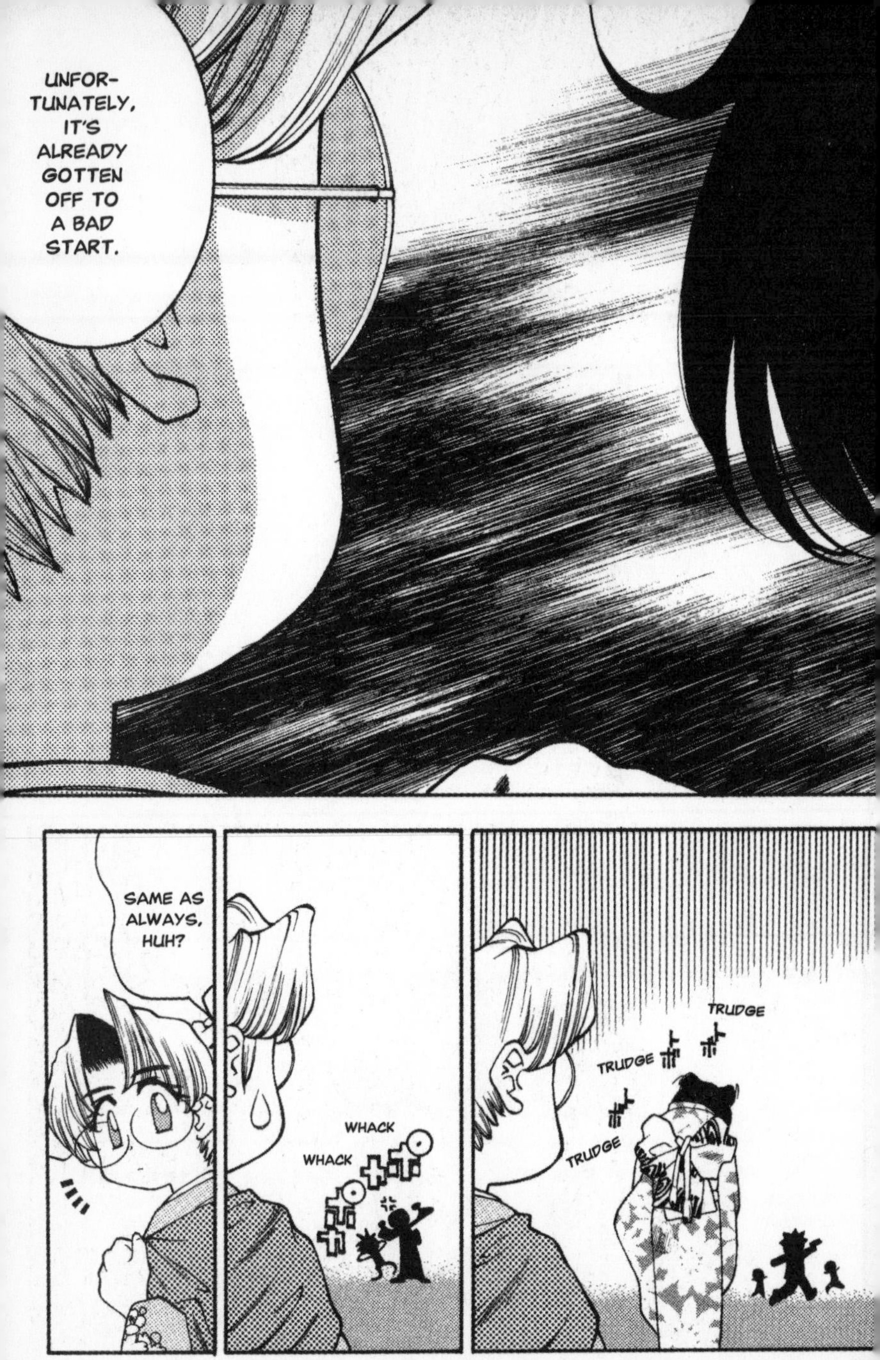
UNFORTUNATELY, IT'S ALREADY GOTTEN OFF TO A BAD START.
SAME AS ALWAYS, HUH?
WHACK
WHACK
TRUDGE
TRUDGE
TRUDGE

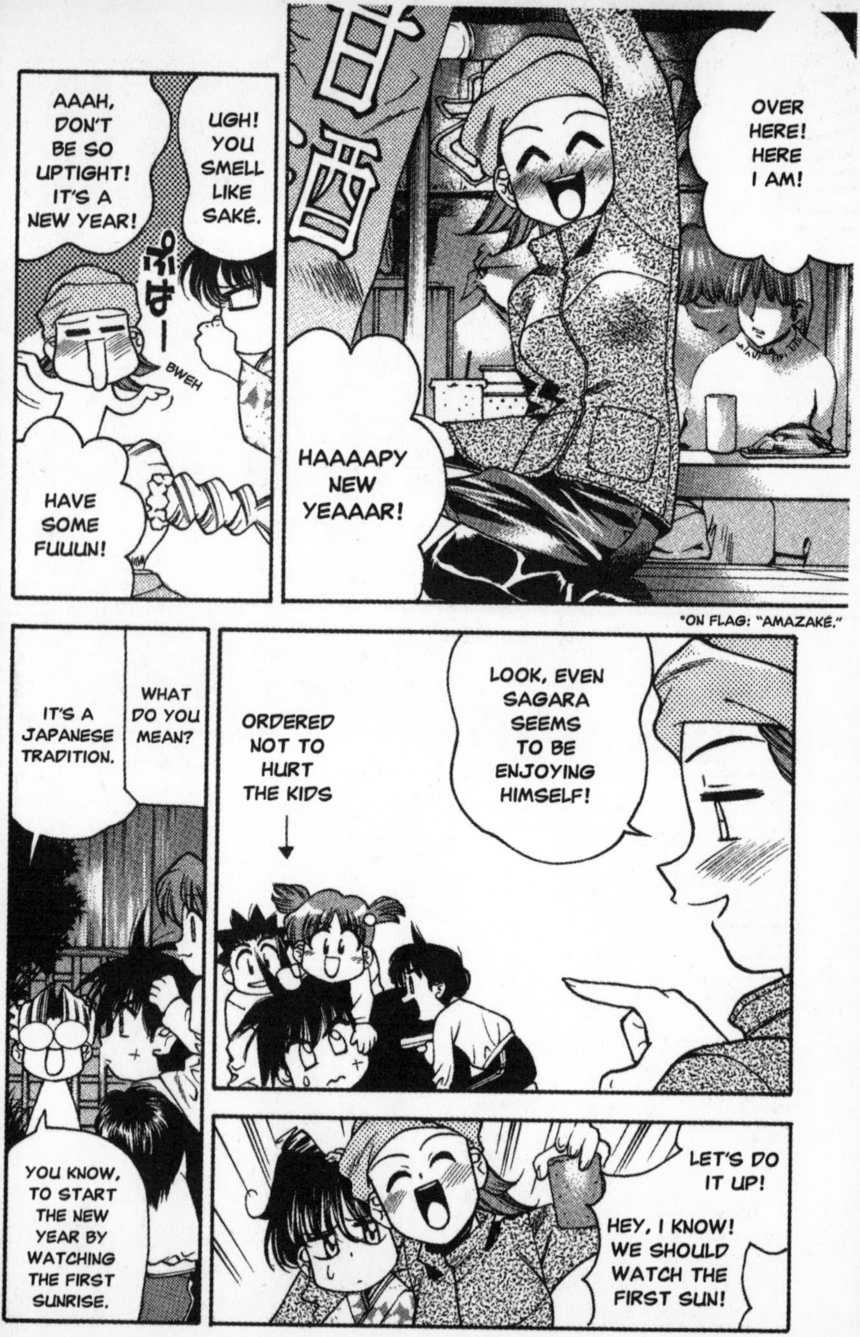
OVER HERE! HERE I AM!
HAAAAPY NEW YEAAAR!
UGH! YOU SMELL LIKE SAKÉ.
AAAH, DON'T BE SO UPTIGHT! IT'S A NEW YEAR!
ぷはー
BWEH
HAVE SOME FUUUN!
*ON FLAG: "AMAZAKÉ."
LOOK, EVEN SAGARA SEEMS TO BE ENJOYING HIMSELF!
ORDERED NOT TO HURT THE KIDS
LET'S DO IT UP!
HEY, I KNOW! WE SHOULD WATCH THE FIRST SUN!
WHAT DO YOU MEAN?
IT'S A JAPANESE TRADITION.
YOU KNOW, TO START THE NEW YEAR BY WATCHING THE FIRST SUNRISE.

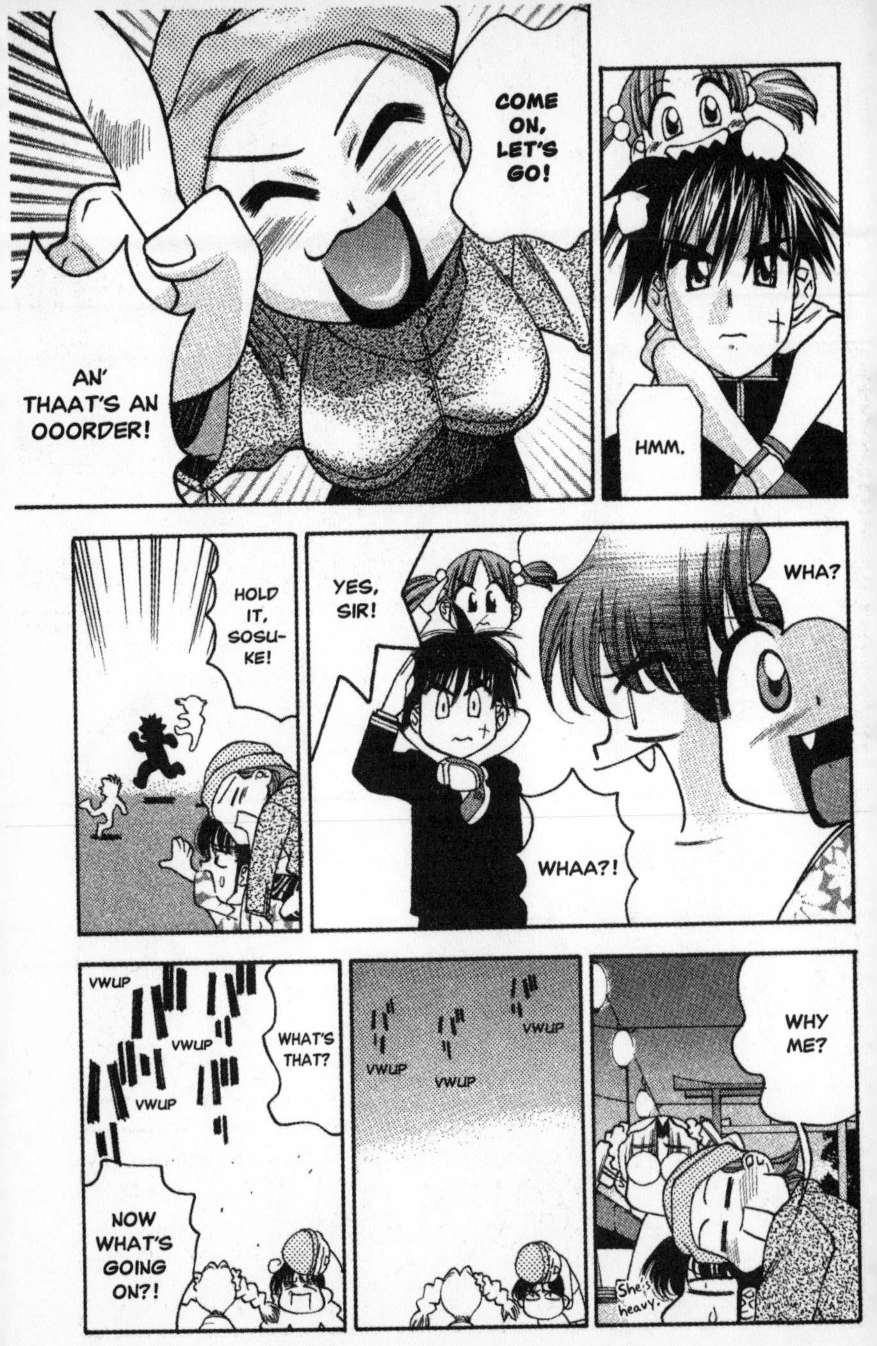
COME ON, LET'S GO!
AN' THAAT'S AN OOORDER!
HMM.
HOLD IT, SOSUKE!
YES, SIR!
WHA?
WHAA?!
VWUP
VWUP
VWUP
WHAT'S THAT?
NOW WHAT'S GOING ON?!
VWUP
VWUP
VWUP
WHY ME?
She's heavy.

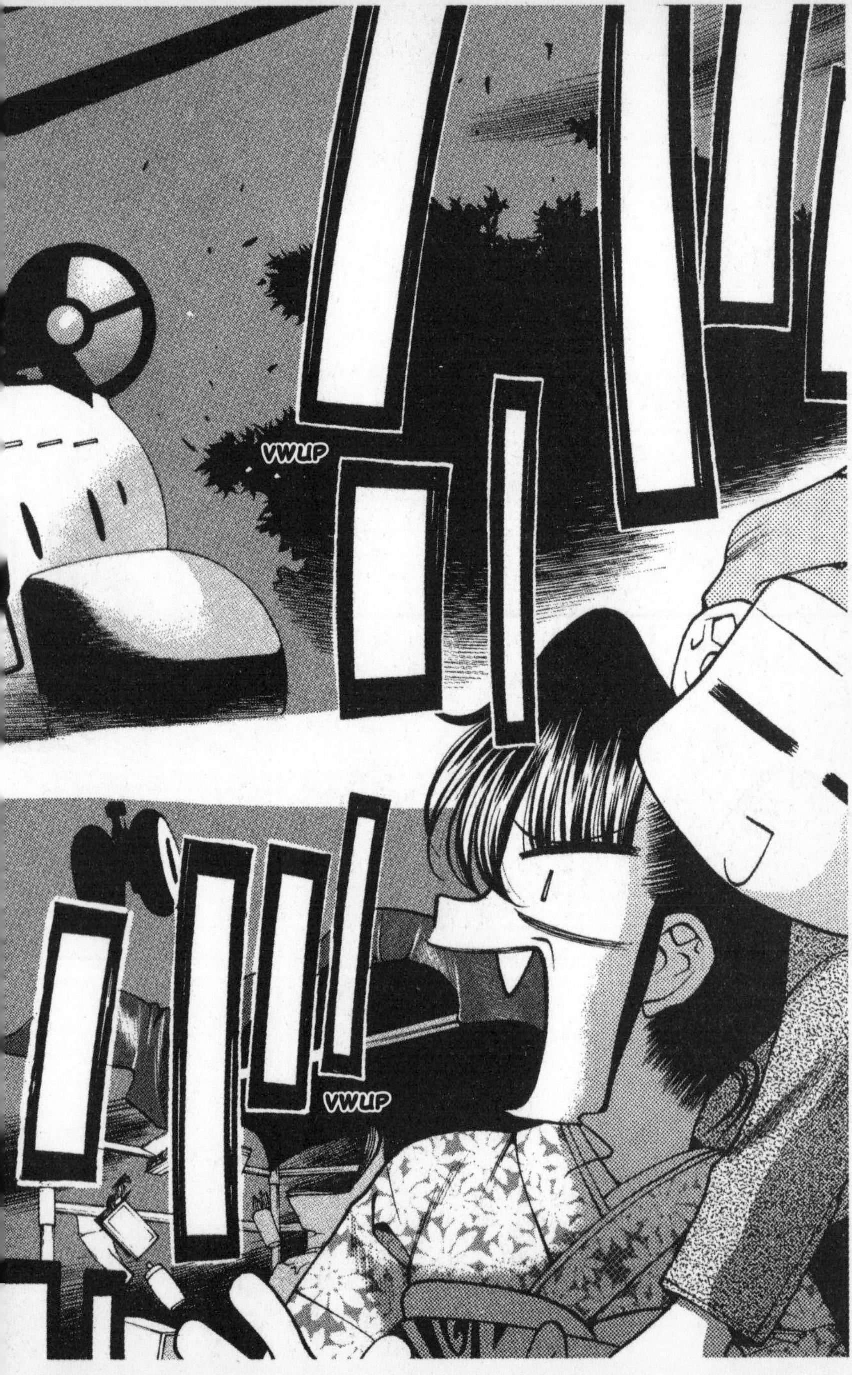
VWUP
VWUP

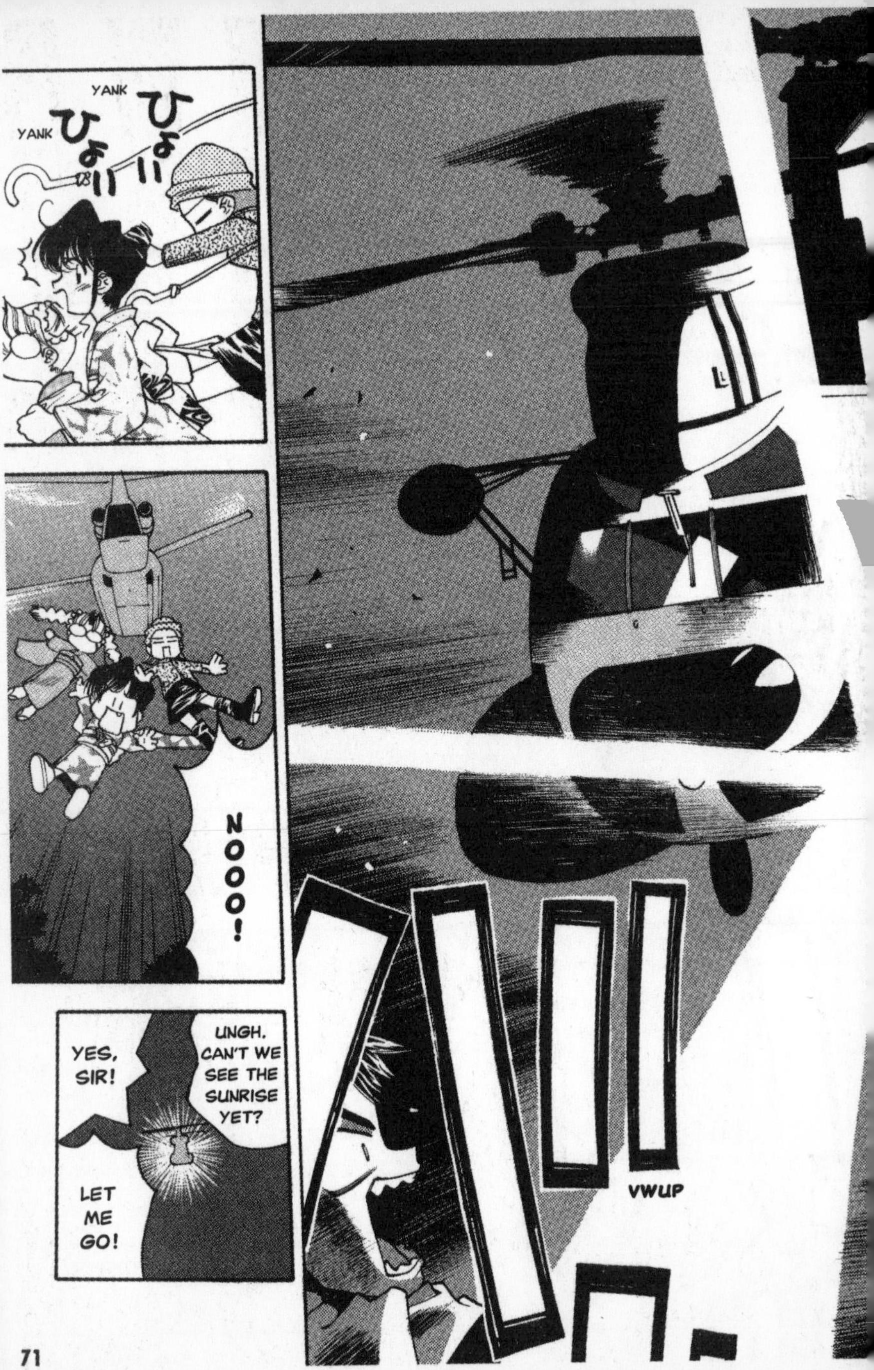

VWUP
ひょい
YANK
ひょい
YANK
NOOOO!
UNGH. CAN'T WE SEE THE SUNRISE YET?
YES, SIR!
LET ME GO!

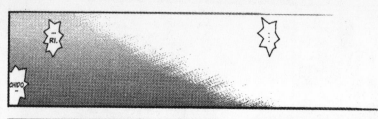

...RI.

...

CHIDO...

HM?

CHIDORI!

SOSUKE?

GOOD, YOU'RE AWAKE.

WHERE AM !?

IS IT SNOWING?

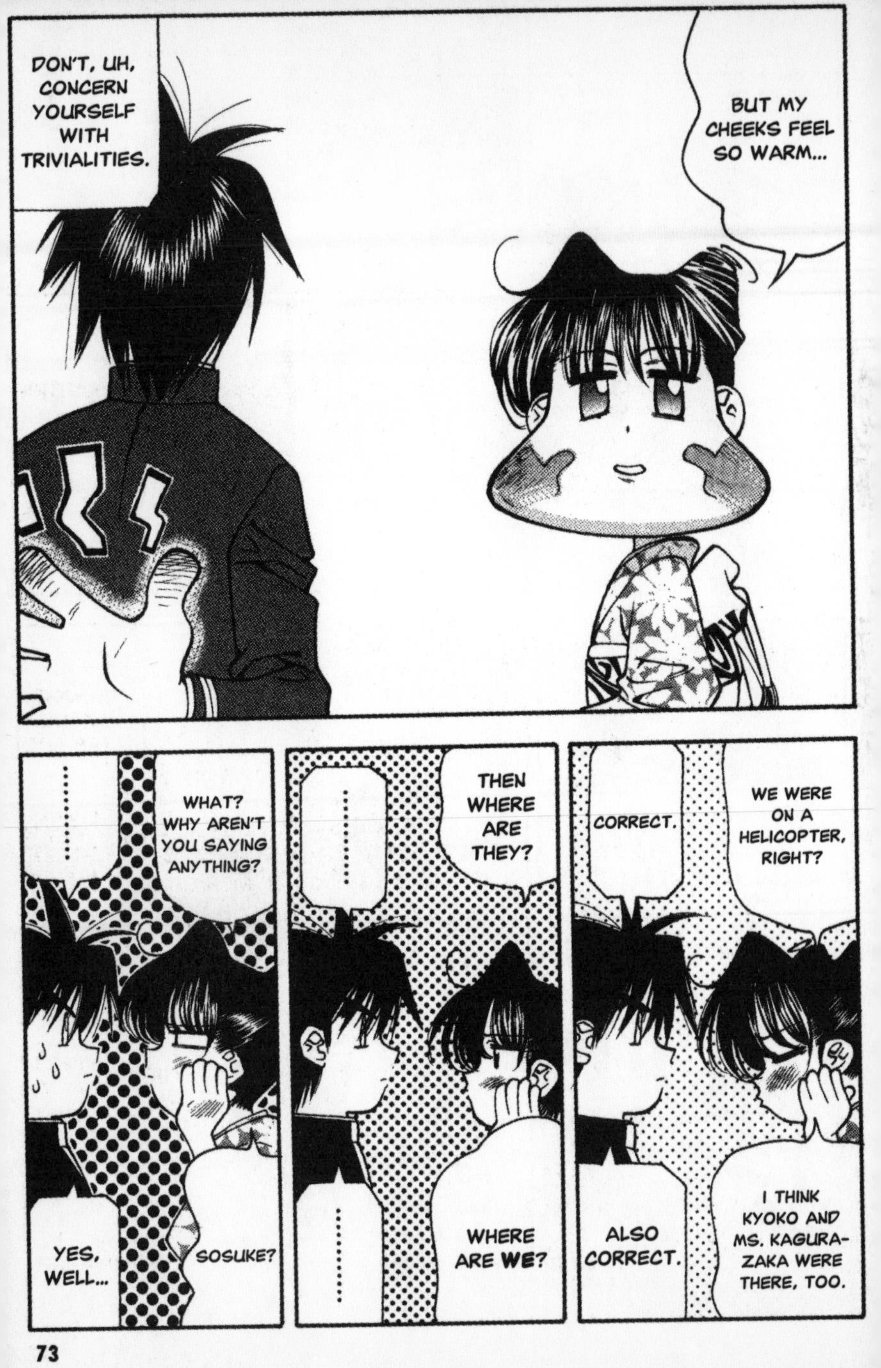

BUT MY CHEEKS FEEL SO WARM...
DON'T, UH, CONCERN YOURSELF WITH TRIVIALITIES.
WE WERE ON A HELICOPTER, RIGHT?
CORRECT.
I THINK KYOKO AND MS. KAGURA-ZAKA WERE THERE, TOO.
ALSO CORRECT.
THEN WHERE ARE THEY?
......
WHERE ARE **WE**?
......
WHAT? WHY AREN'T YOU SAYING ANYTHING?
......
SOSUKE?
YES, WELL...

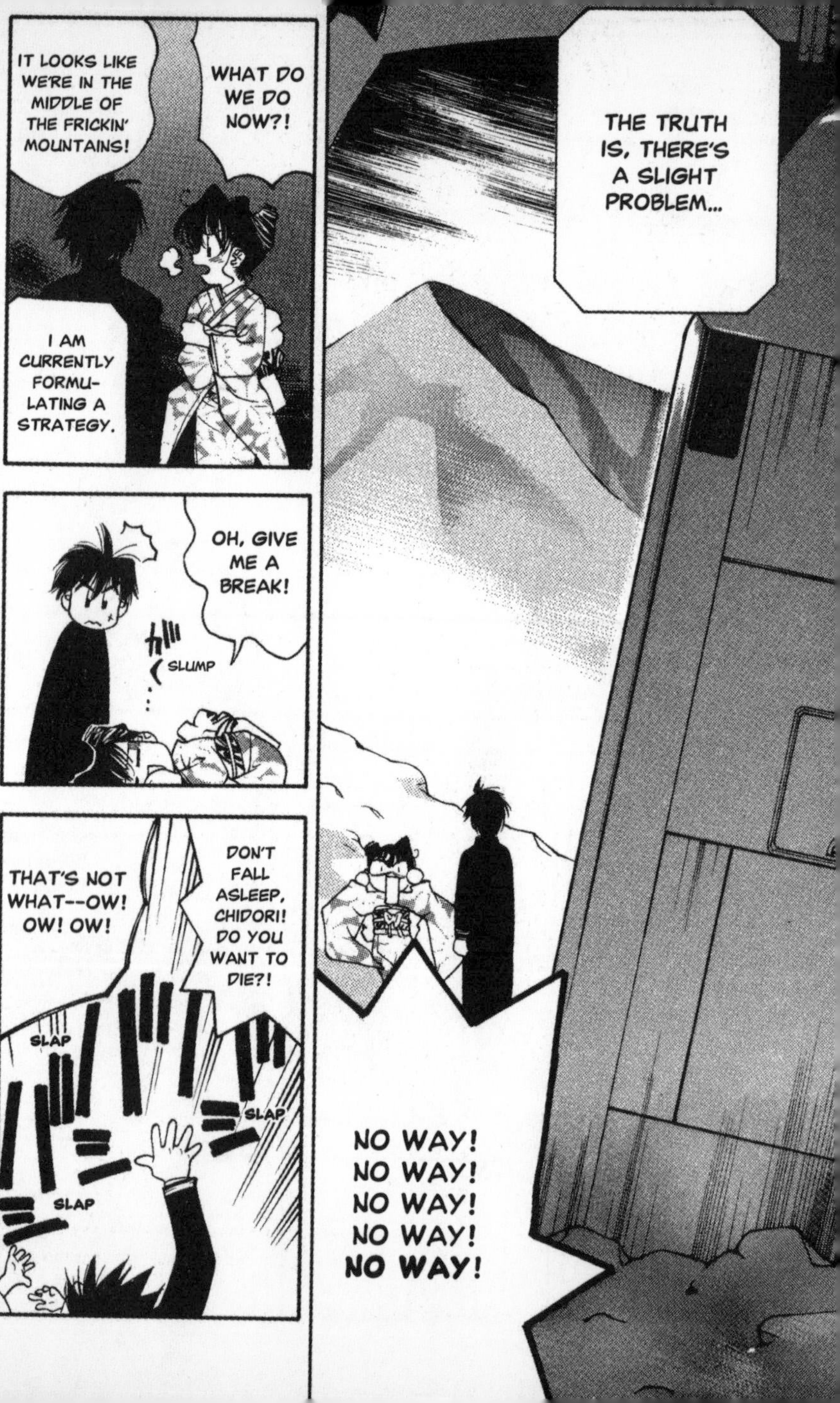
THE TRUTH IS, THERE'S A SLIGHT PROBLEM...
NO WAY! NO WAY! NO WAY! NO WAY! NO WAY!
IT LOOKS LIKE WE'RE IN THE MIDDLE OF THE FRICKIN' MOUNTAINS!
WHAT DO WE DO NOW?!
I AM CURRENTLY FORMU-LATING A STRATEGY.
OH, GIVE ME A BREAK!
SLUMP
DON'T FALL ASLEEP, CHIDORI! DO YOU WANT TO DIE?!
THAT'S NOT WHAT--OW! OW! OW!
SLAP
SLAP
SLAP

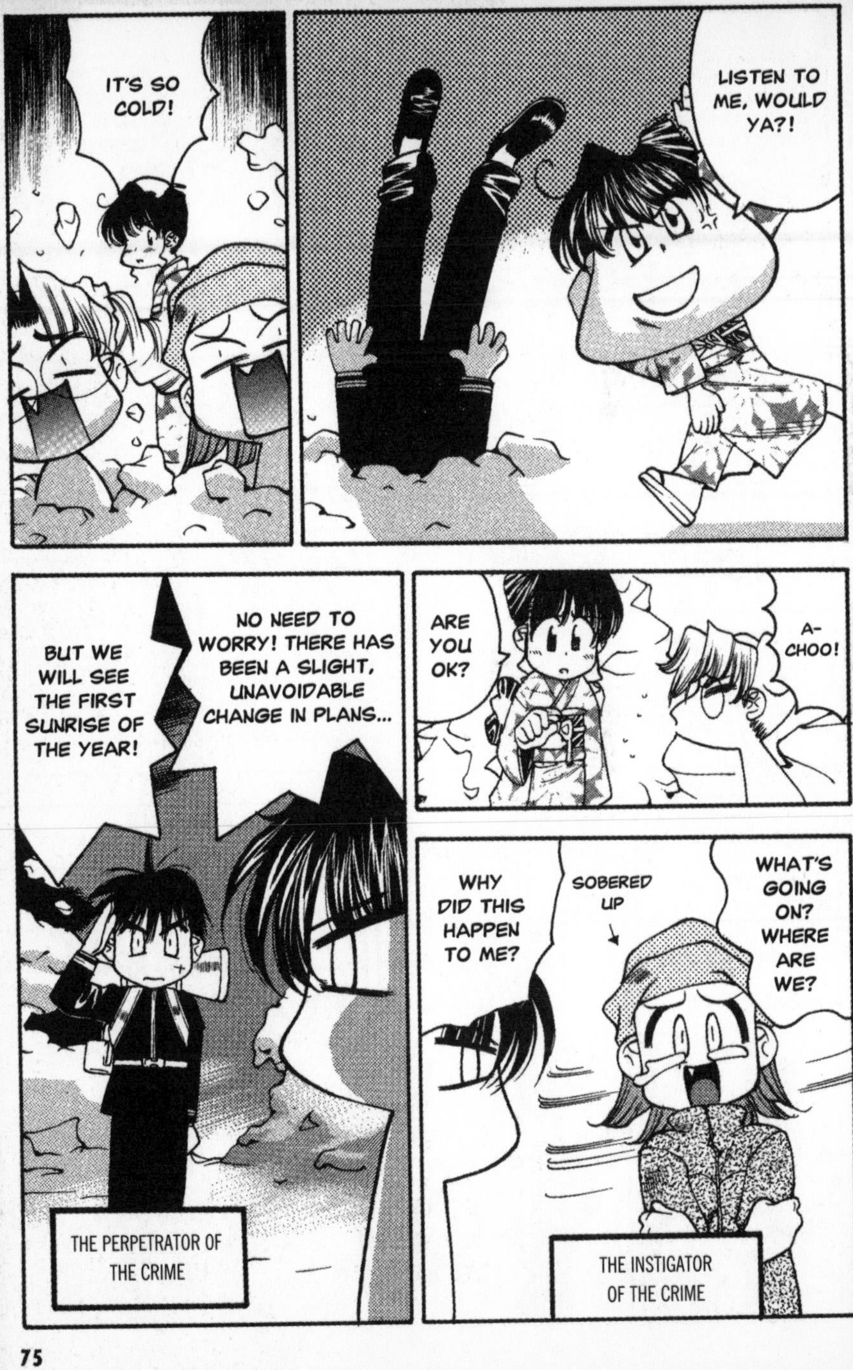
LISTEN TO ME, WOULD YA?!
IT'S SO COLD!
ARE YOU OK?
A-CHOO!
NO NEED TO WORRY! THERE HAS BEEN A SLIGHT, UNAVOIDABLE CHANGE IN PLANS...
BUT WE WILL SEE THE FIRST SUNRISE OF THE YEAR!
THE PERPETRATOR OF THE CRIME
WHAT'S GOING ON? WHERE ARE WE?
SOBERED UP
WHY DID THIS HAPPEN TO ME?
THE INSTIGATOR OF THE CRIME

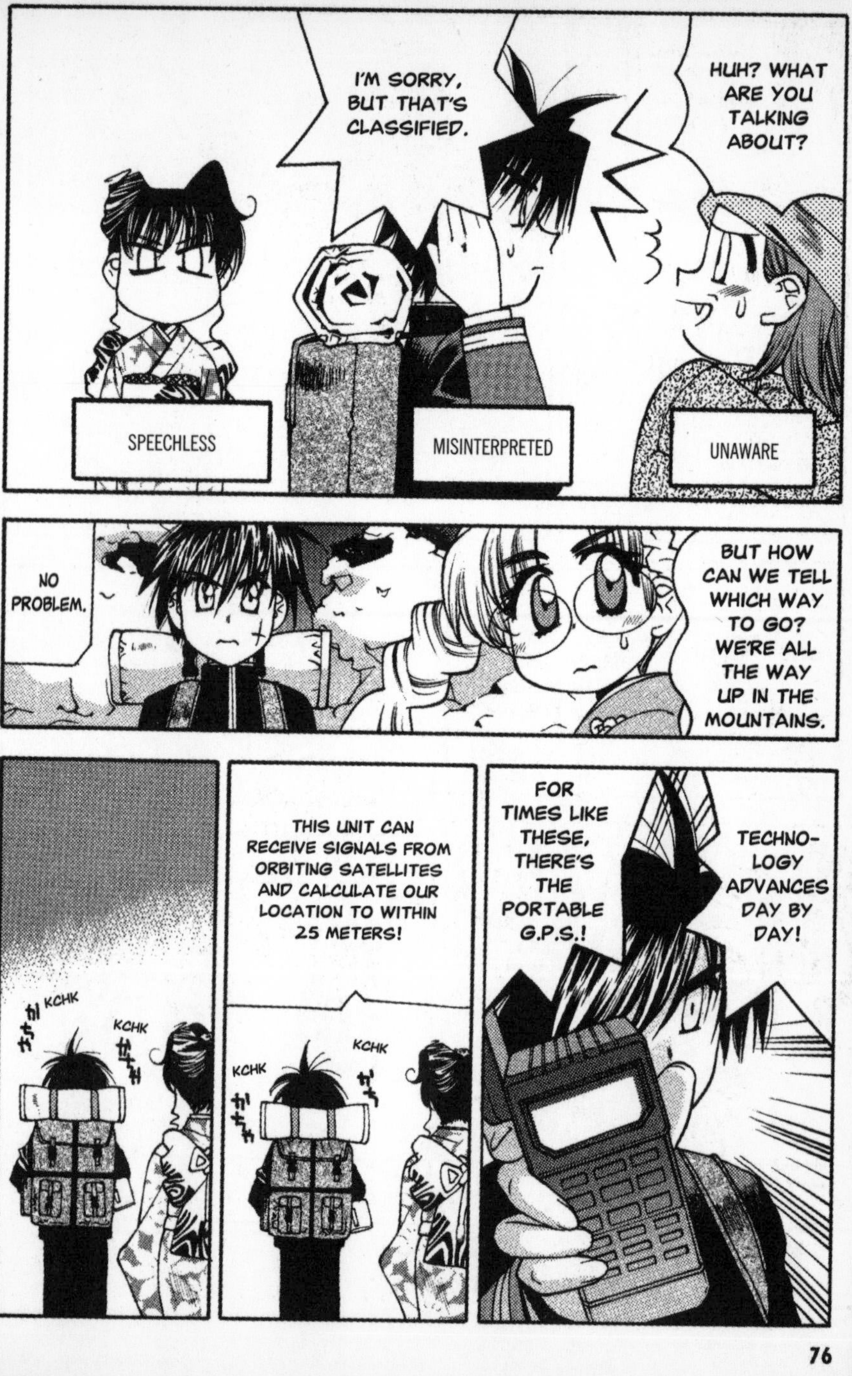
HUH? WHAT ARE YOU TALKING ABOUT?
I'M SORRY, BUT THAT'S CLASSIFIED.
UNAWARE
MISINTERPRETED
SPEECHLESS
BUT HOW CAN WE TELL WHICH WAY TO GO? WE'RE ALL THE WAY UP IN THE MOUNTAINS.
NO PROBLEM.
FOR TIMES LIKE THESE, THERE'S THE PORTABLE G.P.S.!
TECHNO-LOGY ADVANCES DAY BY DAY!
THIS UNIT CAN RECEIVE SIGNALS FROM ORBITING SATELLITES AND CALCULATE OUR LOCATION TO WITHIN 25 METERS!
KCHK
KCHK
KCHK
KCHK

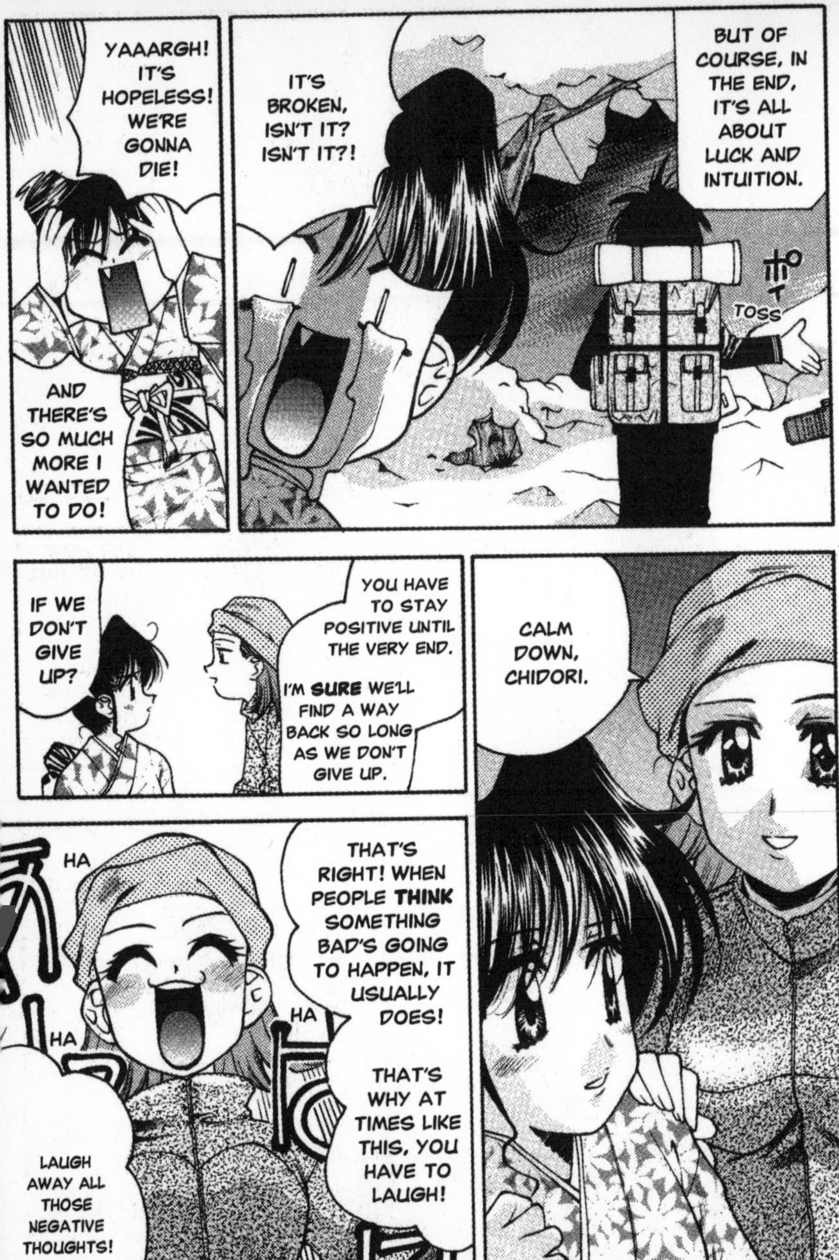

BUT OF COURSE, IN THE END, IT'S ALL ABOUT LUCK AND INTUITION.
TOSS
IT'S BROKEN, ISN'T IT? ISN'T IT?!
YAAARGH! IT'S HOPELESS! WE'RE GONNA DIE!
AND THERE'S SO MUCH MORE I WANTED TO DO!
CALM DOWN, CHIDORI.
YOU HAVE TO STAY POSITIVE UNTIL THE VERY END.
I'M **SURE** WE'LL FIND A WAY BACK SO LONG AS WE DON'T GIVE UP.
IF WE DON'T GIVE UP?
THAT'S RIGHT! WHEN PEOPLE **THINK** SOMETHING BAD'S GOING TO HAPPEN, IT USUALLY DOES!
THAT'S WHY AT TIMES LIKE THIS, YOU HAVE TO LAUGH!
HA
HA
HA
LAUGH AWAY ALL THOSE NEGATIVE THOUGHTS!

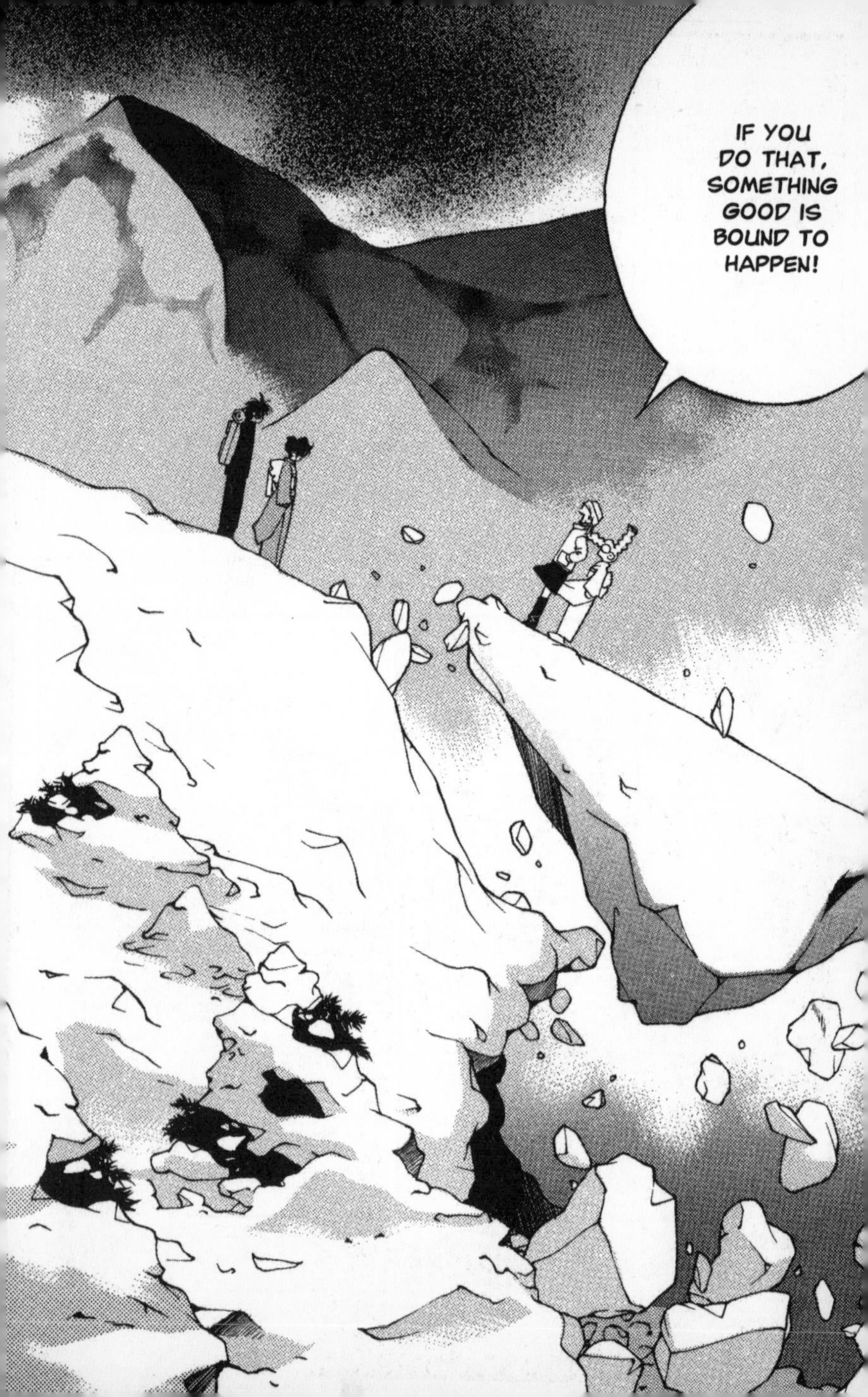
IF YOU DO THAT, SOMETHING GOOD IS BOUND TO HAPPEN!

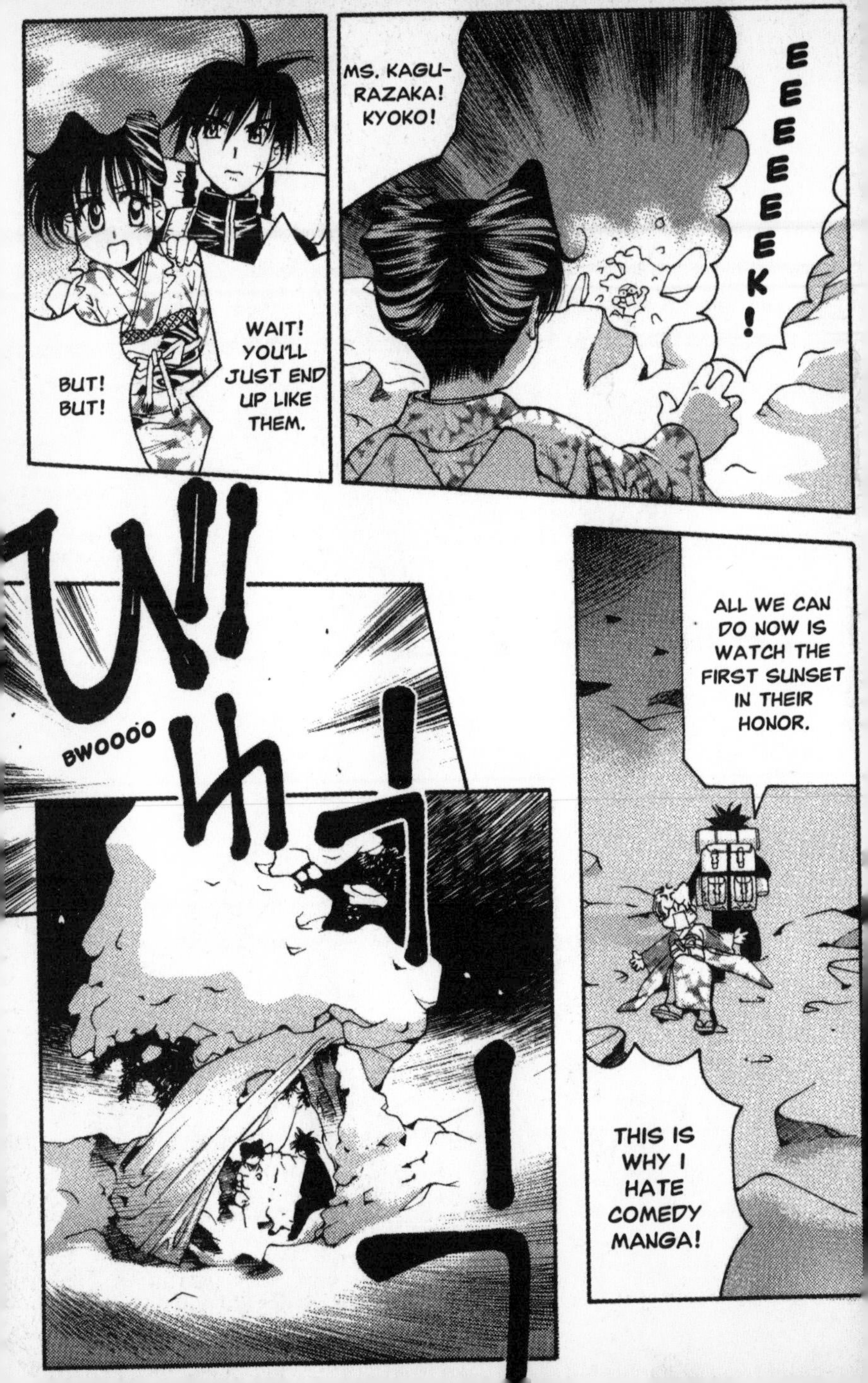
EEEEEEK!
MS. KAGURAZAKA! KYOKO!
WAIT! YOU'LL JUST END UP LIKE THEM.
BUT! BUT!
BWOOOO
ALL WE CAN DO NOW IS WATCH THE FIRST SUNSET IN THEIR HONOR.
THIS IS WHY I HATE COMEDY MANGA!

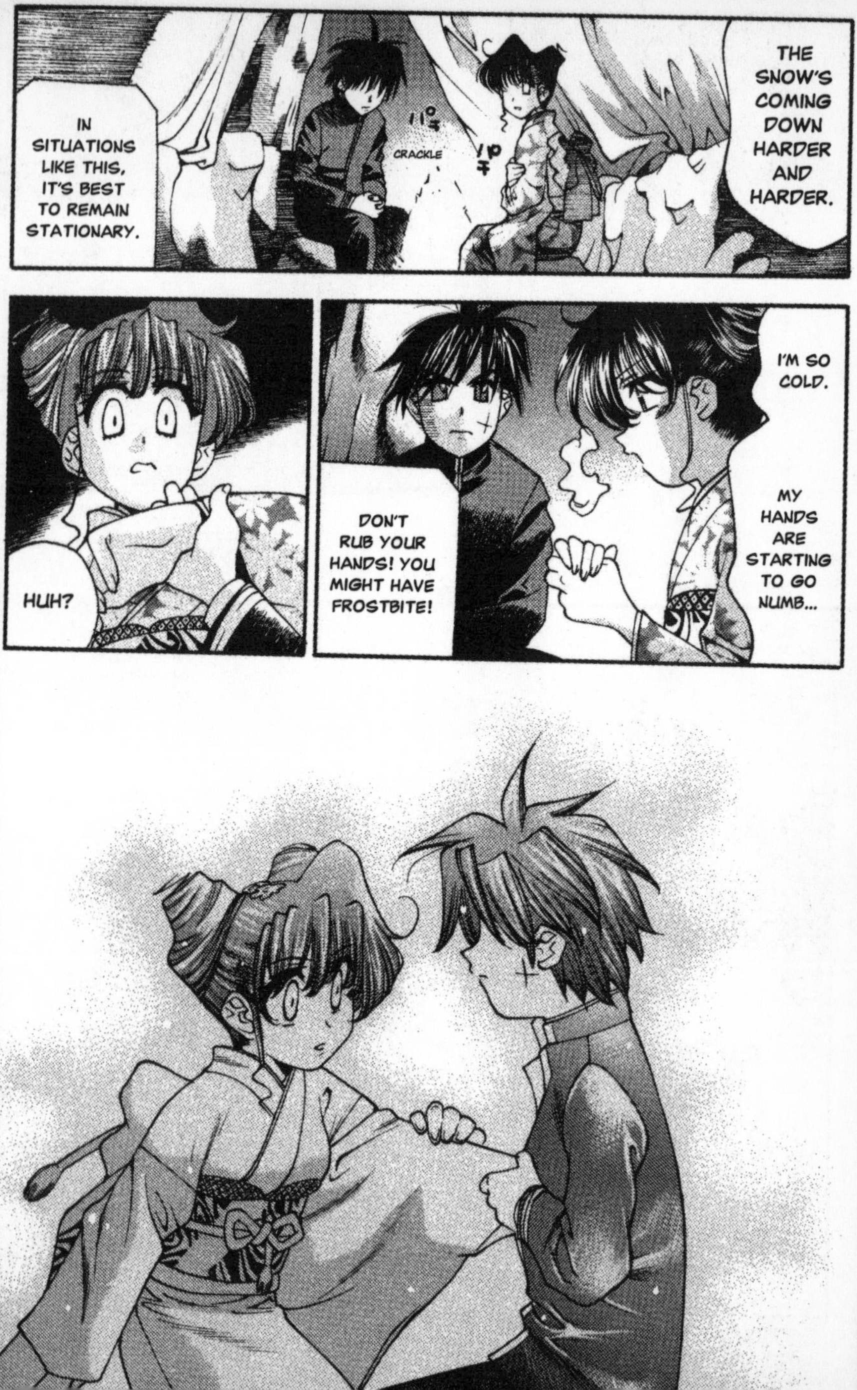
THE SNOW'S COMING DOWN HARDER AND HARDER.
パチ
CRACKLE
パチ
IN SITUATIONS LIKE THIS, IT'S BEST TO REMAIN STATIONARY.
I'M SO COLD.
MY HANDS ARE STARTING TO GO NUMB...
DON'T RUB YOUR HANDS! YOU MIGHT HAVE FROSTBITE!
HUH?

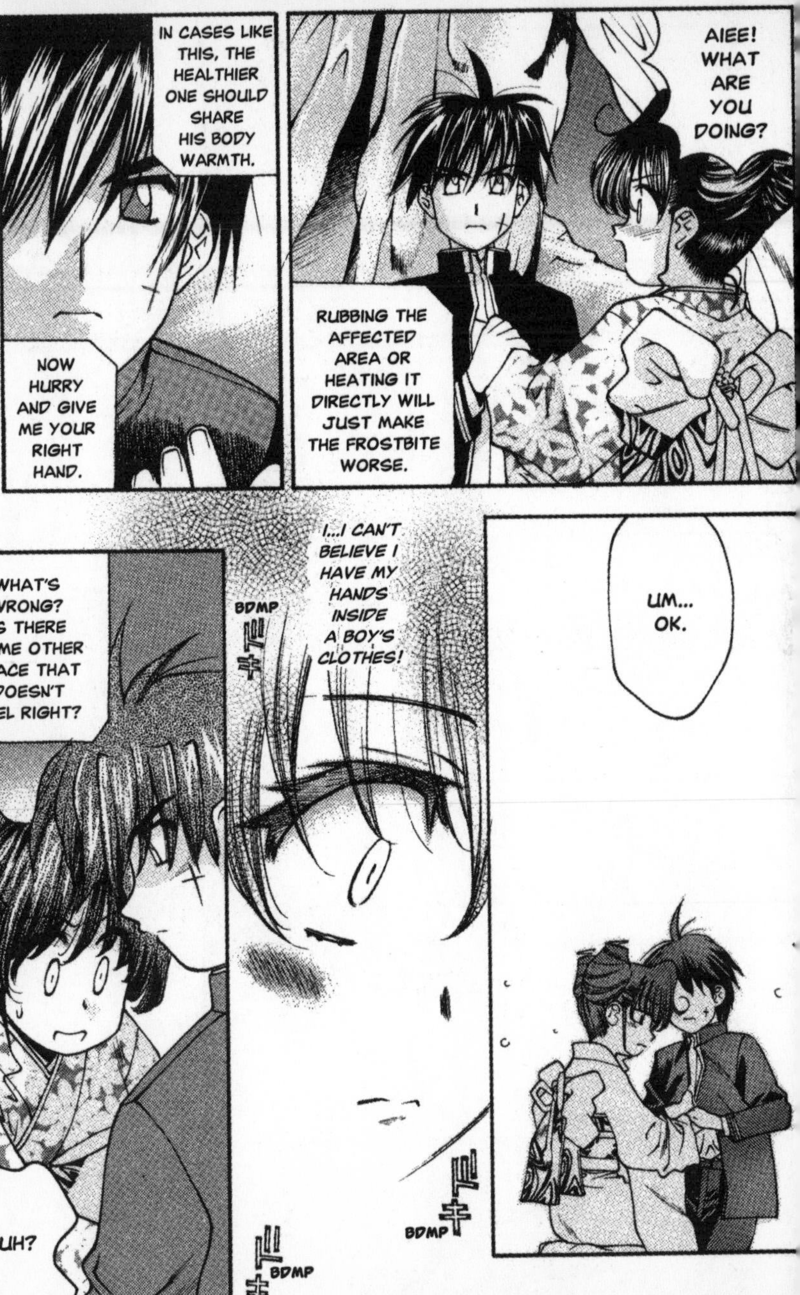
AIEE! WHAT ARE YOU DOING?
RUBBING THE AFFECTED AREA OR HEATING IT DIRECTLY WILL JUST MAKE THE FROSTBITE WORSE.
IN CASES LIKE THIS, THE HEALTHIER ONE SHOULD SHARE HIS BODY WARMTH.
NOW HURRY AND GIVE ME YOUR RIGHT HAND.
UM... OK.
BDMP
I...I CAN'T BELIEVE I HAVE MY HANDS INSIDE A BOY'S CLOTHES!
BDMP
BDMP
WHAT'S WRONG? IS THERE SOME OTHER PLACE THAT DOESN'T FEEL RIGHT?
HUH?

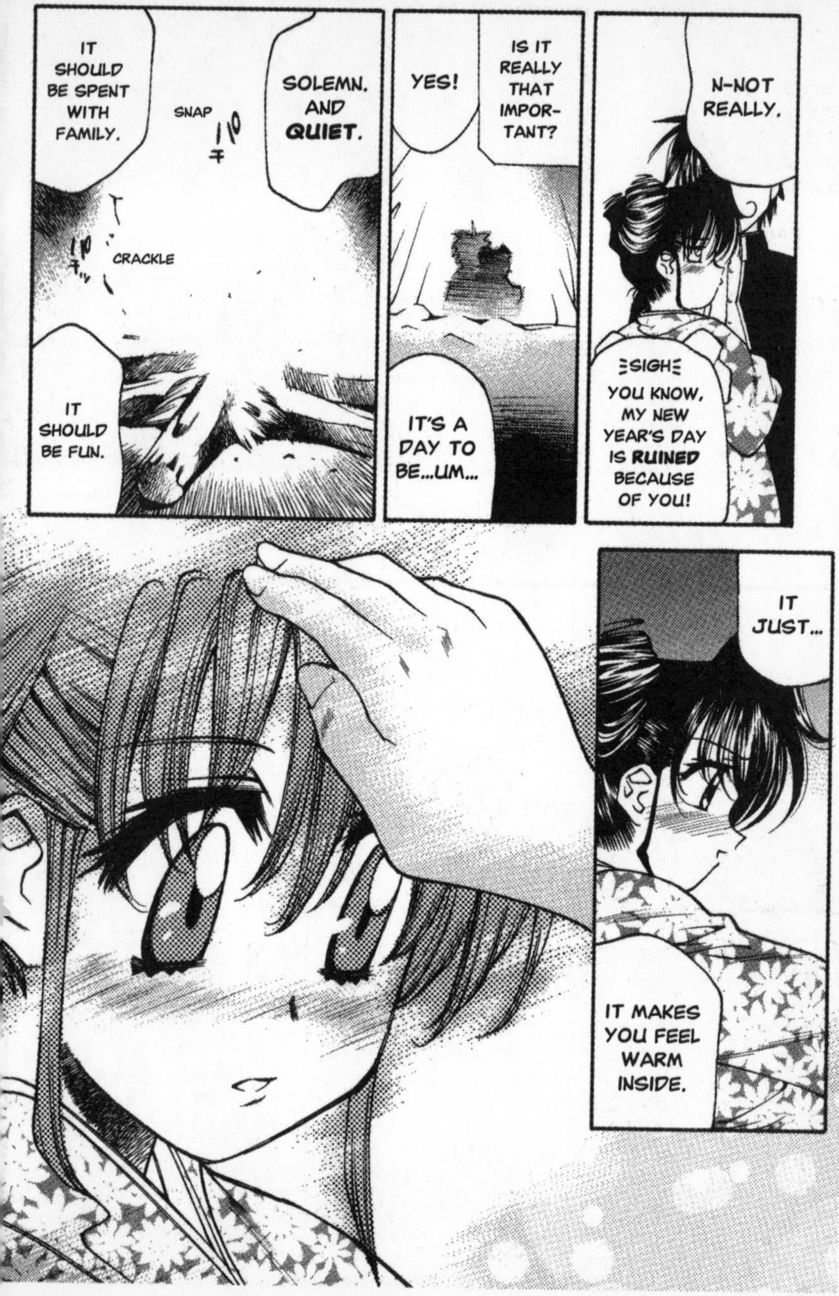
IT SHOULD BE SPENT WITH FAMILY.
SNAP
SOLEMN. AND **QUIET**.
CRACKLE
IT SHOULD BE FUN.
YES!
IS IT REALLY THAT IMPORTANT?
IT'S A DAY TO BE...UM...
N-NOT REALLY.
≡SIGH≡ YOU KNOW, MY NEW YEAR'S DAY IS **RUINED** BECAUSE OF YOU!
IT JUST...
IT MAKES YOU FEEL WARM INSIDE.

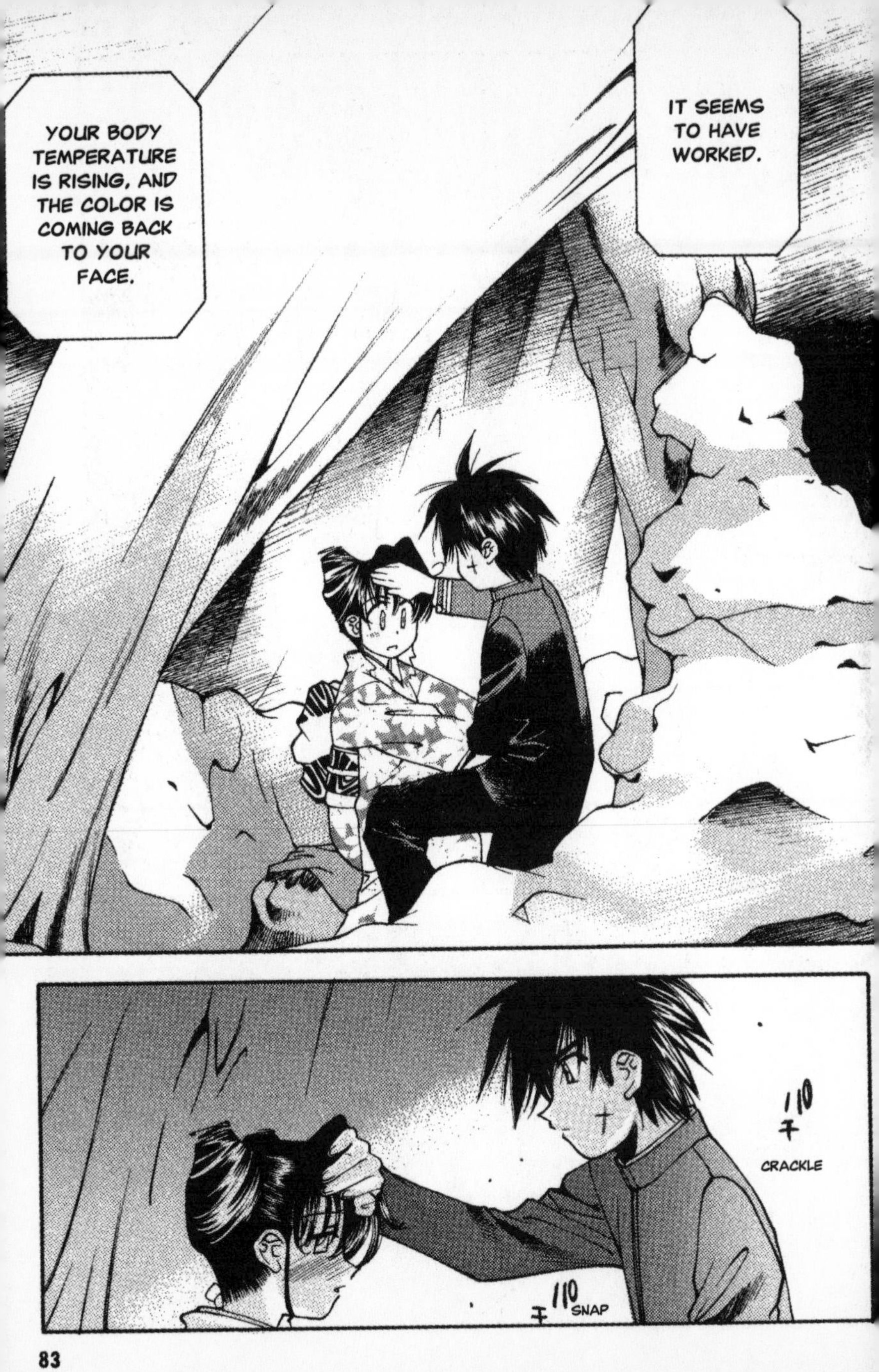
IT SEEMS TO HAVE WORKED.
YOUR BODY TEMPERATURE IS RISING, AND THE COLOR IS COMING BACK TO YOUR FACE.
CRACKLE
SNAP

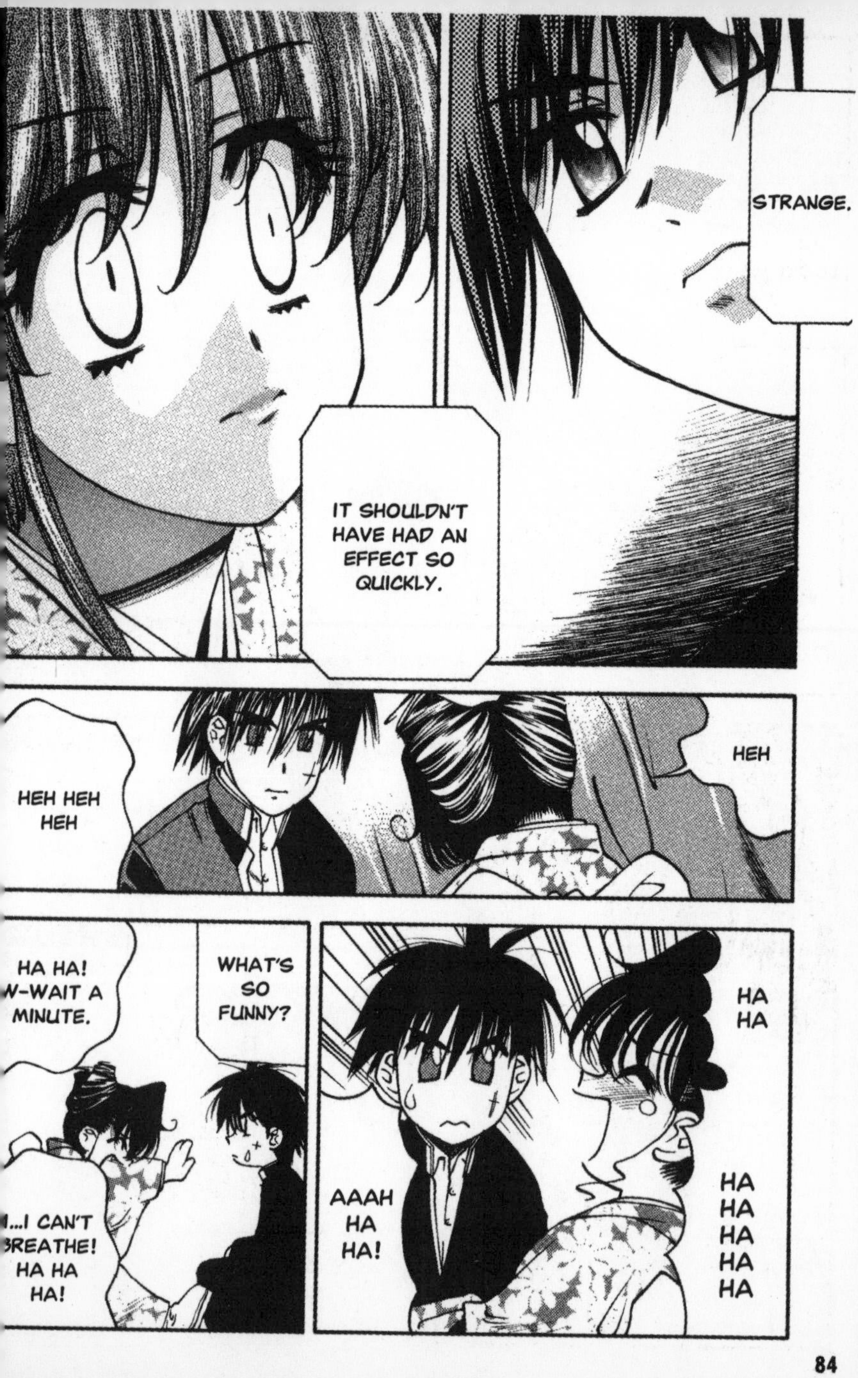
STRANGE.
IT SHOULDN'T HAVE HAD AN EFFECT SO QUICKLY.
HEH
HEH HEH HEH
HA HA
HA HA HA HA HA
AAAH HA HA!
WHAT'S SO FUNNY?
HA HA! W-WAIT A MINUTE.
...I CAN'T BREATHE! HA HA HA!

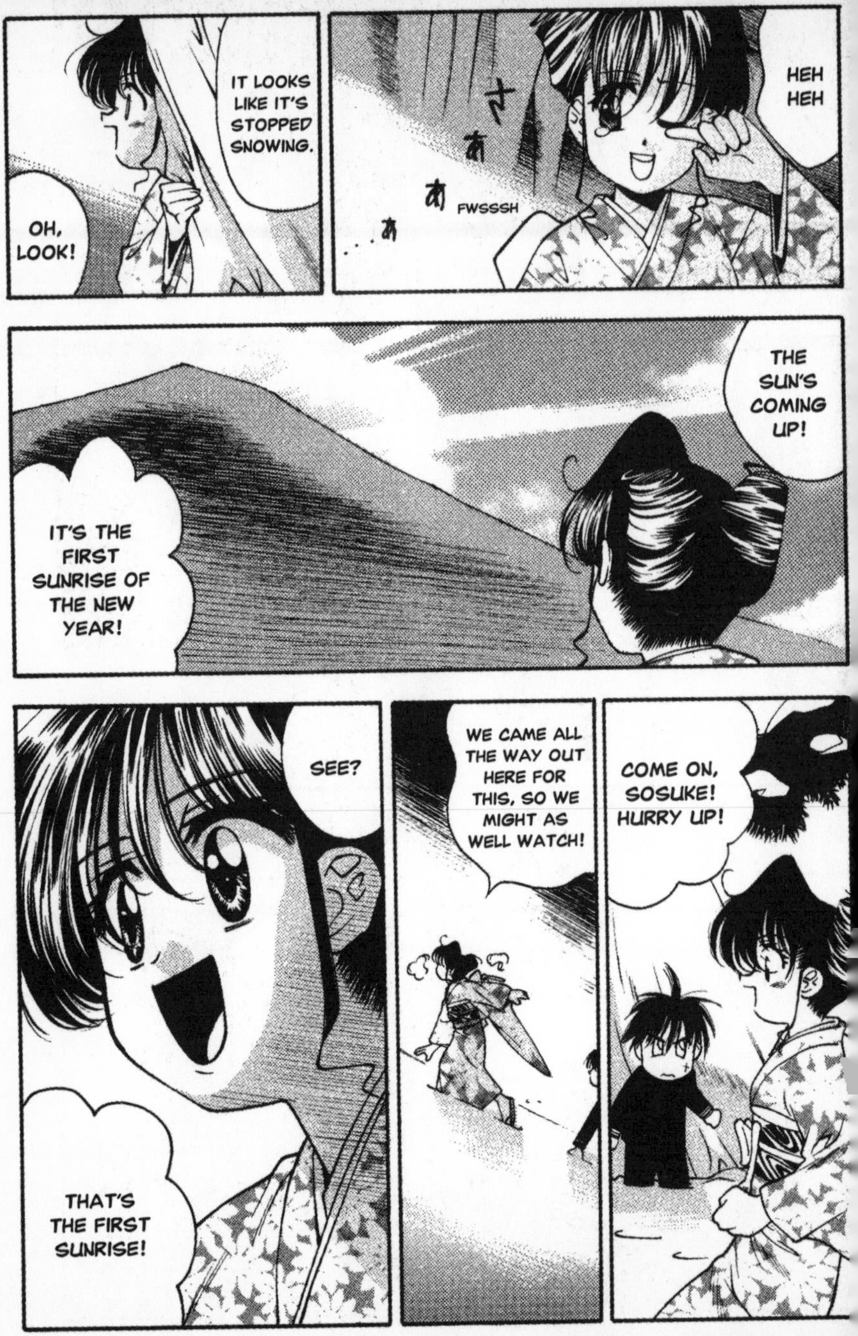
OH, LOOK!
IT LOOKS LIKE IT'S STOPPED SNOWING.
さ
あ
あ
あ
FWSSSH
HEH HEH
THE SUN'S COMING UP!
IT'S THE FIRST SUNRISE OF THE NEW YEAR!
SEE?
THAT'S THE FIRST SUNRISE!
WE CAME ALL THE WAY OUT HERE FOR THIS, SO WE MIGHT AS WELL WATCH!
COME ON, SOSUKE! HURRY UP!

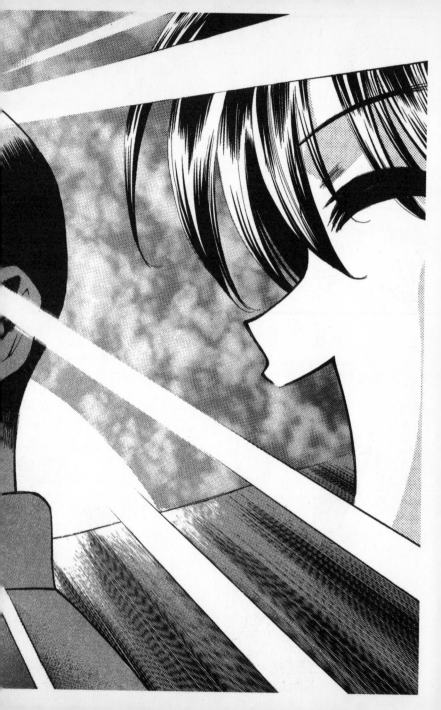

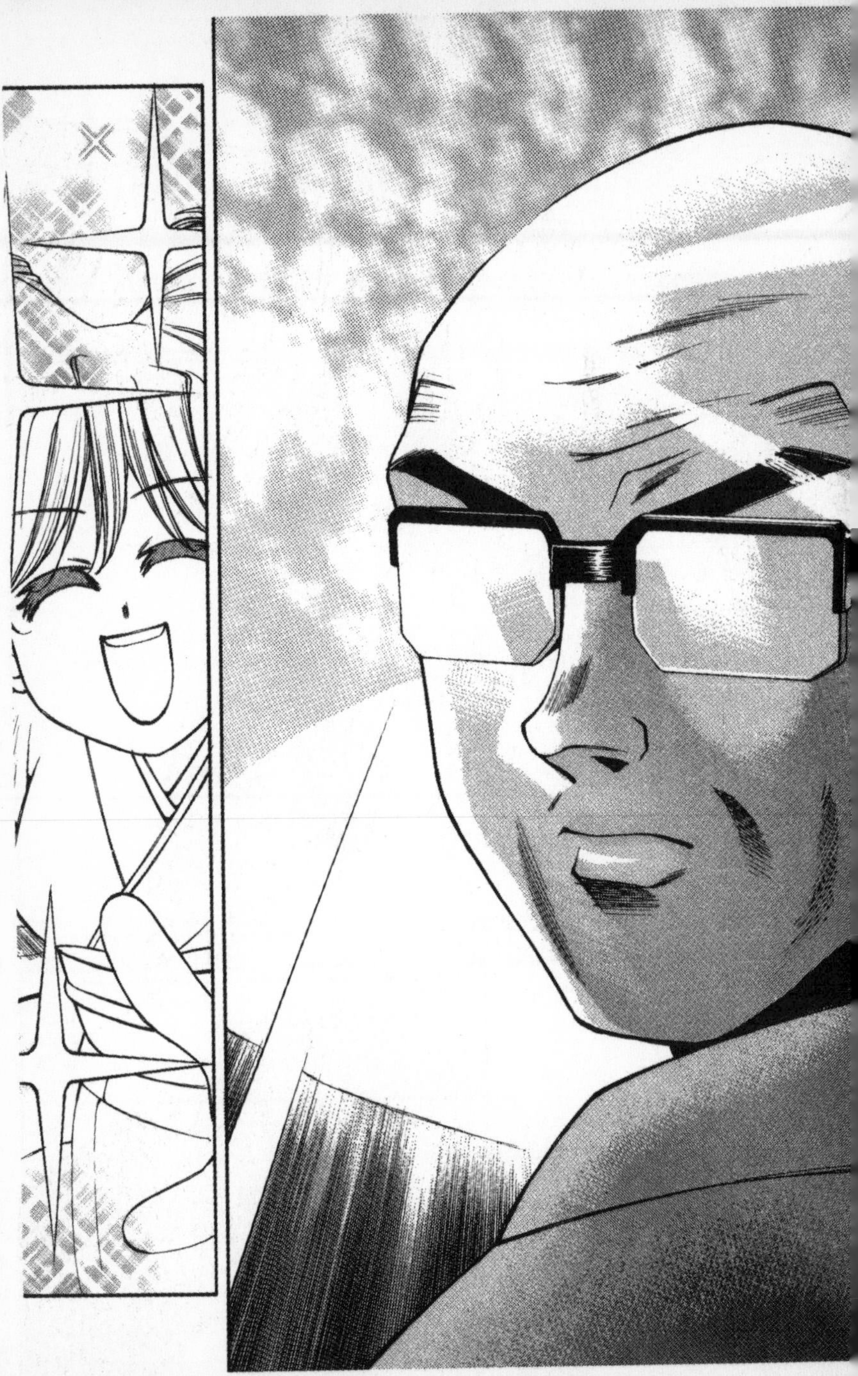

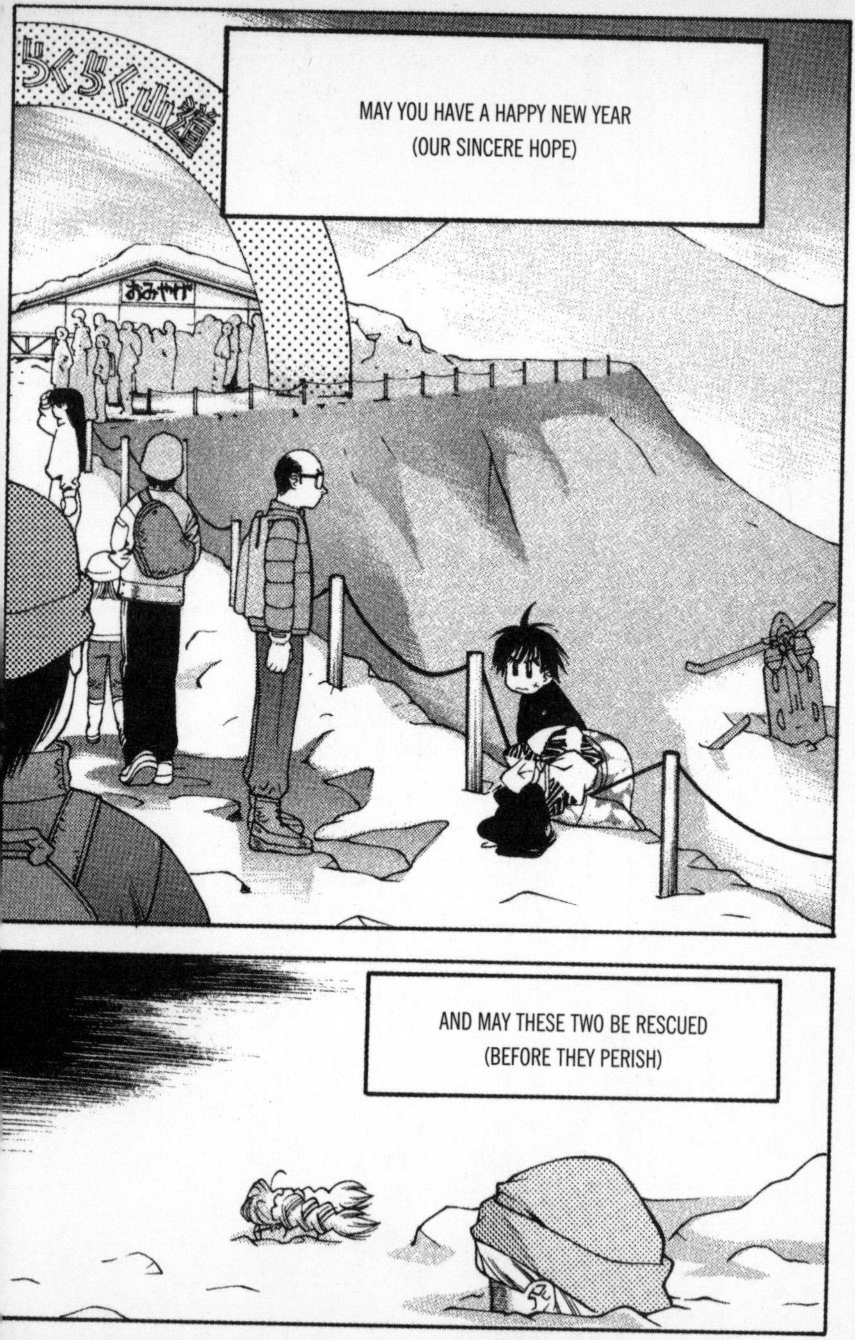
MAY YOU HAVE A HAPPY NEW YEAR
(OUR SINCERE HOPE)
らくらく山道
おみやげ
AND MAY THESE TWO BE RESCUED
(BEFORE THEY PERISH)

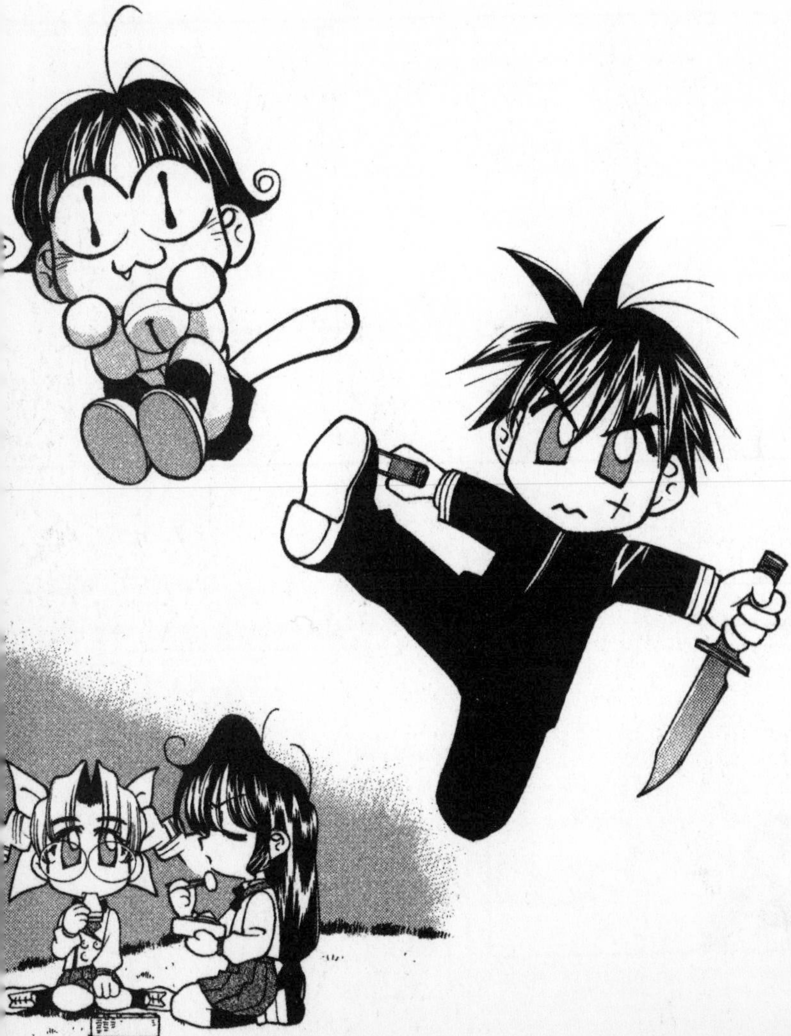

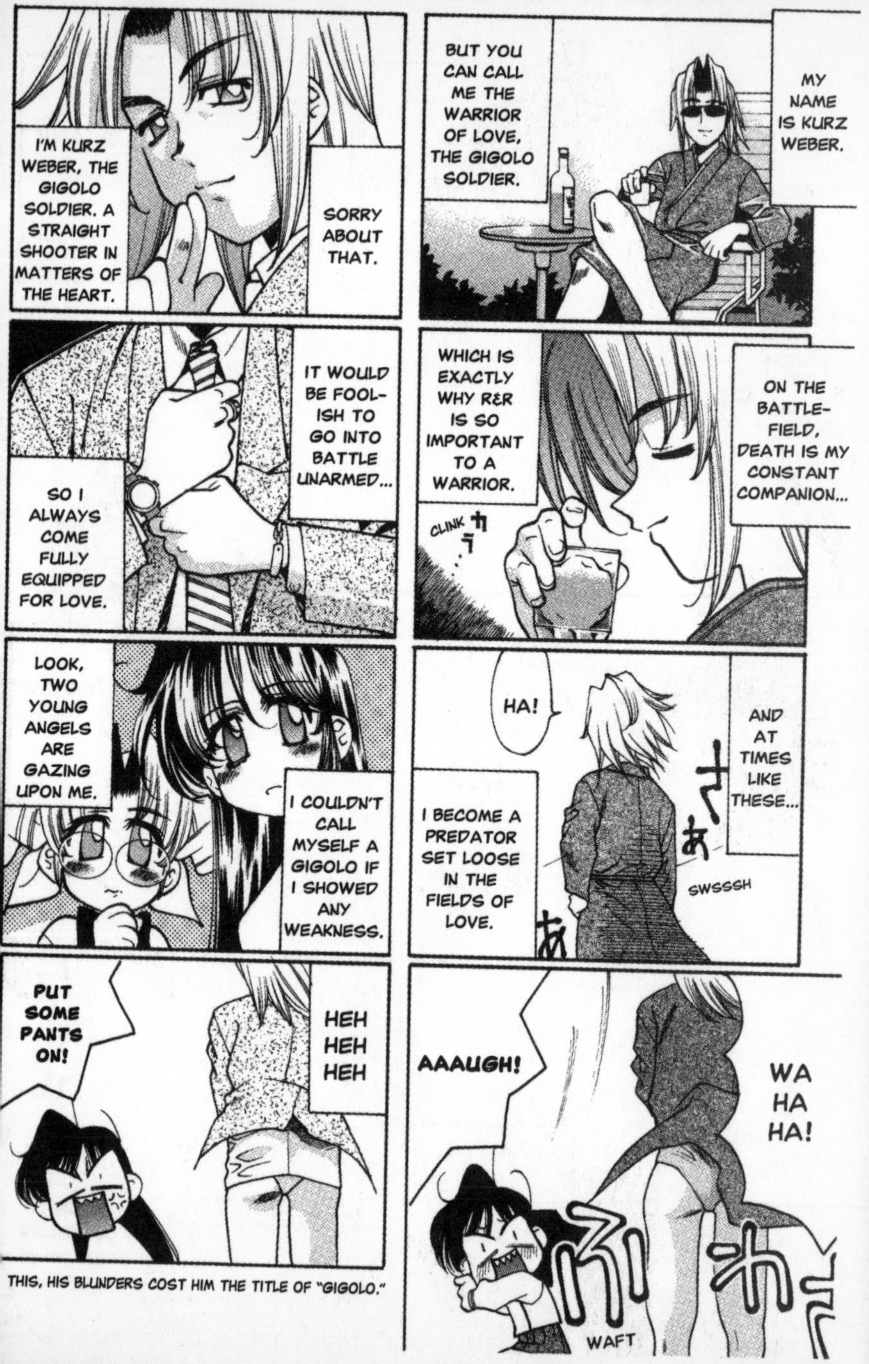
MY NAME IS KURZ WEBER.
BUT YOU CAN CALL ME THE WARRIOR OF LOVE, THE GIGOLO SOLDIER.
ON THE BATTLE-FIELD, DEATH IS MY CONSTANT COMPANION...
WHICH IS EXACTLY WHY R&R IS SO IMPORTANT TO A WARRIOR.
CLINK
AND AT TIMES LIKE THESE...
HA!
I BECOME A PREDATOR SET LOOSE IN THE FIELDS OF LOVE.
SWSSSH
WA HA HA!
AAAUGH!
WAFT
SORRY ABOUT THAT.
I'M KURZ WEBER, THE GIGOLO SOLDIER. A STRAIGHT SHOOTER IN MATTERS OF THE HEART.
IT WOULD BE FOOL-ISH TO GO INTO BATTLE UNARMED...
SO I ALWAYS COME FULLY EQUIPPED FOR LOVE.
I COULDN'T CALL MYSELF A GIGOLO IF I SHOWED ANY WEAKNESS.
LOOK, TWO YOUNG ANGELS ARE GAZING UPON ME.
HEH HEH HEH
PUT SOME PANTS ON!
THIS, HIS BLUNDERS COST HIM THE TITLE OF "GIGOLO."

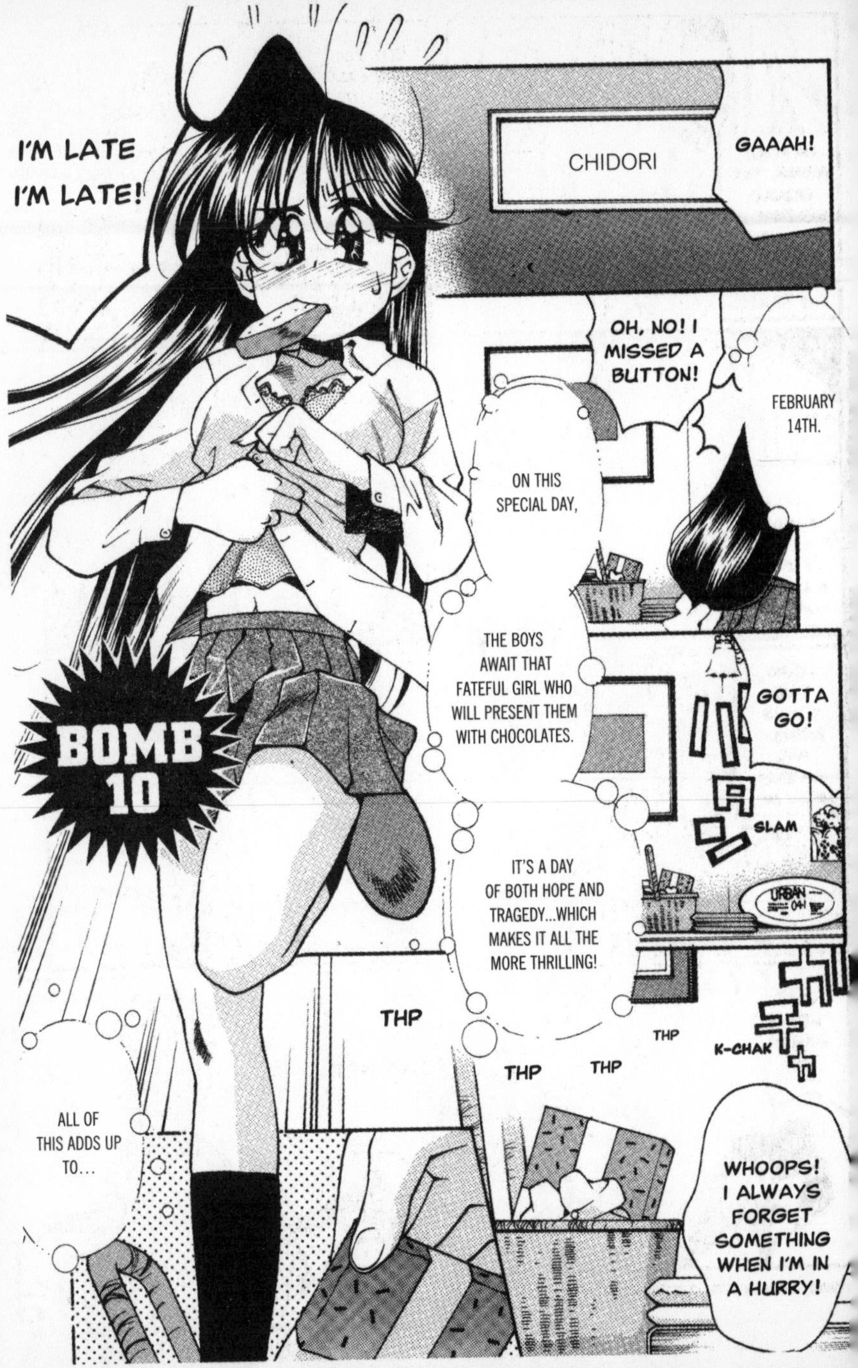
GAAAH!
CHIDORI
I'M LATE I'M LATE!
BOMB 10
FEBRUARY 14TH.
OH, NO! I MISSED A BUTTON!
ON THIS SPECIAL DAY,
THE BOYS AWAIT THAT FATEFUL GIRL WHO WILL PRESENT THEM WITH CHOCOLATES.
GOTTA GO!
SLAM
IT'S A DAY OF BOTH HOPE AND TRAGEDY...WHICH MAKES IT ALL THE MORE THRILLING!
THP
THP
THP
THP
K-CHAK
WHOOPS! I ALWAYS FORGET SOMETHING WHEN I'M IN A HURRY!
ALL OF THIS ADDS UP TO...

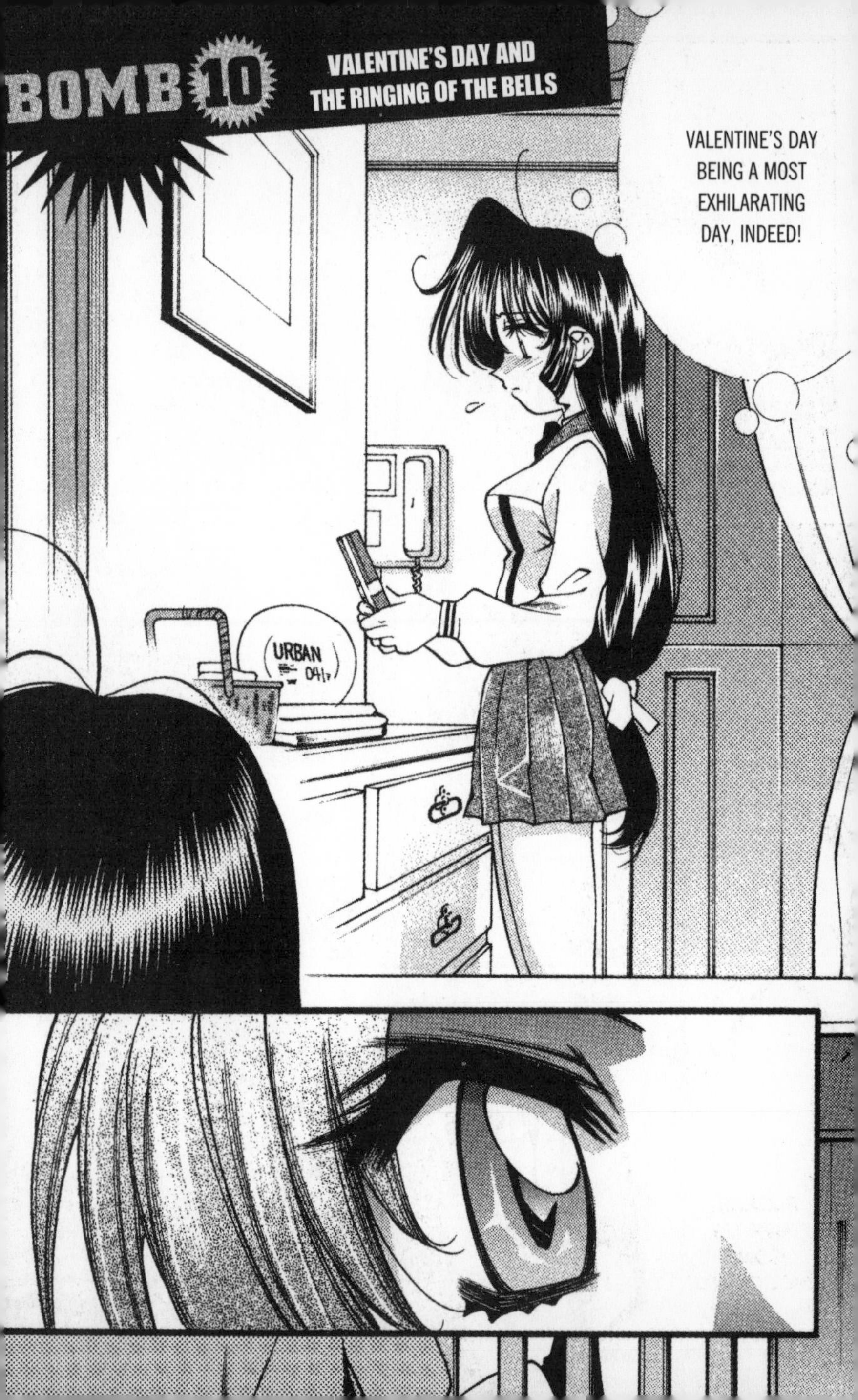
BOMB 10
VALENTINE'S DAY AND THE RINGING OF THE BELLS
VALENTINE'S DAY BEING A MOST EXHILARATING DAY, INDEED!
URBAN

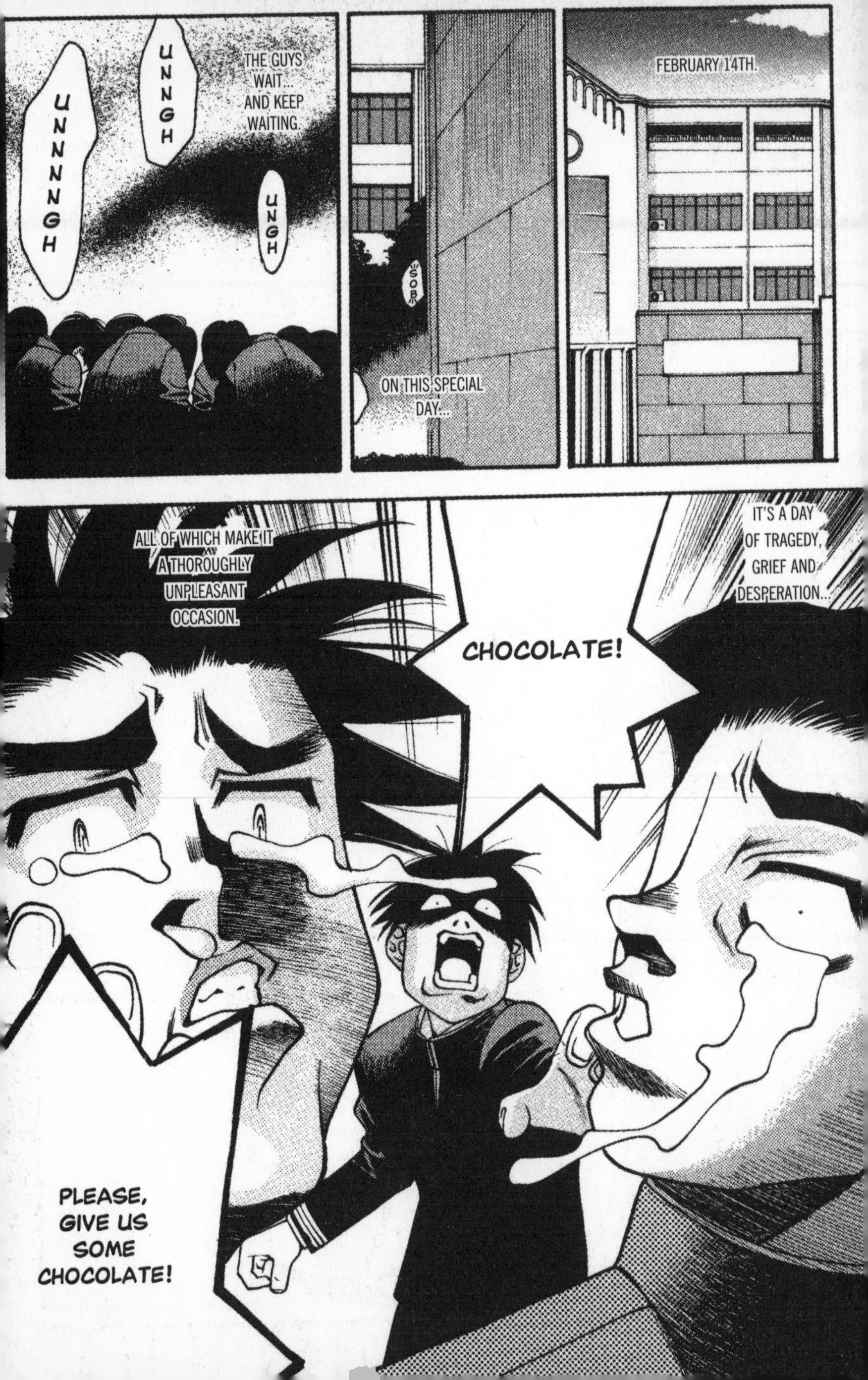
FEBRUARY 14TH.
ON THIS SPECIAL DAY...
SOB
THE GUYS WAIT... AND KEEP WAITING.
UNNGH
UNGH
UNNNNNGH
IT'S A DAY OF TRAGEDY, GRIEF AND DESPERATION...
ALL OF WHICH MAKE IT A THOROUGHLY UNPLEASANT OCCASION.
CHOCOLATE!
PLEASE, GIVE US SOME CHOCOLATE!

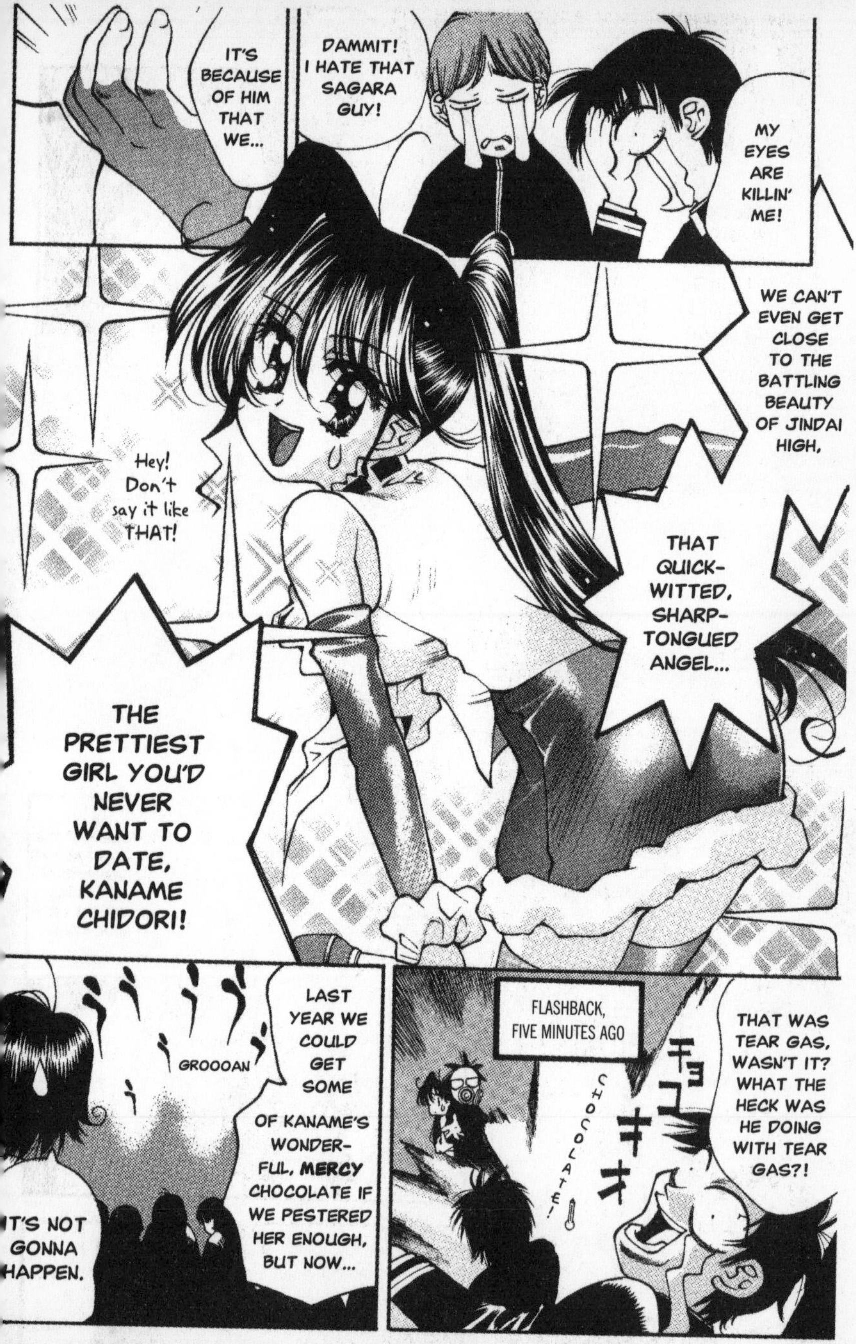
IT'S BECAUSE OF HIM THAT WE...
DAMMIT! I HATE THAT SAGARA GUY!
MY EYES ARE KILLIN' ME!
WE CAN'T EVEN GET CLOSE TO THE BATTLING BEAUTY OF JINDAI HIGH,
THAT QUICK-WITTED, SHARP-TONGUED ANGEL...
THE PRETTIEST GIRL YOU'D NEVER WANT TO DATE, KANAME CHIDORI!
Hey! Don't say it like THAT!
GROOOAN
LAST YEAR WE COULD GET SOME OF KANAME'S WONDERFUL, **MERCY** CHOCOLATE IF WE PESTERED HER ENOUGH, BUT NOW...
IT'S NOT GONNA HAPPEN.
FLASHBACK, FIVE MINUTES AGO
CHOCOLATE!
THAT WAS TEAR GAS, WASN'T IT? WHAT THE HECK WAS HE DOING WITH TEAR GAS?!

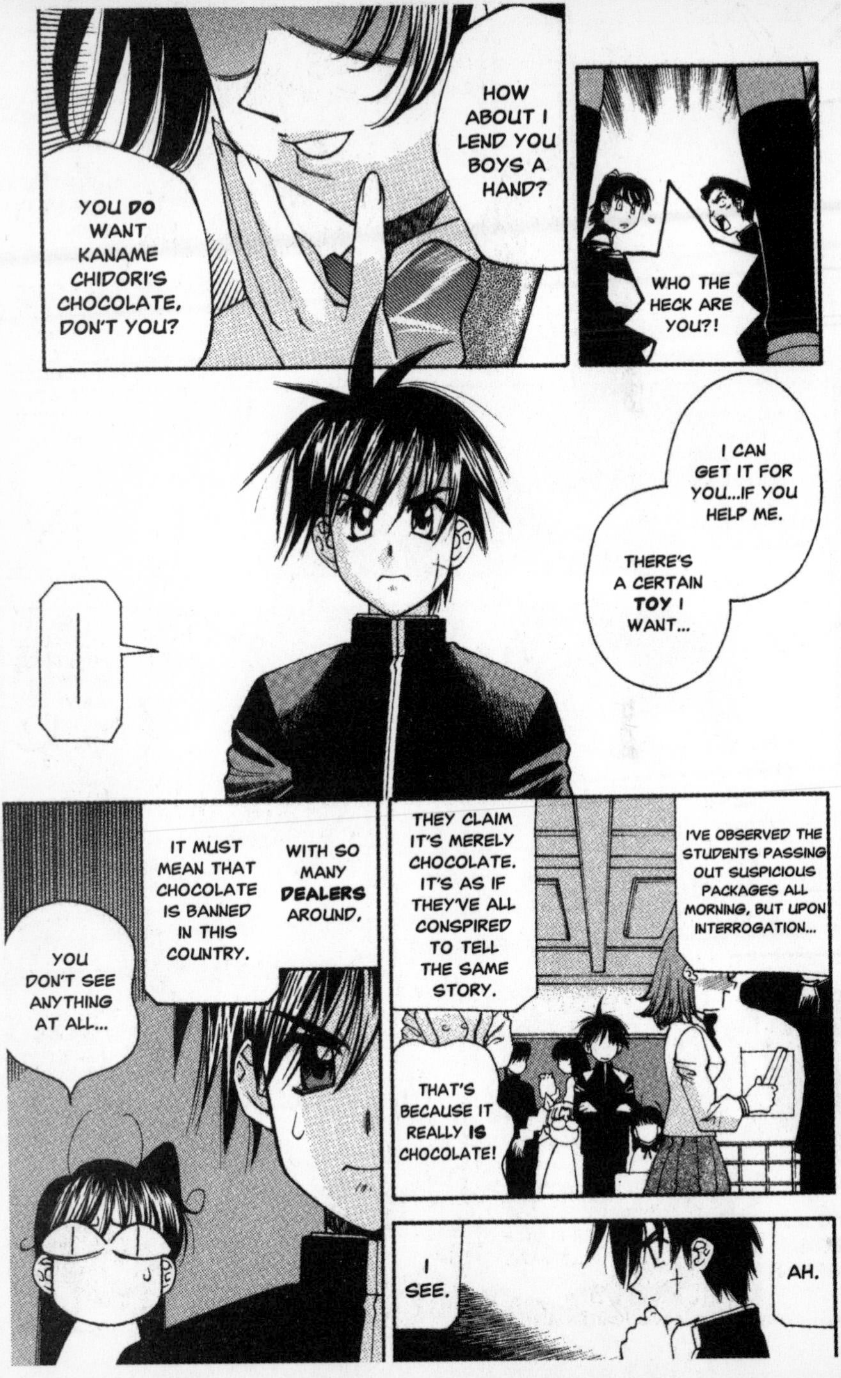
WHO THE HECK ARE YOU?!
HOW ABOUT I LEND YOU BOYS A HAND?
YOU DO WANT KANAME CHIDORI'S CHOCOLATE, DON'T YOU?
I CAN GET IT FOR YOU...IF YOU HELP ME.
THERE'S A CERTAIN TOY I WANT...
I'VE OBSERVED THE STUDENTS PASSING OUT SUSPICIOUS PACKAGES ALL MORNING, BUT UPON INTERROGATION...
THEY CLAIM IT'S MERELY CHOCOLATE. IT'S AS IF THEY'VE ALL CONSPIRED TO TELL THE SAME STORY.
THAT'S BECAUSE IT REALLY IS CHOCOLATE!
AH.
I SEE.
WITH SO MANY DEALERS AROUND,
IT MUST MEAN THAT CHOCOLATE IS BANNED IN THIS COUNTRY.
YOU DON'T SEE ANYTHING AT ALL...

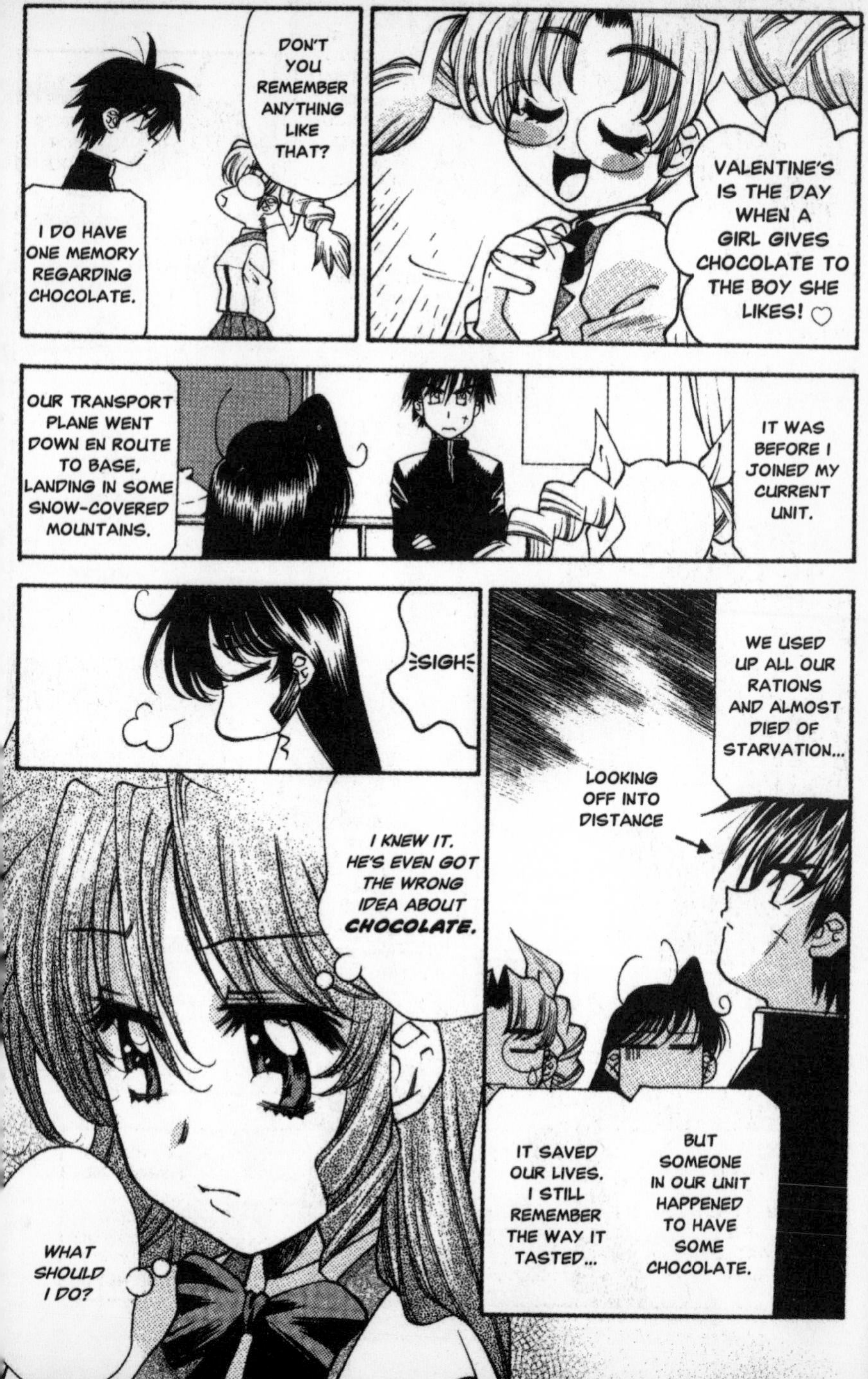
VALENTINE'S IS THE DAY WHEN A GIRL GIVES CHOCOLATE TO THE BOY SHE LIKES! ♡
DON'T YOU REMEMBER ANYTHING LIKE THAT?
I DO HAVE ONE MEMORY REGARDING CHOCOLATE.
IT WAS BEFORE I JOINED MY CURRENT UNIT.
OUR TRANSPORT PLANE WENT DOWN EN ROUTE TO BASE, LANDING IN SOME SNOW-COVERED MOUNTAINS.
WE USED UP ALL OUR RATIONS AND ALMOST DIED OF STARVATION...
LOOKING OFF INTO DISTANCE
BUT SOMEONE IN OUR UNIT HAPPENED TO HAVE SOME CHOCOLATE.
IT SAVED OUR LIVES. I STILL REMEMBER THE WAY IT TASTED...
SIGH
I KNEW IT. HE'S EVEN GOT THE WRONG IDEA ABOUT CHOCOLATE.
WHAT SHOULD I DO?

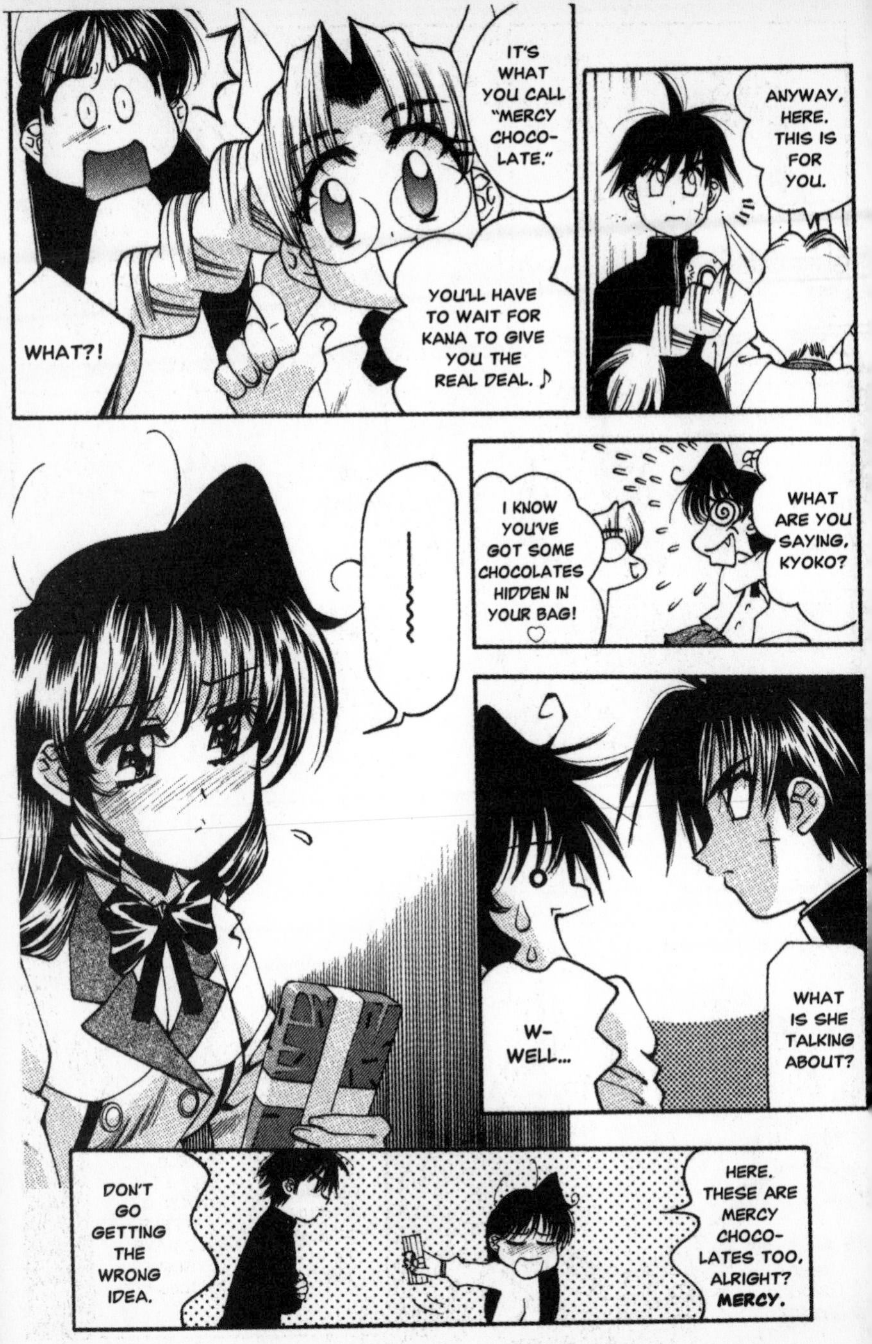
ANYWAY, HERE. THIS IS FOR YOU.
IT'S WHAT YOU CALL "MERCY CHOCOLATE."
WHAT?!
YOU'LL HAVE TO WAIT FOR KANA TO GIVE YOU THE REAL DEAL. ♪
WHAT ARE YOU SAYING, KYOKO?
I KNOW YOU'VE GOT SOME CHOCOLATES HIDDEN IN YOUR BAG! ♡
WHAT IS SHE TALKING ABOUT?
W-WELL...
HERE. THESE ARE MERCY CHOCOLATES TOO, ALRIGHT? MERCY.
DON'T GO GETTING THE WRONG IDEA.

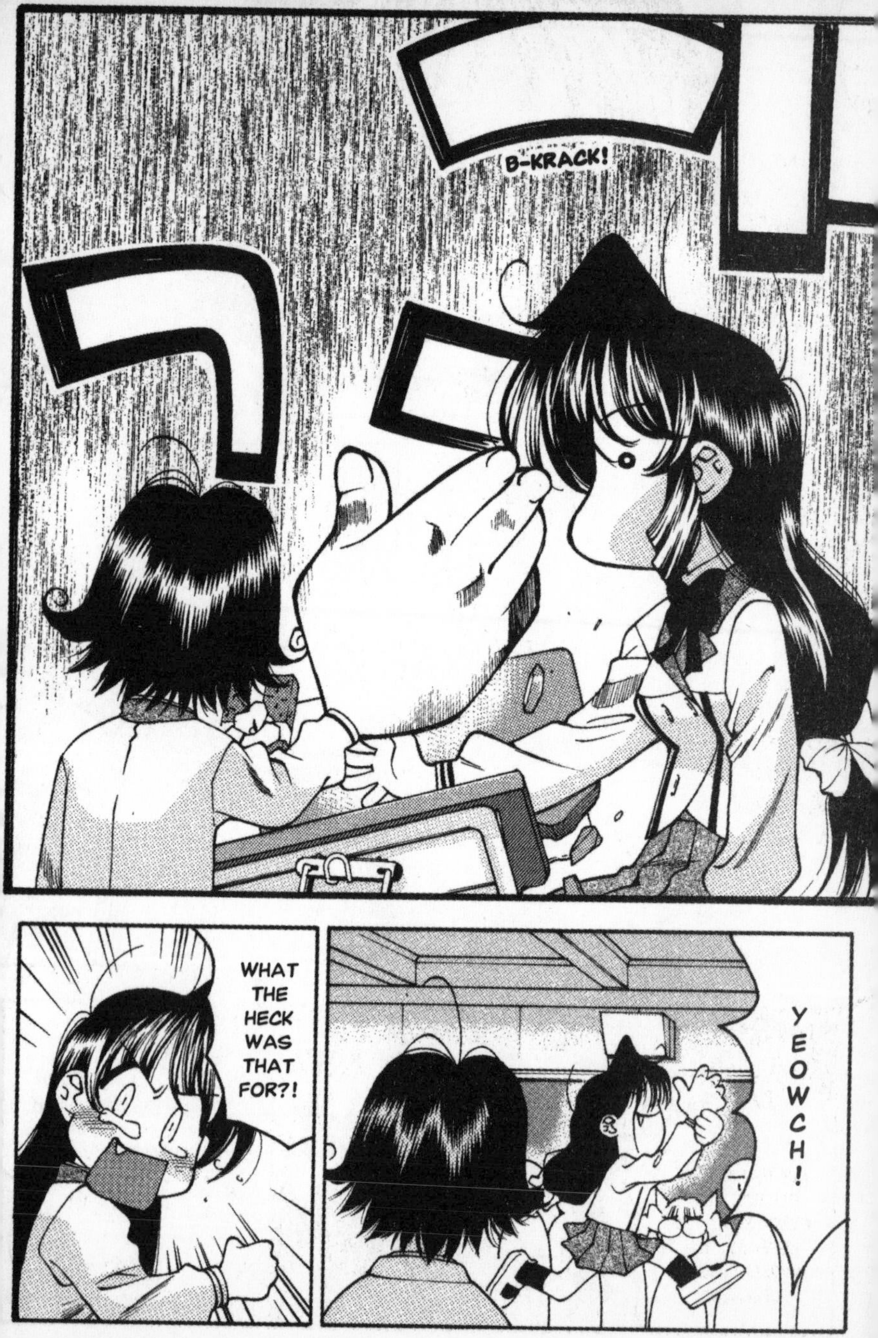
B-KRACK!
WHAT THE HECK WAS THAT FOR?!
YEOWCH!

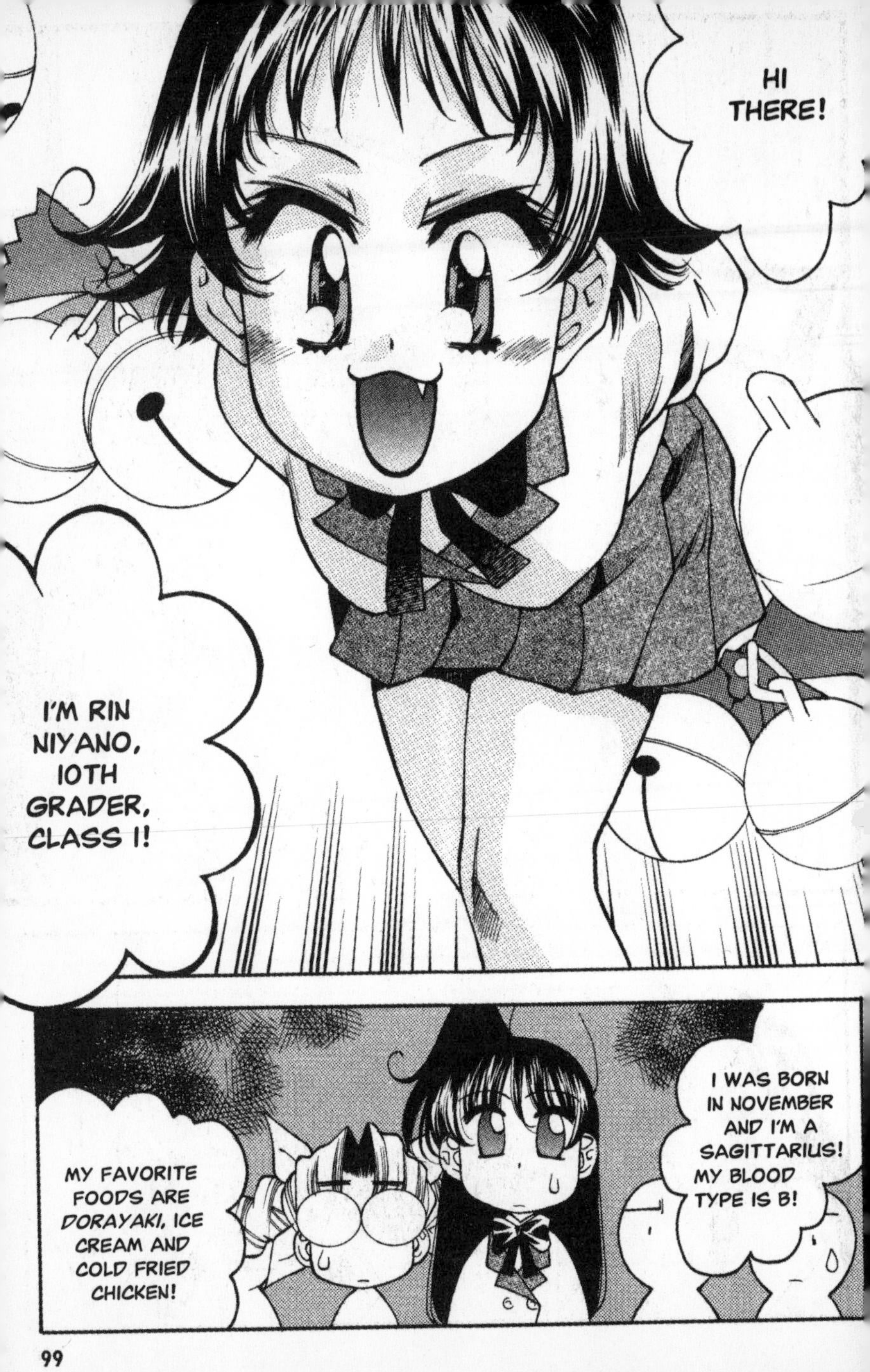
HI THERE!
I'M RIN NIYANO, 10TH GRADER, CLASS 1!
I WAS BORN IN NOVEMBER AND I'M A SAGITTARIUS! MY BLOOD TYPE IS B!
MY FAVORITE FOODS ARE *DORAYAKI*, ICE CREAM AND COLD FRIED CHICKEN!

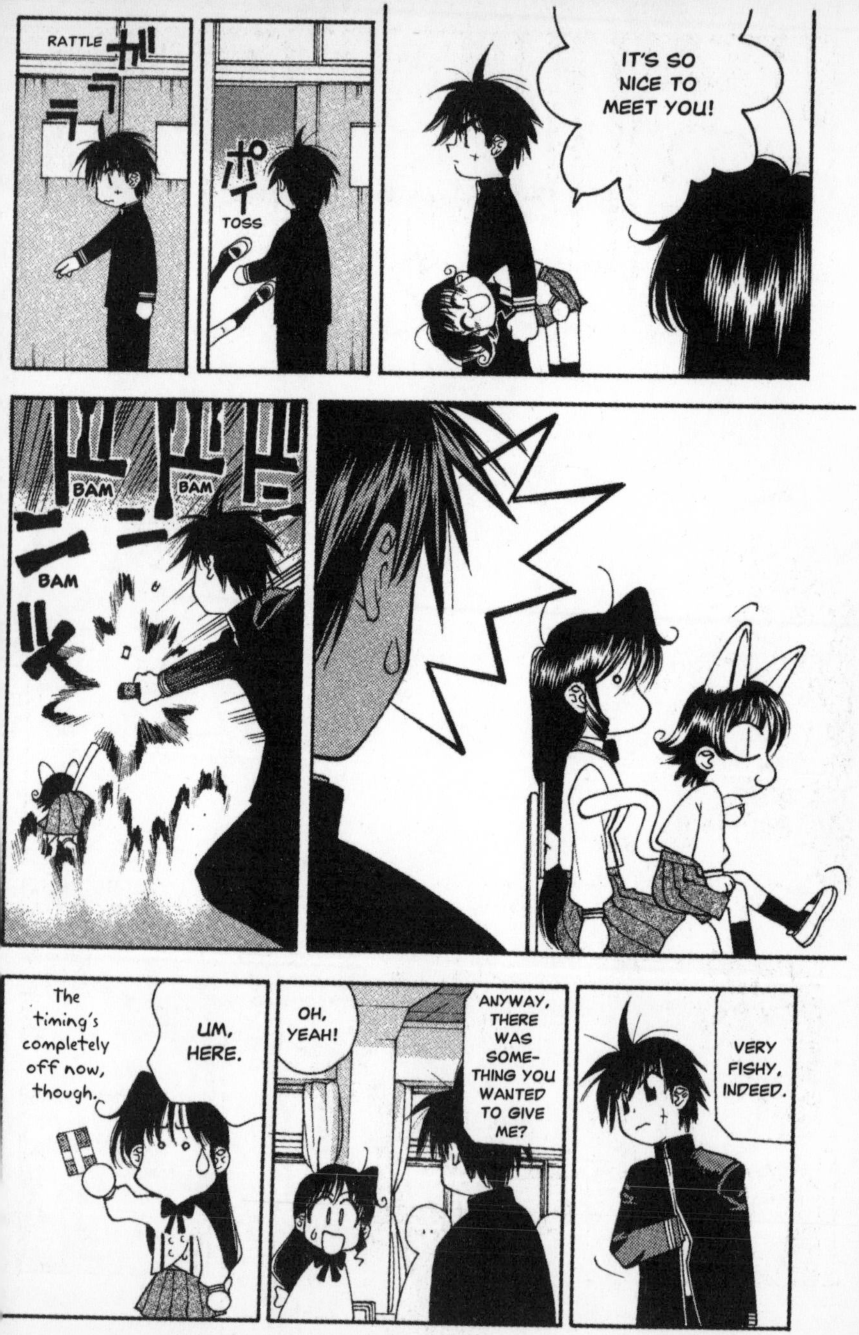

IT'S SO NICE TO MEET YOU!
TOSS
RATTLE
BAM
BAM
BAM
VERY FISHY, INDEED.
ANYWAY, THERE WAS SOME-THING YOU WANTED TO GIVE ME?
OH, YEAH!
UM, HERE.
The timing's completely off now, though.

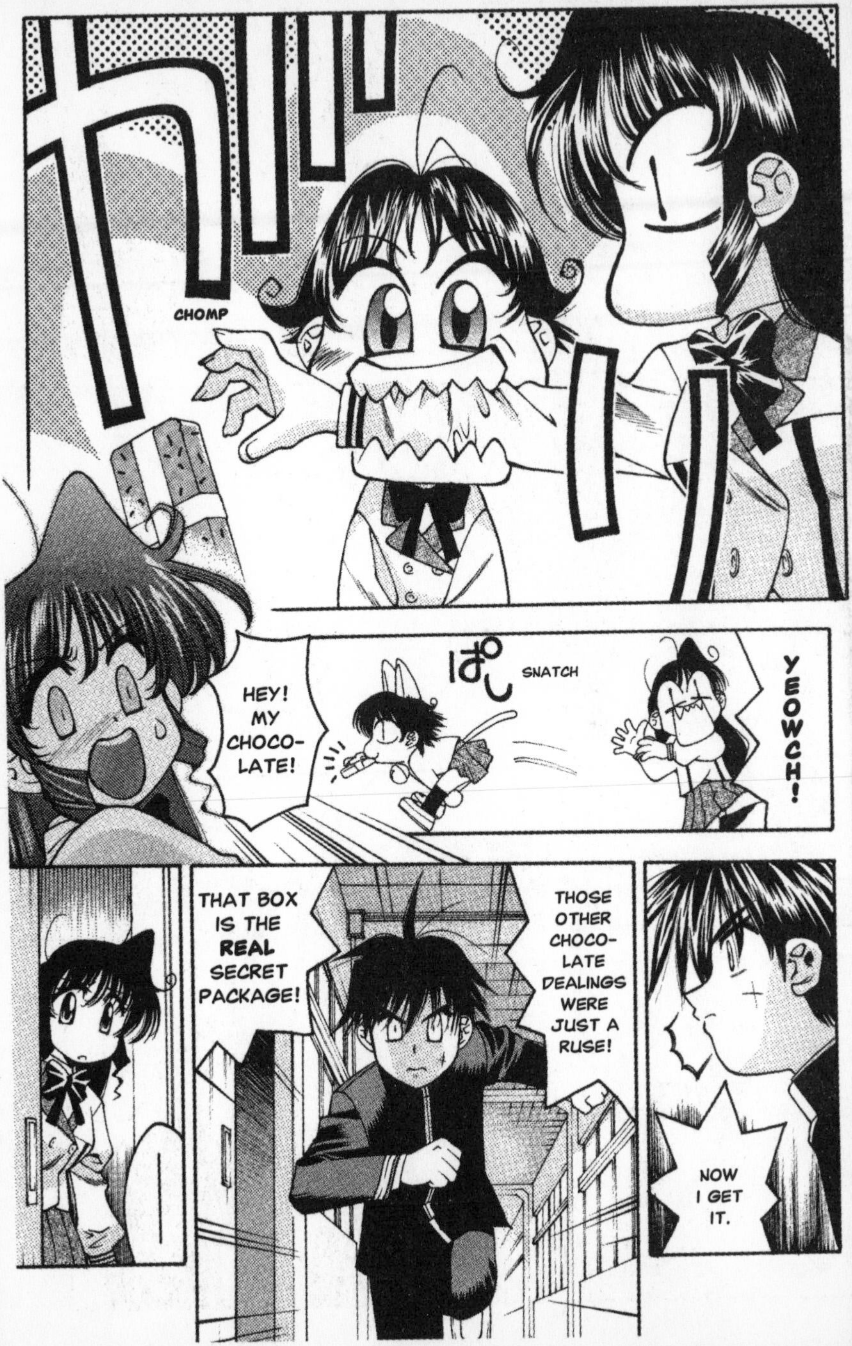
CHOMP
YEOWCH!
ぱし
SNATCH
HEY! MY CHOCOLATE!
NOW I GET IT.
THOSE OTHER CHOCOLATE DEALINGS WERE JUST A RUSE!
THAT BOX IS THE REAL SECRET PACKAGE!

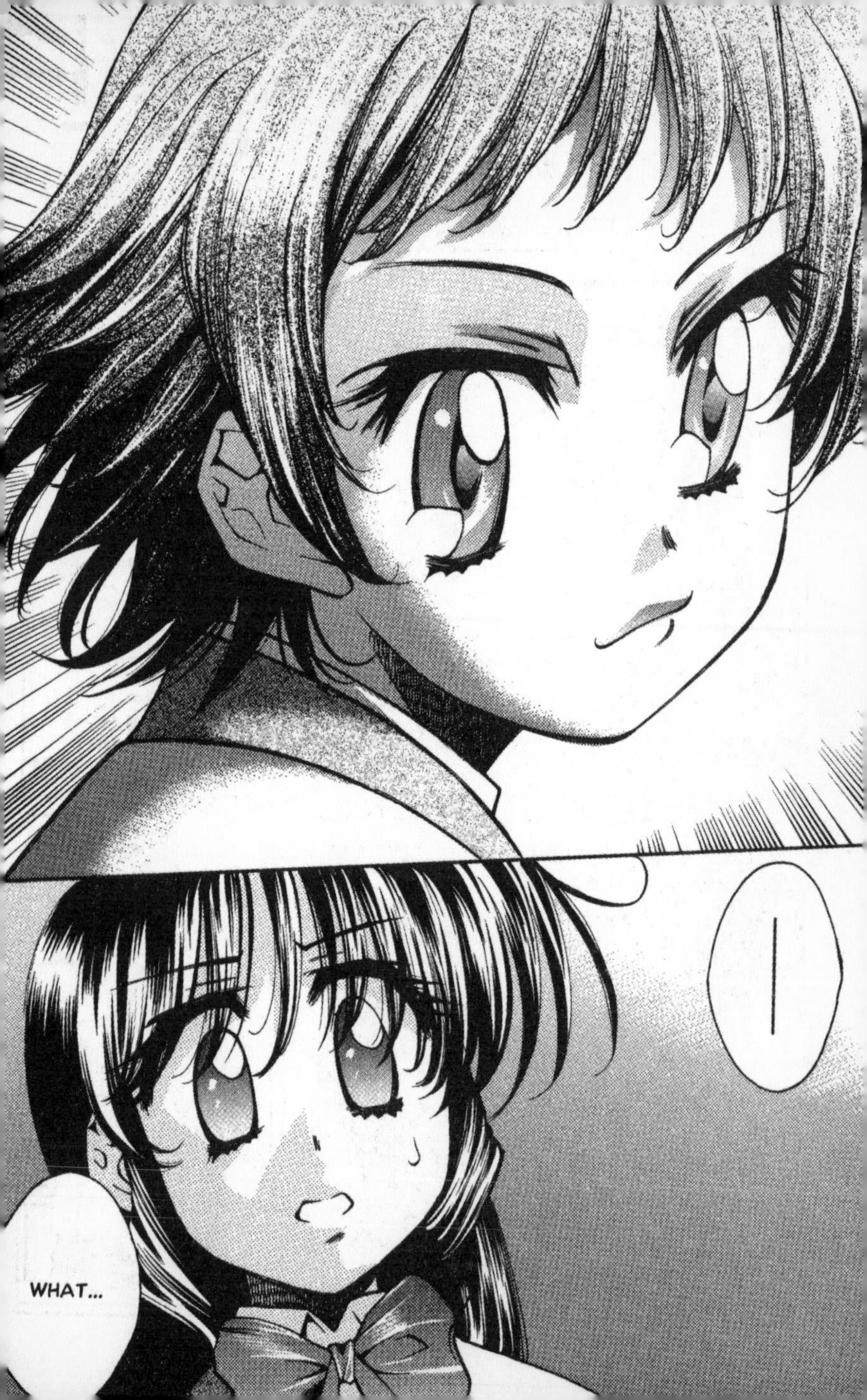

!
WHAT...

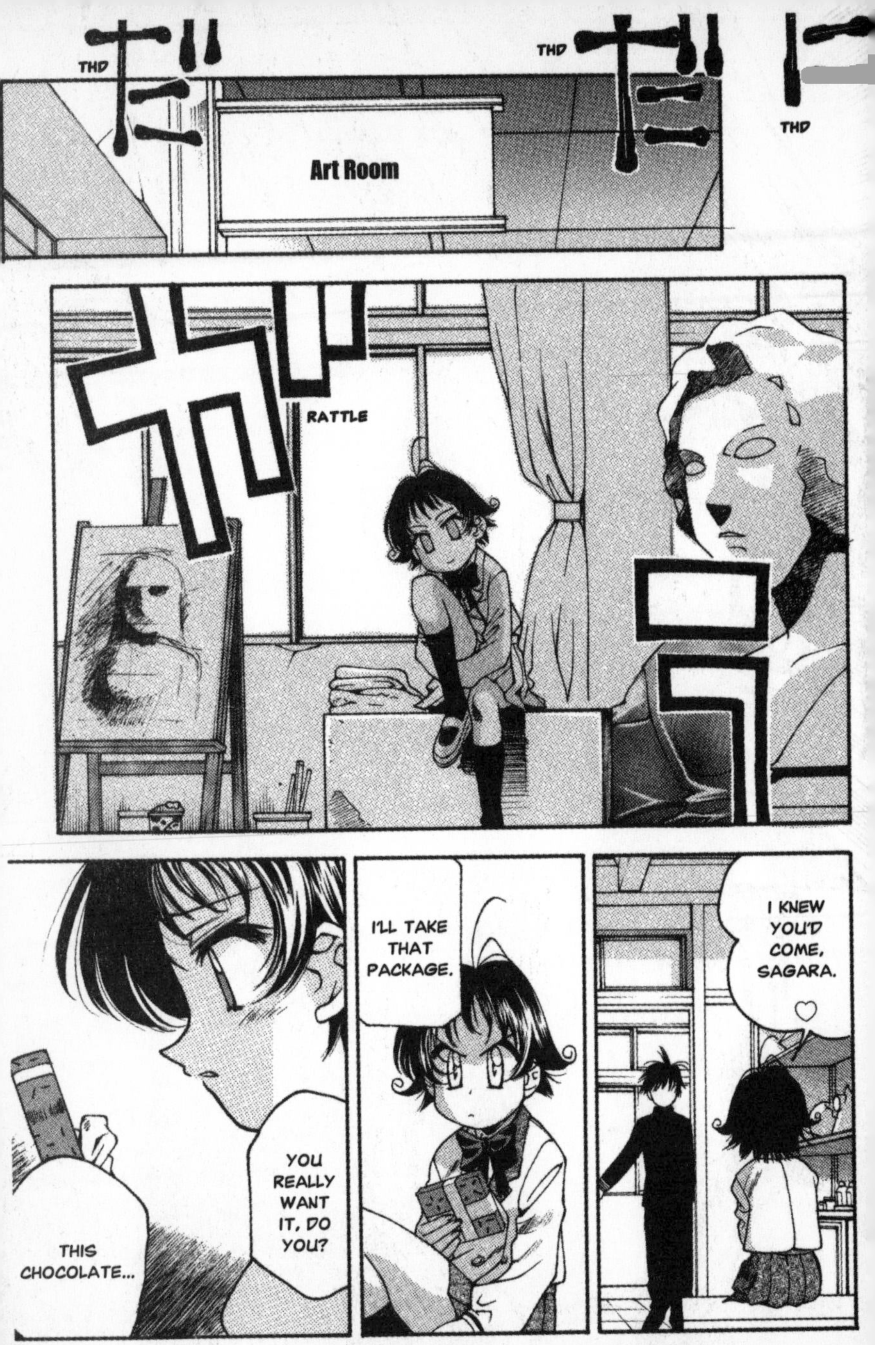
THD
THD
THD
Art Room
RATTLE
I KNEW YOU'D COME, SAGARA. ♡
I'LL TAKE THAT PACKAGE.
YOU REALLY WANT IT, DO YOU?
THIS CHOCOLATE...

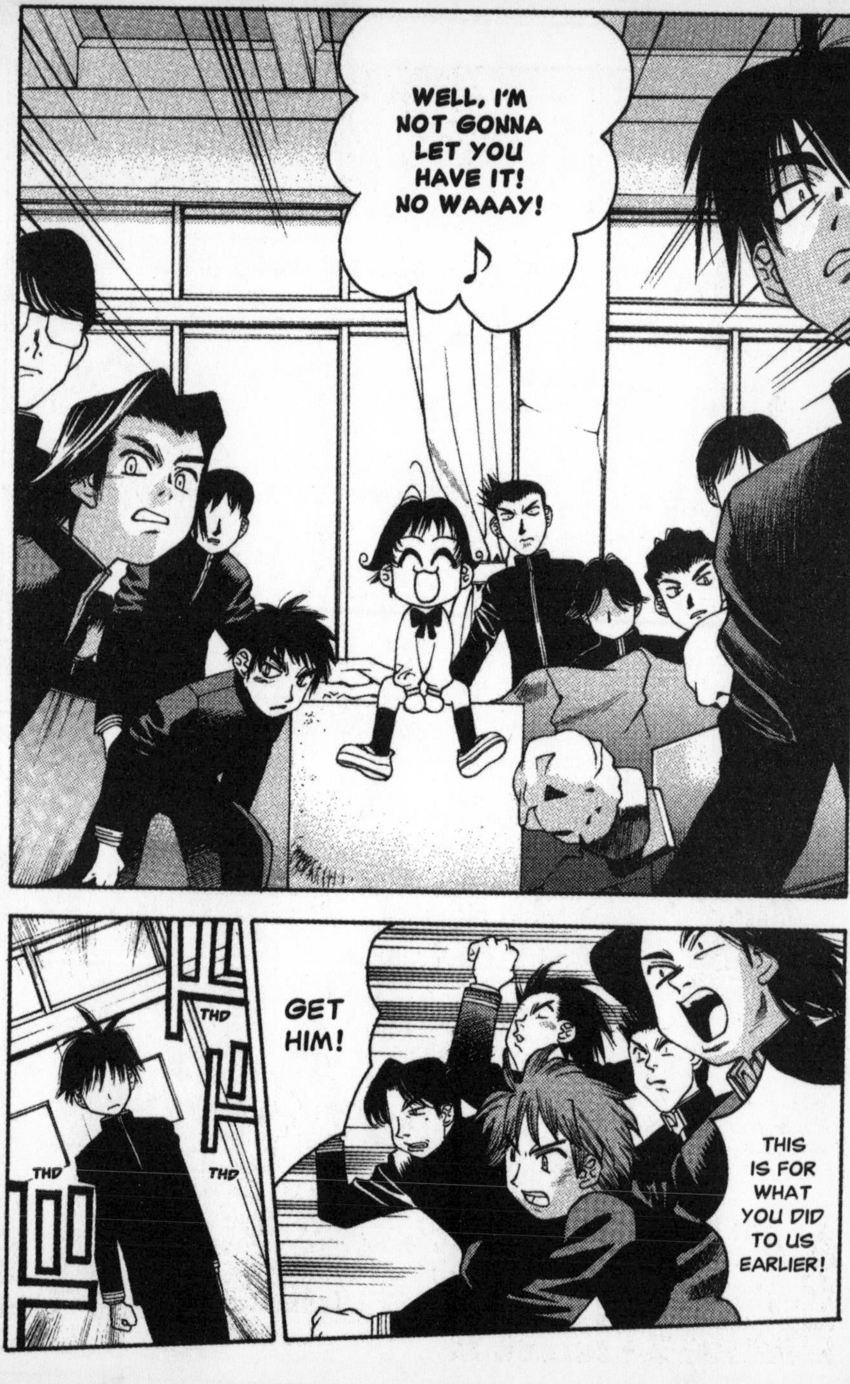
WELL, I'M NOT GONNA LET YOU HAVE IT! NO WAAAY! ♪
THIS IS FOR WHAT YOU DID TO US EARLIER!
GET HIM!
THD
THD
THD

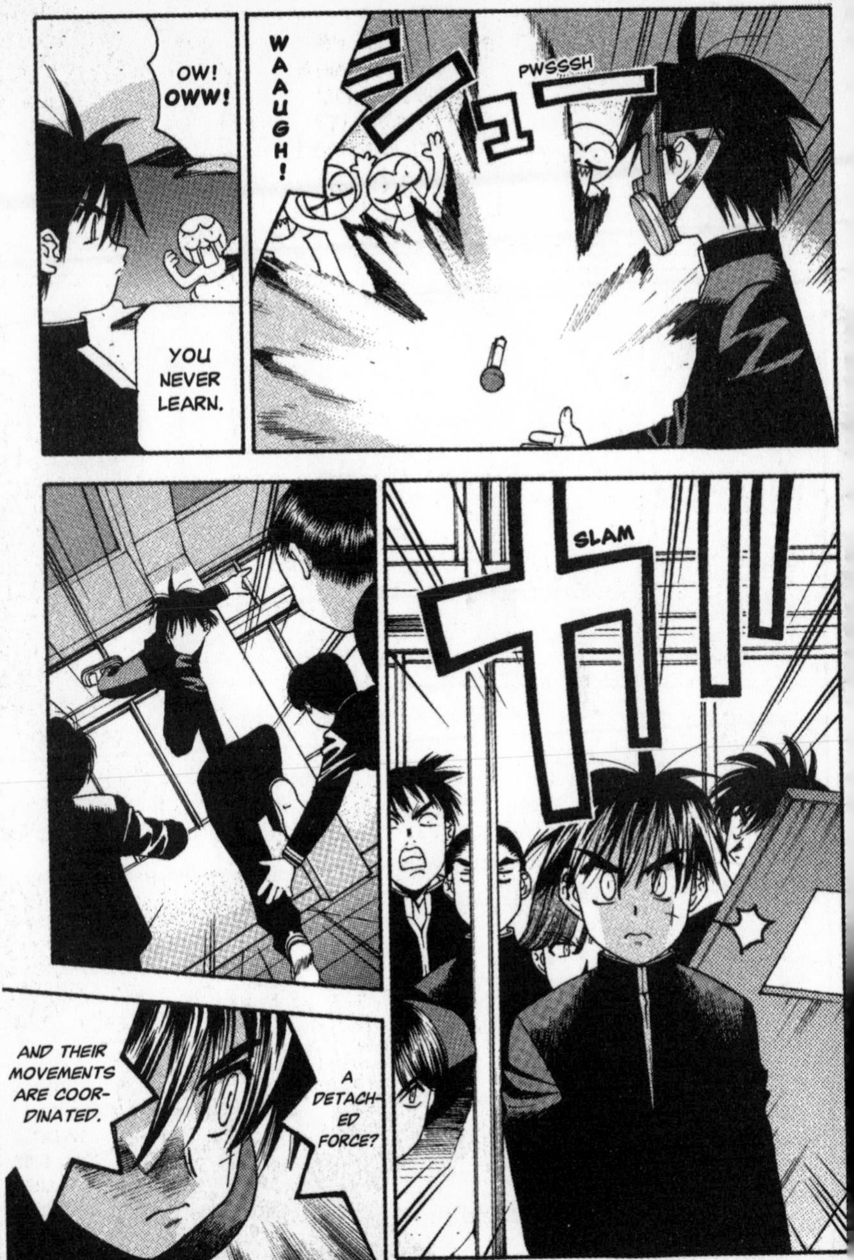
PWSSSH
WAAAUGH!
OW! OWW!
YOU NEVER LEARN.
SLAM
A DETACH-ED FORCE?
AND THEIR MOVEMENTS ARE COOR-DINATED.

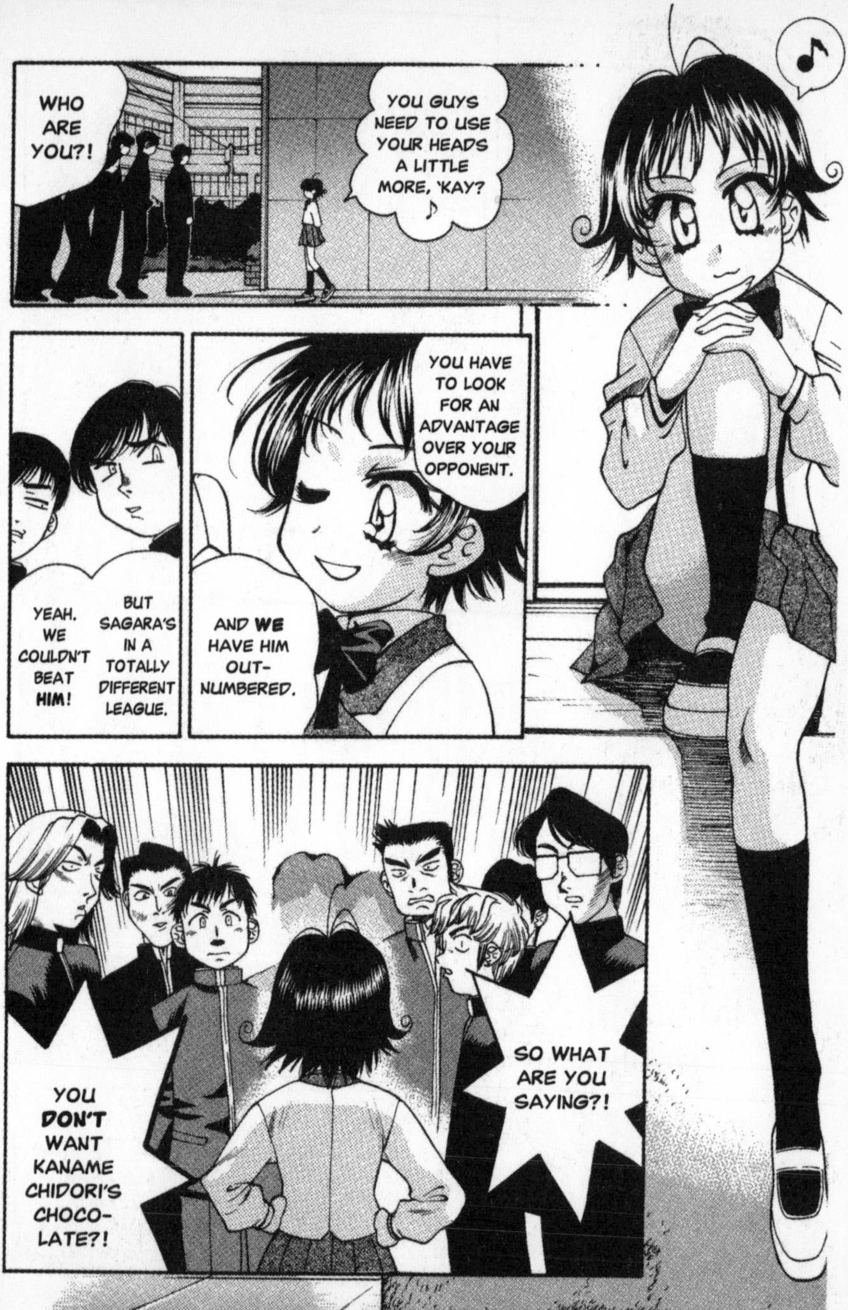
WHO ARE YOU?!
YOU GUYS NEED TO USE YOUR HEADS A LITTLE MORE, 'KAY? ♪
♪
YOU HAVE TO LOOK FOR AN ADVANTAGE OVER YOUR OPPONENT.
YEAH. WE COULDN'T BEAT HIM!
BUT SAGARA'S IN A TOTALLY DIFFERENT LEAGUE.
AND WE HAVE HIM OUT-NUMBERED.
SO WHAT ARE YOU SAYING?!
YOU DON'T WANT KANAME CHIDORI'S CHOCO-LATE?!

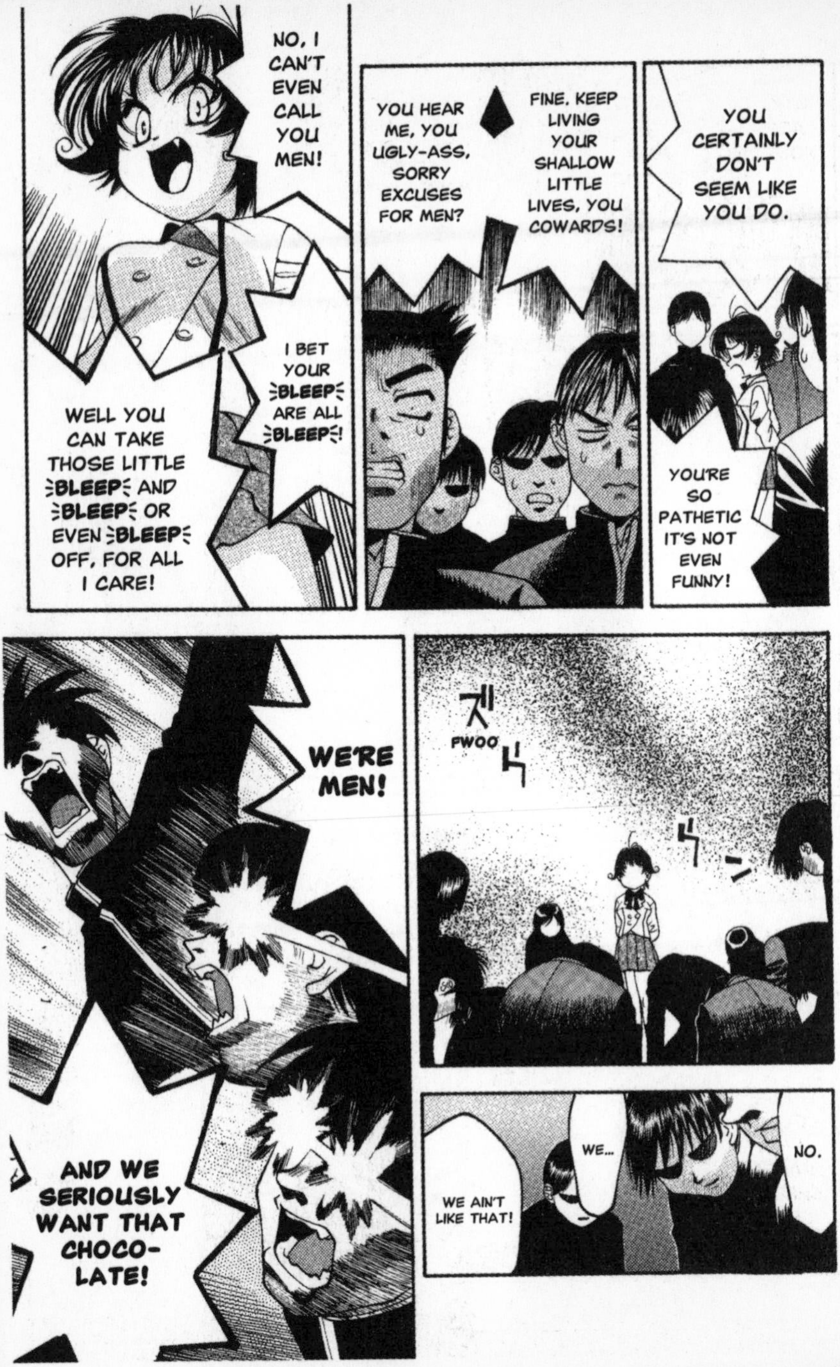
YOU CERTAINLY DON'T SEEM LIKE YOU DO.
YOU'RE SO PATHETIC IT'S NOT EVEN FUNNY!
FINE. KEEP LIVING YOUR SHALLOW LITTLE LIVES, YOU COWARDS!
YOU HEAR ME, YOU UGLY-ASS, SORRY EXCUSES FOR MEN?
NO, I CAN'T EVEN CALL YOU MEN!
I BET YOUR BLEEP ARE ALL BLEEP!
WELL YOU CAN TAKE THOSE LITTLE BLEEP AND BLEEP OR EVEN BLEEP OFF, FOR ALL I CARE!
FWOO
NO.
WE...
WE AIN'T LIKE THAT!
WE'RE MEN!
AND WE SERIOUSLY WANT THAT CHOCO-LATE!

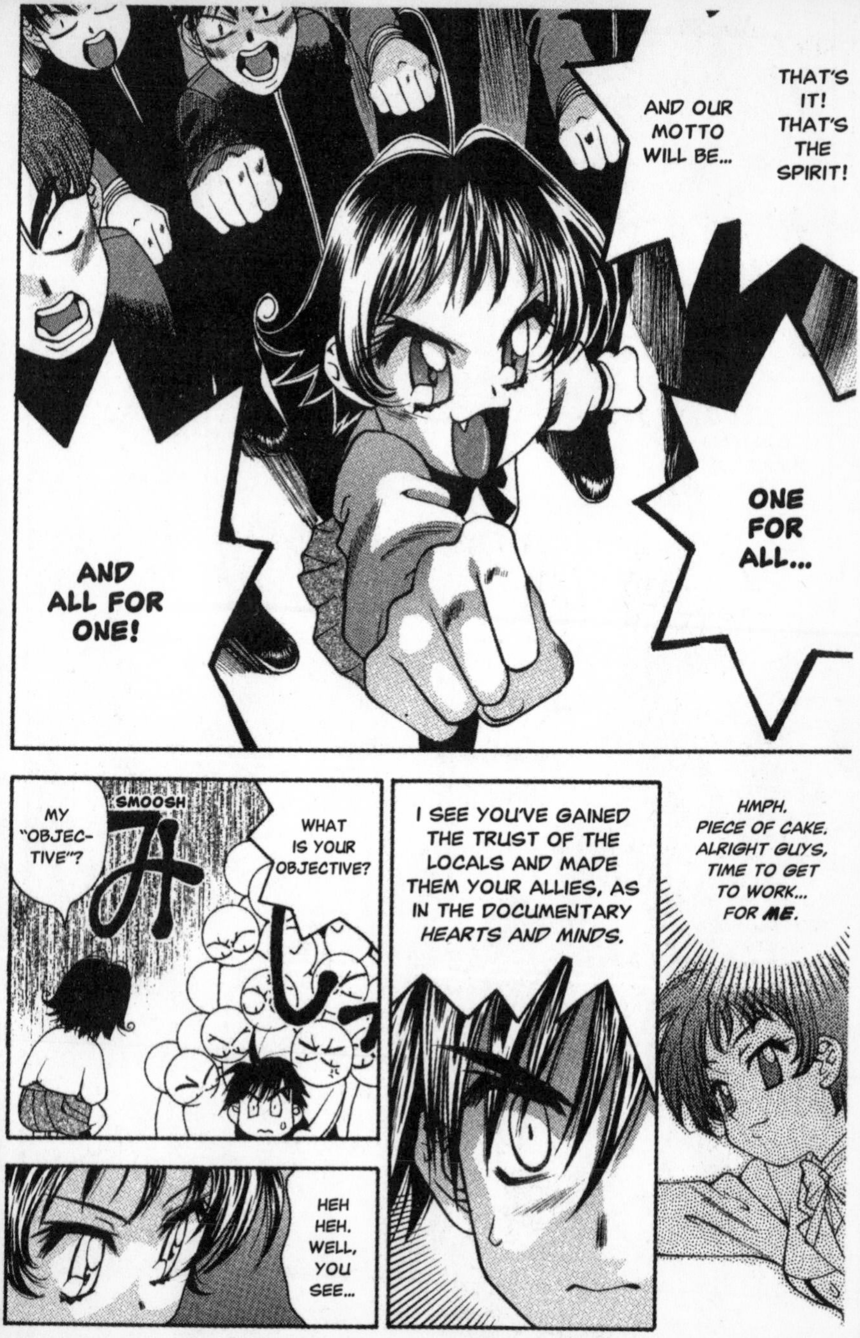
THAT'S IT! THAT'S THE SPIRIT!
AND OUR MOTTO WILL BE...
ONE FOR ALL...
AND ALL FOR ONE!
HMPH. PIECE OF CAKE. ALRIGHT GUYS, TIME TO GET TO WORK... FOR ME.
I SEE YOU'VE GAINED THE TRUST OF THE LOCALS AND MADE THEM YOUR ALLIES, AS IN THE DOCUMENTARY HEARTS AND MINDS.
WHAT IS YOUR OBJECTIVE?
SMOOSH
みしっ
MY "OBJECTIVE"?
HEH HEH. WELL, YOU SEE...

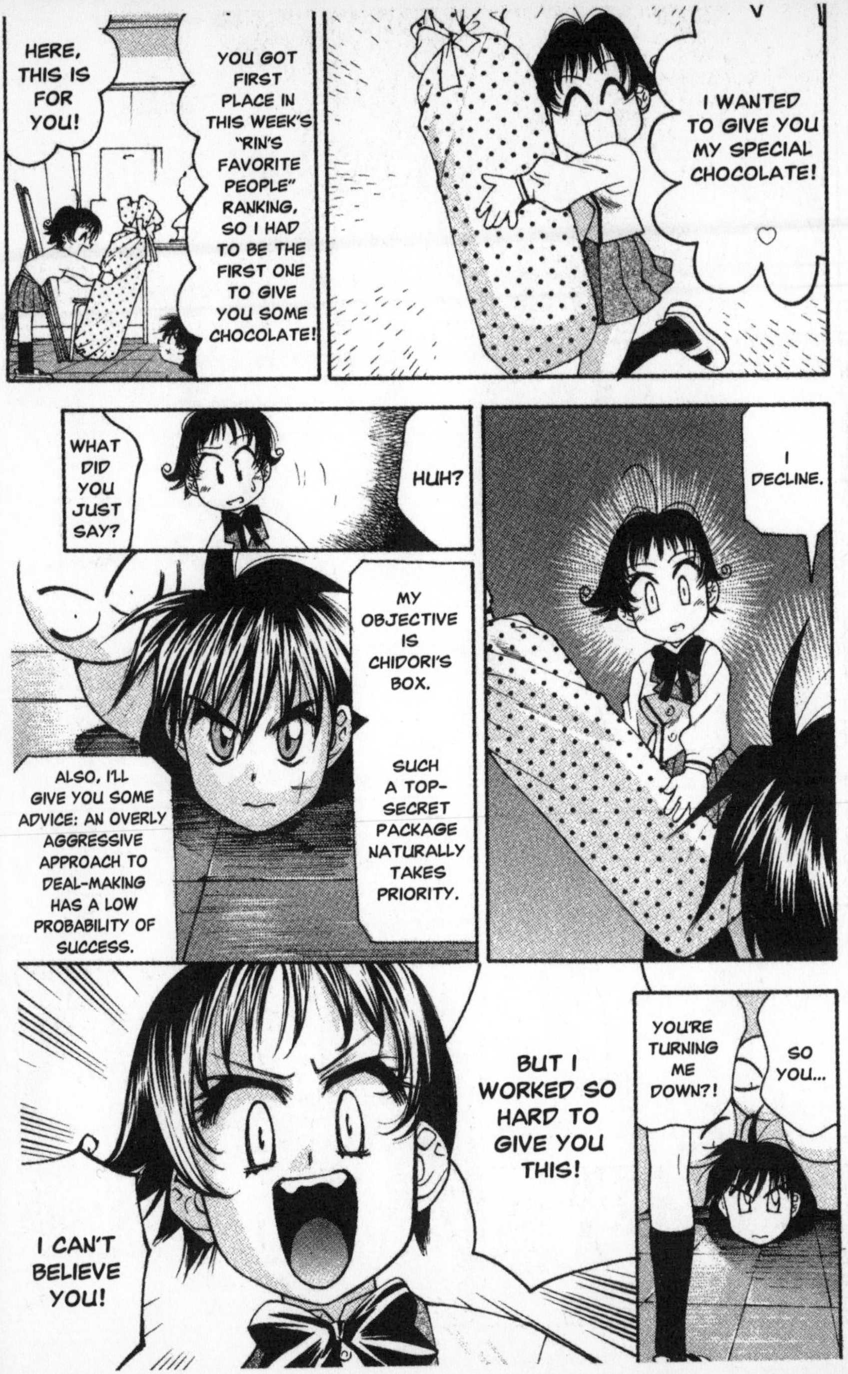
I WANTED TO GIVE YOU MY SPECIAL CHOCOLATE!
YOU GOT FIRST PLACE IN THIS WEEK'S "RIN'S FAVORITE PEOPLE" RANKING, SO I HAD TO BE THE FIRST ONE TO GIVE YOU SOME CHOCOLATE!
HERE, THIS IS FOR YOU!
I DECLINE.
HUH?
WHAT DID YOU JUST SAY?
MY OBJECTIVE IS CHIDORI'S BOX.
SUCH A TOP-SECRET PACKAGE NATURALLY TAKES PRIORITY.
ALSO, I'LL GIVE YOU SOME ADVICE: AN OVERLY AGGRESSIVE APPROACH TO DEAL-MAKING HAS A LOW PROBABILITY OF SUCCESS.
SO YOU...
YOU'RE TURNING ME DOWN?!
BUT I WORKED SO HARD TO GIVE YOU THIS!
I CAN'T BELIEVE YOU!

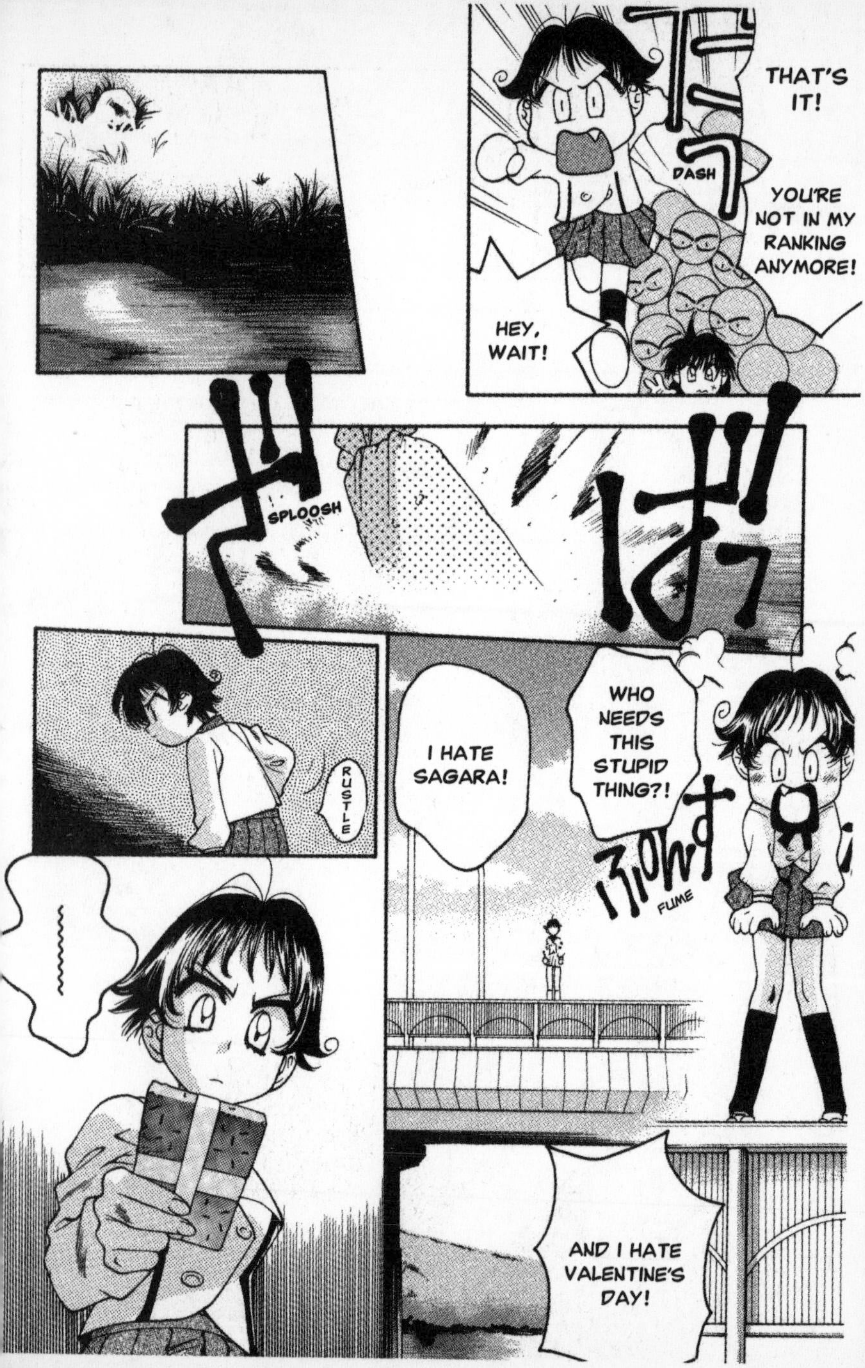
THAT'S IT!
DASH
YOU'RE NOT IN MY RANKING ANYMORE!
HEY, WAIT!
SPLOOSH
WHO NEEDS THIS STUPID THING?!
FUME
I HATE SAGARA!
AND I HATE VALENTINE'S DAY!
RUSTLE

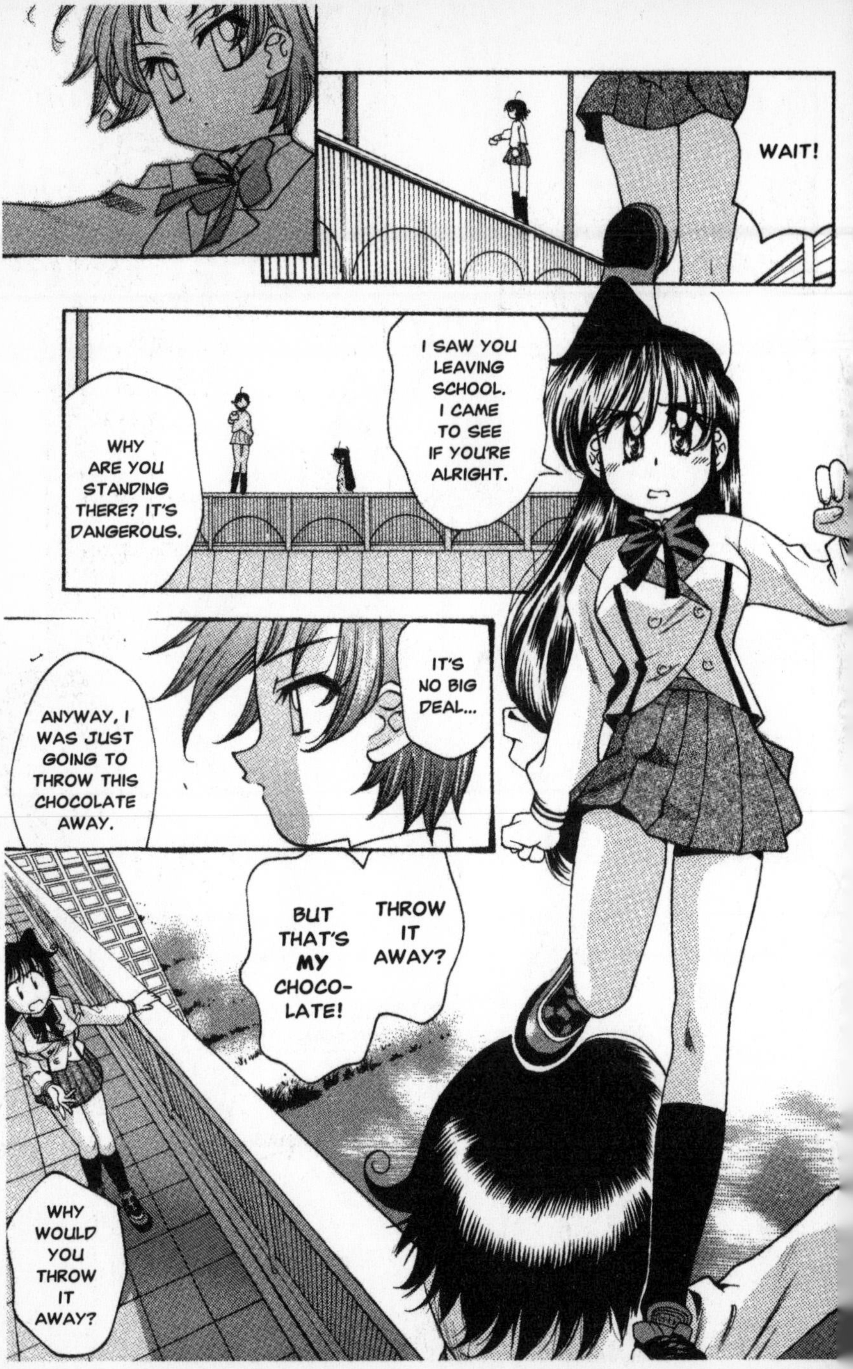
WAIT!
I SAW YOU LEAVING SCHOOL. I CAME TO SEE IF YOU'RE ALRIGHT.
WHY ARE YOU STANDING THERE? IT'S DANGEROUS.
IT'S NO BIG DEAL...
ANYWAY, I WAS JUST GOING TO THROW THIS CHOCOLATE AWAY.
THROW IT AWAY?
BUT THAT'S **MY** CHOCO-LATE!
WHY WOULD YOU THROW IT AWAY?

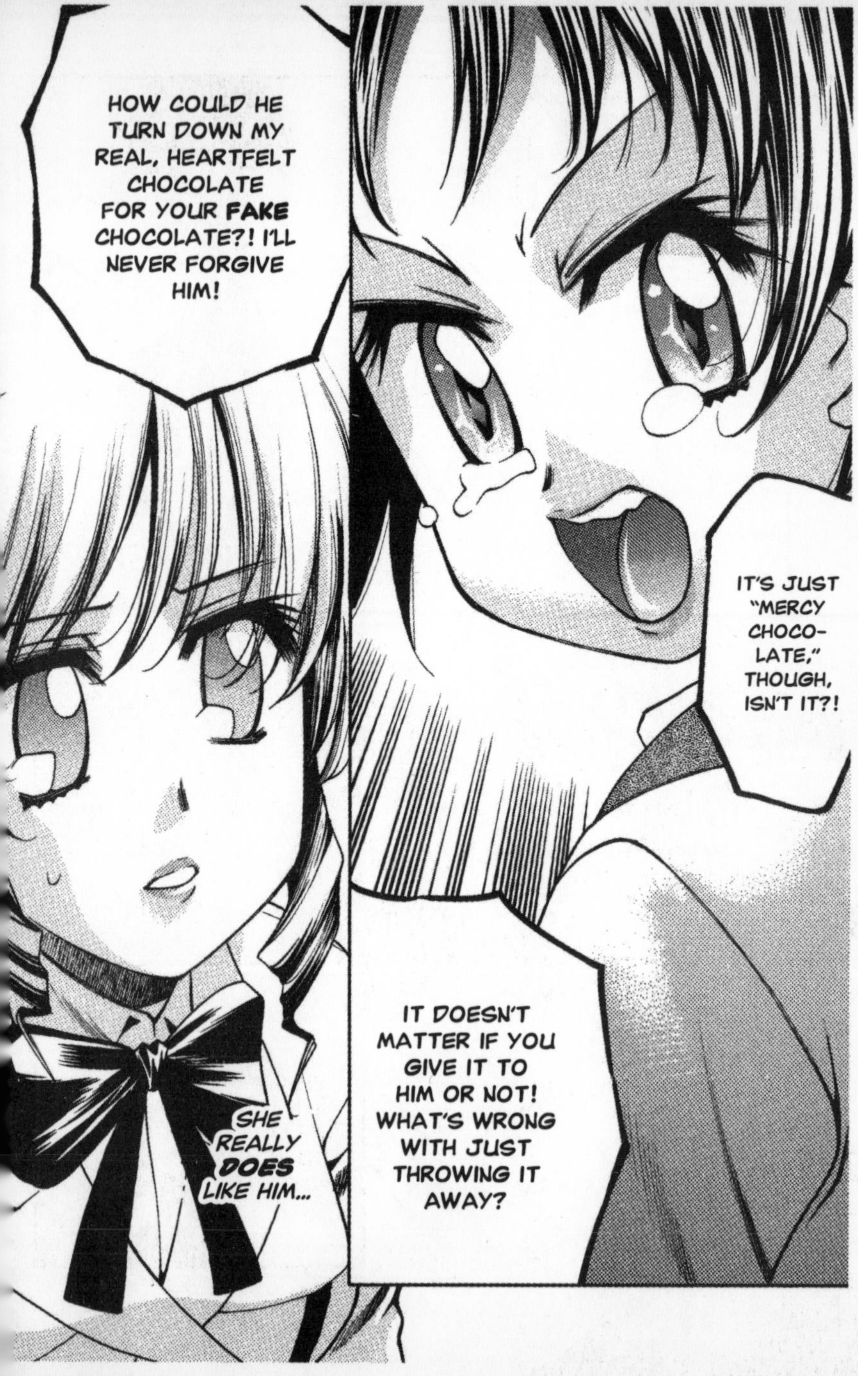
HOW COULD HE TURN DOWN MY REAL, HEARTFELT CHOCOLATE FOR YOUR FAKE CHOCOLATE?! I'LL NEVER FORGIVE HIM!
IT'S JUST "MERCY CHOCOLATE," THOUGH, ISN'T IT?!
IT DOESN'T MATTER IF YOU GIVE IT TO HIM OR NOT! WHAT'S WRONG WITH JUST THROWING IT AWAY?
SHE REALLY DOES LIKE HIM...

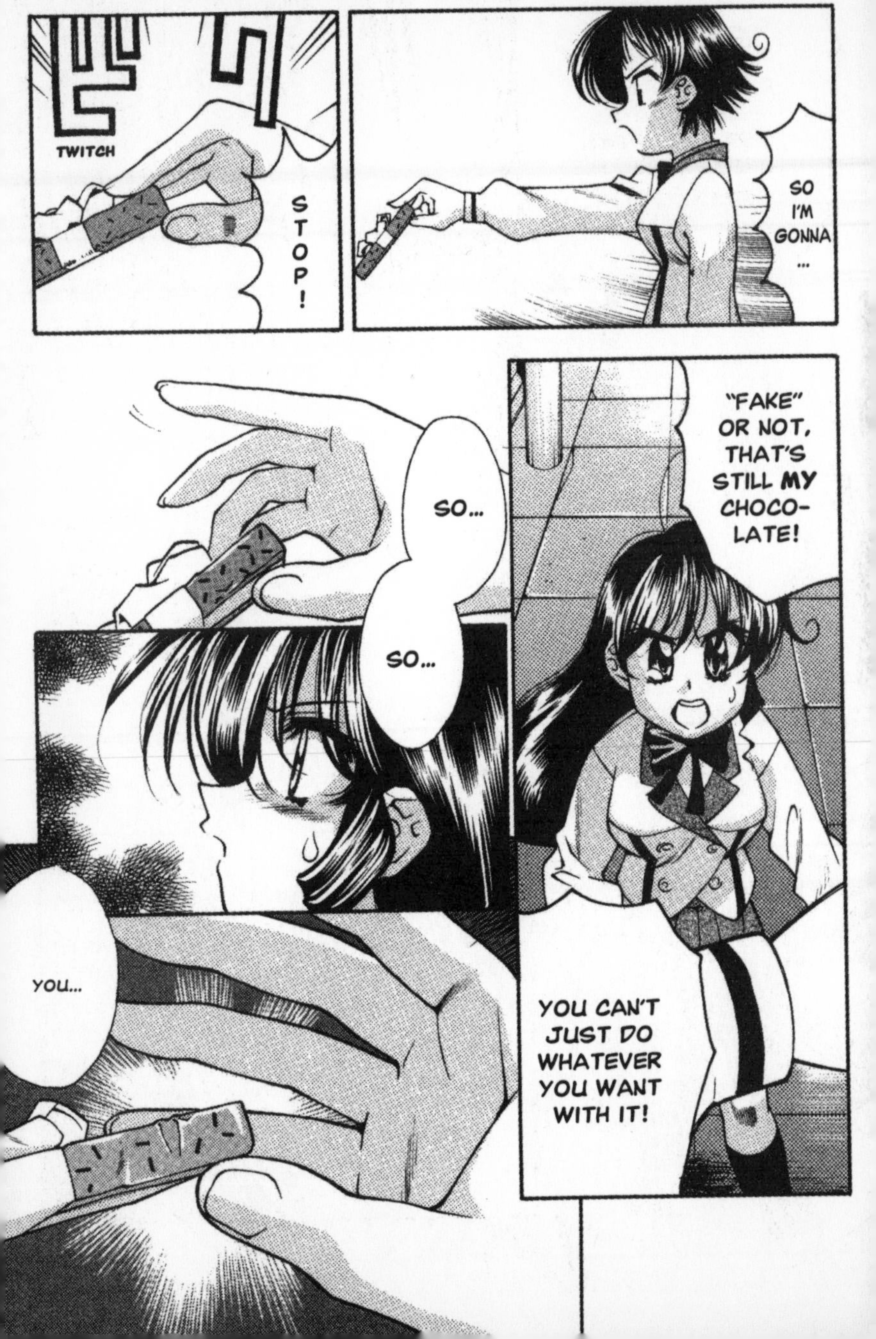
SO I'M GONNA ...
STOP!
TWITCH
"FAKE" OR NOT, THAT'S STILL MY CHOCOLATE!
YOU CAN'T JUST DO WHATEVER YOU WANT WITH IT!
SO...
SO...
YOU...

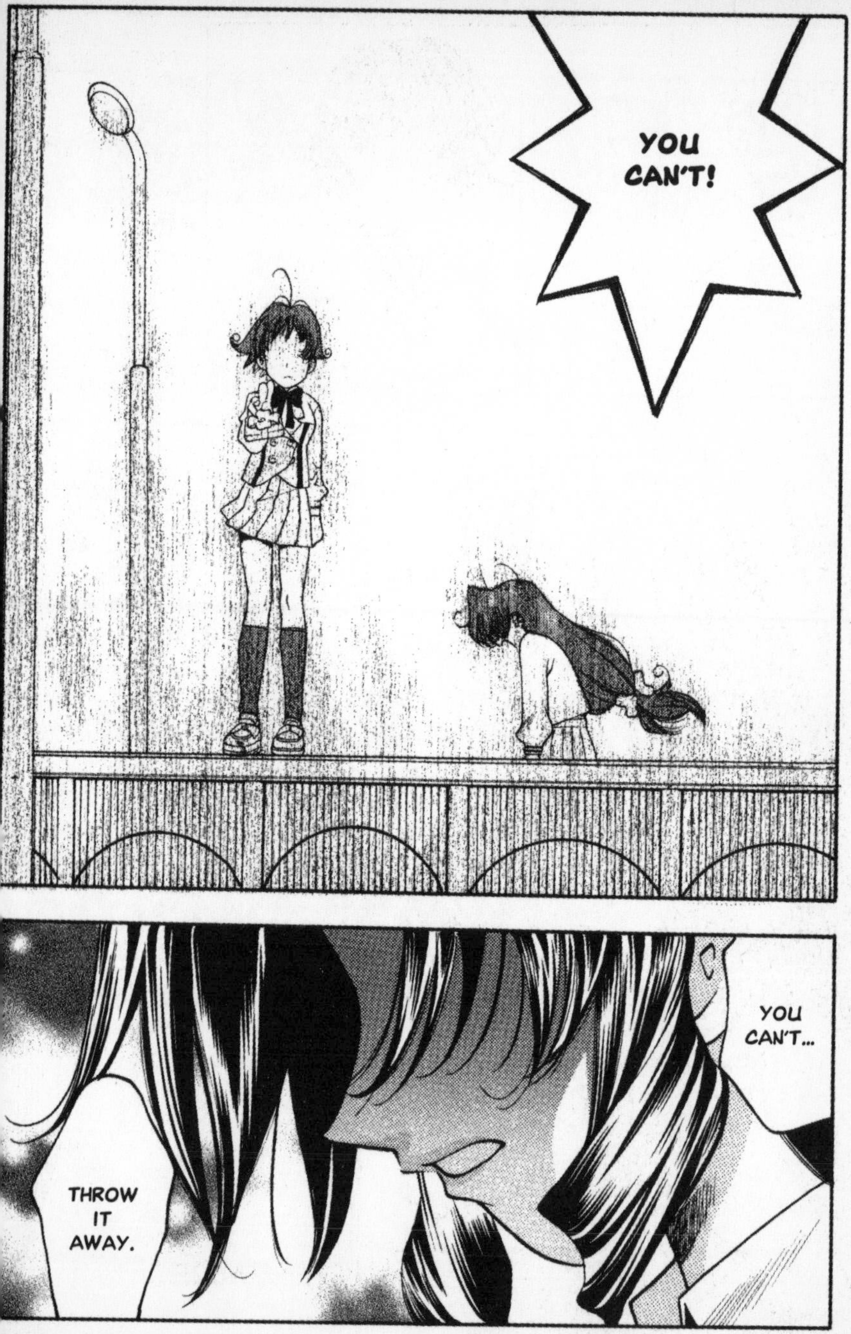
YOU CAN'T!
YOU CAN'T...
THROW IT AWAY.

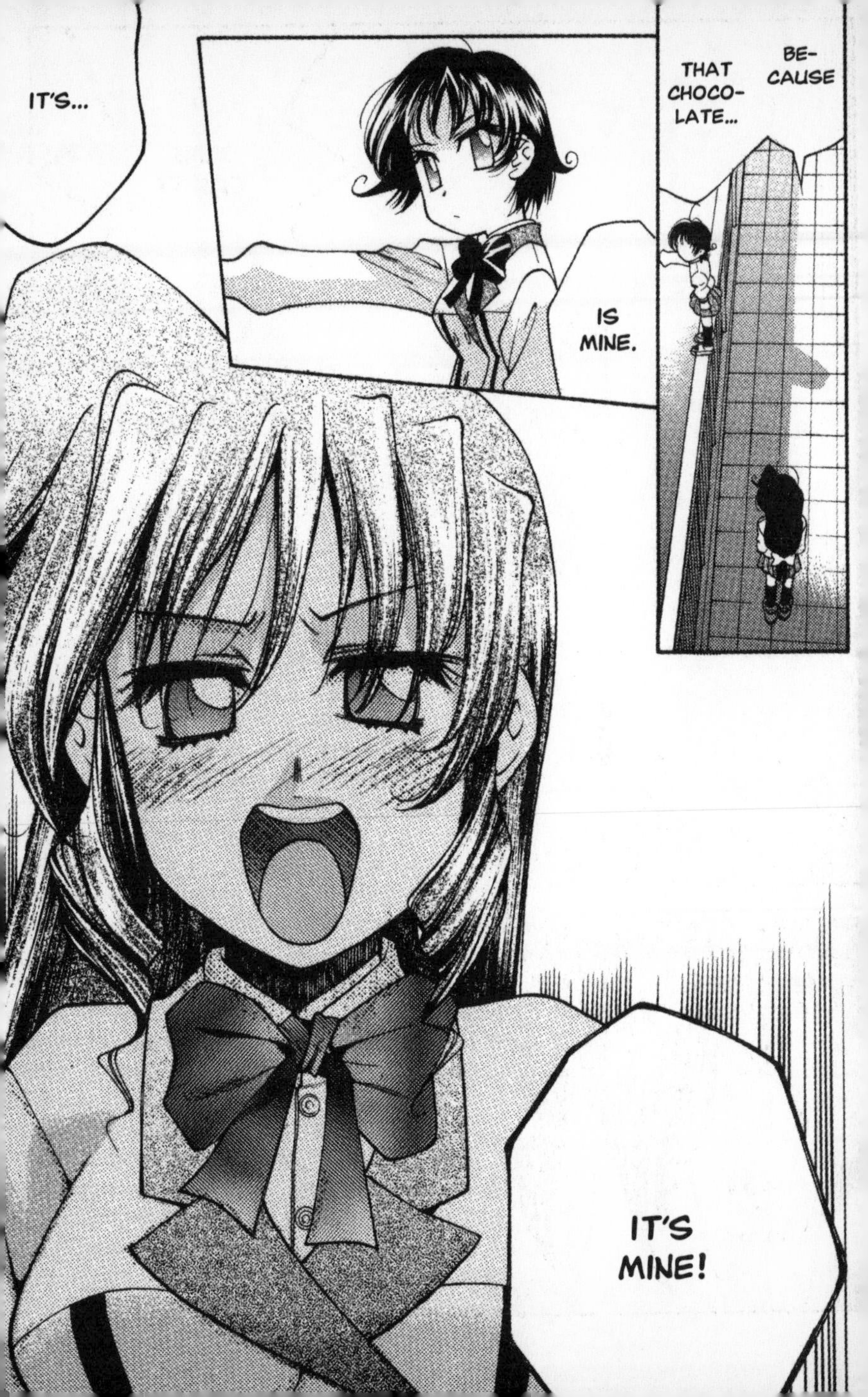
BE-CAUSE
THAT CHOCO-LATE...
IS MINE.
IT'S...
IT'S MINE!

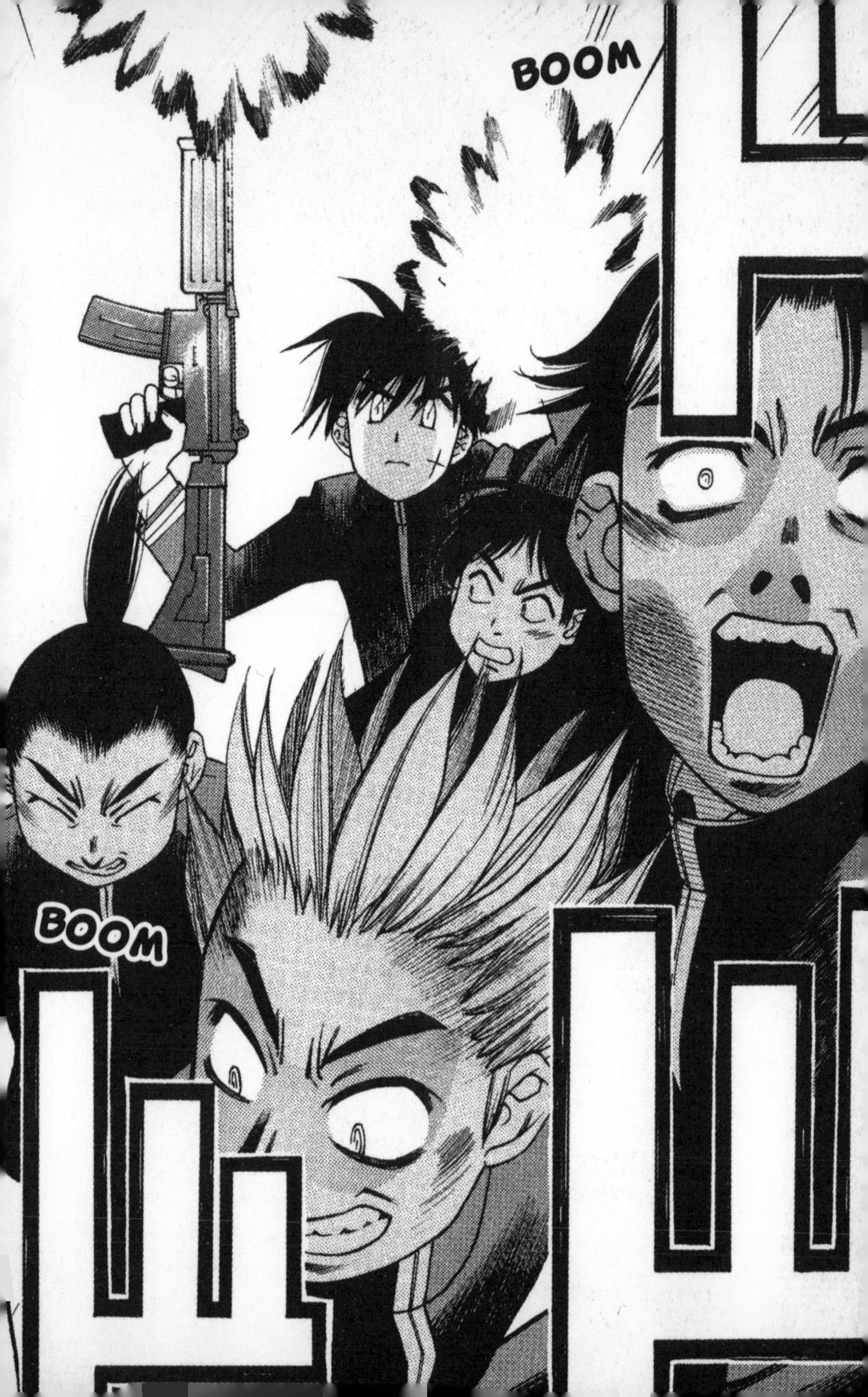
BOOM
BOOM

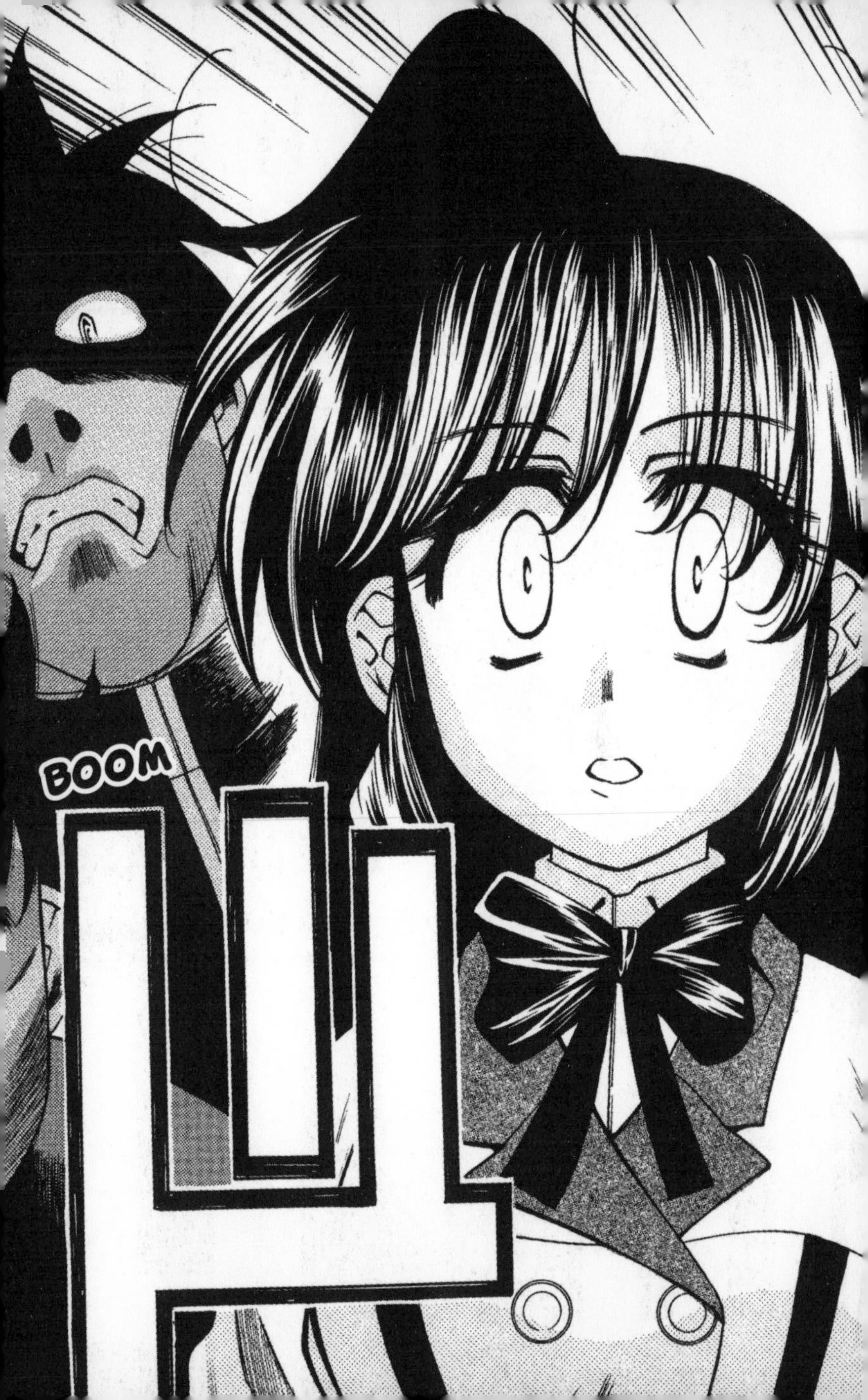
BOOM

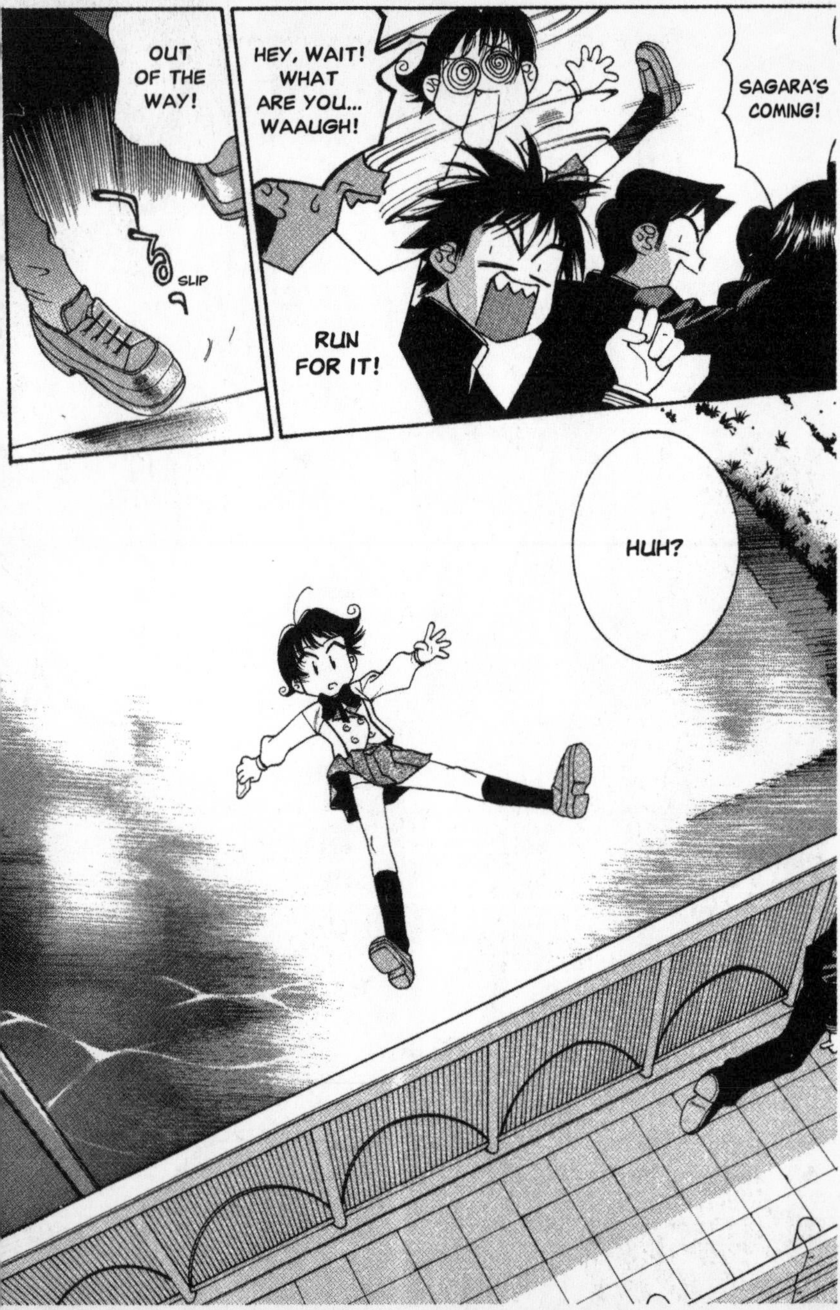
SAGARA'S COMING!
RUN FOR IT!
HEY, WAIT! WHAT ARE YOU... WAAUGH!
OUT OF THE WAY!
SLIP
HUH?

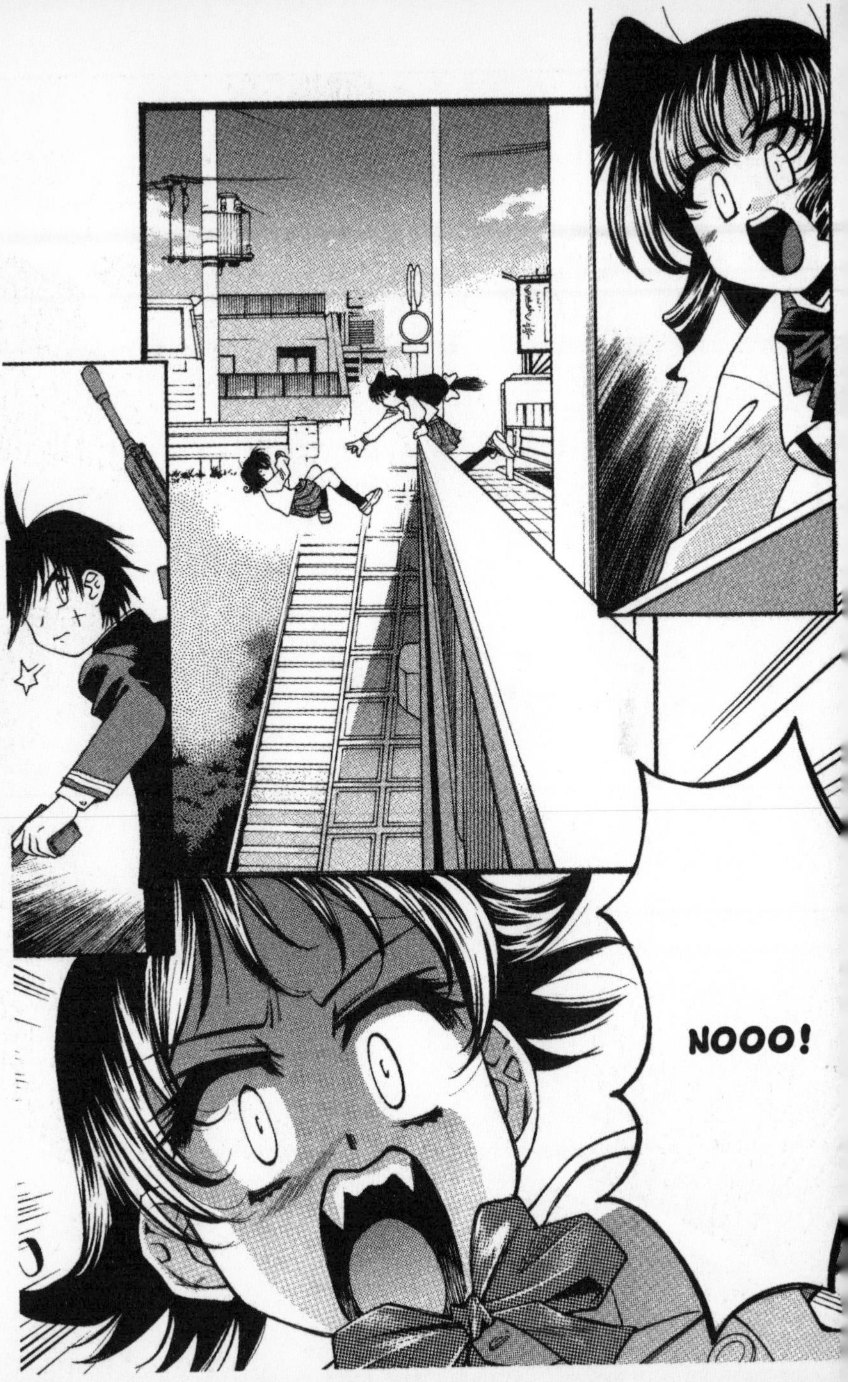
NOOO!

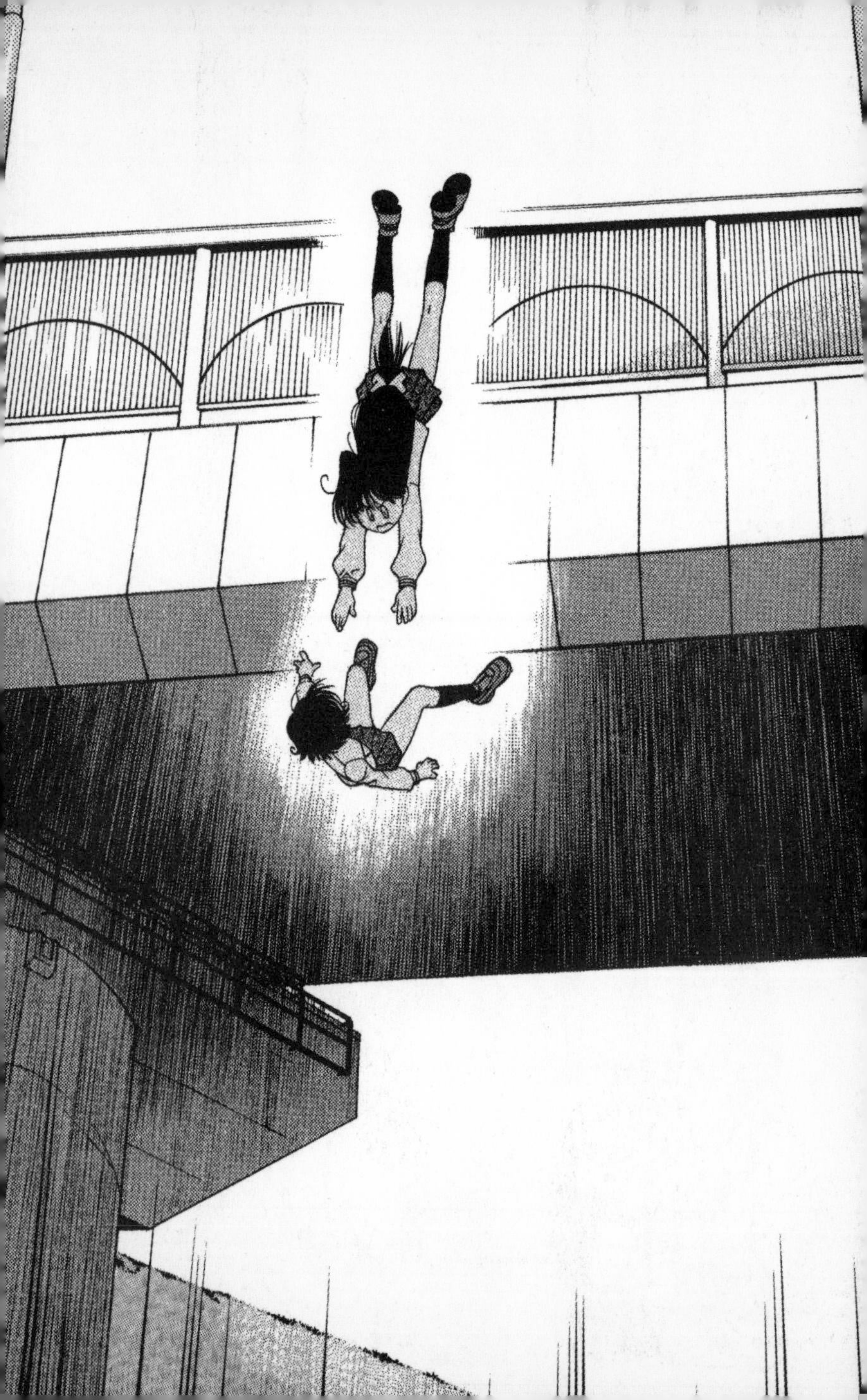

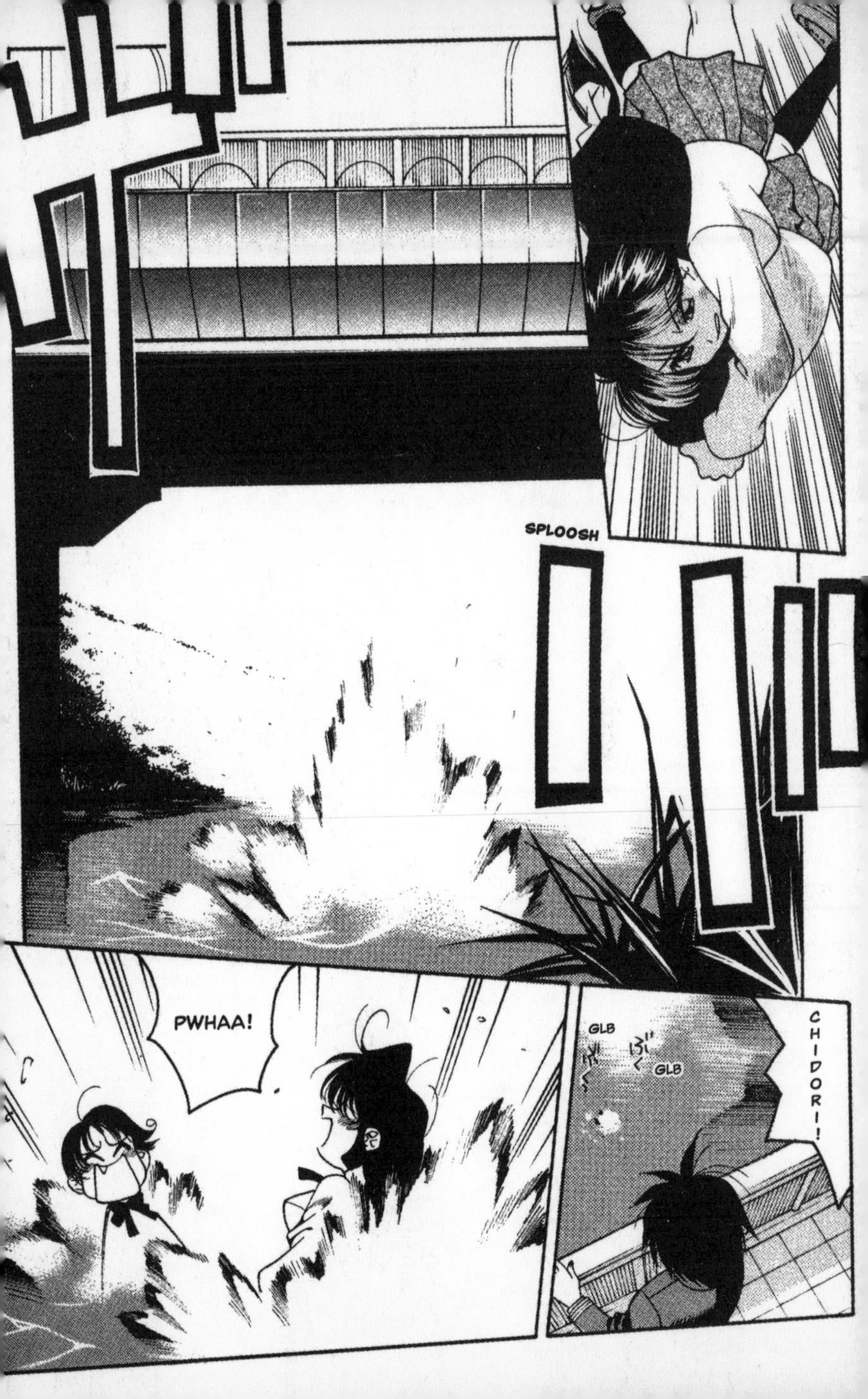
SPLOOSH
CHIDORI!
GLB
GLB
PWHAA!

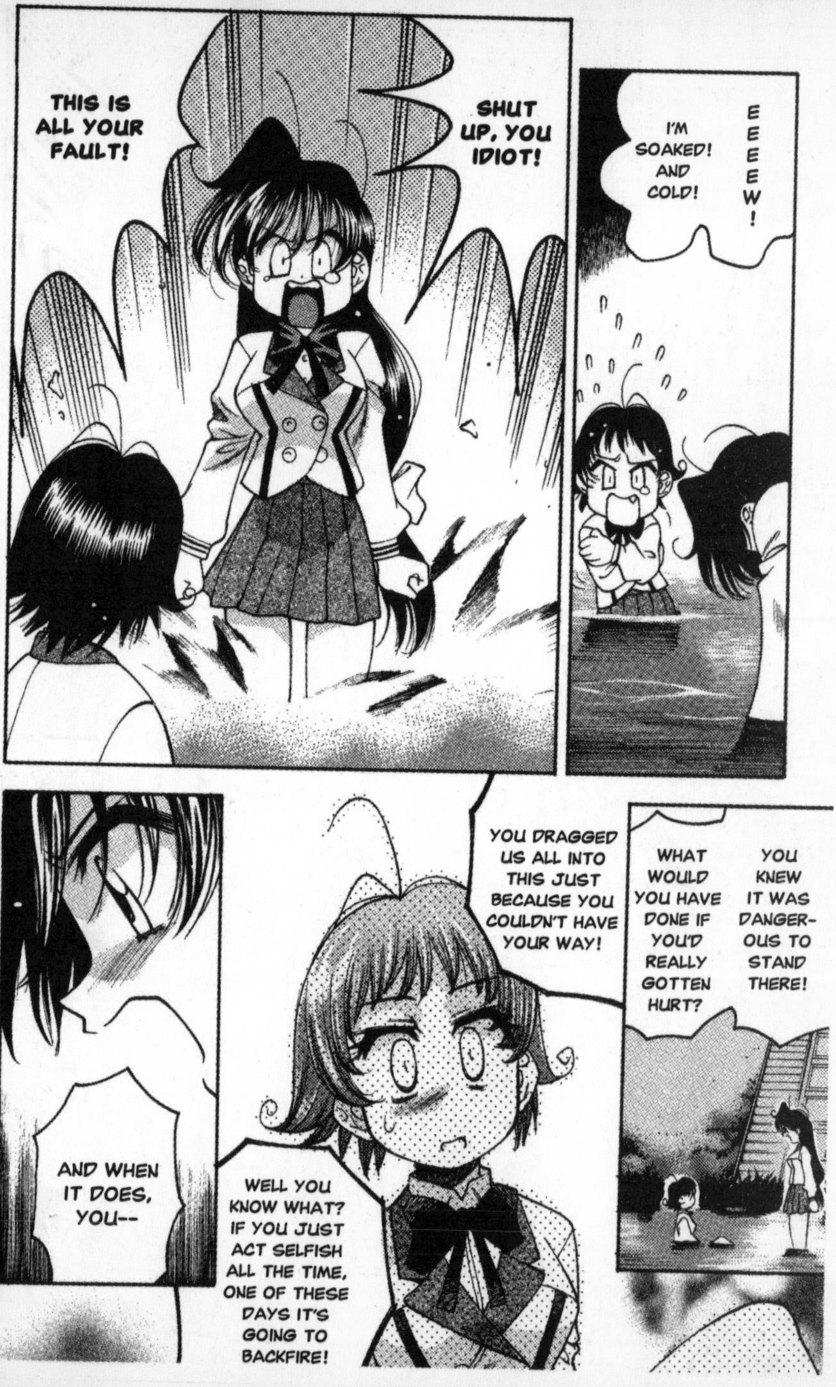
I'M SOAKED! AND COLD!
EEEEEW!
SHUT UP, YOU IDIOT!
THIS IS ALL YOUR FAULT!
YOU KNEW IT WAS DANGER-OUS TO STAND THERE!
WHAT WOULD YOU HAVE DONE IF YOU'D REALLY GOTTEN HURT?
YOU DRAGGED US ALL INTO THIS JUST BECAUSE YOU COULDN'T HAVE YOUR WAY!
WELL YOU KNOW WHAT? IF YOU JUST ACT SELFISH ALL THE TIME, ONE OF THESE DAYS IT'S GOING TO BACKFIRE!
AND WHEN IT DOES, YOU--

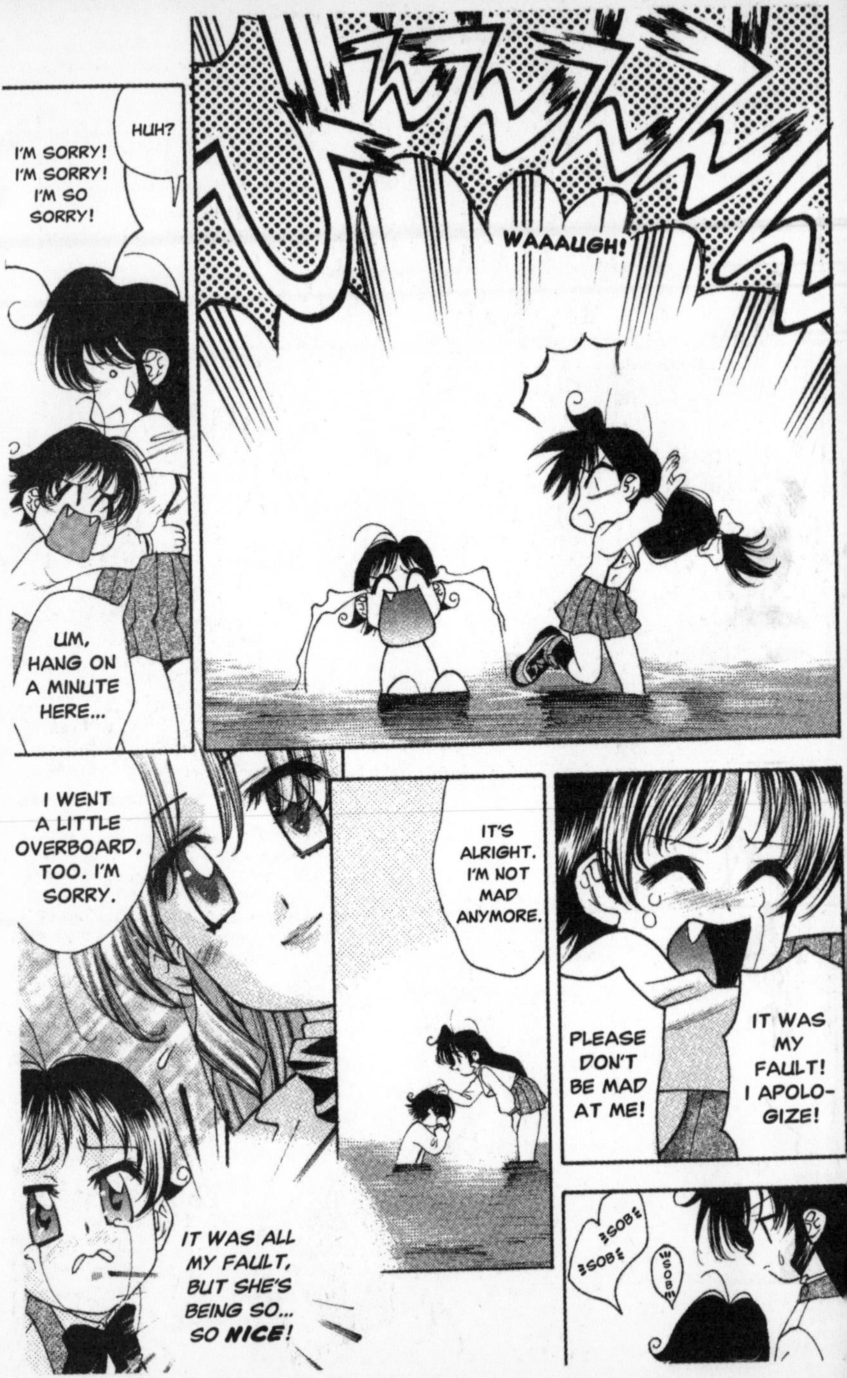
WAAAUGH!
HUH?
I'M SORRY! I'M SORRY! I'M SO SORRY!
UM, HANG ON A MINUTE HERE...
IT WAS MY FAULT! I APOLO-GIZE!
PLEASE DON'T BE MAD AT ME!
IT'S ALRIGHT. I'M NOT MAD ANYMORE.
SOB
SOB
SOB
I WENT A LITTLE OVERBOARD, TOO. I'M SORRY.
IT WAS ALL MY FAULT, BUT SHE'S BEING SO... SO NICE!

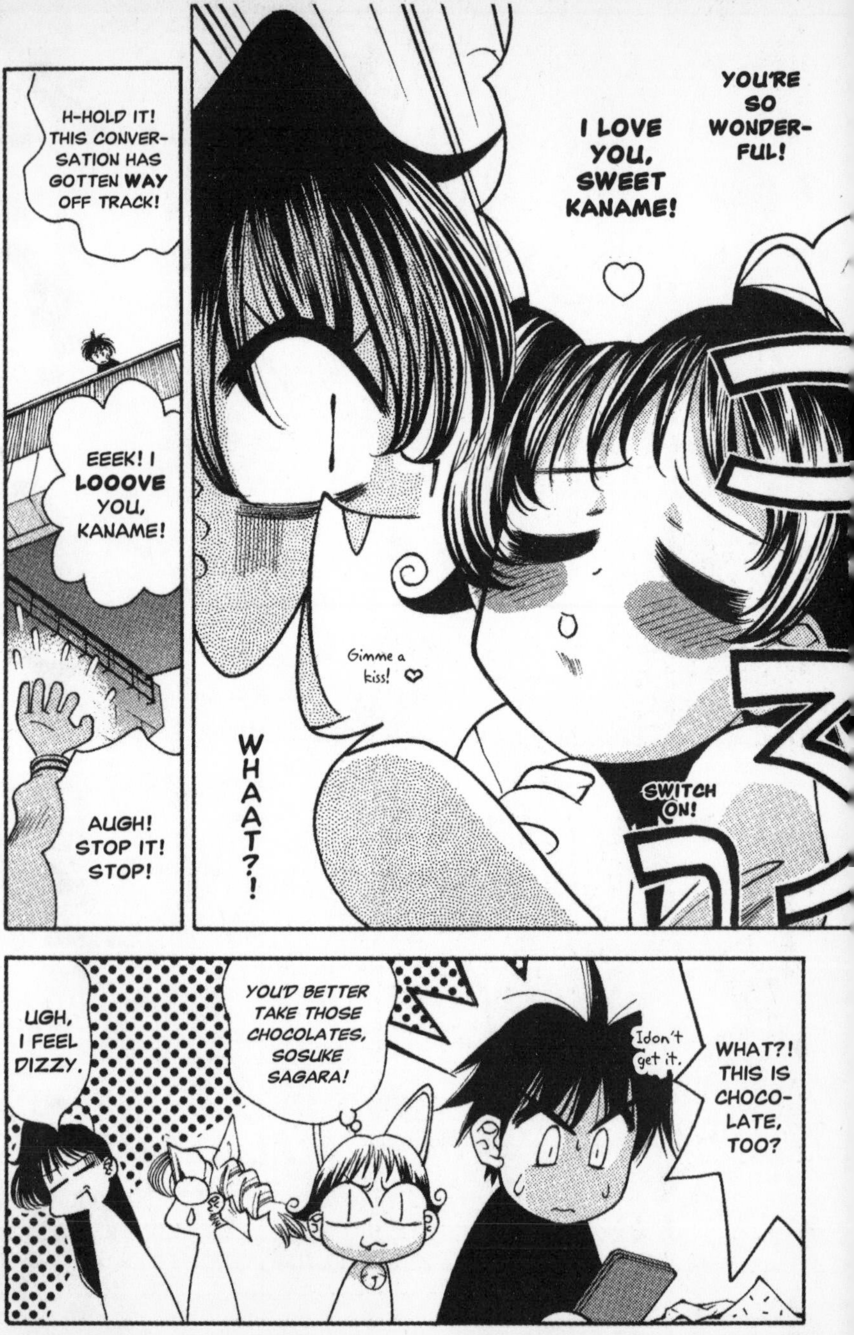
YOU'RE SO WONDERFUL!
I LOVE YOU, SWEET KANAME!
Gimme a kiss!
SWITCH ON!
WHAAAT?!
H-HOLD IT! THIS CONVERSATION HAS GOTTEN WAY OFF TRACK!
EEEK! I LOOOVE YOU, KANAME!
AUGH! STOP IT! STOP!
WHAT?! THIS IS CHOCOLATE, TOO?
I don't get it.
YOU'D BETTER TAKE THOSE CHOCOLATES, SOSUKE SAGARA!
UGH, I FEEL DIZZY.

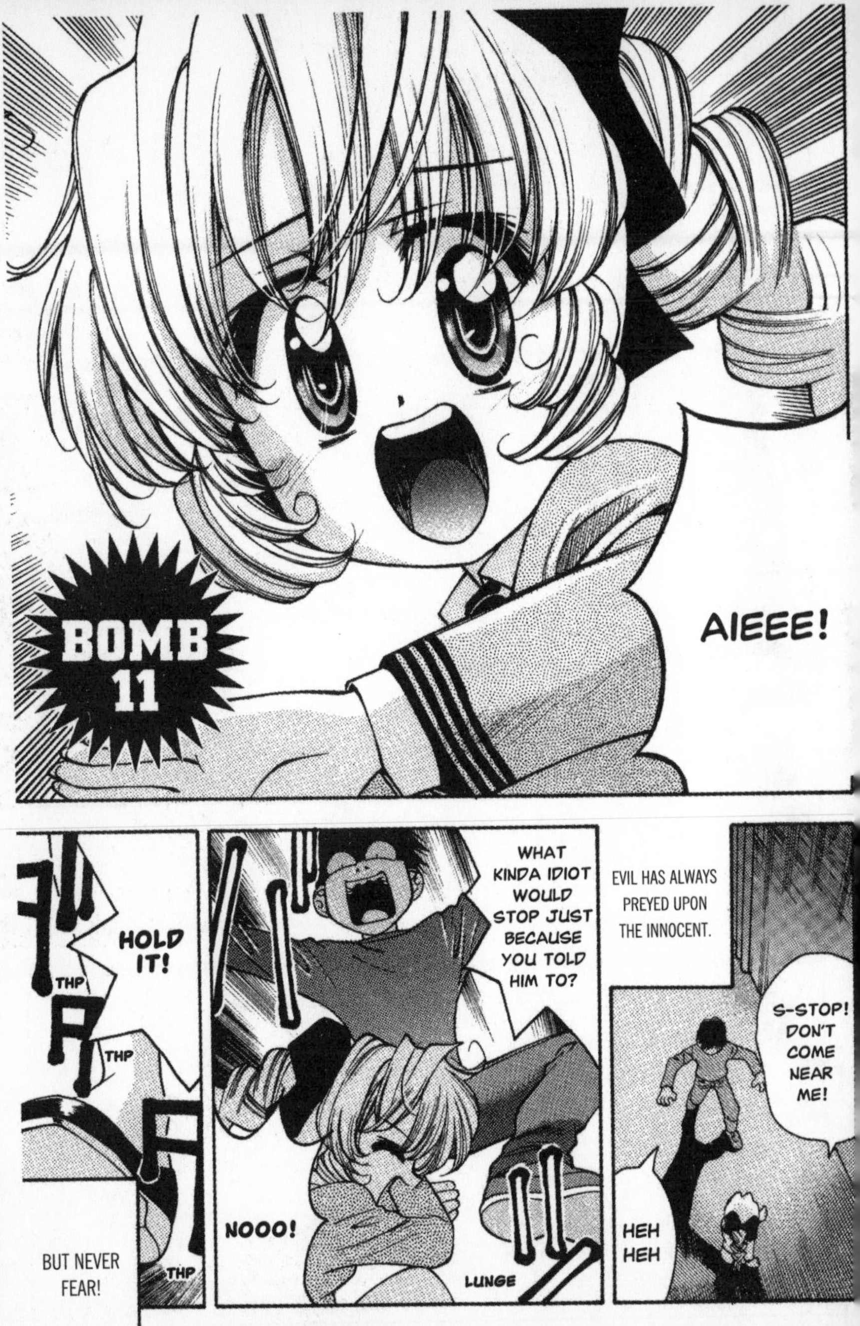
AIEEE!
BOMB 11
EVIL HAS ALWAYS PREYED UPON THE INNOCENT.
S-STOP! DON'T COME NEAR ME!
HEH HEH
WHAT KINDA IDIOT WOULD STOP JUST BECAUSE YOU TOLD HIM TO?
NOOO!
LUNGE
HOLD IT!
THP
THP
THP
BUT NEVER FEAR!

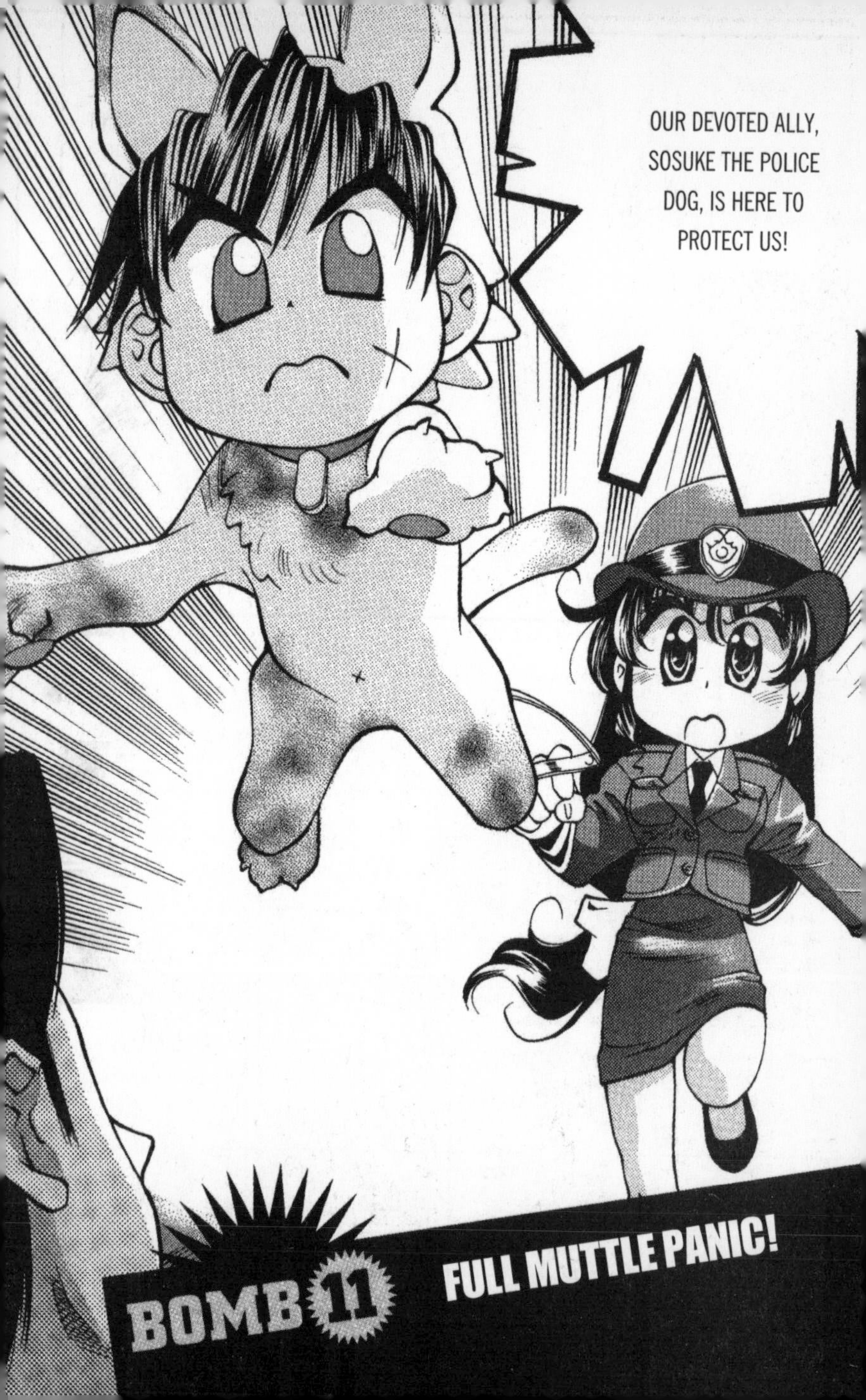
OUR DEVOTED ALLY, SOSUKE THE POLICE DOG, IS HERE TO PROTECT US!
BOMB 11
FULL MUTTLE PANIC!

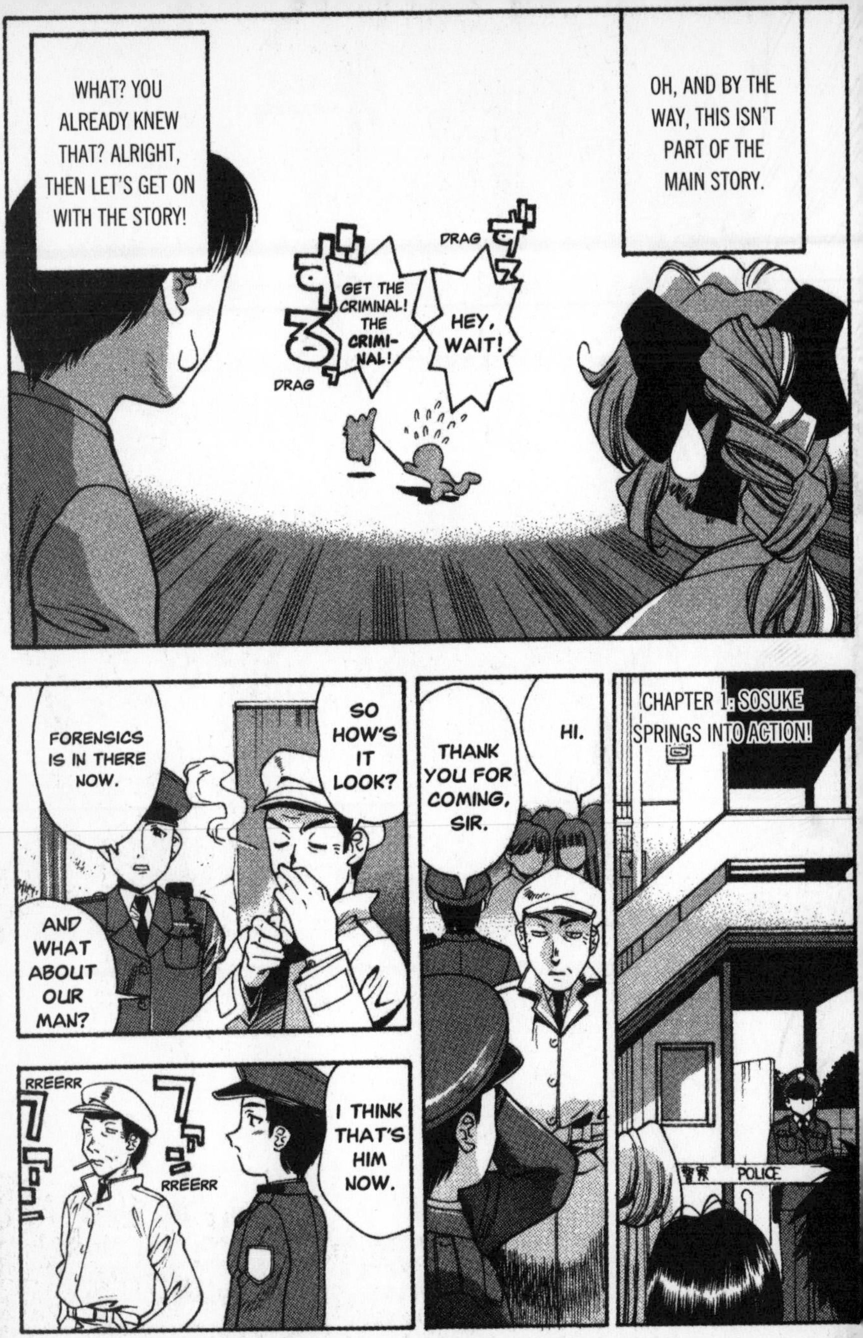
OH, AND BY THE WAY, THIS ISN'T PART OF THE MAIN STORY.
WHAT? YOU ALREADY KNEW THAT? ALRIGHT, THEN LET'S GET ON WITH THE STORY!
DRAG
HEY, WAIT!
GET THE CRIMINAL! THE CRIMINAL!
DRAG
CHAPTER 1: SOSUKE SPRINGS INTO ACTION!
POLICE
HI.
THANK YOU FOR COMING, SIR.
SO HOW'S IT LOOK?
FORENSICS IS IN THERE NOW.
AND WHAT ABOUT OUR MAN?
I THINK THAT'S HIM NOW.
RREERR
RREERR

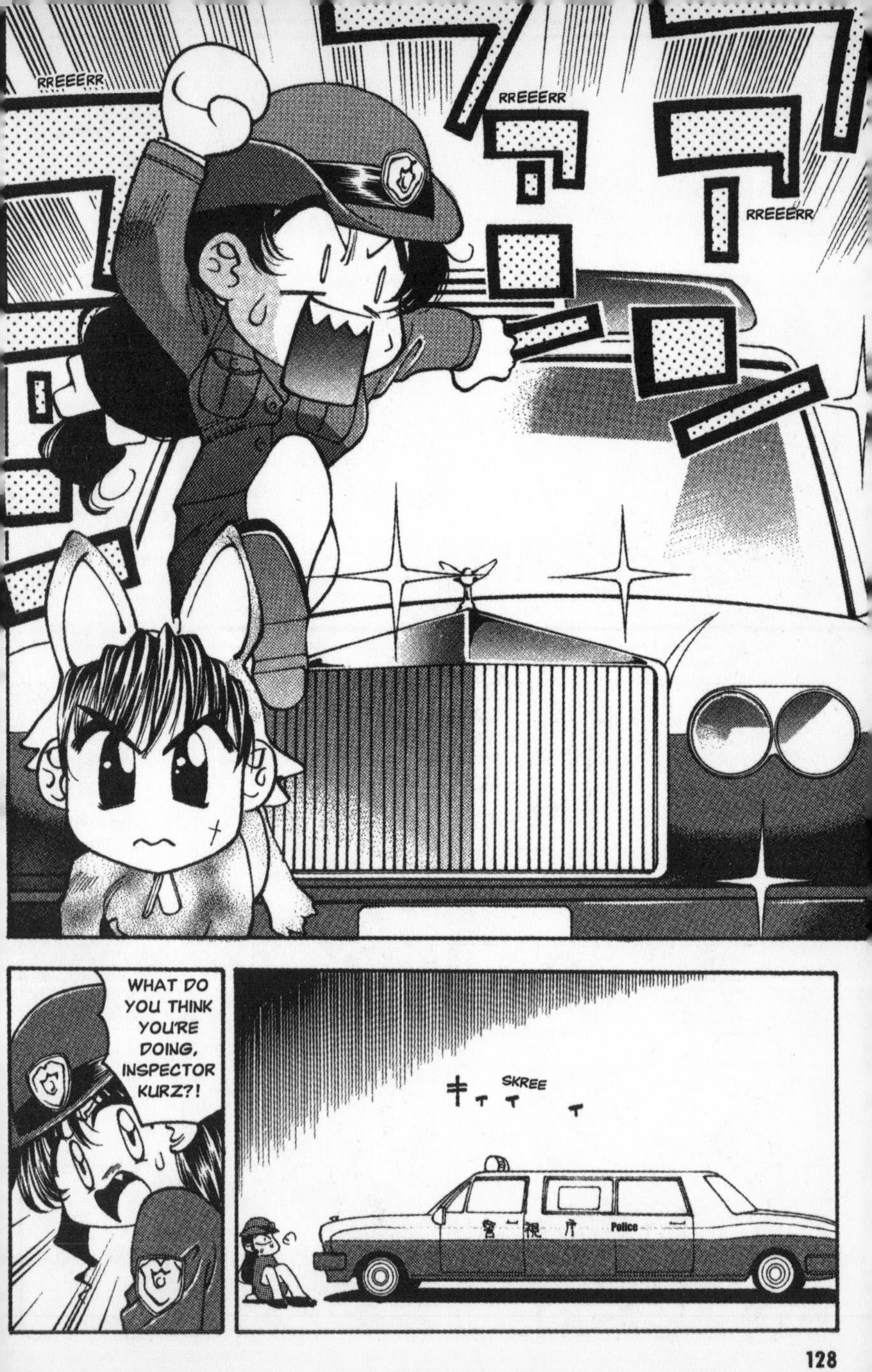
RREEERR
RREEERR
RREEERR
SKREE
WHAT DO YOU THINK YOU'RE DOING, INSPECTOR KURZ?!

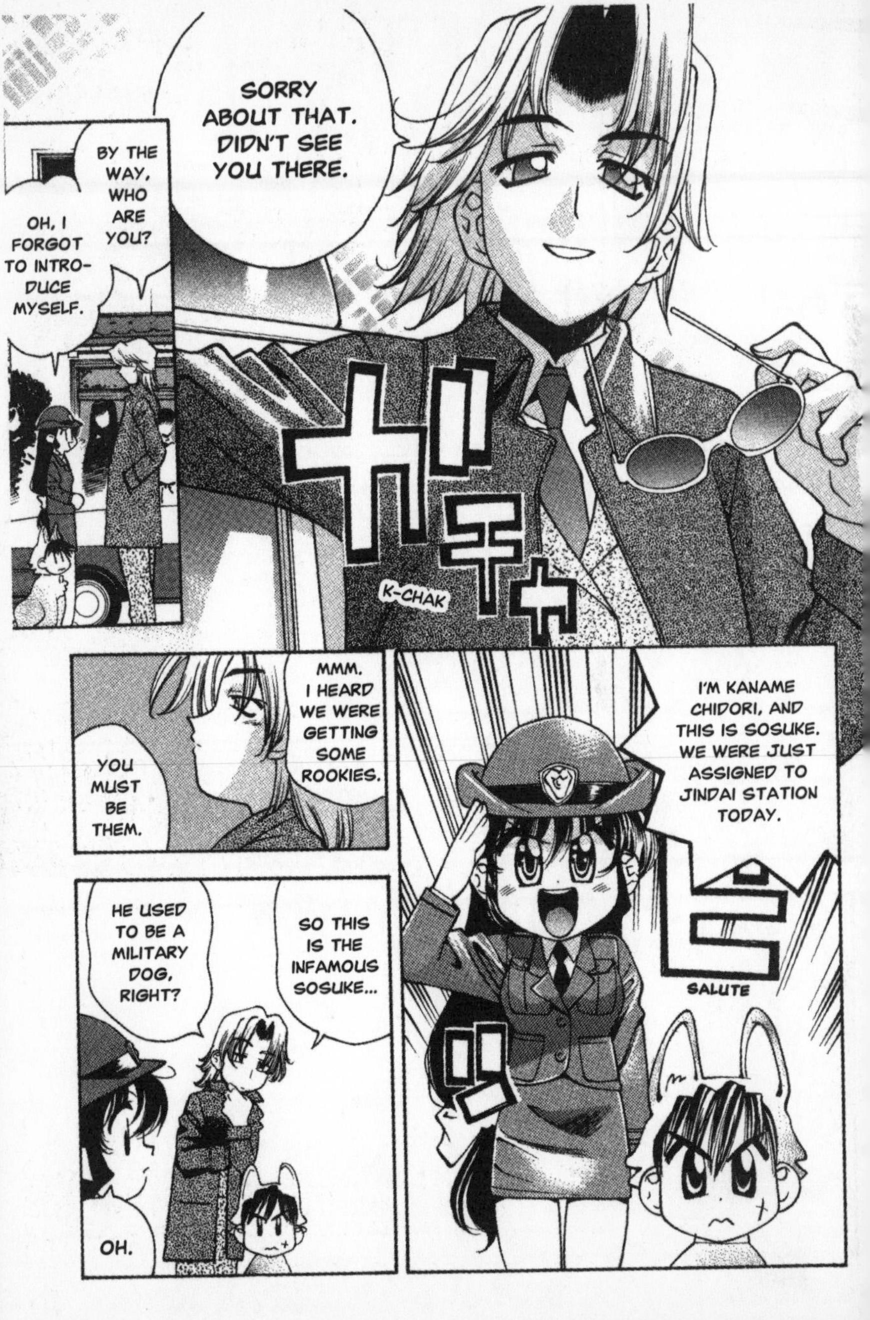
SORRY ABOUT THAT. DIDN'T SEE YOU THERE.
K-CHAK
BY THE WAY, WHO ARE YOU?
OH, I FORGOT TO INTRO-DUCE MYSELF.
I'M KANAME CHIDORI, AND THIS IS SOSUKE. WE WERE JUST ASSIGNED TO JINDAI STATION TODAY.
SALUTE
MMM. I HEARD WE WERE GETTING SOME ROOKIES.
YOU MUST BE THEM.
SO THIS IS THE INFAMOUS SOSUKE...
HE USED TO BE A MILITARY DOG, RIGHT?
OH.

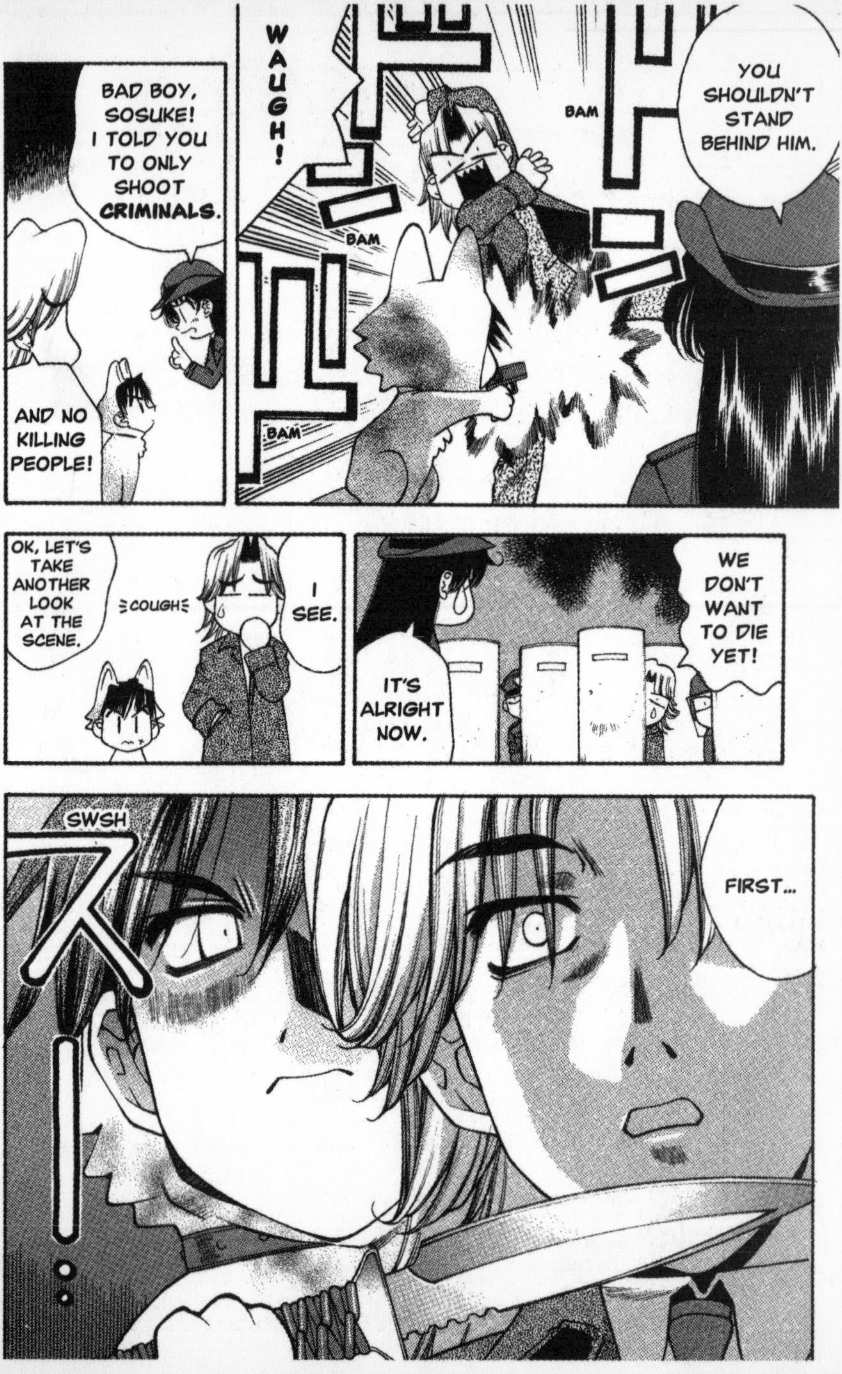
YOU SHOULDN'T STAND BEHIND HIM.
BAM
WAUGH!
BAM
BAM
BAD BOY, SOSUKE! I TOLD YOU TO ONLY SHOOT CRIMINALS.
AND NO KILLING PEOPLE!
WE DON'T WANT TO DIE YET!
IT'S ALRIGHT NOW.
I SEE.
COUGH
OK, LET'S TAKE ANOTHER LOOK AT THE SCENE.
FIRST...
SWSH

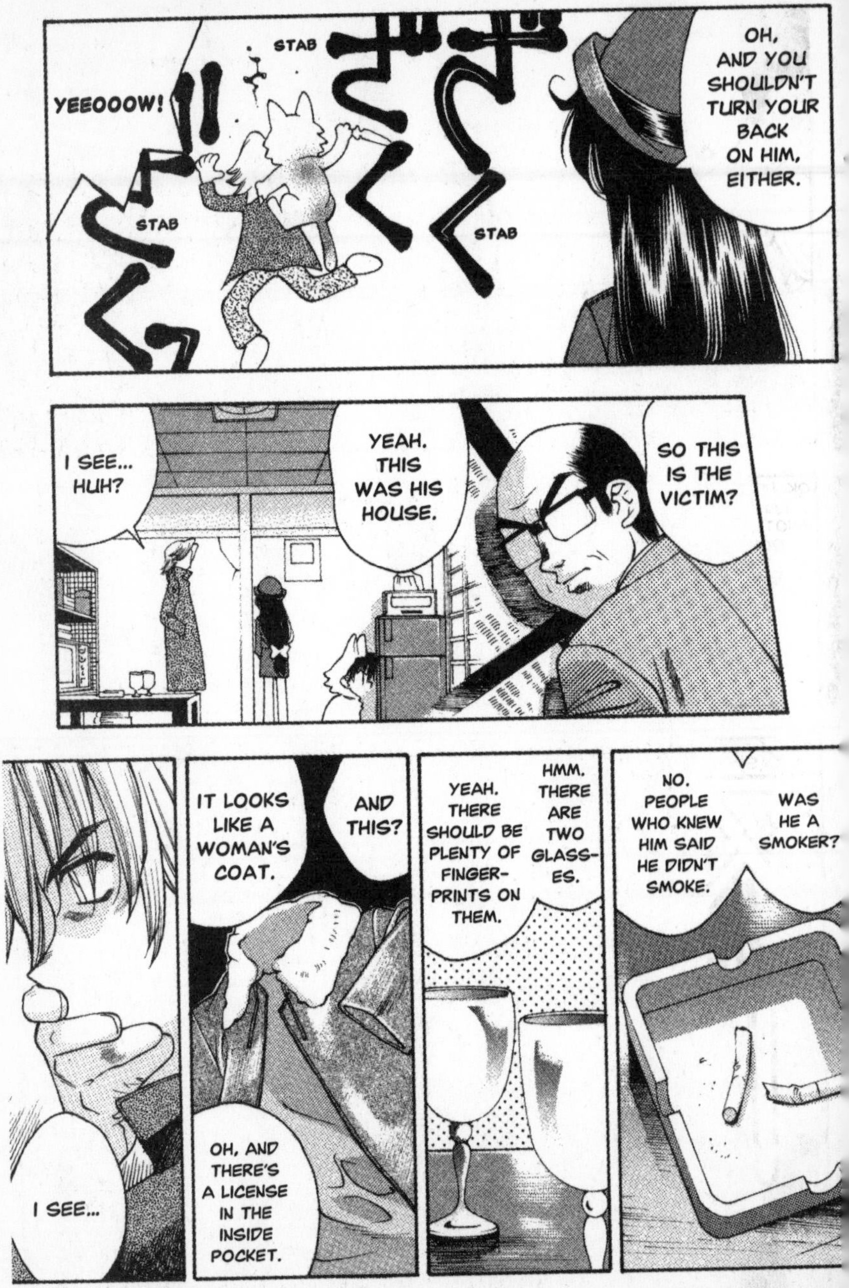
OH, AND YOU SHOULDN'T TURN YOUR BACK ON HIM, EITHER.
STAB
STAB
STAB
YEEOOOW!
SO THIS IS THE VICTIM?
YEAH. THIS WAS HIS HOUSE.
I SEE... HUH?
WAS HE A SMOKER?
NO. PEOPLE WHO KNEW HIM SAID HE DIDN'T SMOKE.
HMM. THERE ARE TWO GLASSES.
YEAH. THERE SHOULD BE PLENTY OF FINGERPRINTS ON THEM.
AND THIS?
IT LOOKS LIKE A WOMAN'S COAT.
OH, AND THERE'S A LICENSE IN THE INSIDE POCKET.
I SEE...

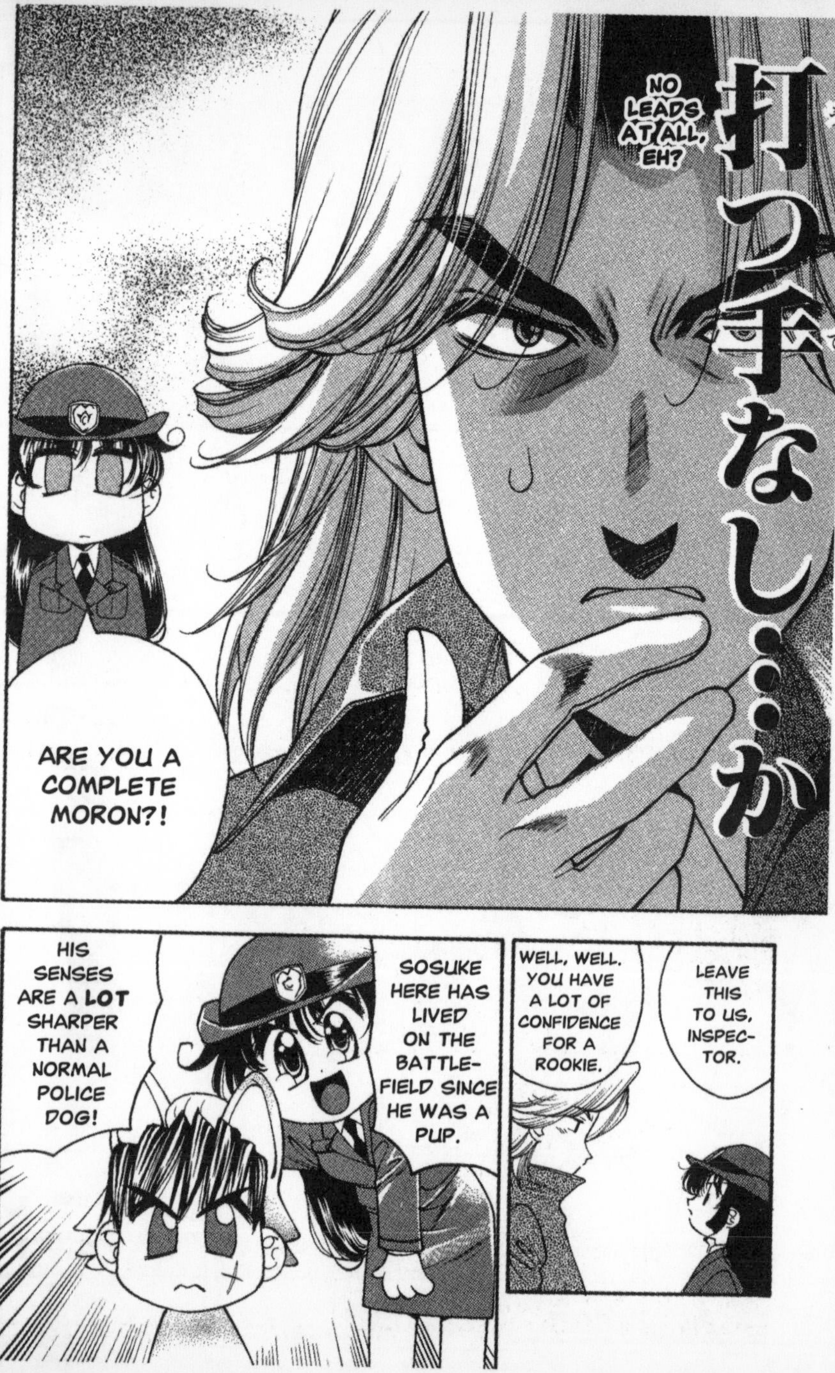
打つ手なし…か
NO LEADS AT ALL, EH?
ARE YOU A COMPLETE MORON?!
LEAVE THIS TO US, INSPECTOR.
WELL, WELL. YOU HAVE A LOT OF CONFIDENCE FOR A ROOKIE.
SOSUKE HERE HAS LIVED ON THE BATTLEFIELD SINCE HE WAS A PUP.
HIS SENSES ARE A **LOT** SHARPER THAN A NORMAL POLICE DOG!

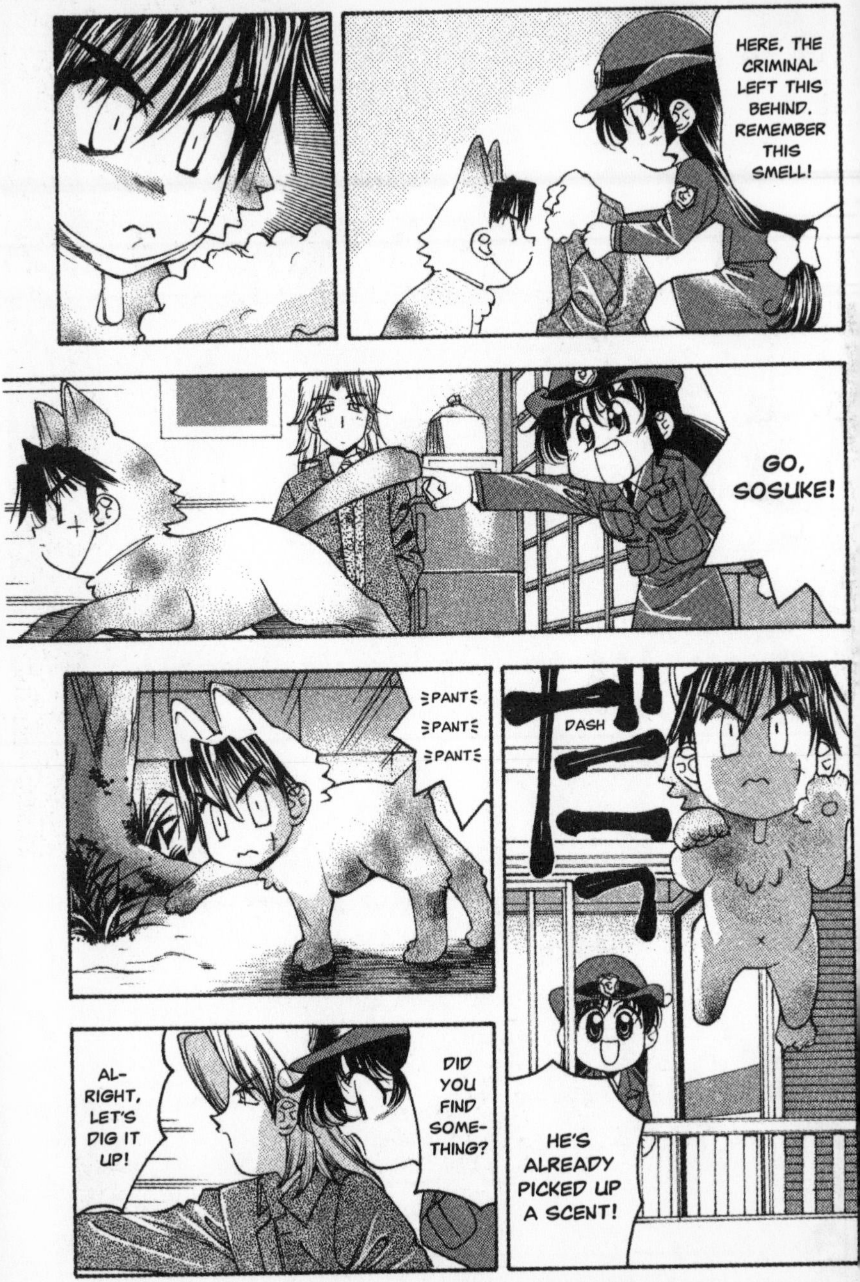
HERE, THE CRIMINAL LEFT THIS BEHIND. REMEMBER THIS SMELL!
GO, SOSUKE!
DASH
HE'S ALREADY PICKED UP A SCENT!
PANT PANT PANT
DID YOU FIND SOME-THING?
AL-RIGHT, LET'S DIG IT UP!

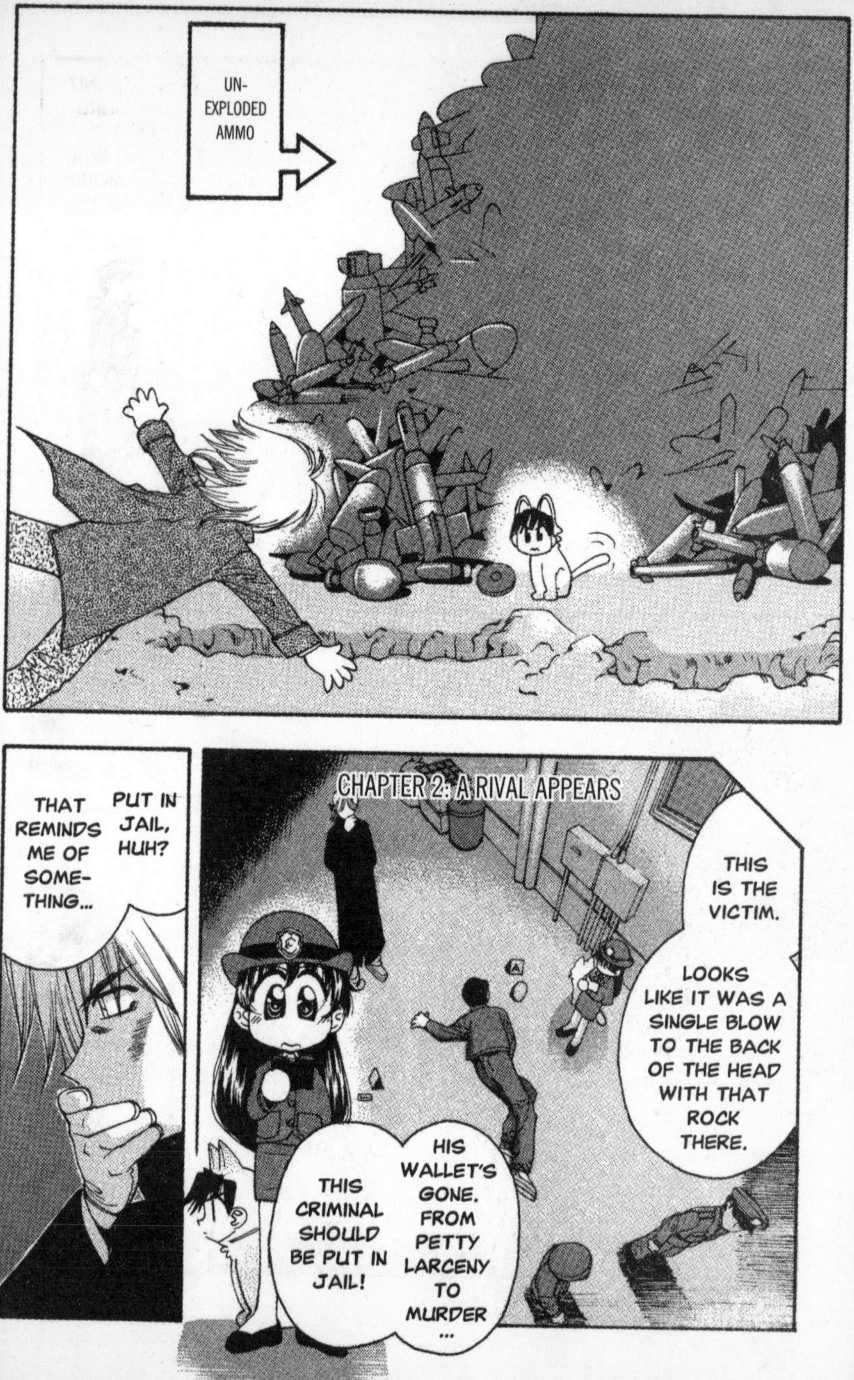
UN-EXPLODED AMMO
CHAPTER 2: A RIVAL APPEARS
THIS IS THE VICTIM.
LOOKS LIKE IT WAS A SINGLE BLOW TO THE BACK OF THE HEAD WITH THAT ROCK THERE.
HIS WALLET'S GONE. FROM PETTY LARCENY TO MURDER...
THIS CRIMINAL SHOULD BE PUT IN JAIL!
PUT IN JAIL, HUH?
THAT REMINDS ME OF SOMETHING...

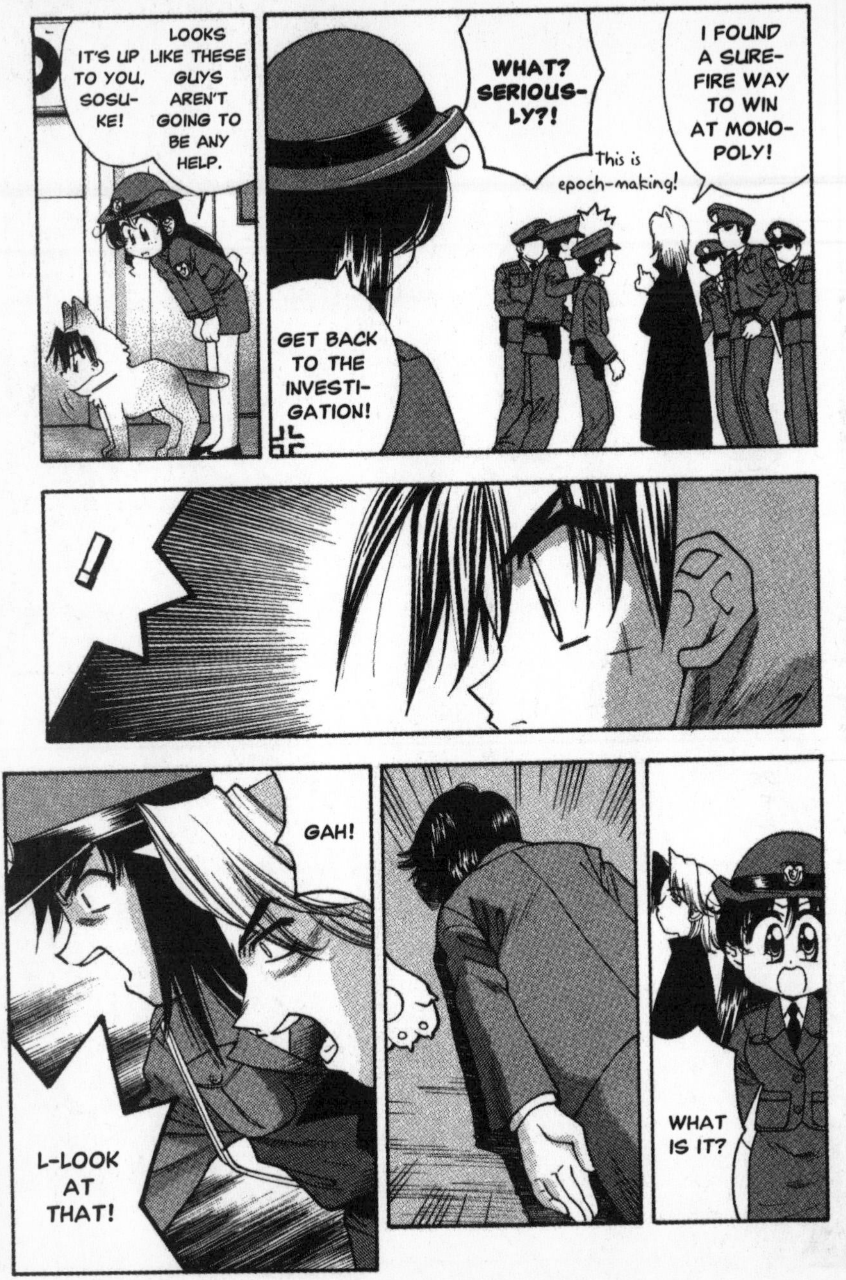
I FOUND A SURE-FIRE WAY TO WIN AT MONO-POLY!
WHAT? SERIOUS-LY?!
This is epoch-making!
GET BACK TO THE INVESTI-GATION!
LOOKS LIKE THESE GUYS AREN'T GOING TO BE ANY HELP.
IT'S UP TO YOU, SOSU-KE!
!
WHAT IS IT?
GAH!
L-LOOK AT THAT!

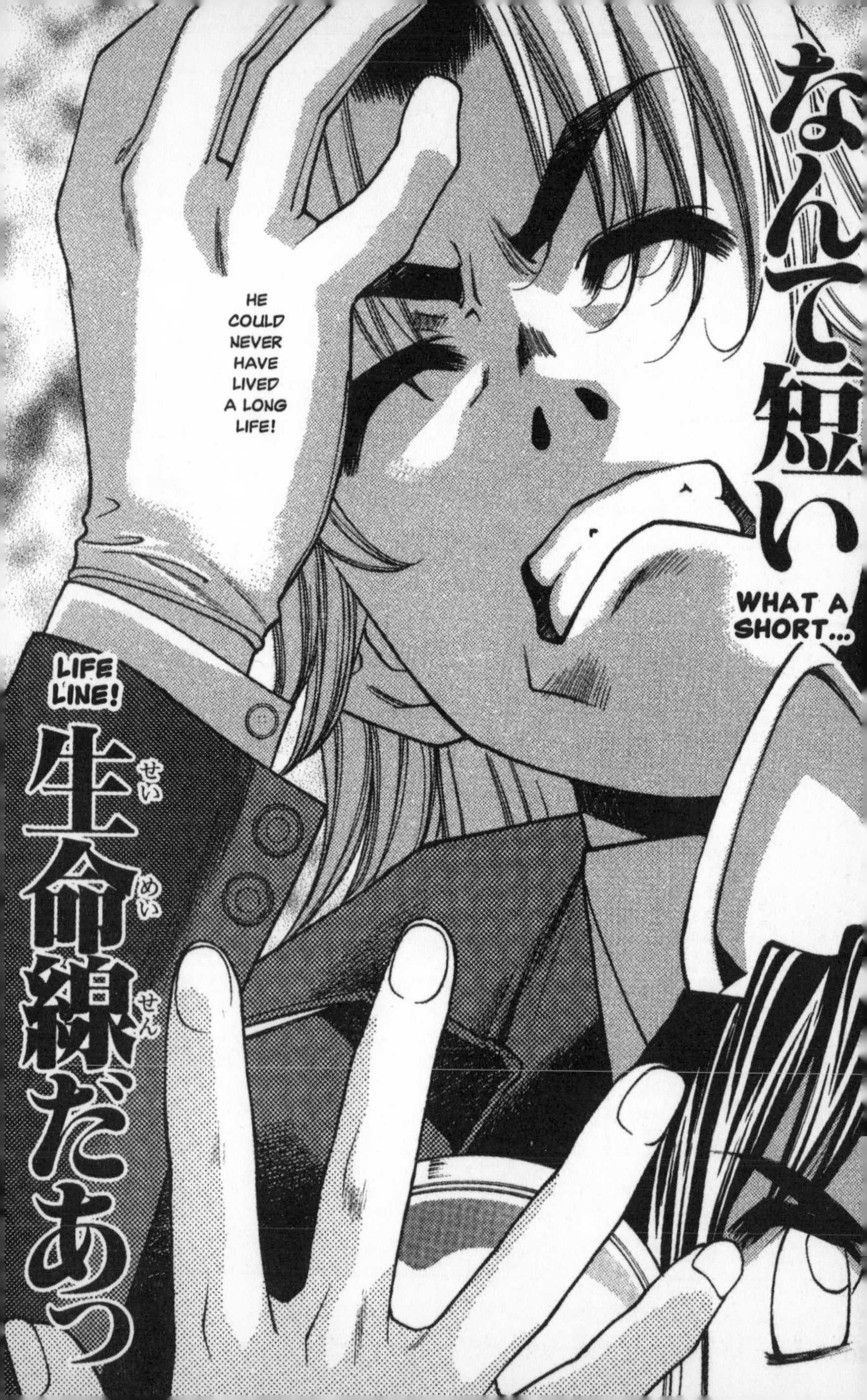
なんて短い
WHAT A SHORT...
生命線だあっ
LIFE LINE!
HE COULD NEVER HAVE LIVED A LONG LIFE!

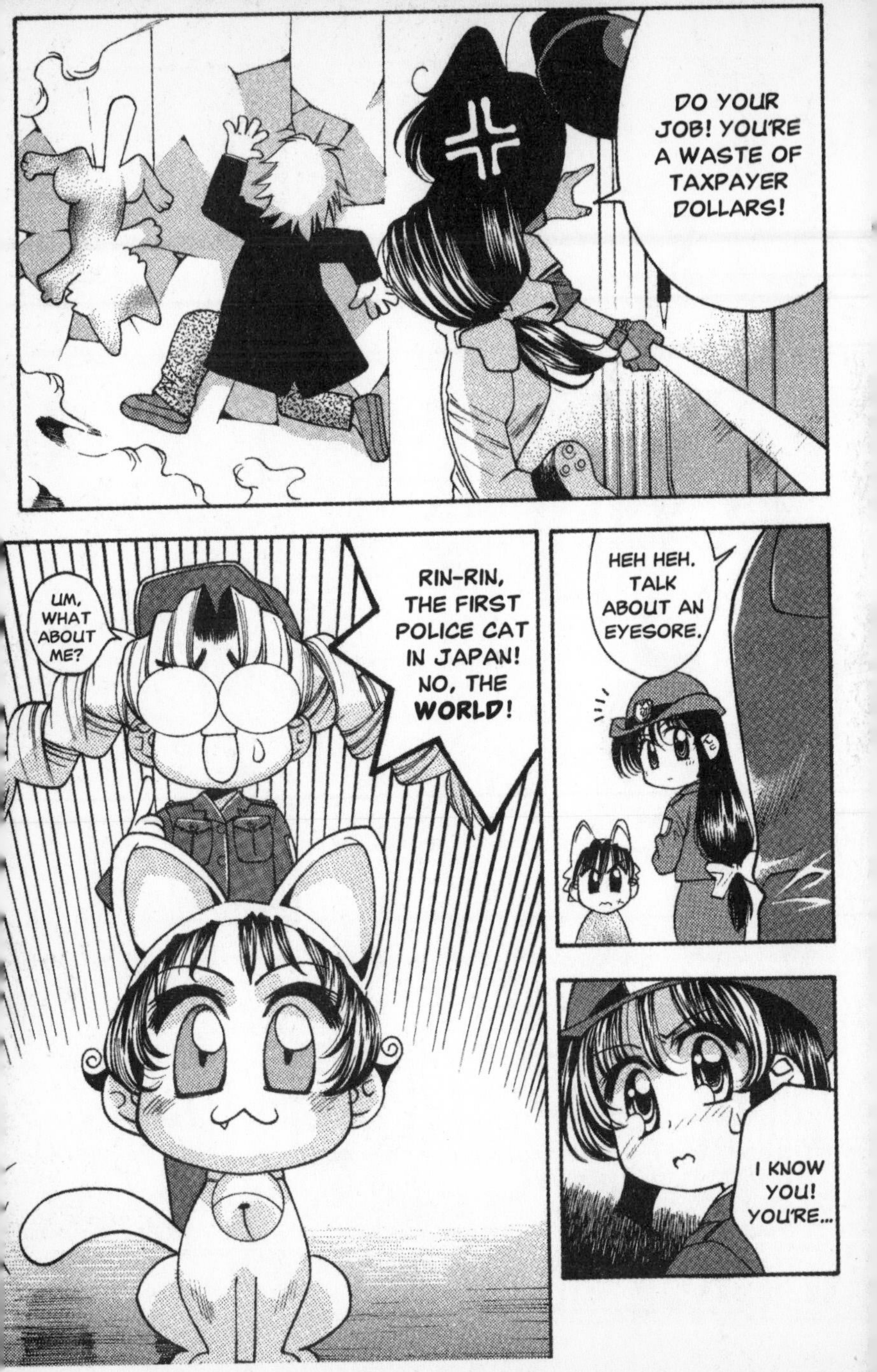
DO YOUR JOB! YOU'RE A WASTE OF TAXPAYER DOLLARS!
HEH HEH. TALK ABOUT AN EYESORE.
RIN-RIN, THE FIRST POLICE CAT IN JAPAN! NO, THE **WORLD**!
UM, WHAT ABOUT ME?
I KNOW YOU! YOU'RE...

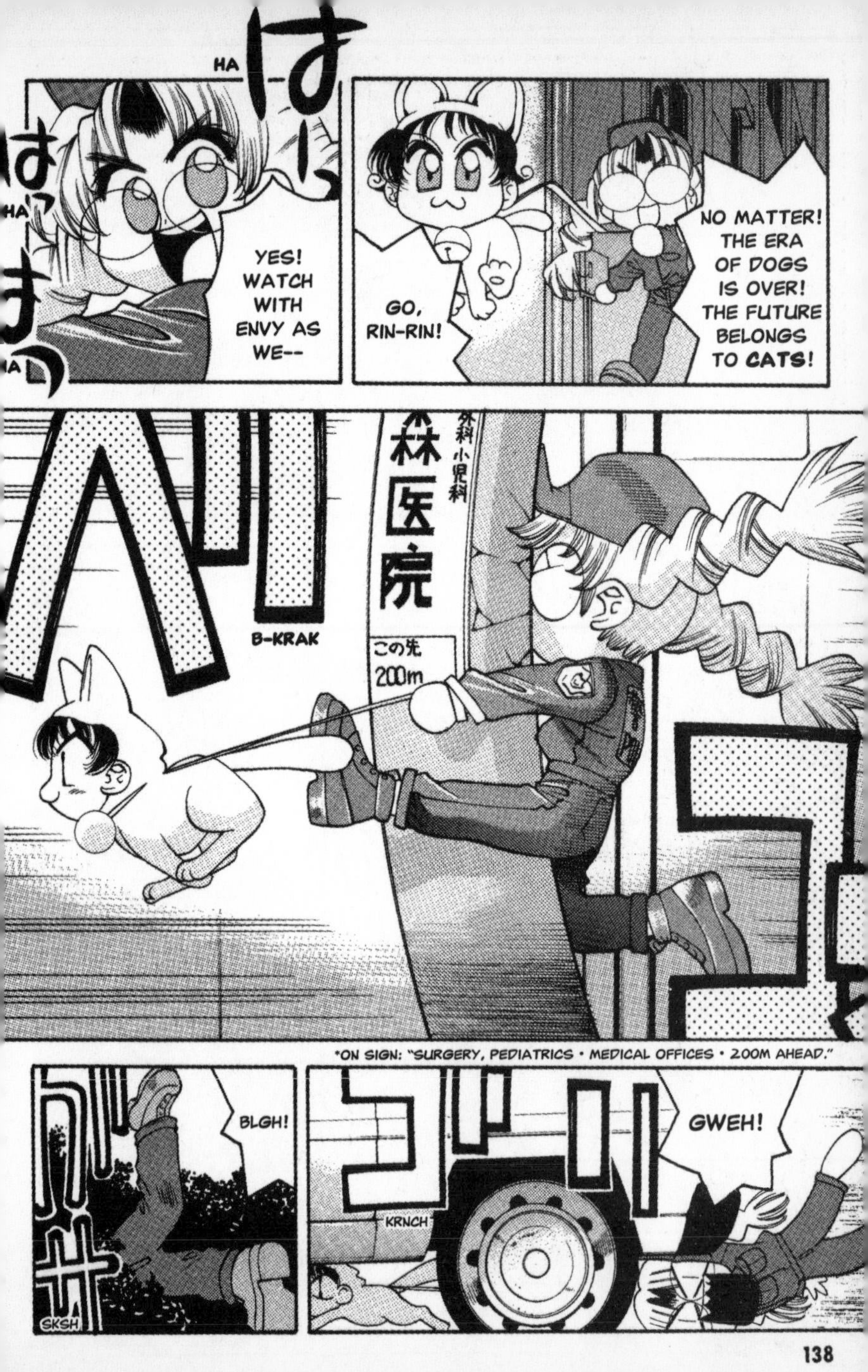
NO MATTER! THE ERA OF DOGS IS OVER! THE FUTURE BELONGS TO **CATS**!
GO, RIN-RIN!
YES! WATCH WITH ENVY AS WE--
HA
HA
HA
B-KRAK
外科小児科
森医院
この先
200m
*ON SIGN: "SURGERY, PEDIATRICS • MEDICAL OFFICES • 200M AHEAD."
GWEH!
KRNCH
BLGH!
SKSH

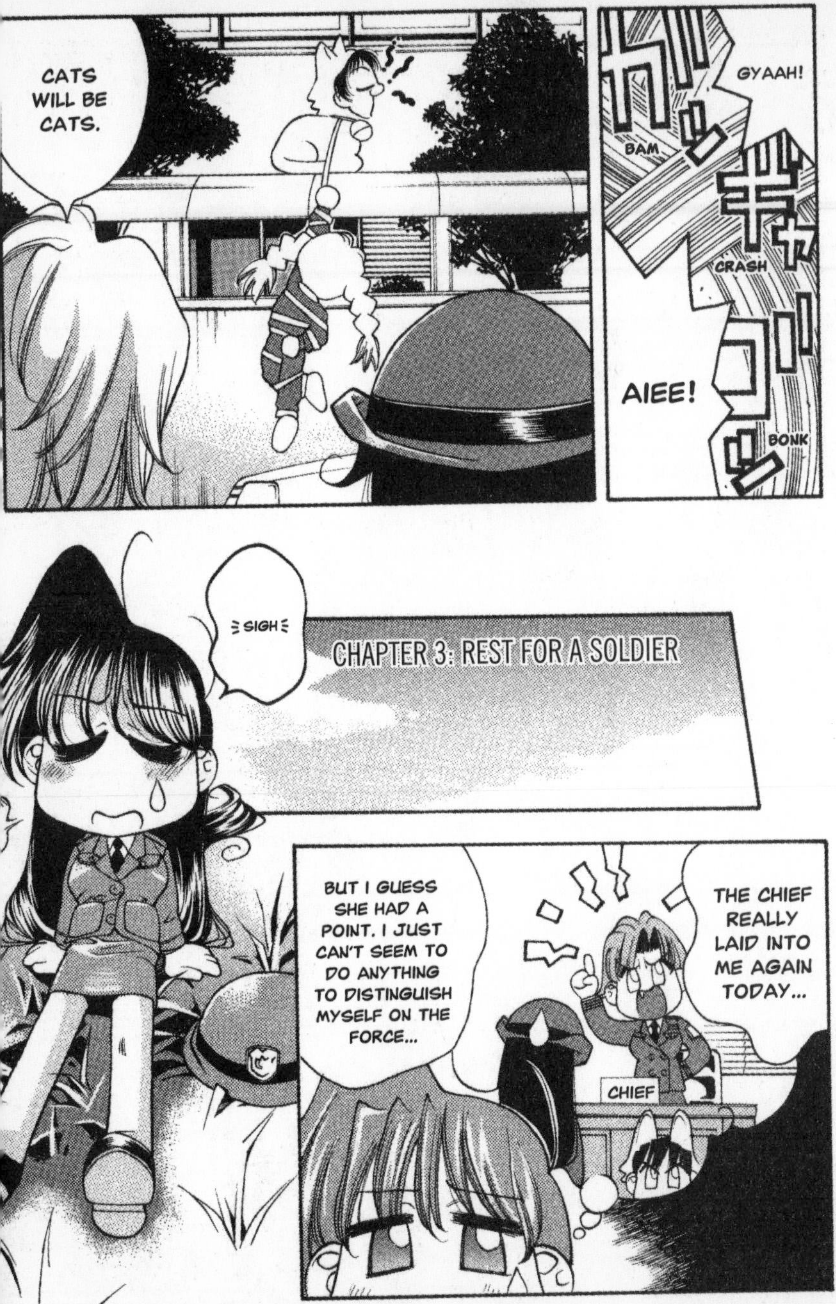
GYAAH!
BAM
CRASH
AIEE!
BONK
CATS WILL BE CATS.
SIGH
CHAPTER 3: REST FOR A SOLDIER
THE CHIEF REALLY LAID INTO ME AGAIN TODAY...
BUT I GUESS SHE HAD A POINT. I JUST CAN'T SEEM TO DO ANYTHING TO DISTINGUISH MYSELF ON THE FORCE...
CHIEF

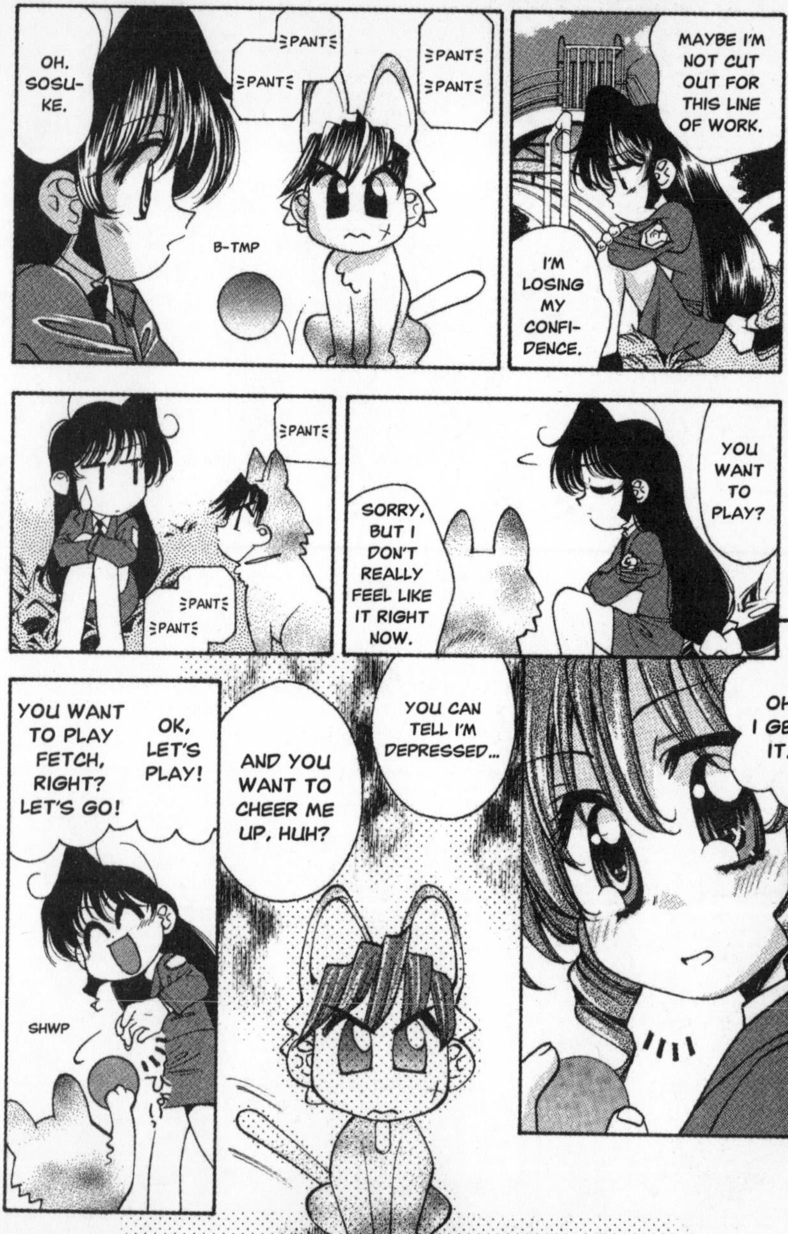
MAYBE I'M NOT CUT OUT FOR THIS LINE OF WORK.
I'M LOSING MY CONFIDENCE.
PANT PANT
PANT PANT
PANT
OH. SOSUKE.
B-TMP
YOU WANT TO PLAY?
SORRY, BUT I DON'T REALLY FEEL LIKE IT RIGHT NOW.
PANT
PANT
PANT
OH I GET IT.
YOU CAN TELL I'M DEPRESSED...
AND YOU WANT TO CHEER ME UP, HUH?
OK, LET'S PLAY!
YOU WANT TO PLAY FETCH, RIGHT? LET'S GO!
SHWP

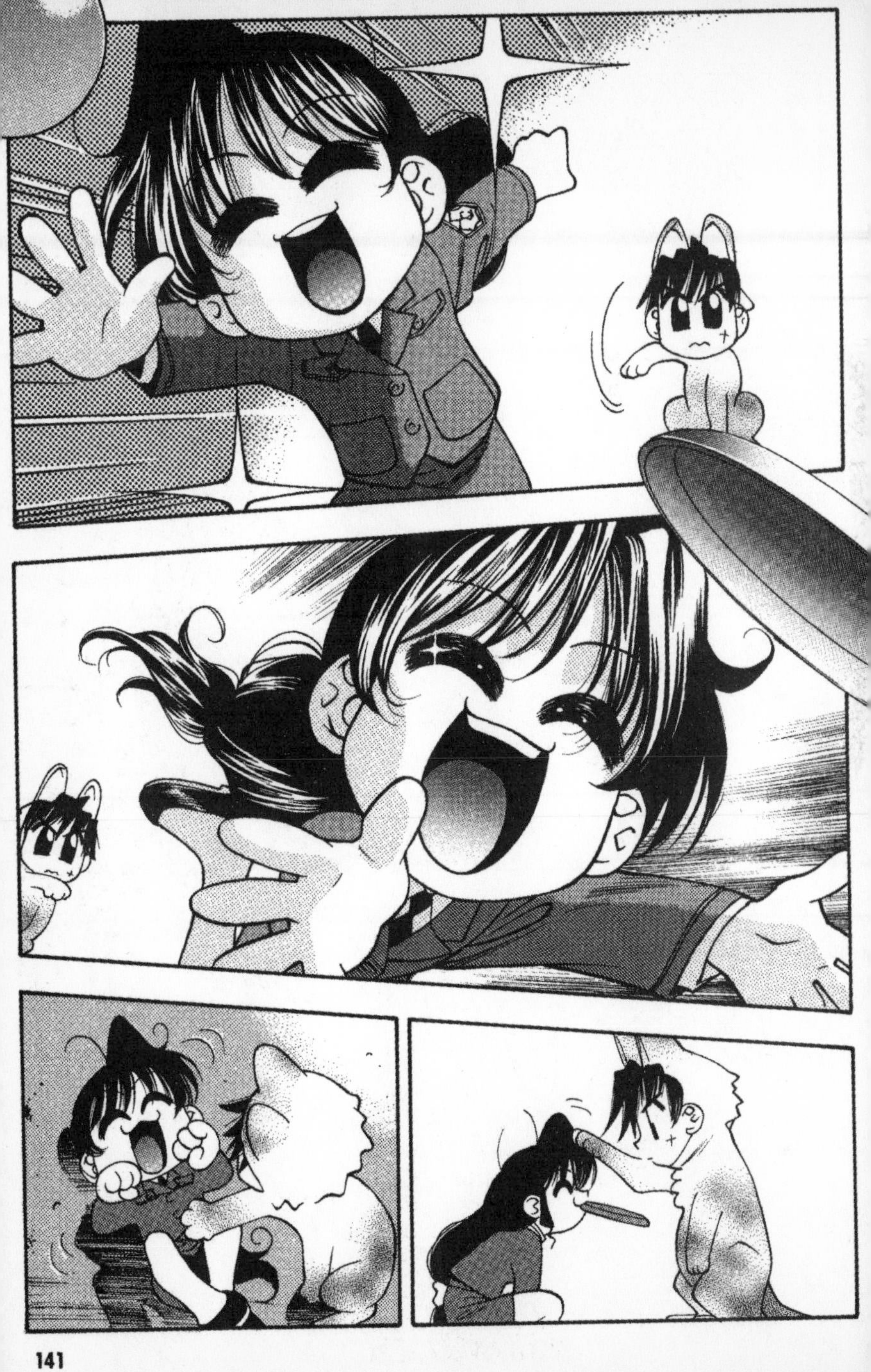

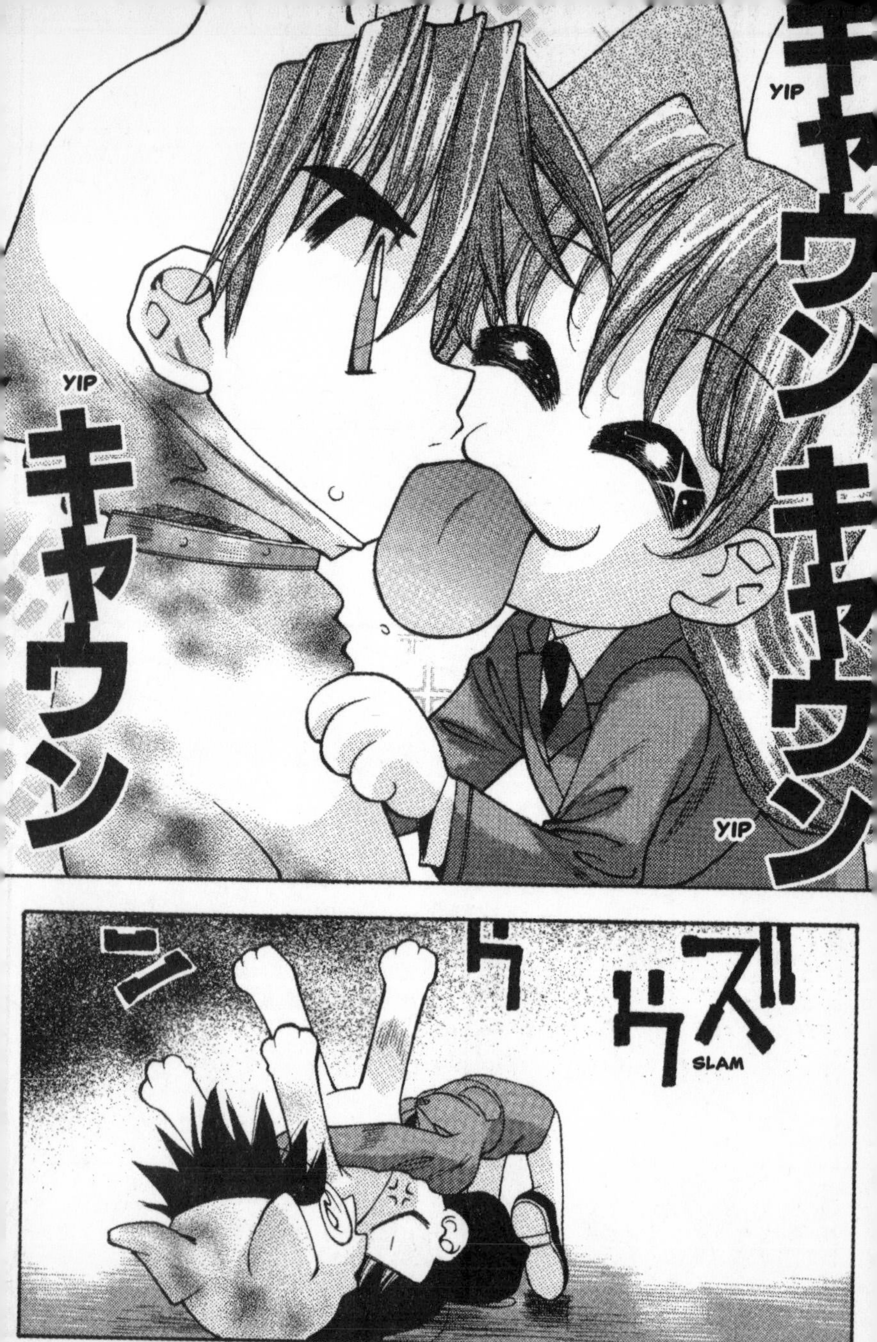
キャウンキャウン
YIP
YIP
キャウン
YIP
SLAM

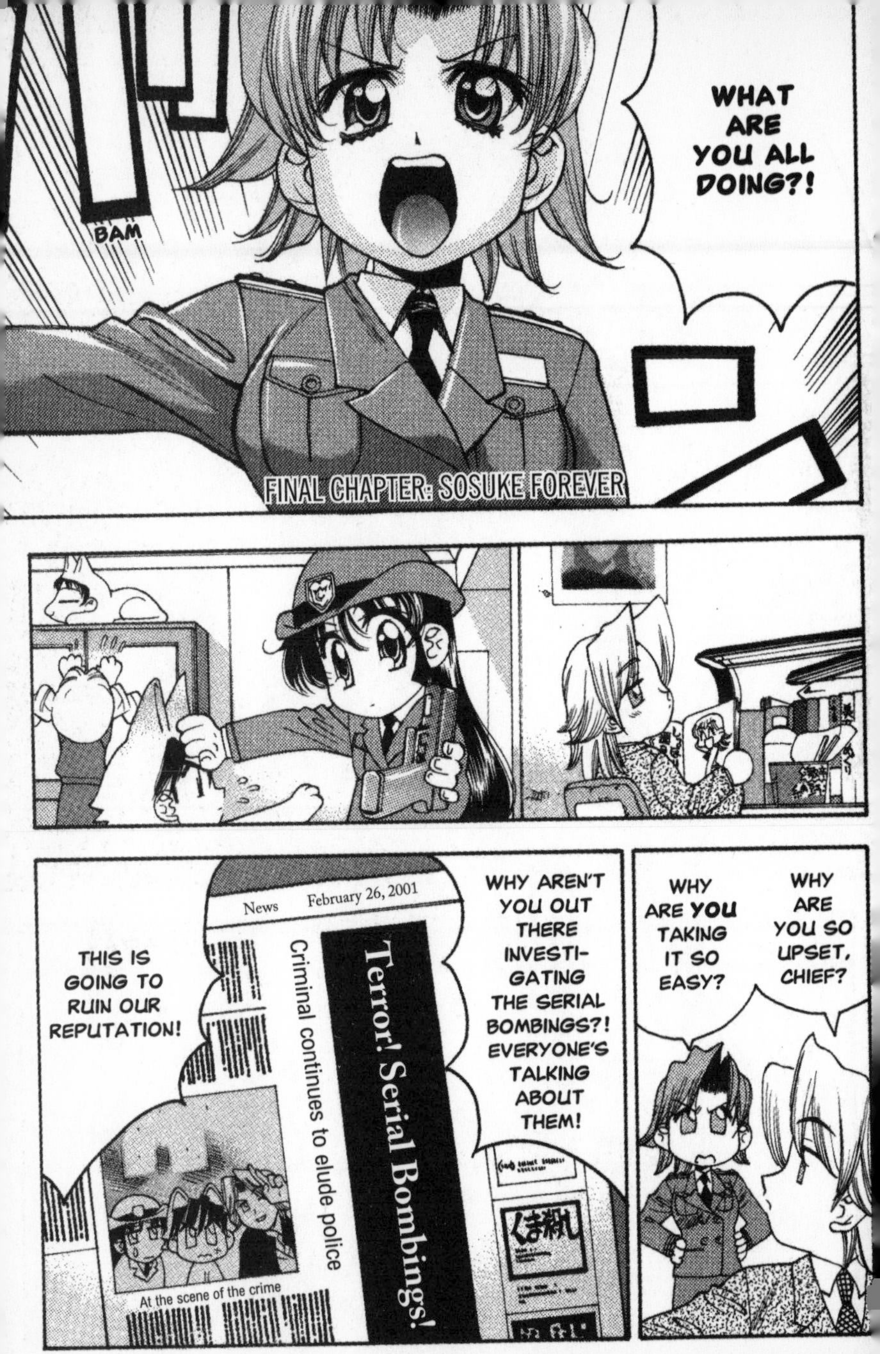
WHAT ARE YOU ALL DOING?!
BAM
FINAL CHAPTER: SOSUKE FOREVER
WHY ARE YOU SO UPSET, CHIEF?
WHY ARE YOU TAKING IT SO EASY?
WHY AREN'T YOU OUT THERE INVESTI-GATING THE SERIAL BOMBINGS?! EVERYONE'S TALKING ABOUT THEM!
News February 26, 2001
Terror! Serial Bombings!
Criminal continues to elude police
At the scene of the crime
THIS IS GOING TO RUIN OUR REPUTATION!

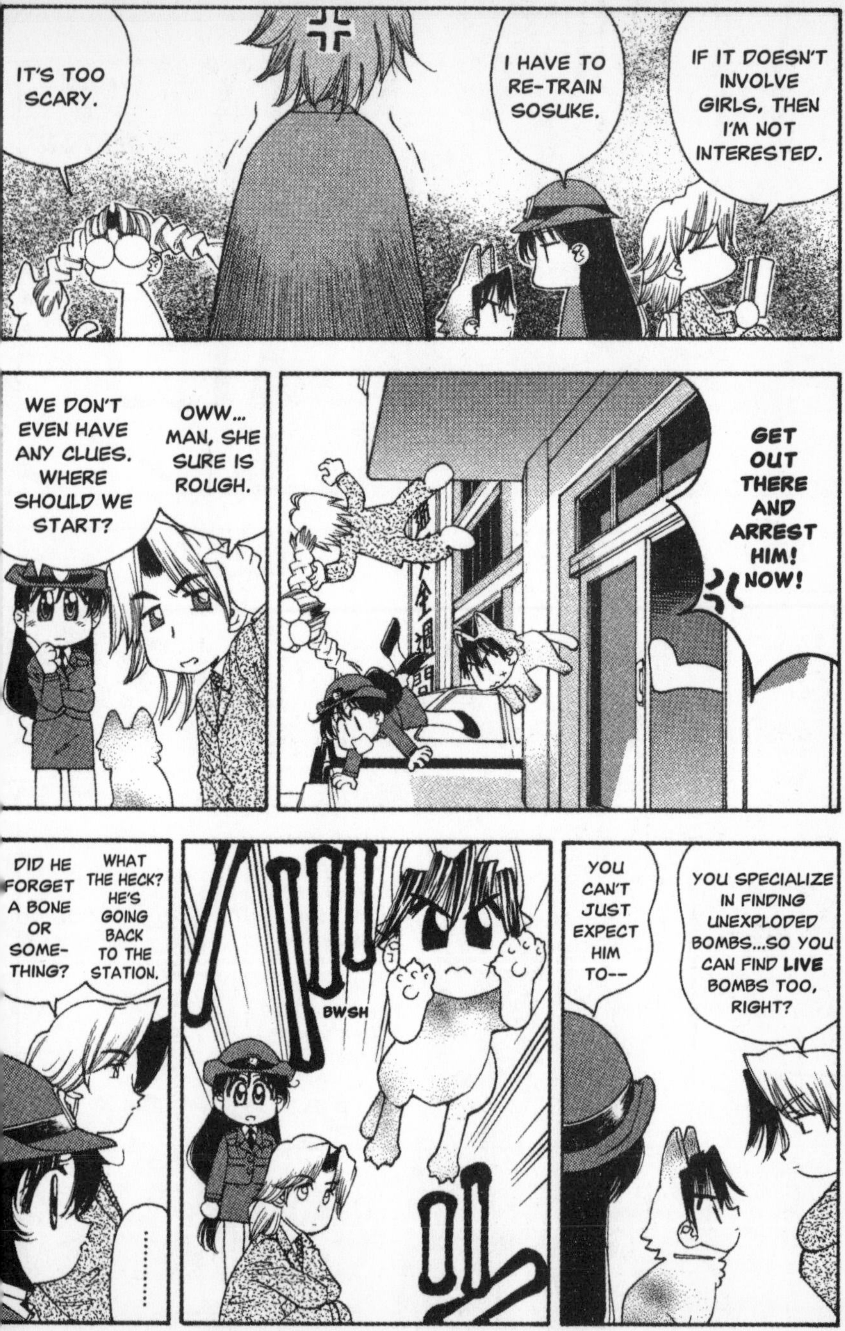
IF IT DOESN'T INVOLVE GIRLS, THEN I'M NOT INTERESTED.
I HAVE TO RE-TRAIN SOSUKE.
IT'S TOO SCARY.
GET OUT THERE AND ARREST HIM! NOW!
OWW... MAN, SHE SURE IS ROUGH.
WE DON'T EVEN HAVE ANY CLUES. WHERE SHOULD WE START?
YOU SPECIALIZE IN FINDING UNEXPLODED BOMBS...SO YOU CAN FIND **LIVE** BOMBS TOO, RIGHT?
YOU CAN'T JUST EXPECT HIM TO--
BWSH
WHAT THE HECK? HE'S GOING BACK TO THE STATION.
DID HE FORGET A BONE OR SOME-THING?
....

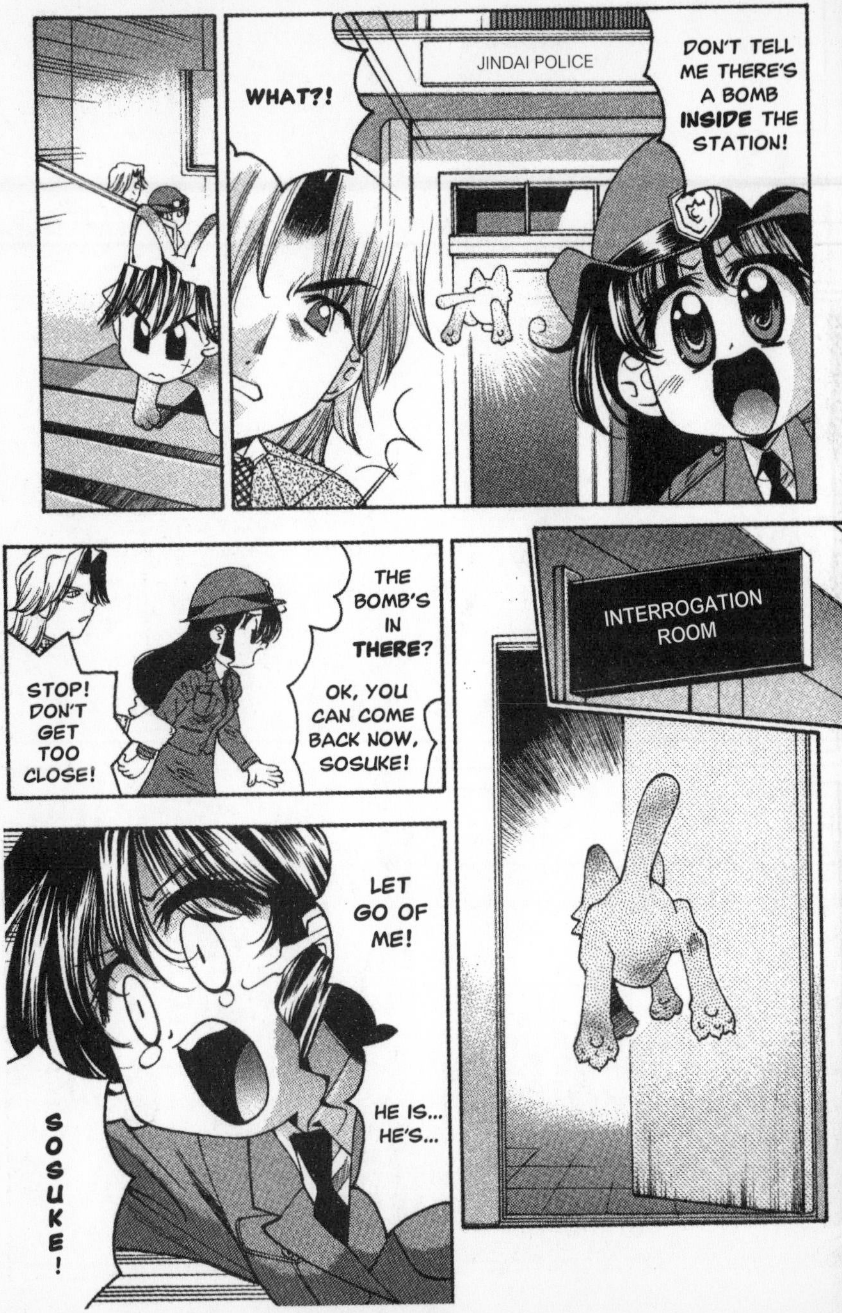
JINDAI POLICE
DON'T TELL ME THERE'S A BOMB **INSIDE** THE STATION!
WHAT?!
INTERROGATION ROOM
THE BOMB'S IN **THERE**?
OK, YOU CAN COME BACK NOW, SOSUKE!
STOP! DON'T GET TOO CLOSE!
LET GO OF ME!
HE IS... HE'S...
SOSUKE!

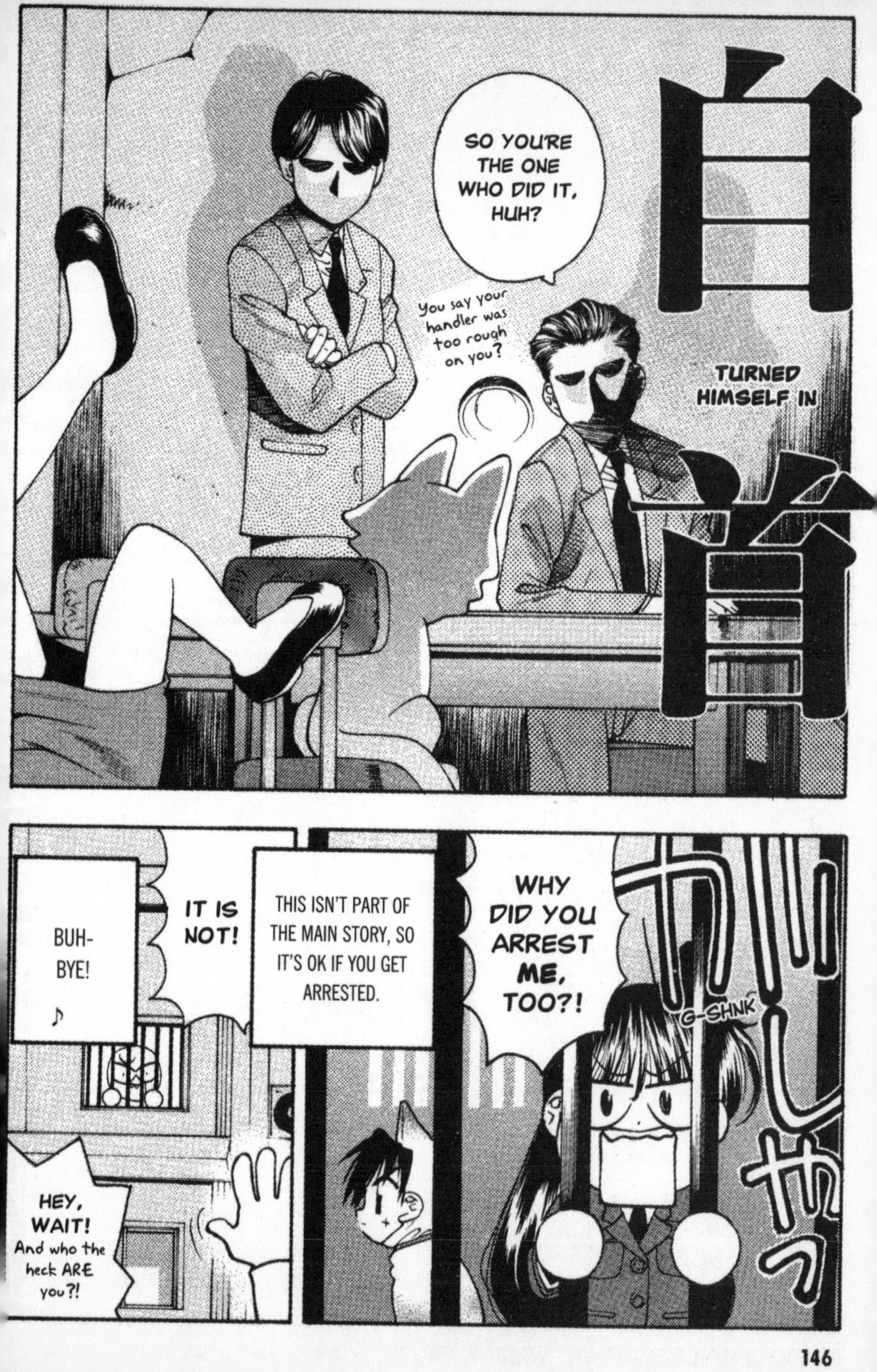
自首
TURNED HIMSELF IN
SO YOU'RE THE ONE WHO DID IT, HUH?
You say your handler was too rough on you?
WHY DID YOU ARREST ME, TOO?!
がしゃっ
G-SHNK
THIS ISN'T PART OF THE MAIN STORY, SO IT'S OK IF YOU GET ARRESTED.
IT IS NOT!
BUH-BYE! ♪
HEY, WAIT! And who the heck ARE you?!

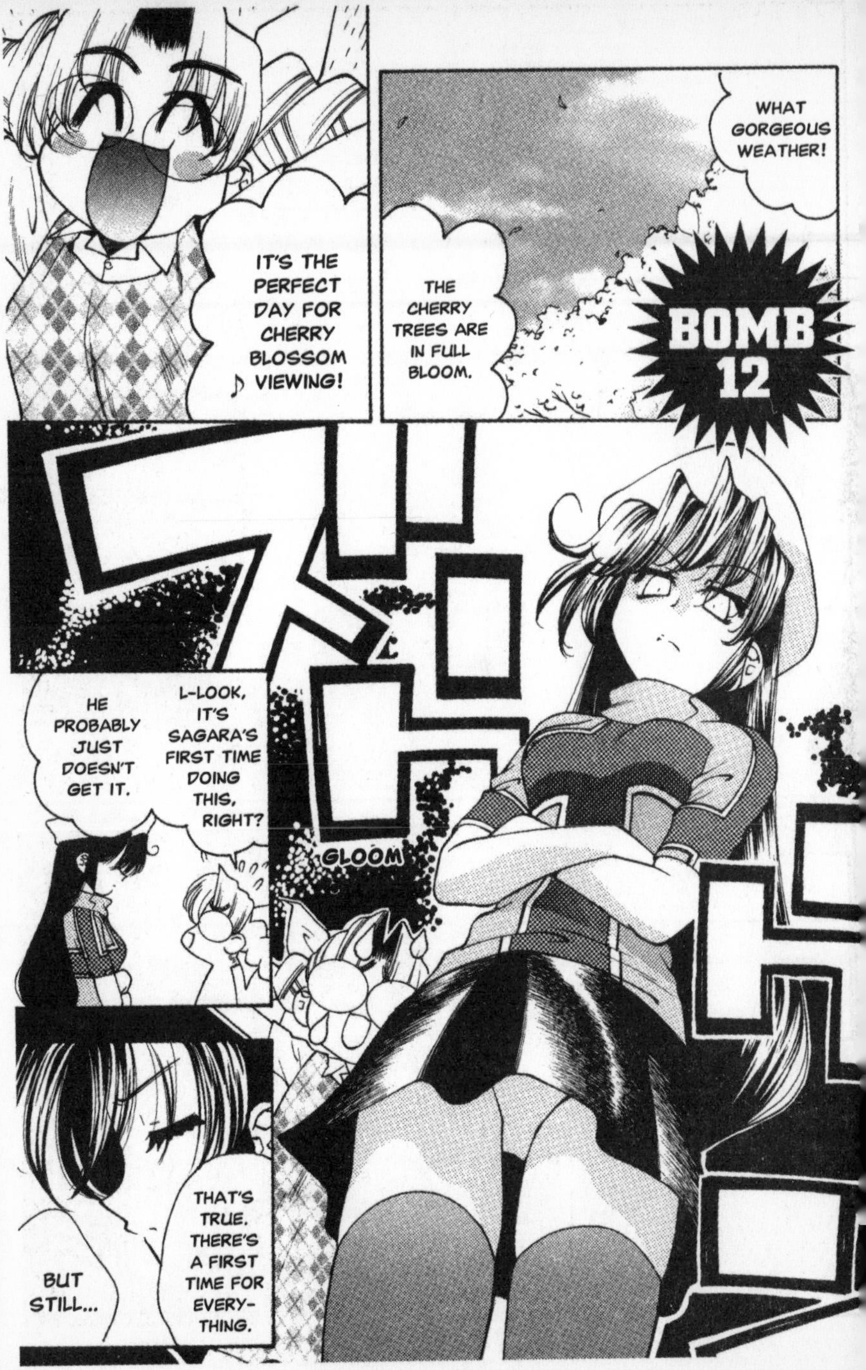
BOMB 12
WHAT GORGEOUS WEATHER!
THE CHERRY TREES ARE IN FULL BLOOM.
IT'S THE PERFECT DAY FOR CHERRY BLOSSOM ♪ VIEWING!
GLOOM
L-LOOK, IT'S SAGARA'S FIRST TIME DOING THIS, RIGHT?
HE PROBABLY JUST DOESN'T GET IT.
THAT'S TRUE. THERE'S A FIRST TIME FOR EVERY-THING.
BUT STILL...

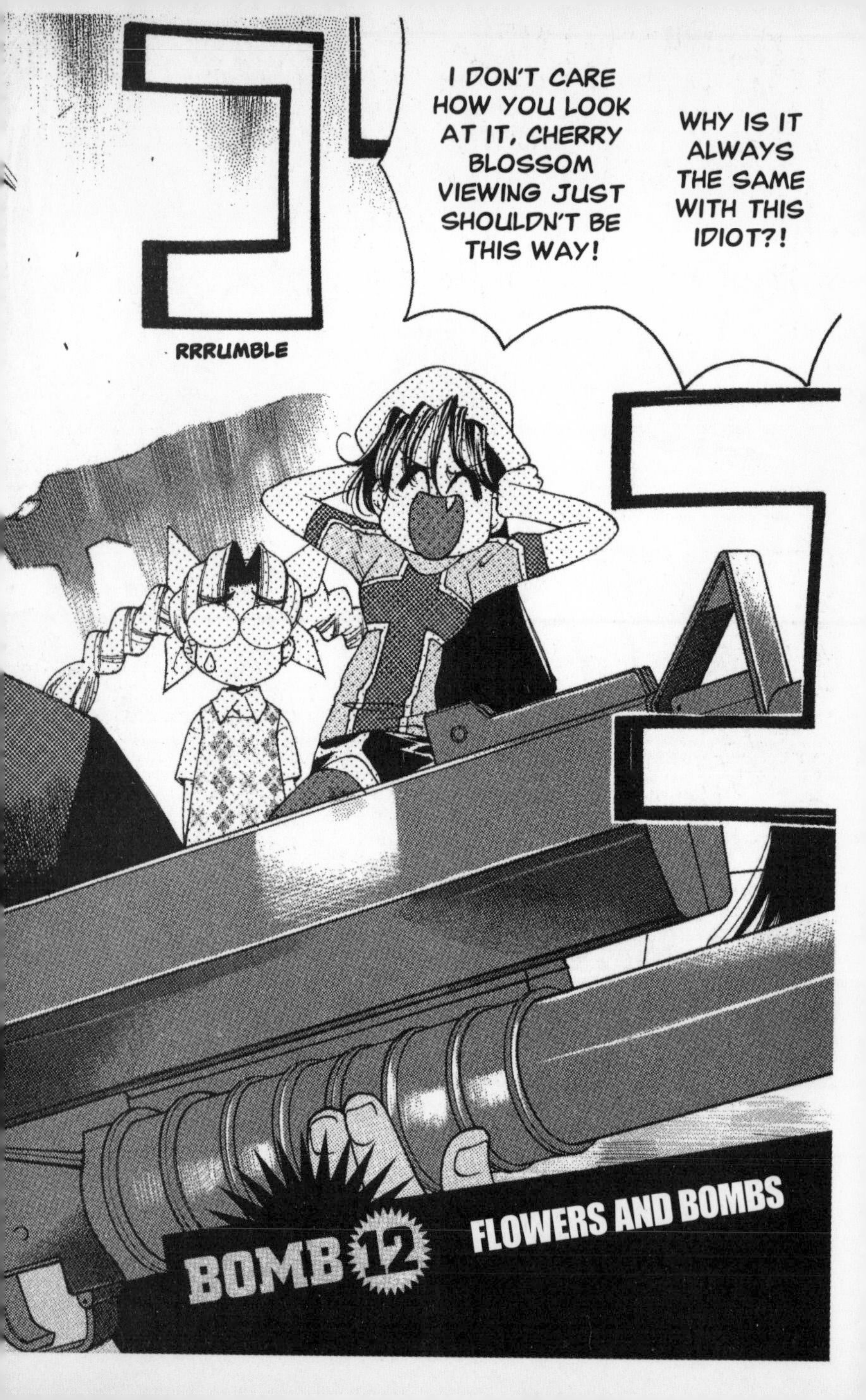
WHY IS IT ALWAYS THE SAME WITH THIS IDIOT?!
I DON'T CARE HOW YOU LOOK AT IT, CHERRY BLOSSOM VIEWING JUST SHOULDN'T BE THIS WAY!
RRRUMBLE
BOMB 12
FLOWERS AND BOMBS

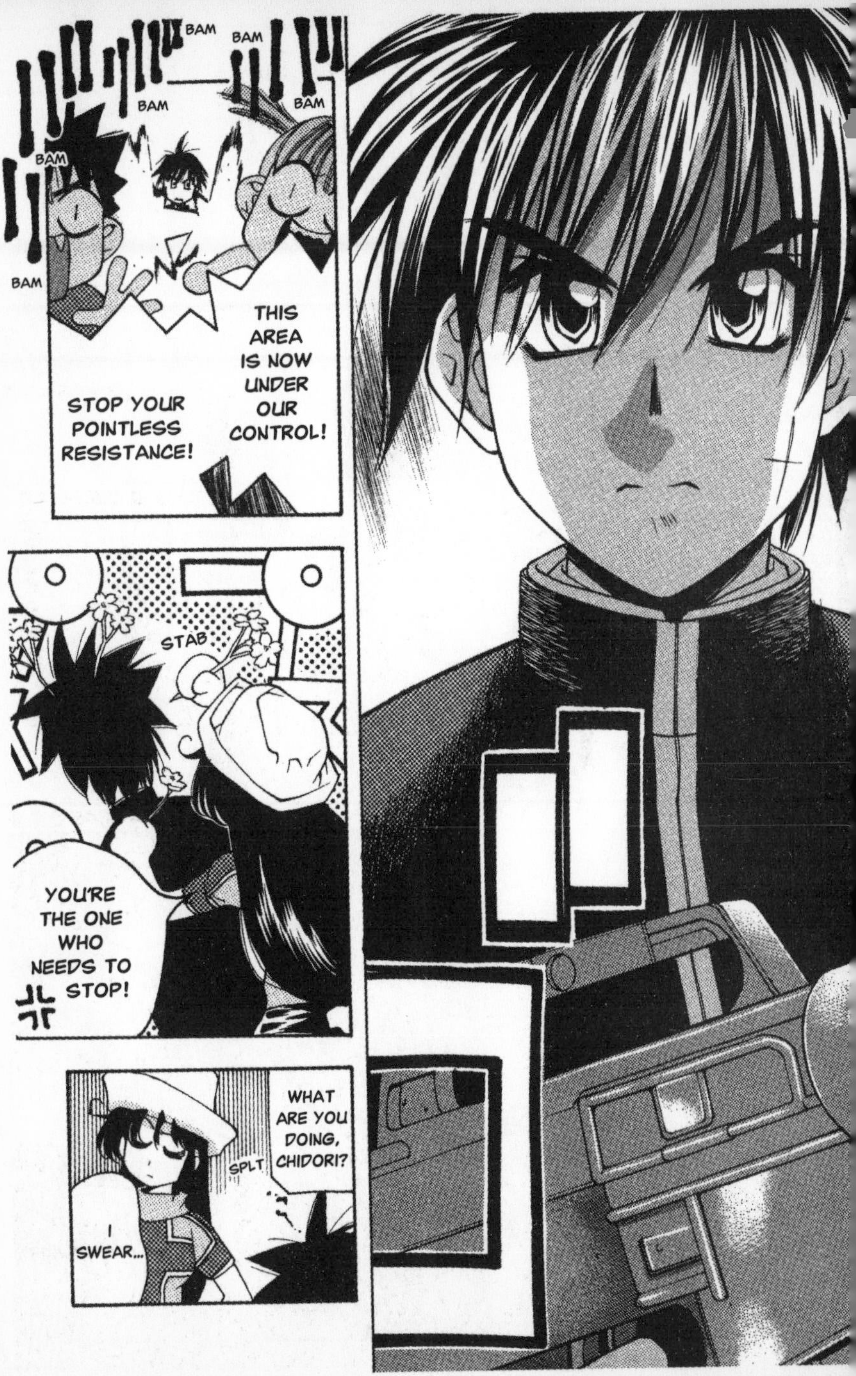
BAM
BAM
BAM
BAM
BAM
BAM
THIS AREA IS NOW UNDER OUR CONTROL!
STOP YOUR POINTLESS RESISTANCE!
STAB
YOU'RE THE ONE WHO NEEDS TO STOP!
WHAT ARE YOU DOING, CHIDORI?
SPLT
I SWEAR...

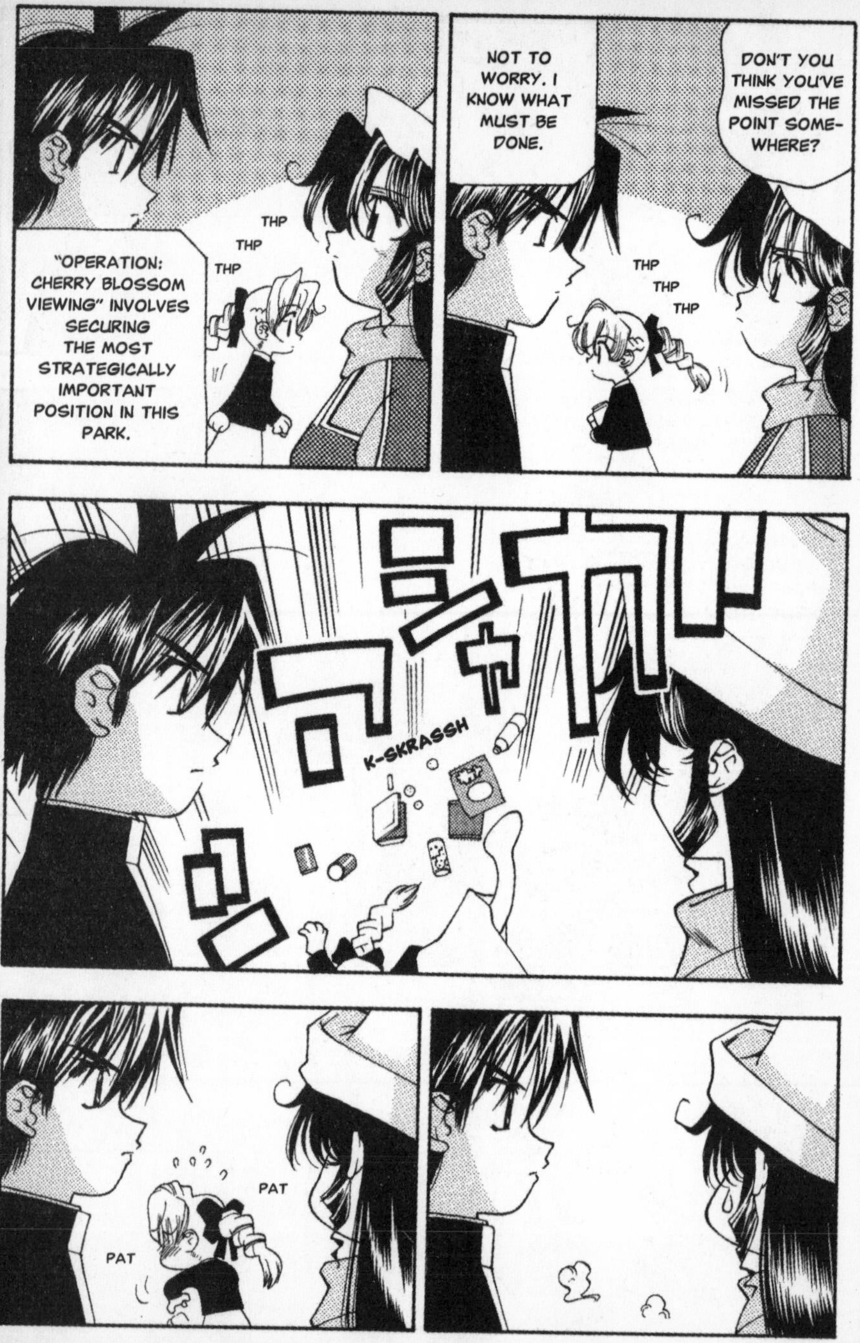
DON'T YOU THINK YOU'VE MISSED THE POINT SOME-WHERE?
NOT TO WORRY. I KNOW WHAT MUST BE DONE.
THP
THP
THP
THP
THP
THP
"OPERATION: CHERRY BLOSSOM VIEWING" INVOLVES SECURING THE MOST STRATEGICALLY IMPORTANT POSITION IN THIS PARK.
K-SKRASSH
PAT
PAT

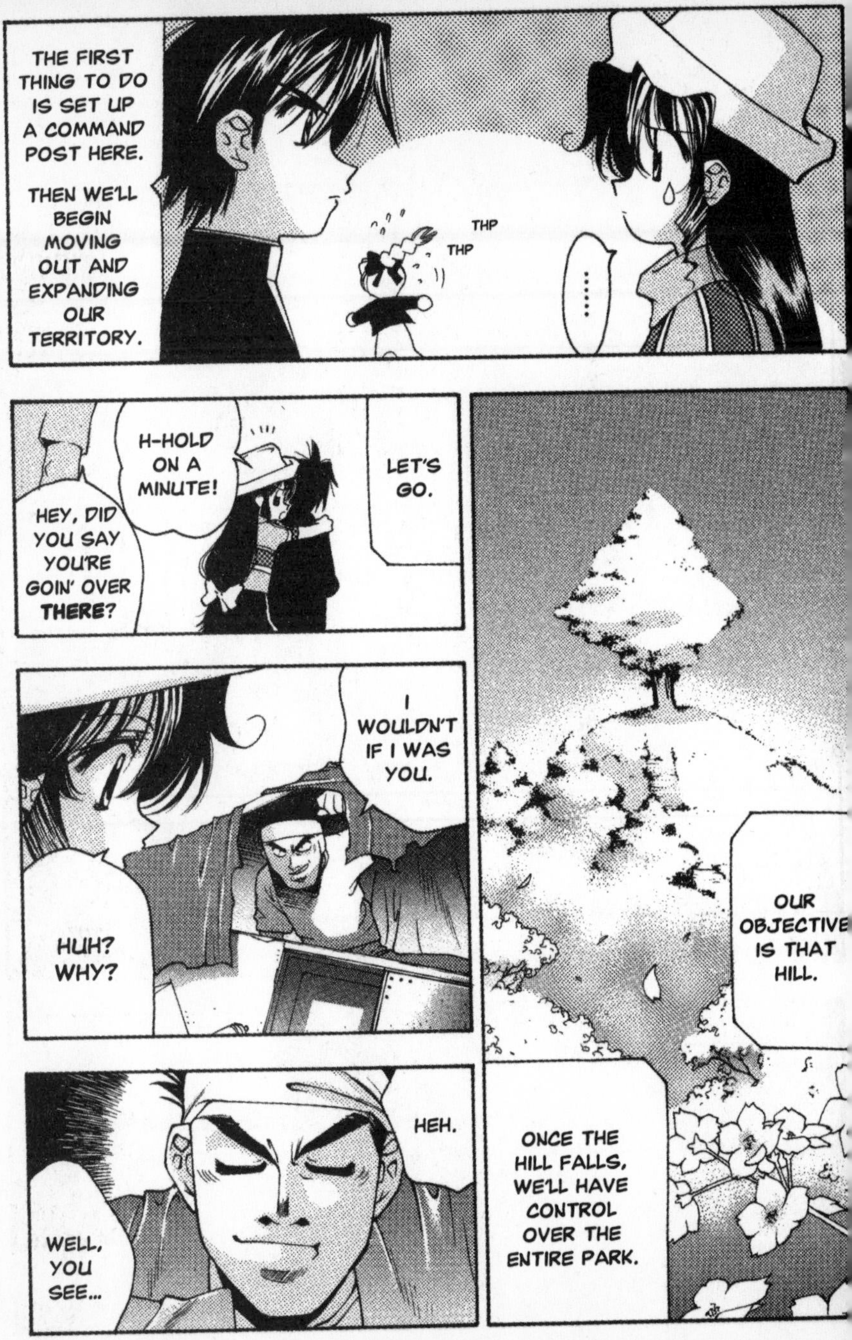
THE FIRST THING TO DO IS SET UP A COMMAND POST HERE.
THEN WE'LL BEGIN MOVING OUT AND EXPANDING OUR TERRITORY.
THP
THP
......
OUR OBJECTIVE IS THAT HILL.
ONCE THE HILL FALLS, WE'LL HAVE CONTROL OVER THE ENTIRE PARK.
LET'S GO.
H-HOLD ON A MINUTE!
HEY, DID YOU SAY YOU'RE GOIN' OVER **THERE**?
I WOULDN'T IF I WAS YOU.
HUH? WHY?
HEH.
WELL, YOU SEE...

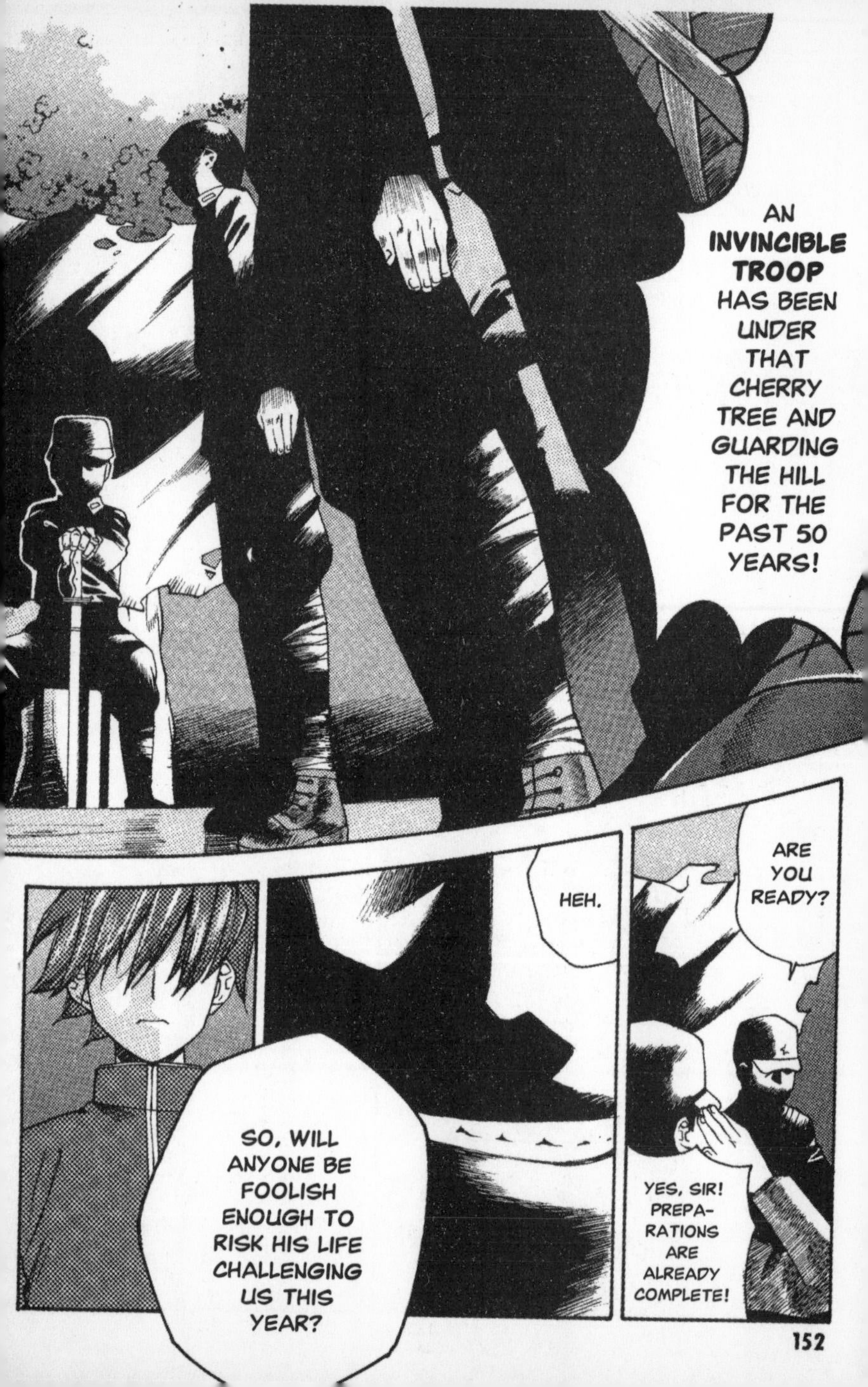
AN **INVINCIBLE TROOP** HAS BEEN UNDER THAT CHERRY TREE AND GUARDING THE HILL FOR THE PAST 50 YEARS!
ARE YOU READY?
YES, SIR! PREPA-RATIONS ARE ALREADY COMPLETE!
HEH.
SO, WILL ANYONE BE FOOLISH ENOUGH TO RISK HIS LIFE CHALLENGING US THIS YEAR?

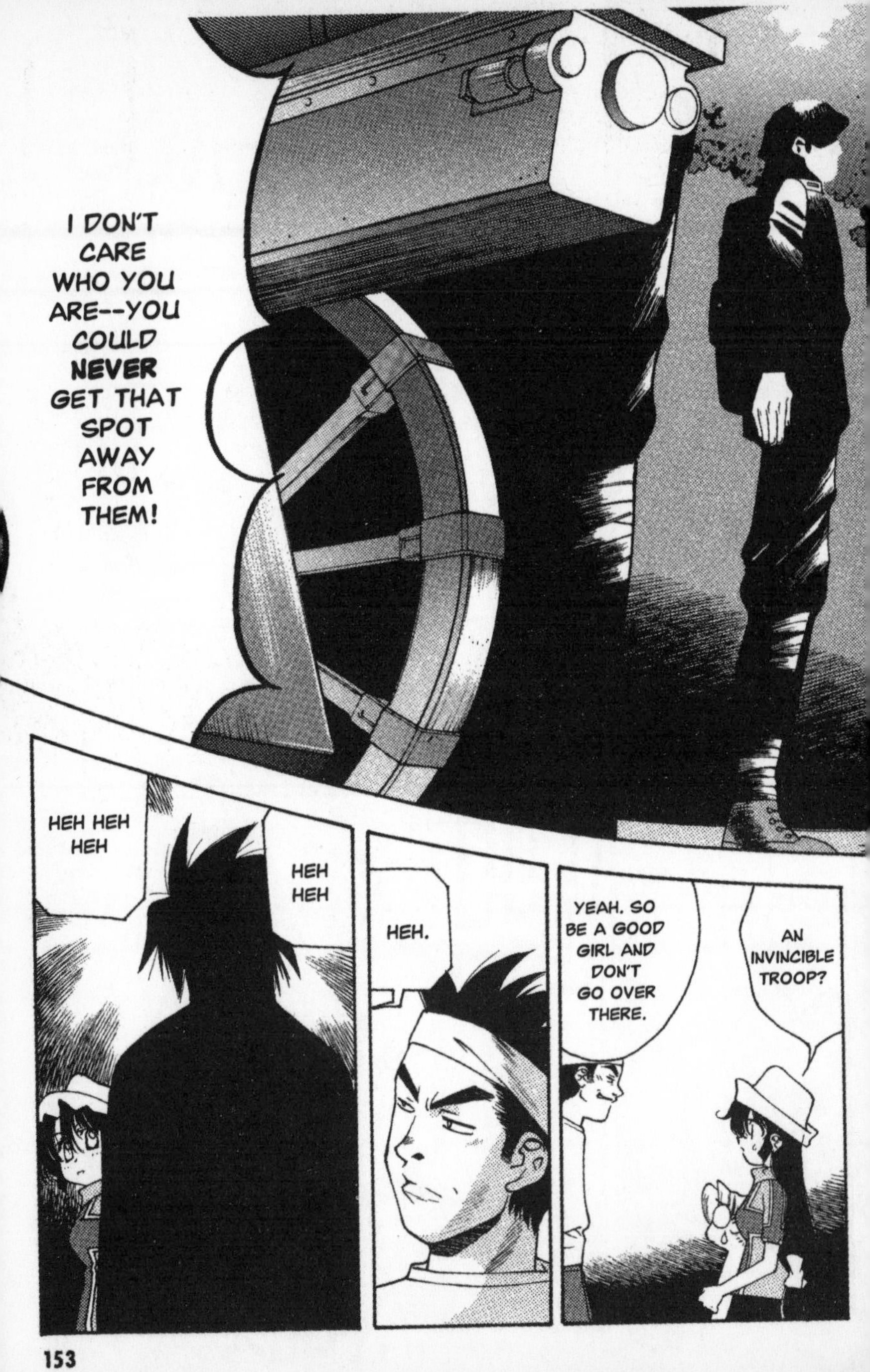
I DON'T CARE WHO YOU ARE--YOU COULD NEVER GET THAT SPOT AWAY FROM THEM!
AN INVINCIBLE TROOP?
YEAH. SO BE A GOOD GIRL AND DON'T GO OVER THERE.
HEH.
HEH HEH
HEH HEH HEH

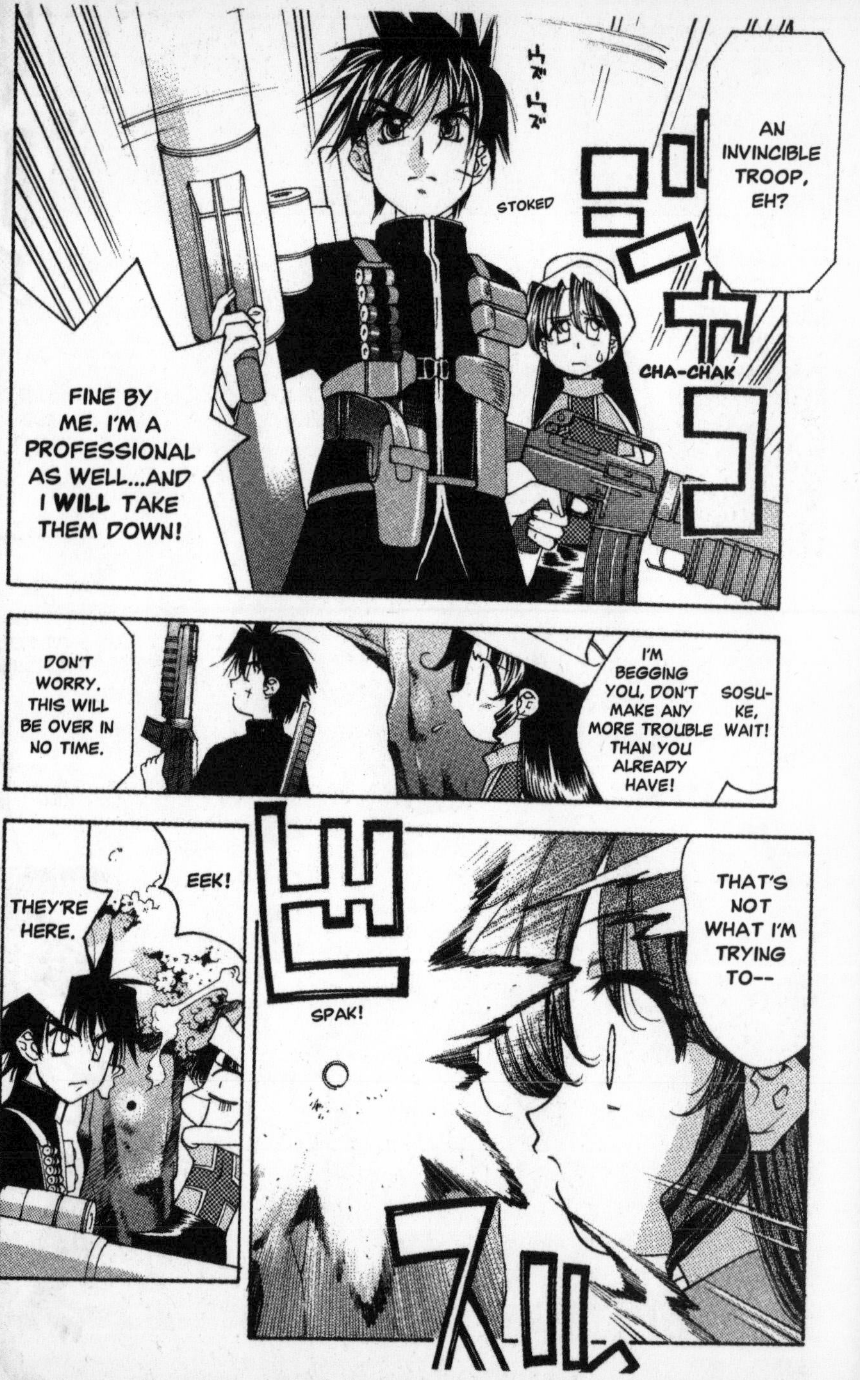
AN INVINCIBLE TROOP, EH?
STOKED
CHA-CHAK
FINE BY ME. I'M A PROFESSIONAL AS WELL...AND I **WILL** TAKE THEM DOWN!
SOSU-KE, WAIT!
I'M BEGGING YOU, DON'T MAKE ANY MORE TROUBLE THAN YOU ALREADY HAVE!
DON'T WORRY. THIS WILL BE OVER IN NO TIME.
THAT'S NOT WHAT I'M TRYING TO--
SPAK!
EEK!
THEY'RE HERE.

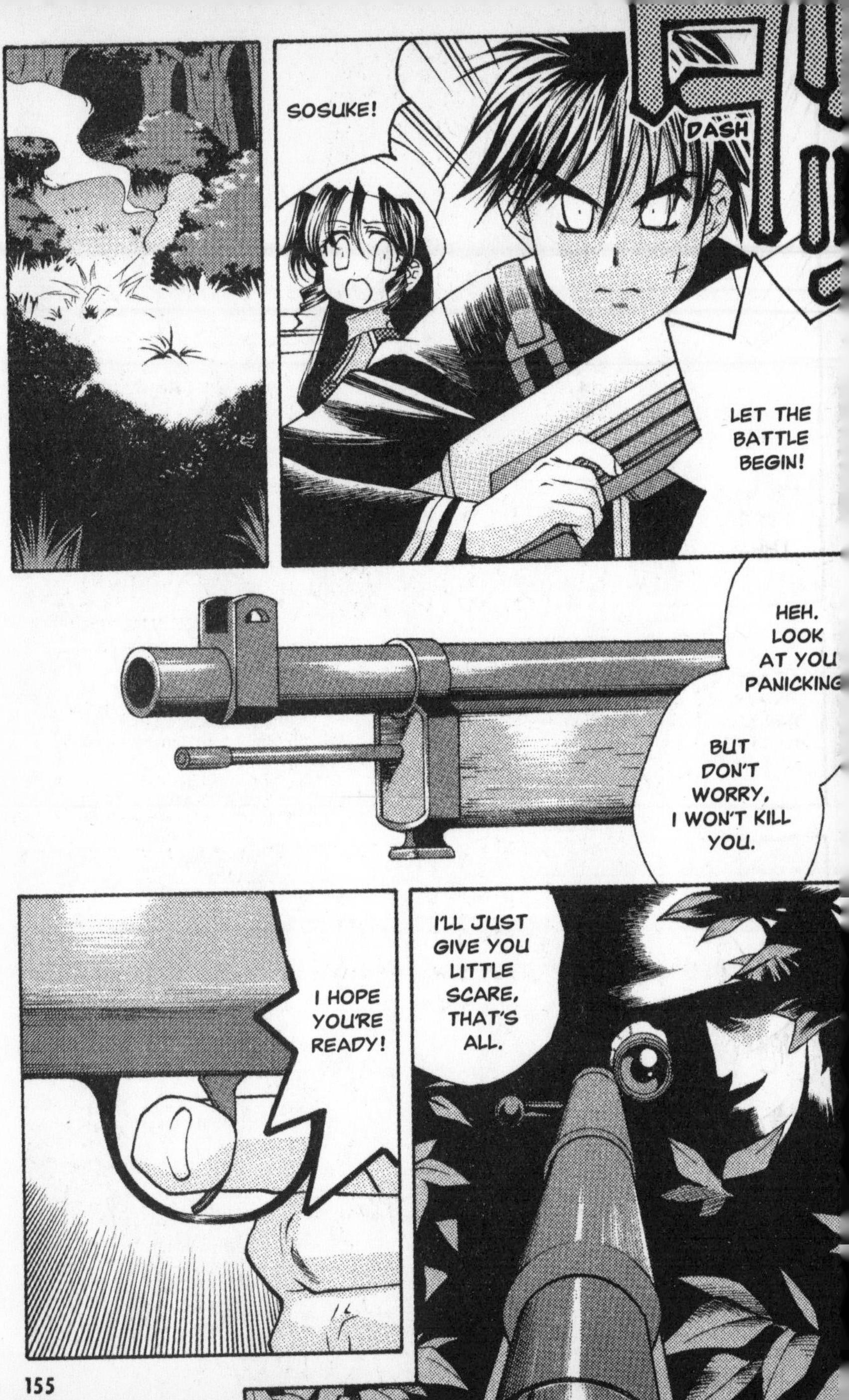
DASH
SOSUKE!
LET THE BATTLE BEGIN!
HEH. LOOK AT YOU PANICKING
BUT DON'T WORRY, I WON'T KILL YOU.
I'LL JUST GIVE YOU LITTLE SCARE, THAT'S ALL.
I HOPE YOU'RE READY!

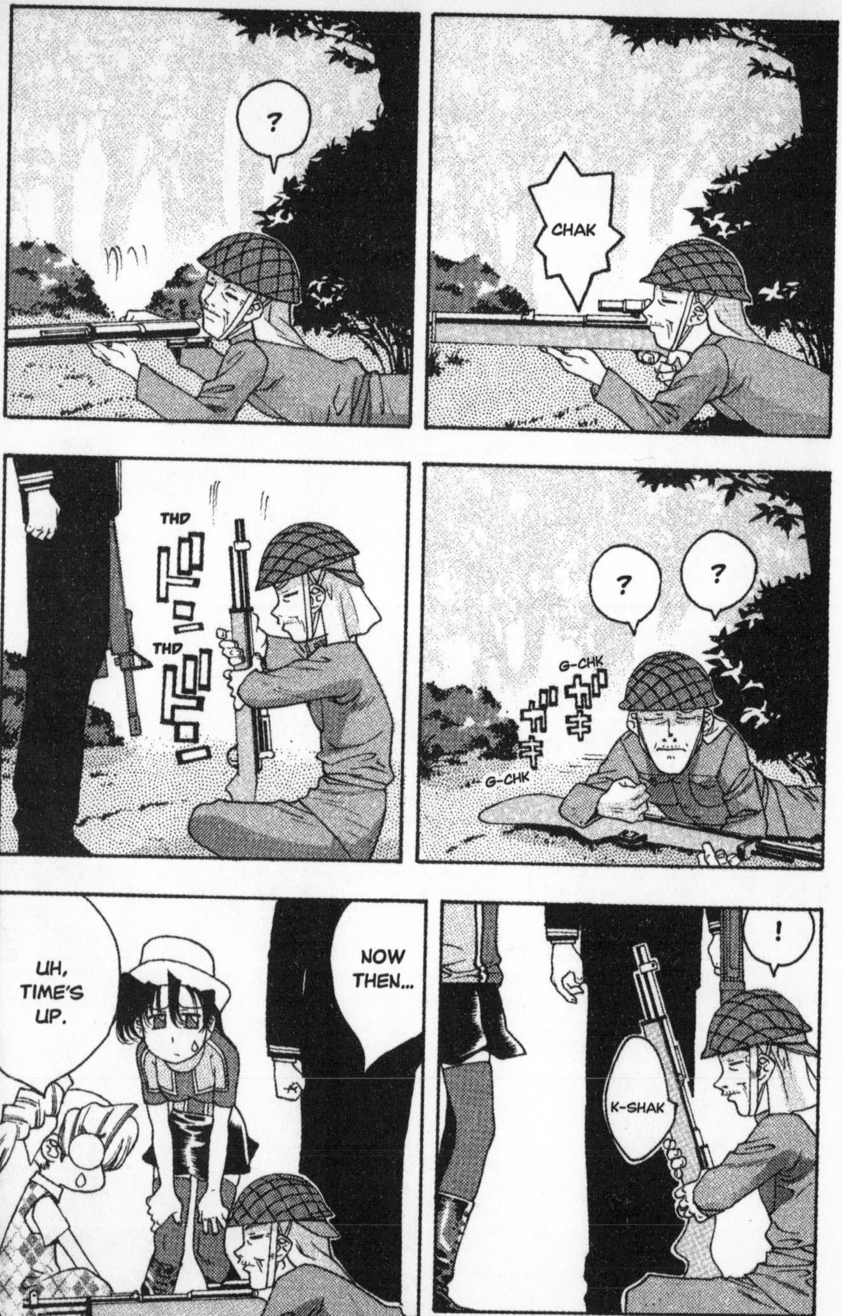
CHAK
?
?
?
G-CHK
G-CHK
THD
THD
!
K-SHAK
NOW THEN...
UH, TIME'S UP.

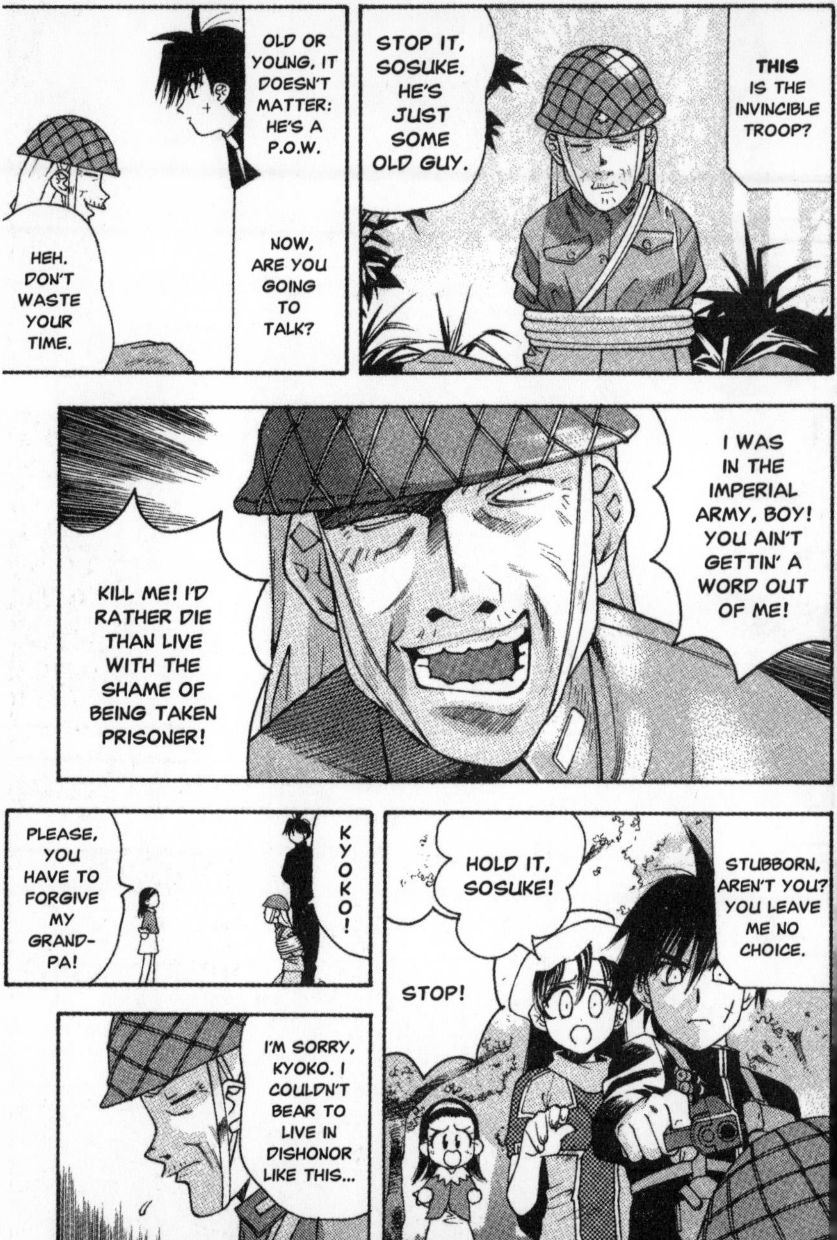

THIS IS THE INVINCIBLE TROOP?
STOP IT, SOSUKE. HE'S JUST SOME OLD GUY.
OLD OR YOUNG, IT DOESN'T MATTER: HE'S A P.O.W.
NOW, ARE YOU GOING TO TALK?
HEH. DON'T WASTE YOUR TIME.
I WAS IN THE IMPERIAL ARMY, BOY! YOU AIN'T GETTIN' A WORD OUT OF ME!
KILL ME! I'D RATHER DIE THAN LIVE WITH THE SHAME OF BEING TAKEN PRISONER!
STUBBORN, AREN'T YOU? YOU LEAVE ME NO CHOICE.
HOLD IT, SOSUKE!
STOP!
KYOKO!
PLEASE, YOU HAVE TO FORGIVE MY GRAND-PA!
I'M SORRY, KYOKO. I COULDN'T BEAR TO LIVE IN DISHONOR LIKE THIS...

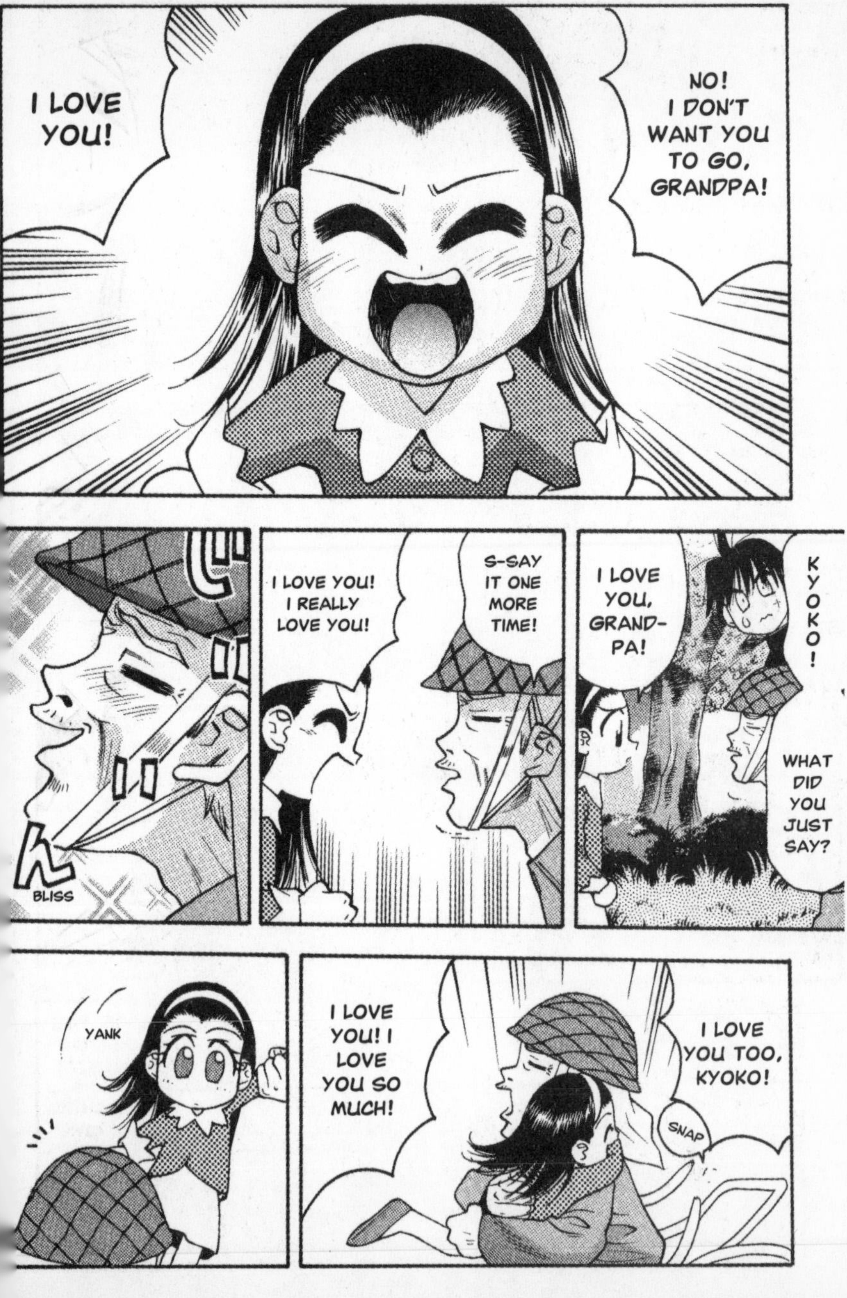
NO! I DON'T WANT YOU TO GO, GRANDPA!
I LOVE YOU!
KYOKO!
I LOVE YOU, GRAND-PA!
WHAT DID YOU JUST SAY?
S-SAY IT ONE MORE TIME!
I LOVE YOU! I REALLY LOVE YOU!
BLISS
I LOVE YOU TOO, KYOKO!
SNAP
I LOVE YOU! I LOVE YOU SO MUCH!
YANK

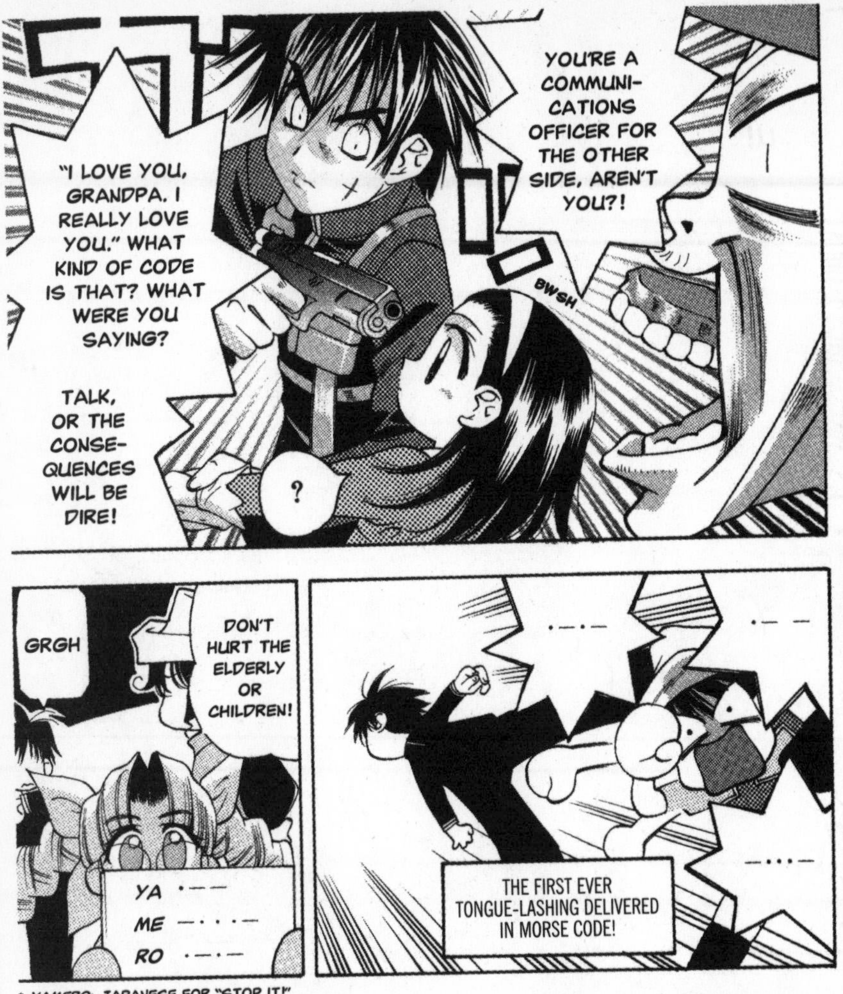
YOU'RE A COMMUNICATIONS OFFICER FOR THE OTHER SIDE, AREN'T YOU?!
BWSH
"I LOVE YOU, GRANDPA. I REALLY LOVE YOU." WHAT KIND OF CODE IS THAT? WHAT WERE YOU SAYING?
TALK, OR THE CONSEQUENCES WILL BE DIRE!
?
THE FIRST EVER TONGUE-LASHING DELIVERED IN MORSE CODE!
DON'T HURT THE ELDERLY OR CHILDREN!
GRGH
YA
ME
RO

* YAMERO: JAPANESE FOR "STOP IT!"

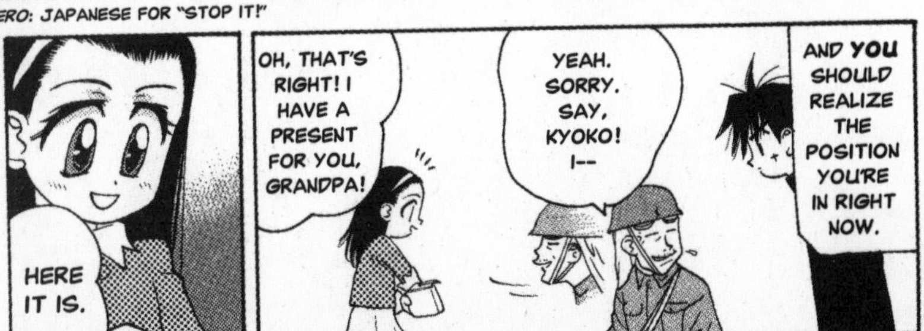
AND YOU SHOULD REALIZE THE POSITION YOU'RE IN RIGHT NOW.
YEAH. SORRY. SAY, KYOKO! I--
OH, THAT'S RIGHT! I HAVE A PRESENT FOR YOU, GRANDPA!
HERE IT IS.

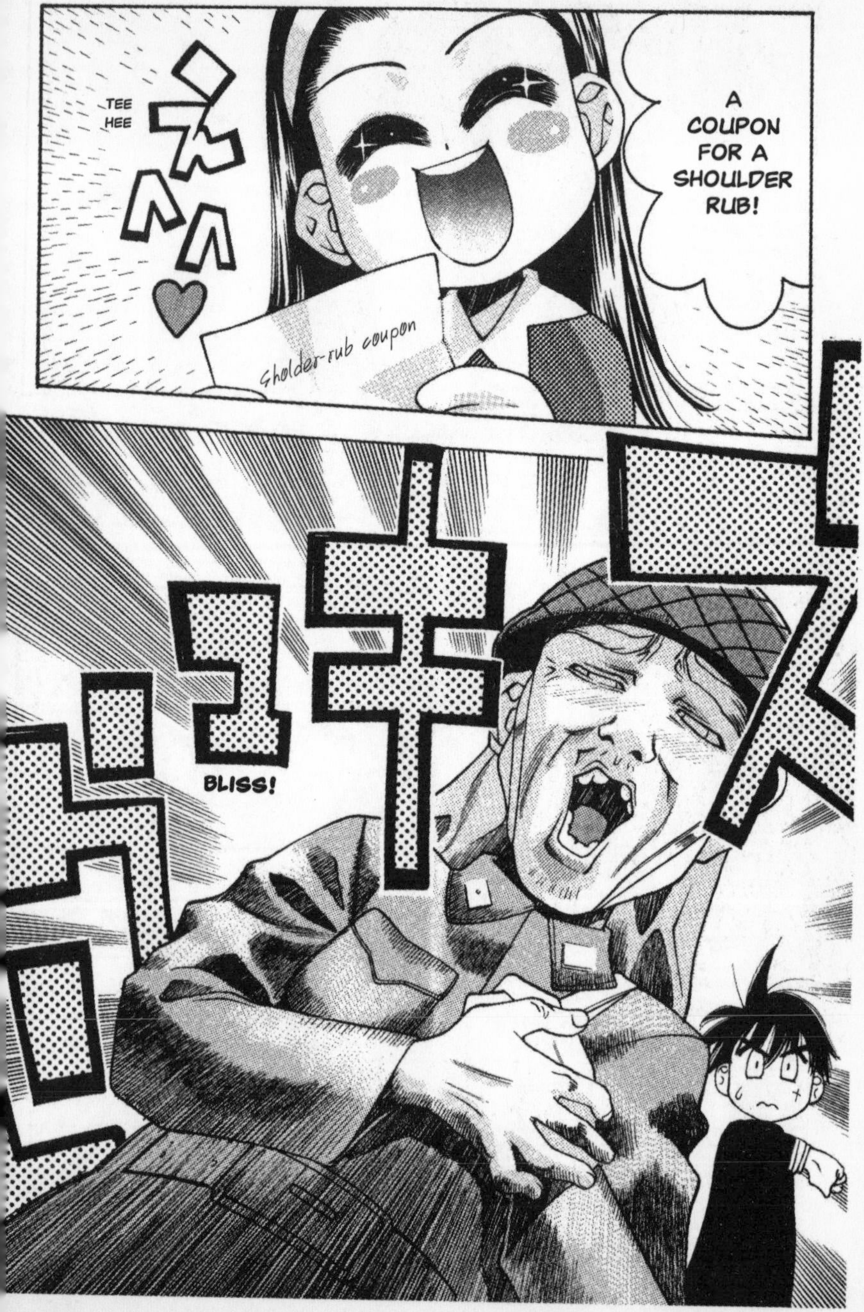
A COUPON FOR A SHOULDER RUB!
TEE HEE
Sholder-rub coupon
BLISS!

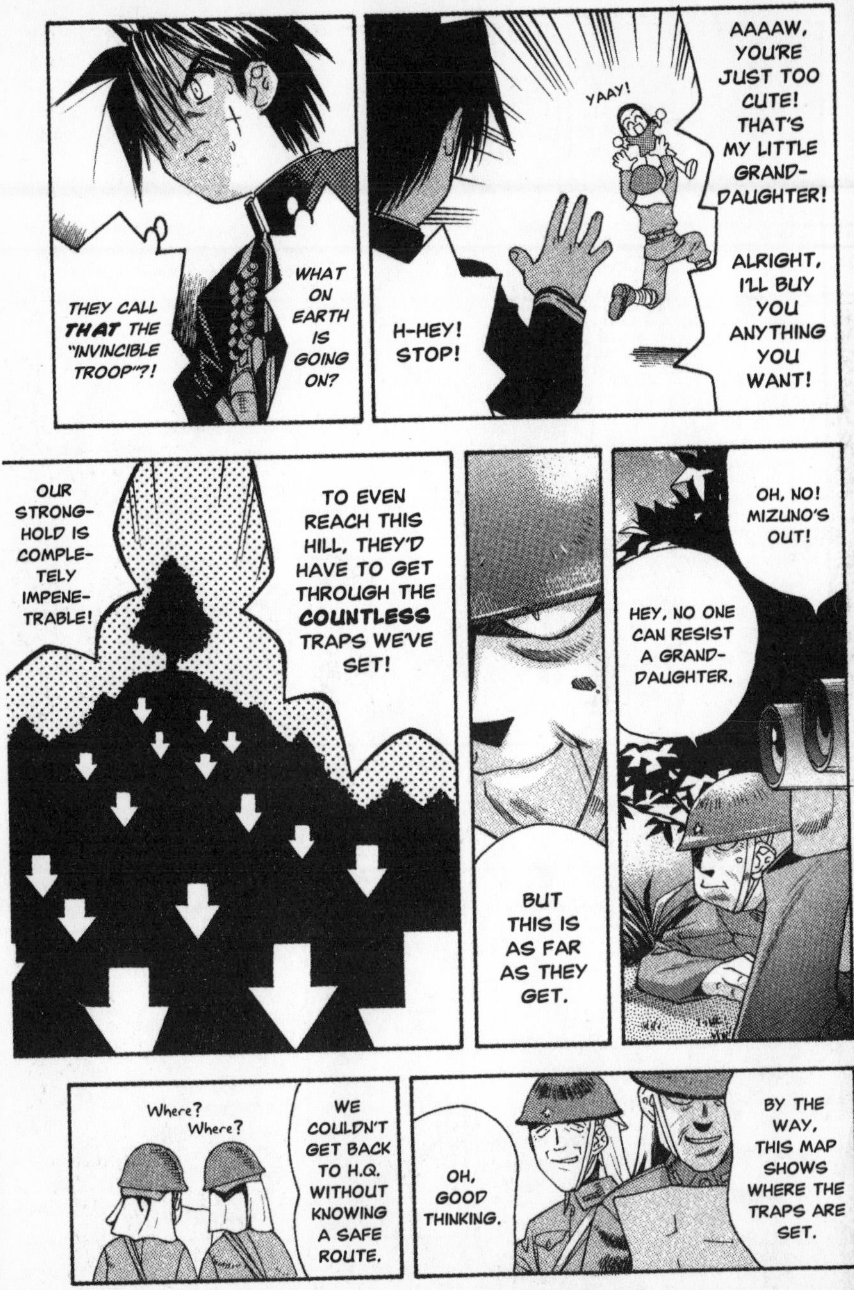
AAAAW, YOU'RE JUST TOO CUTE! THAT'S MY LITTLE GRAND-DAUGHTER!
YAAY!
ALRIGHT, I'LL BUY YOU ANYTHING YOU WANT!
H-HEY! STOP!
WHAT ON EARTH IS GOING ON?
THEY CALL THAT THE "INVINCIBLE TROOP"?!
OH, NO! MIZUNO'S OUT!
HEY, NO ONE CAN RESIST A GRAND-DAUGHTER.
BUT THIS IS AS FAR AS THEY GET.
TO EVEN REACH THIS HILL, THEY'D HAVE TO GET THROUGH THE COUNTLESS TRAPS WE'VE SET!
OUR STRONG-HOLD IS COMPLETE-TELY IMPENE-TRABLE!
BY THE WAY, THIS MAP SHOWS WHERE THE TRAPS ARE SET.
OH, GOOD THINKING.
WE COULDN'T GET BACK TO H.Q. WITHOUT KNOWING A SAFE ROUTE.
Where? Where?

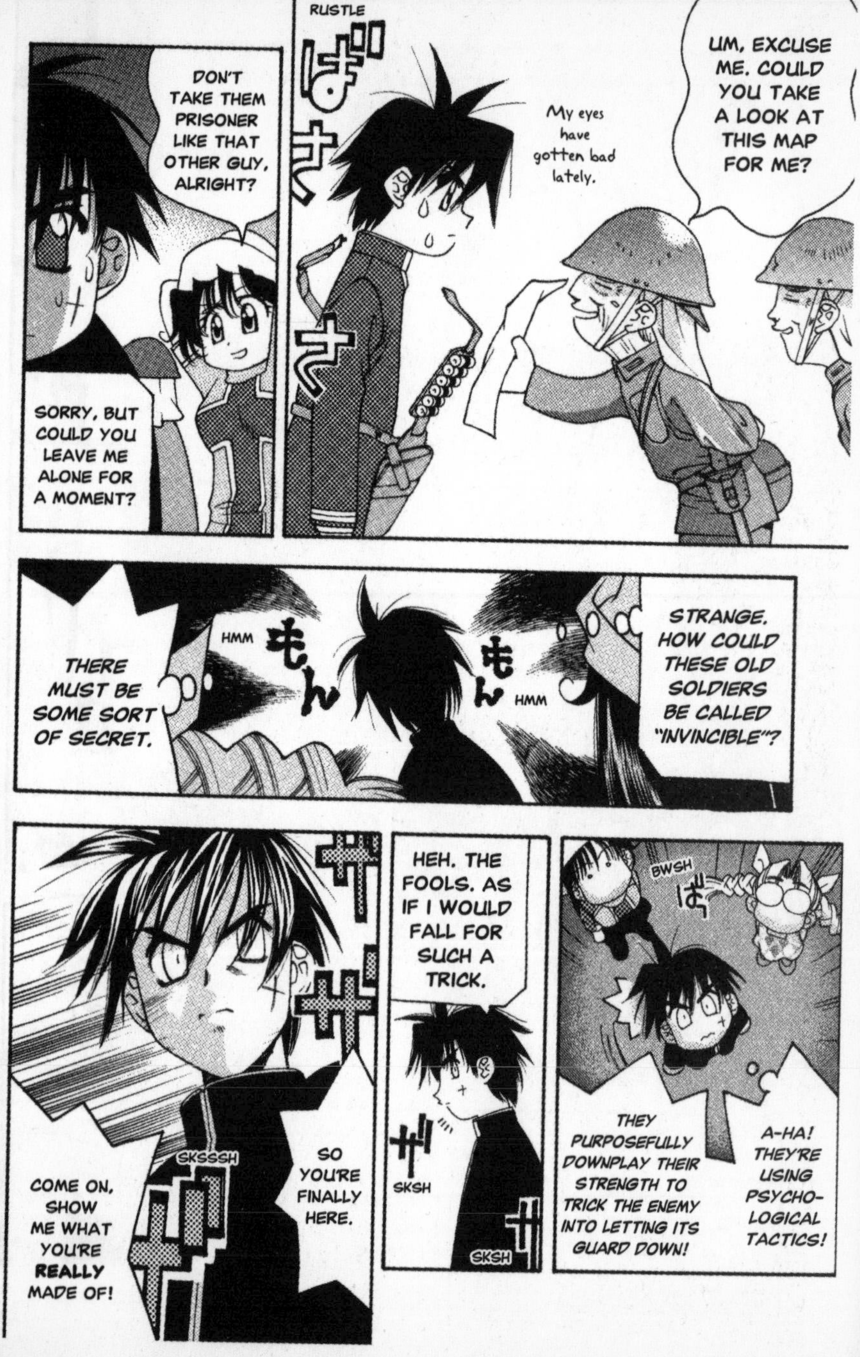

UM, EXCUSE ME. COULD YOU TAKE A LOOK AT THIS MAP FOR ME?
My eyes have gotten bad lately.
RUSTLE
DON'T TAKE THEM PRISONER LIKE THAT OTHER GUY, ALRIGHT?
SORRY, BUT COULD YOU LEAVE ME ALONE FOR A MOMENT?
STRANGE. HOW COULD THESE OLD SOLDIERS BE CALLED "INVINCIBLE"?
HMM
HMM
THERE MUST BE SOME SORT OF SECRET.
BWSH
A-HA! THEY'RE USING PSYCHO-LOGICAL TACTICS!
THEY PURPOSEFULLY DOWNPLAY THEIR STRENGTH TO TRICK THE ENEMY INTO LETTING ITS GUARD DOWN!
HEH. THE FOOLS. AS IF I WOULD FALL FOR SUCH A TRICK.
SKSH
SKSH
SO YOU'RE FINALLY HERE.
SKSSSH
COME ON, SHOW ME WHAT YOU'RE REALLY MADE OF!

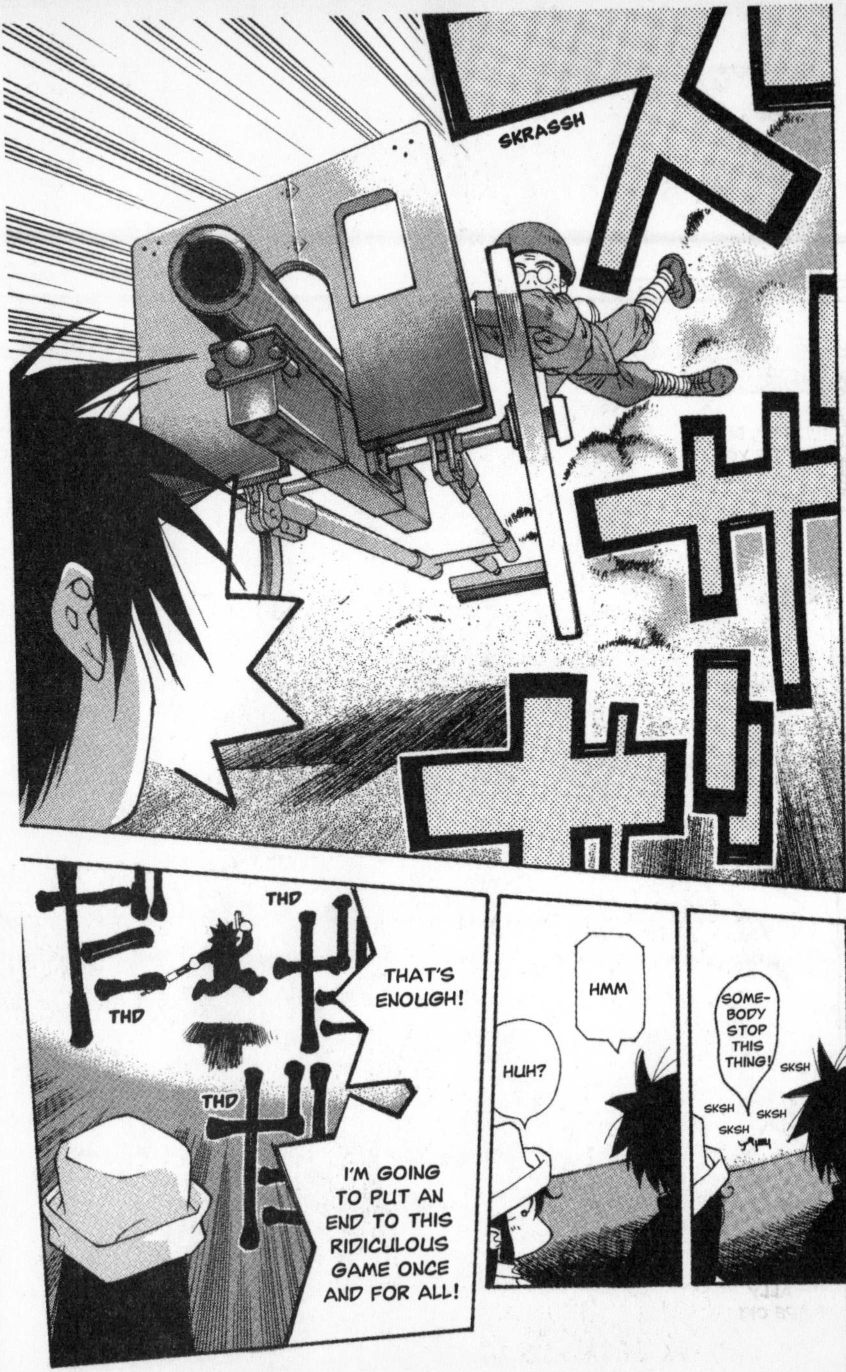

SKRASSH
THD
THD
THD
THAT'S ENOUGH!
I'M GOING TO PUT AN END TO THIS RIDICULOUS GAME ONCE AND FOR ALL!
HMM
HUH?
SOME-BODY STOP THIS THING!
SKSH
SKSH
SKSH
SKSH

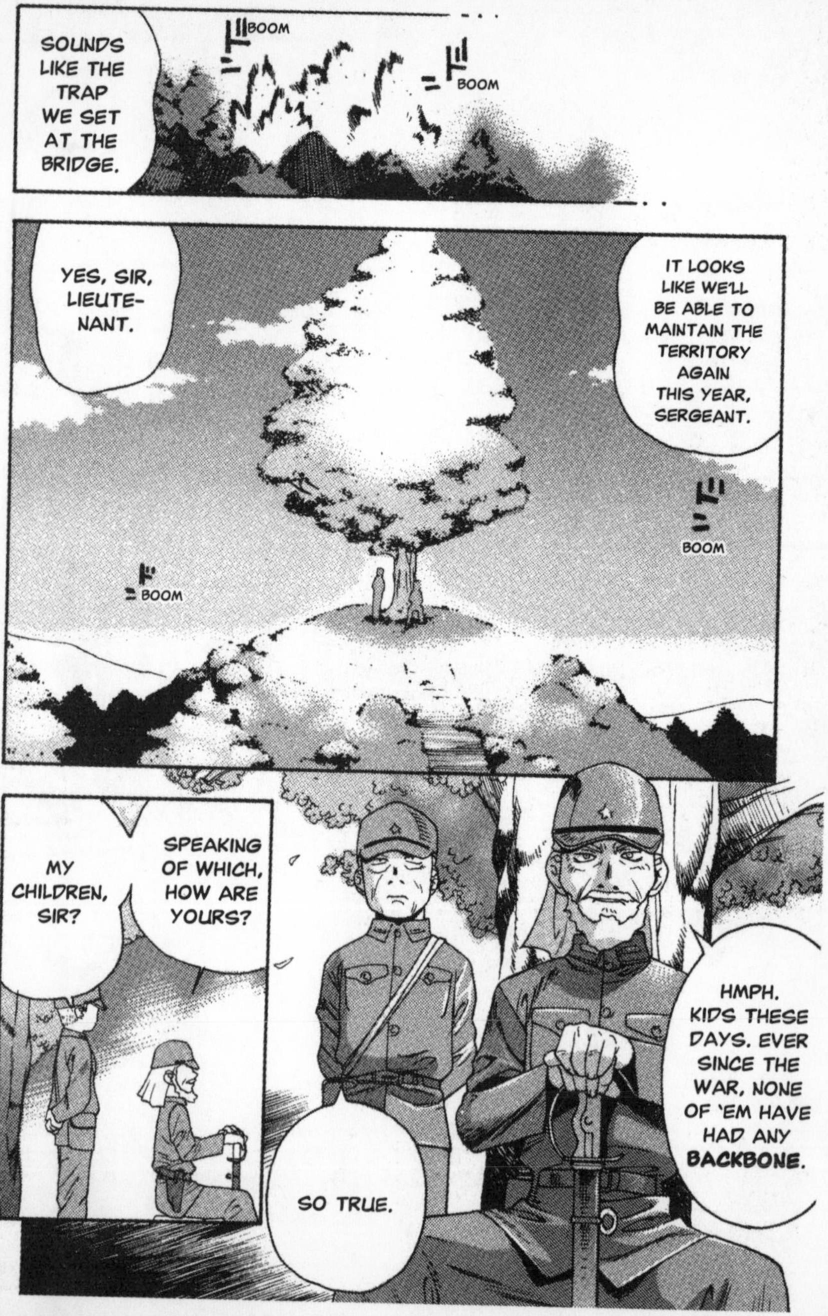

SOUNDS LIKE THE TRAP WE SET AT THE BRIDGE.
BOOM
BOOM
IT LOOKS LIKE WE'LL BE ABLE TO MAINTAIN THE TERRITORY AGAIN THIS YEAR, SERGEANT.
YES, SIR, LIEUTE-NANT.
BOOM
BOOM
SPEAKING OF WHICH, HOW ARE YOURS?
MY CHILDREN, SIR?
HMPH. KIDS THESE DAYS. EVER SINCE THE WAR, NONE OF 'EM HAVE HAD ANY BACKBONE.
SO TRUE.

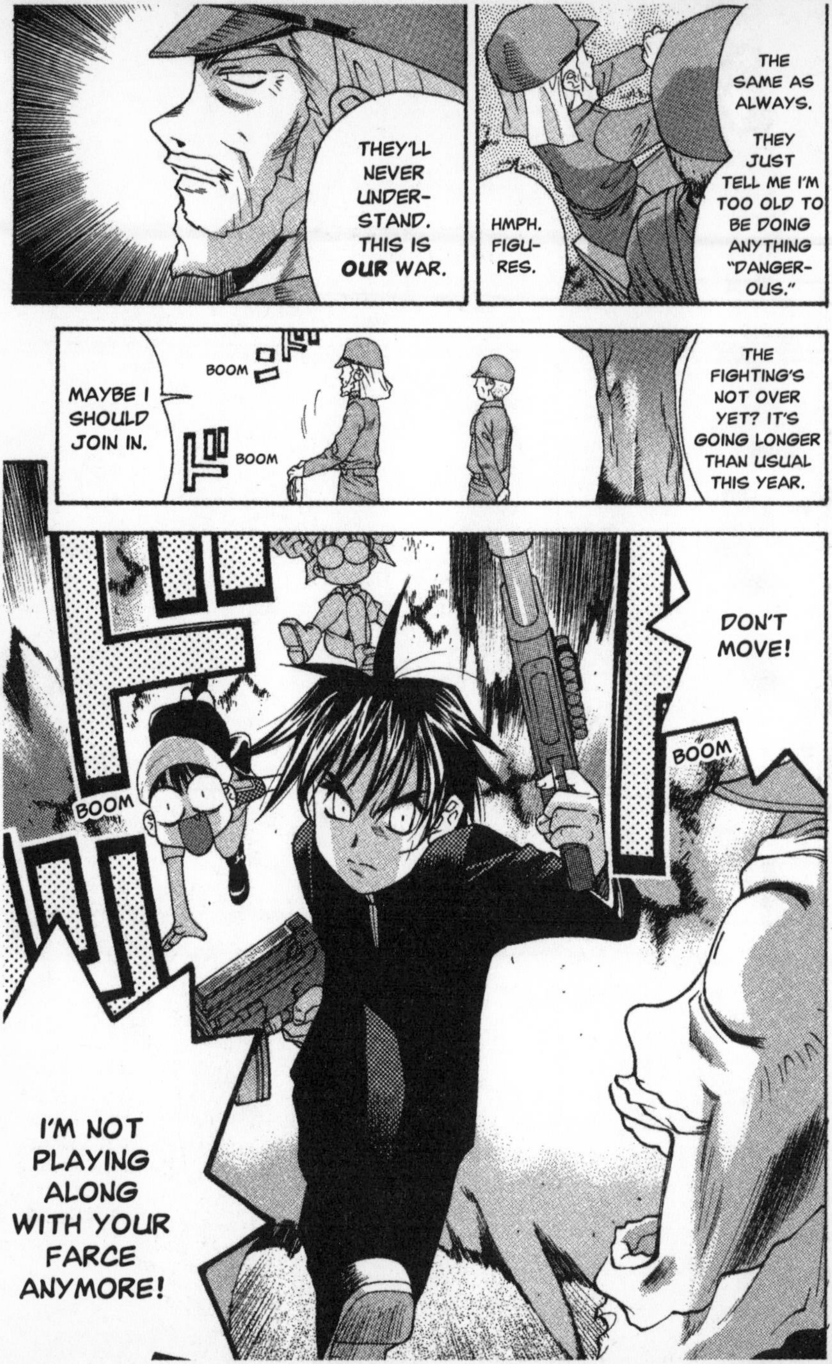
THE SAME AS ALWAYS.
THEY JUST TELL ME I'M TOO OLD TO BE DOING ANYTHING "DANGER-OUS."
HMPH. FIGU-RES.
THEY'LL NEVER UNDER-STAND. THIS IS **OUR** WAR.
THE FIGHTING'S NOT OVER YET? IT'S GOING LONGER THAN USUAL THIS YEAR.
BOOM
BOOM
MAYBE I SHOULD JOIN IN.
DON'T MOVE!
BOOM
BOOM
I'M NOT PLAYING ALONG WITH YOUR FARCE ANYMORE!

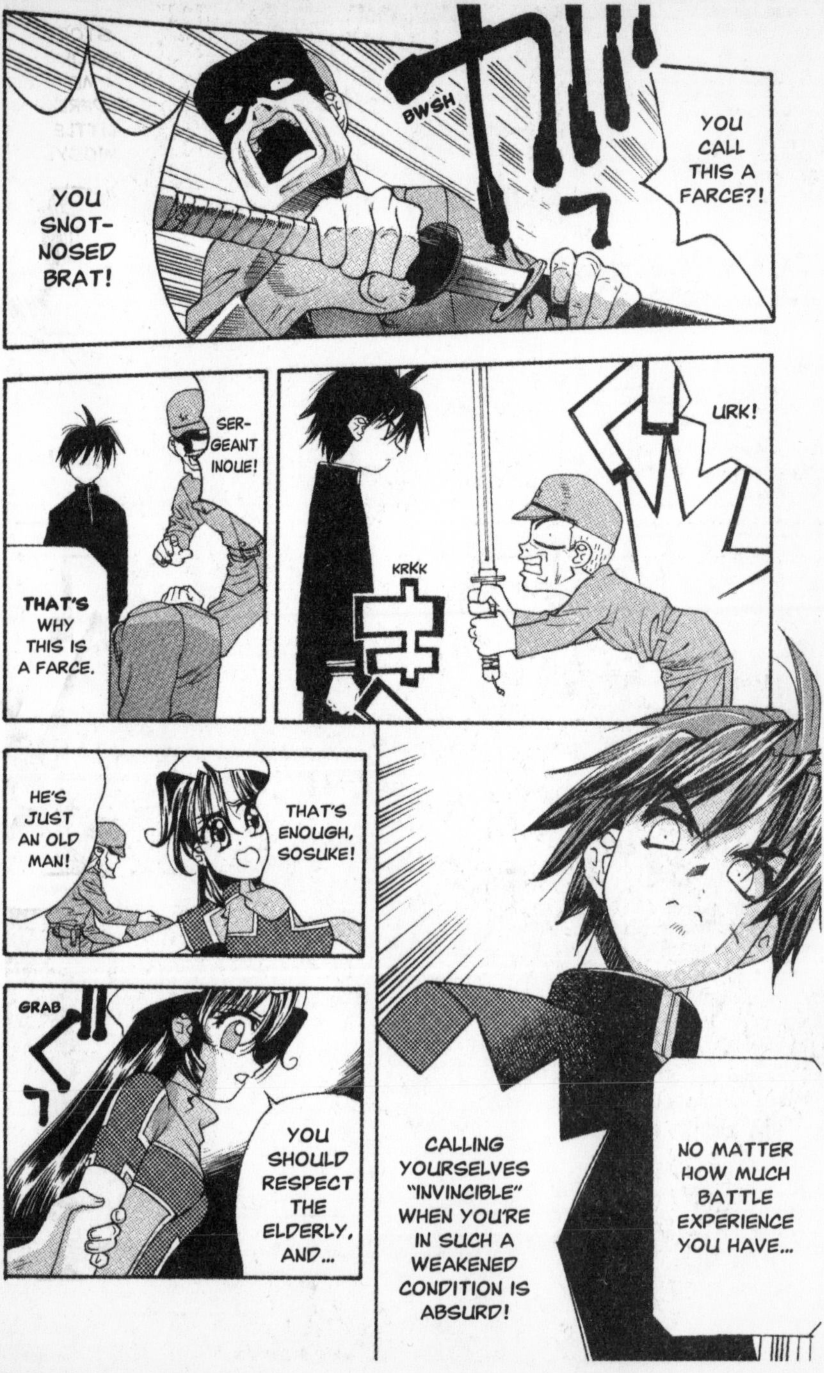

YOU CALL THIS A FARCE?!
BWSH
YOU SNOT-NOSED BRAT!
URK!
KRKK
SER-GEANT INOUE!
THAT'S WHY THIS IS A FARCE.
THAT'S ENOUGH, SOSUKE!
HE'S JUST AN OLD MAN!
NO MATTER HOW MUCH BATTLE EXPERIENCE YOU HAVE...
CALLING YOURSELVES "INVINCIBLE" WHEN YOU'RE IN SUCH A WEAKENED CONDITION IS ABSURD!
GRAB
YOU SHOULD RESPECT THE ELDERLY, AND...

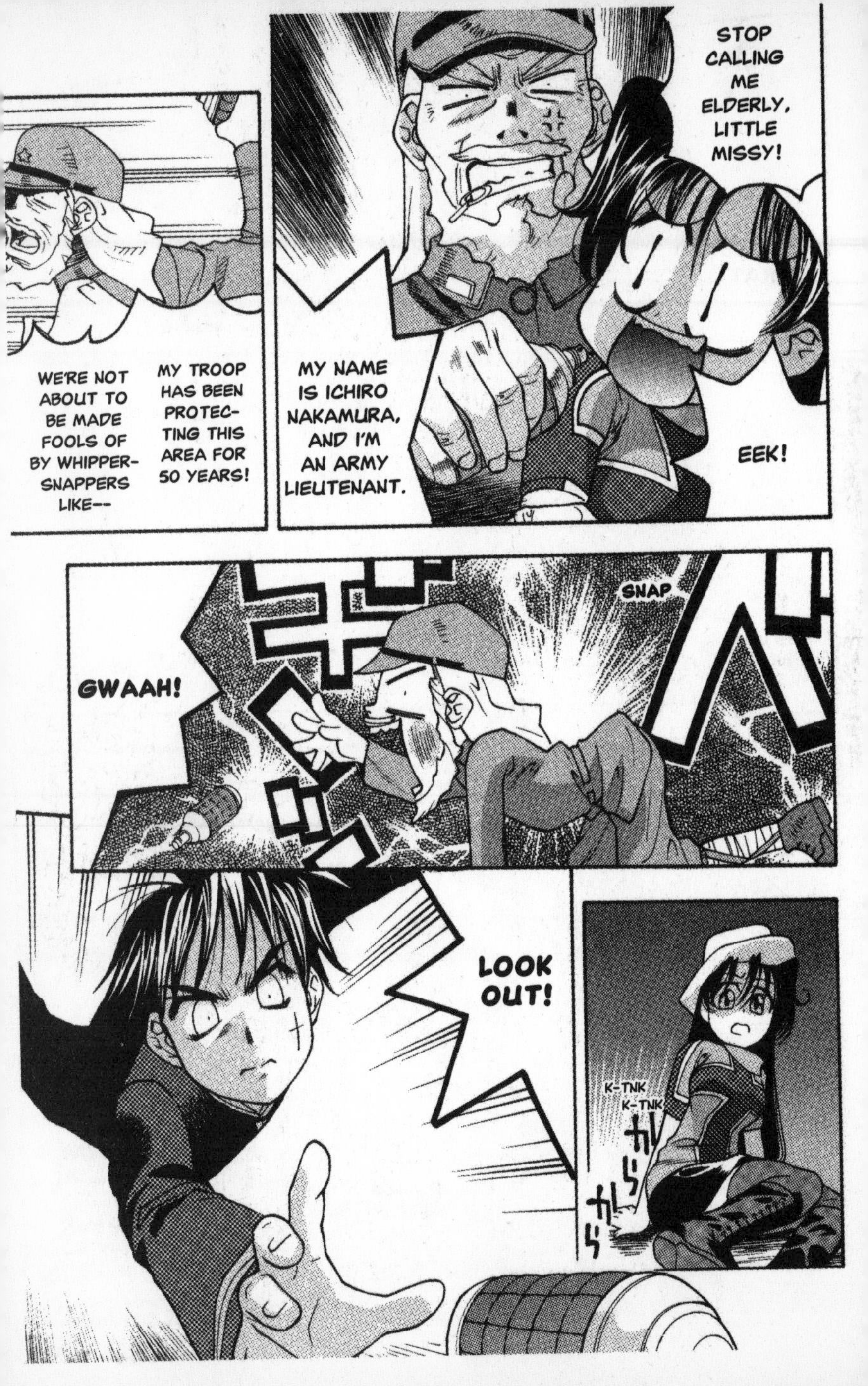
STOP CALLING ME ELDERLY, LITTLE MISSY!
EEK!
MY NAME IS ICHIRO NAKAMURA, AND I'M AN ARMY LIEUTENANT.
MY TROOP HAS BEEN PROTEC-TING THIS AREA FOR 50 YEARS!
WE'RE NOT ABOUT TO BE MADE FOOLS OF BY WHIPPER-SNAPPERS LIKE--
SNAP
GWAAH!
K-TNK
K-TNK
LOOK OUT!

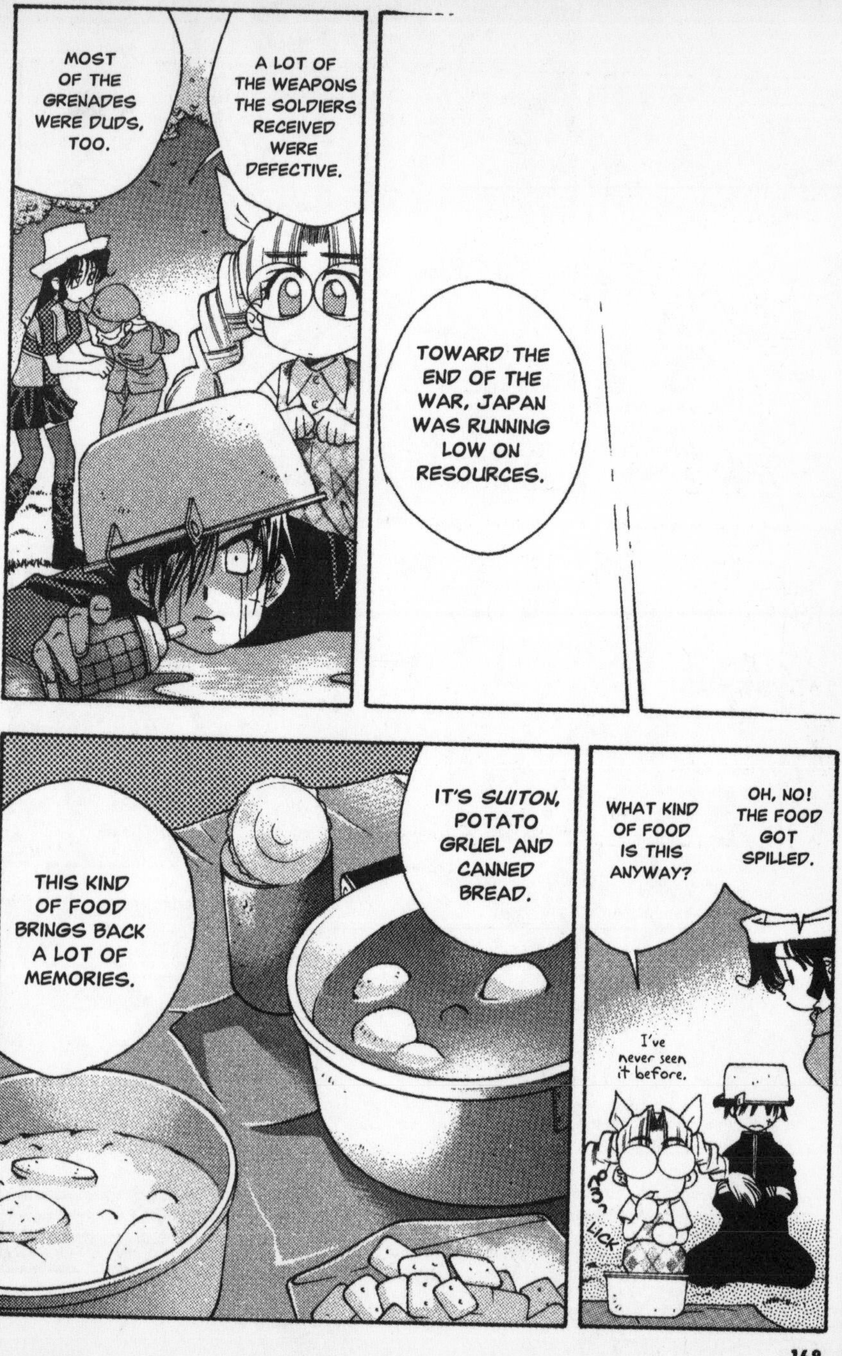
TOWARD THE END OF THE WAR, JAPAN WAS RUNNING LOW ON RESOURCES.
A LOT OF THE WEAPONS THE SOLDIERS RECEIVED WERE DEFECTIVE.
MOST OF THE GRENADES WERE DUDS, TOO.
OH, NO! THE FOOD GOT SPILLED.
WHAT KIND OF FOOD IS THIS ANYWAY?
I've never seen it before.
LICK
IT'S *SUITON*, POTATO GRUEL AND CANNED BREAD.
THIS KIND OF FOOD BRINGS BACK A LOT OF MEMORIES.

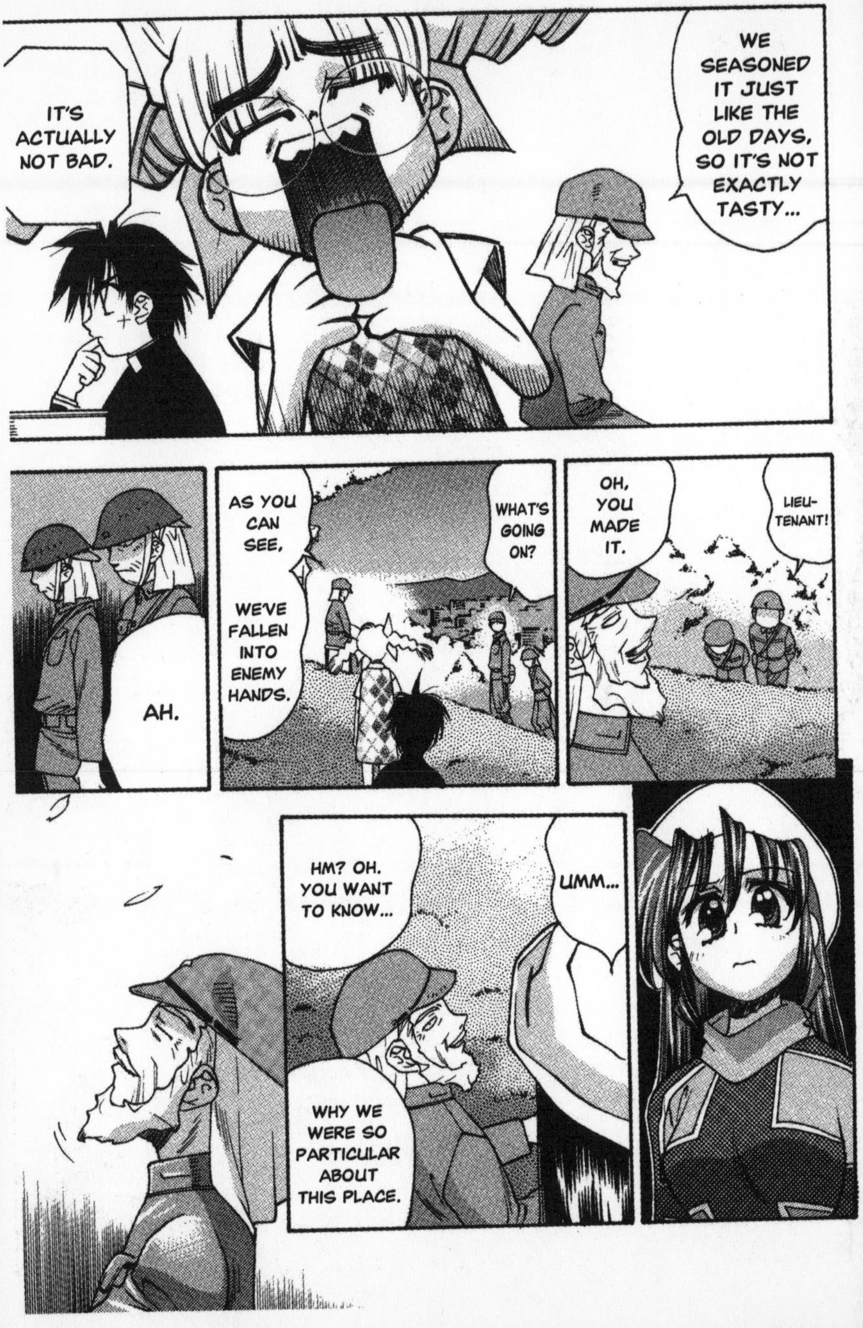
WE SEASONED IT JUST LIKE THE OLD DAYS, SO IT'S NOT EXACTLY TASTY...
IT'S ACTUALLY NOT BAD.
LIEU-TENANT!
OH, YOU MADE IT.
WHAT'S GOING ON?
AS YOU CAN SEE,
WE'VE FALLEN INTO ENEMY HANDS.
AH.
UMM...
HM? OH. YOU WANT TO KNOW...
WHY WE WERE SO PARTICULAR ABOUT THIS PLACE.

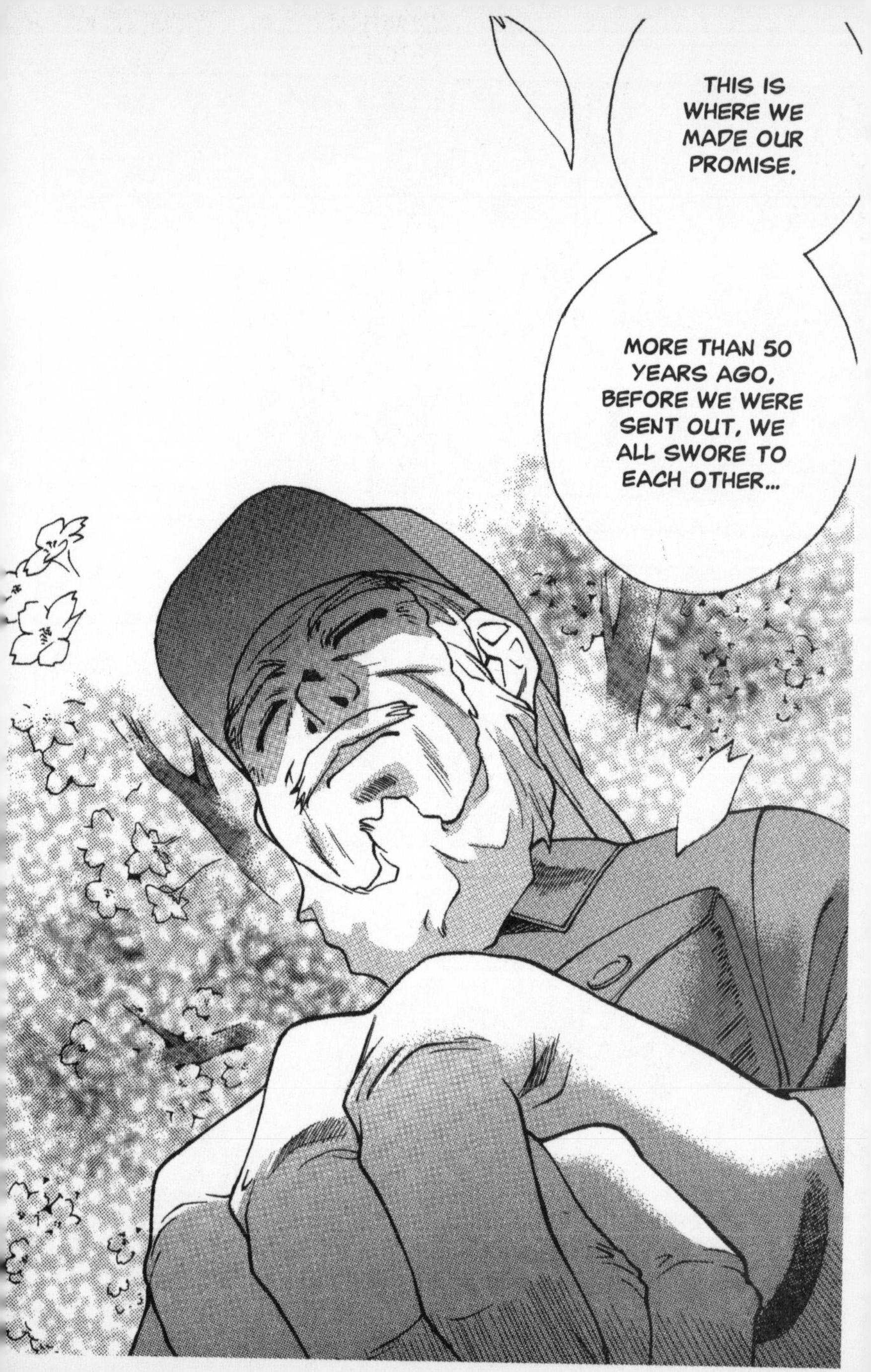
THIS IS WHERE WE MADE OUR PROMISE.
MORE THAN 50 YEARS AGO, BEFORE WE WERE SENT OUT, WE ALL SWORE TO EACH OTHER...

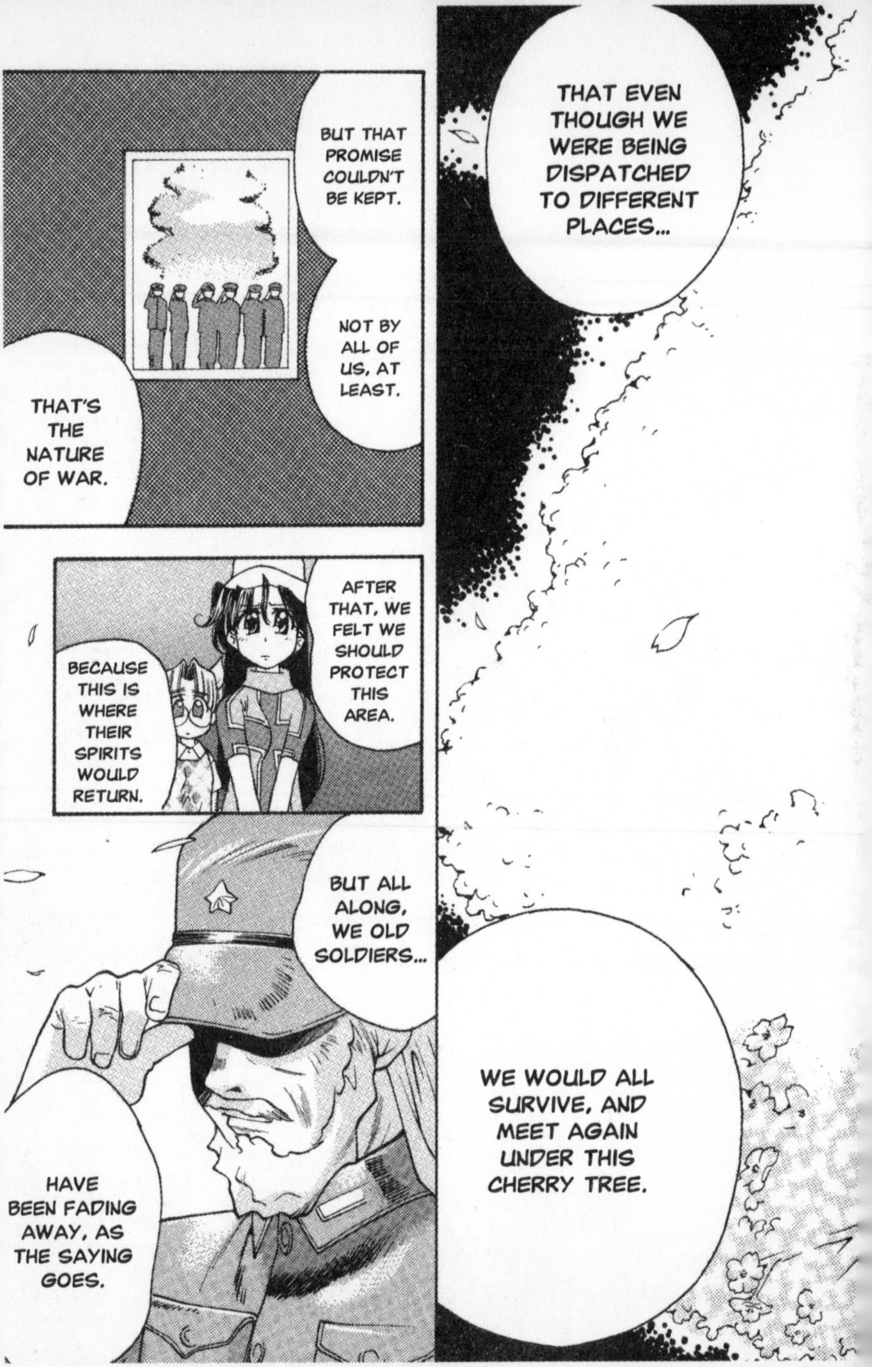
THAT EVEN THOUGH WE WERE BEING DISPATCHED TO DIFFERENT PLACES...
WE WOULD ALL SURVIVE, AND MEET AGAIN UNDER THIS CHERRY TREE.
BUT THAT PROMISE COULDN'T BE KEPT.
NOT BY ALL OF US, AT LEAST.
THAT'S THE NATURE OF WAR.
AFTER THAT, WE FELT WE SHOULD PROTECT THIS AREA.
BECAUSE THIS IS WHERE THEIR SPIRITS WOULD RETURN.
BUT ALL ALONG, WE OLD SOLDIERS...
HAVE BEEN FADING AWAY, AS THE SAYING GOES.

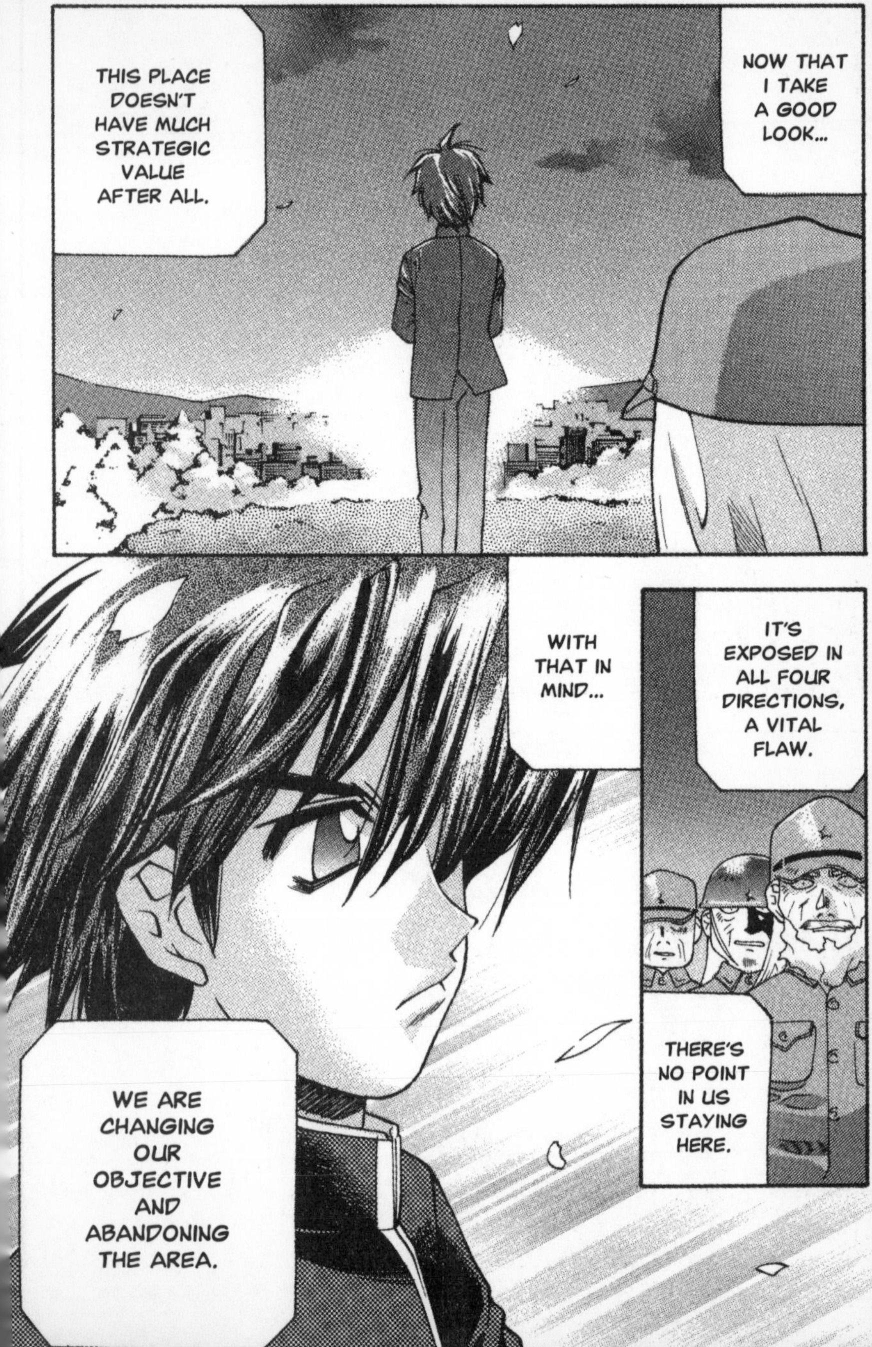
NOW THAT I TAKE A GOOD LOOK...
THIS PLACE DOESN'T HAVE MUCH STRATEGIC VALUE AFTER ALL.
IT'S EXPOSED IN ALL FOUR DIRECTIONS, A VITAL FLAW.
WITH THAT IN MIND...
THERE'S NO POINT IN US STAYING HERE.
WE ARE CHANGING OUR OBJECTIVE AND ABANDONING THE AREA.

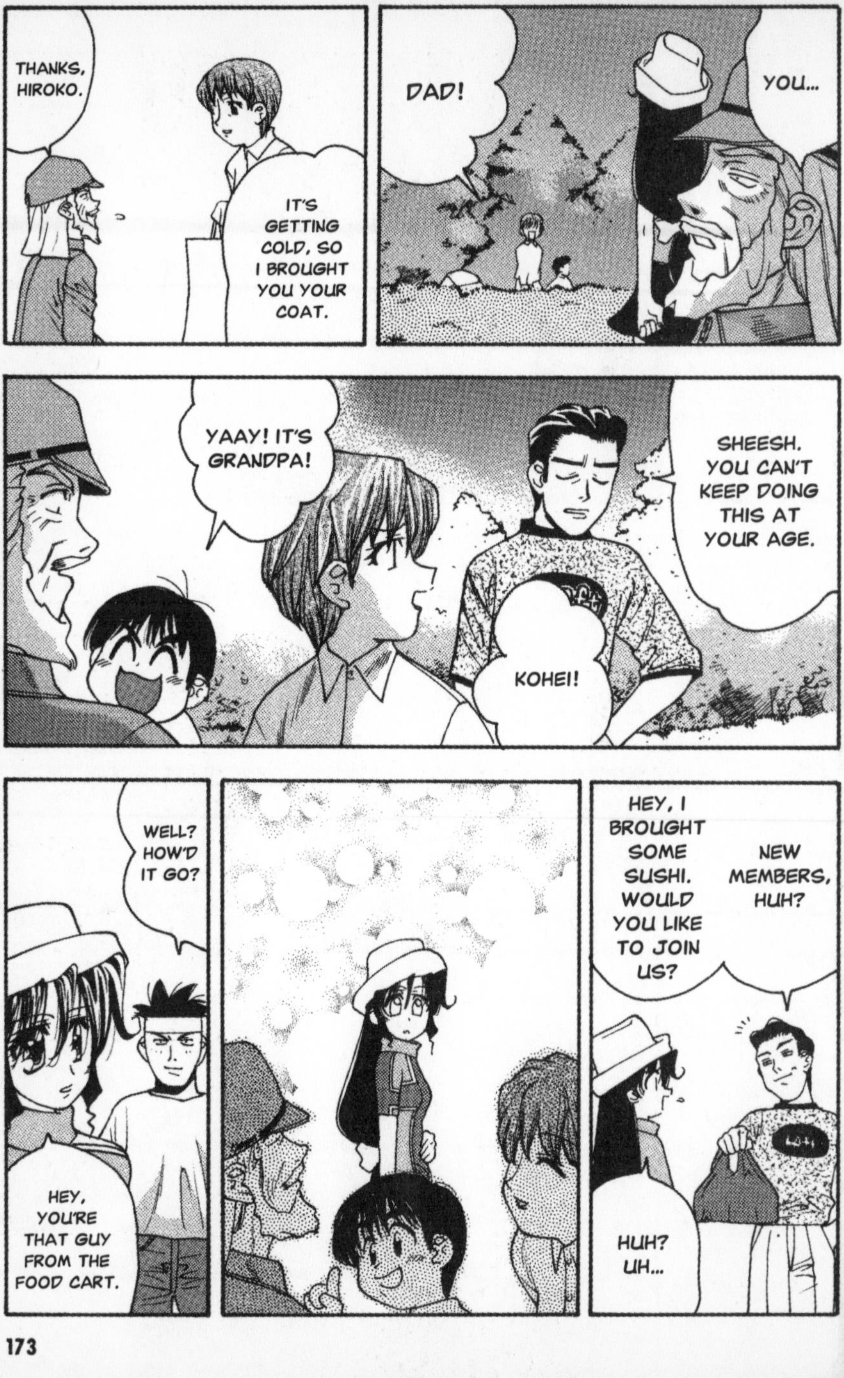
DAD!
YOU...
IT'S GETTING COLD, SO I BROUGHT YOU YOUR COAT.
THANKS, HIROKO.
SHEESH. YOU CAN'T KEEP DOING THIS AT YOUR AGE.
KOHEI!
YAAY! IT'S GRANDPA!
NEW MEMBERS, HUH?
HEY, I BROUGHT SOME SUSHI. WOULD YOU LIKE TO JOIN US?
HUH? UH...
WELL? HOW'D IT GO?
HEY, YOU'RE THAT GUY FROM THE FOOD CART.

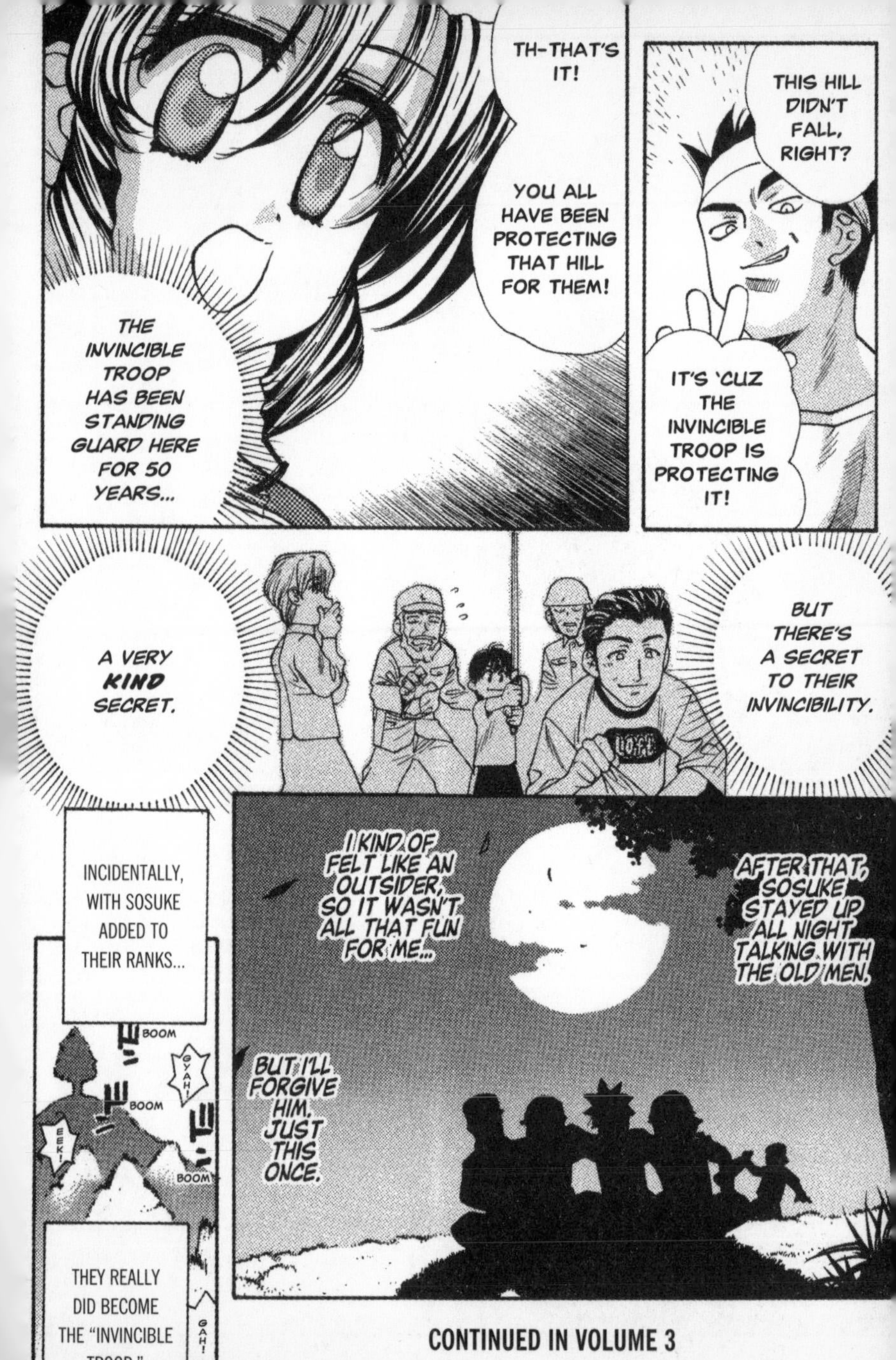
TH-THAT'S IT!
YOU ALL HAVE BEEN PROTECTING THAT HILL FOR THEM!
THIS HILL DIDN'T FALL, RIGHT?
IT'S 'CUZ THE INVINCIBLE TROOP IS PROTECTING IT!
THE INVINCIBLE TROOP HAS BEEN STANDING GUARD HERE FOR 50 YEARS...
BUT THERE'S A SECRET TO THEIR INVINCIBILITY.
A VERY KIND SECRET.
AFTER THAT, SOSUKE STAYED UP ALL NIGHT TALKING WITH THE OLD MEN.
I KIND OF FELT LIKE AN OUTSIDER, SO IT WASN'T ALL THAT FUN FOR ME...
BUT I'LL FORGIVE HIM. JUST THIS ONCE.
INCIDENTALLY, WITH SOSUKE ADDED TO THEIR RANKS...
BOOM
GYAH!
BOOM
EEK!
BOOM
GAH!
THEY REALLY DID BECOME THE "INVINCIBLE TROOP."

CONTINUED IN VOLUME 3

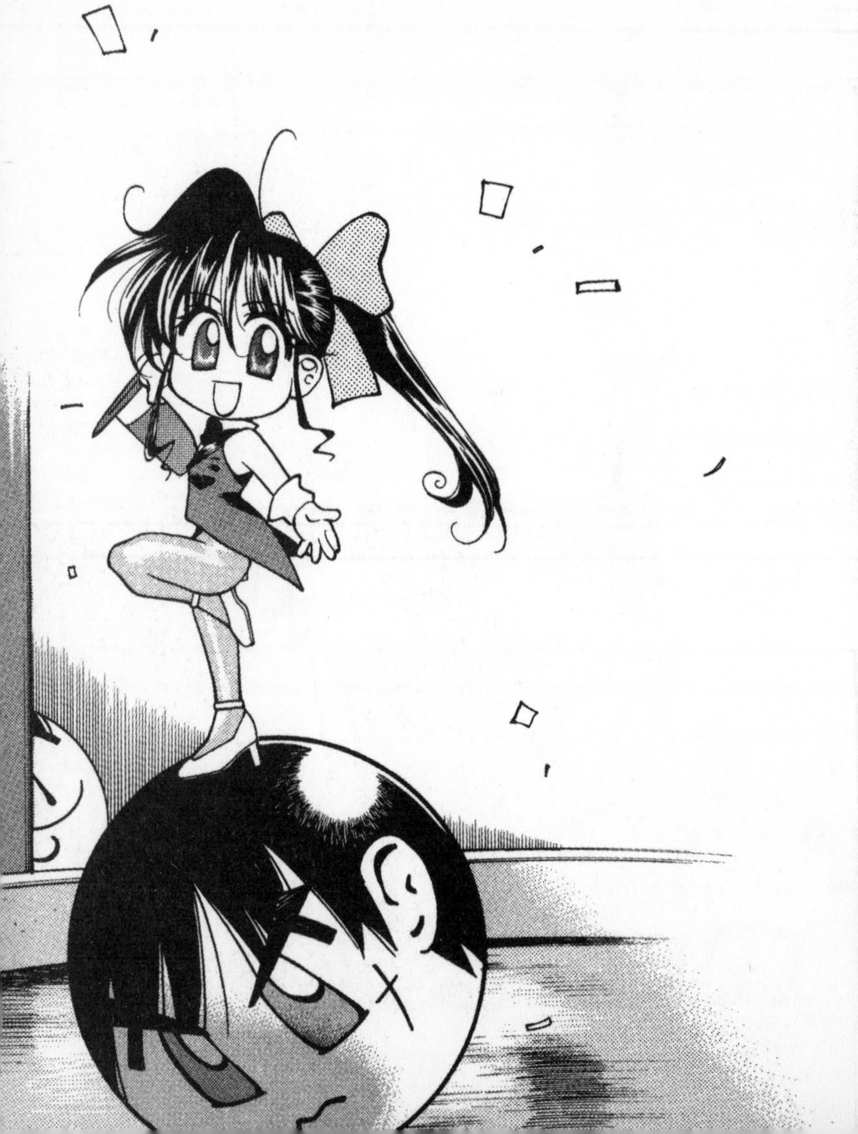

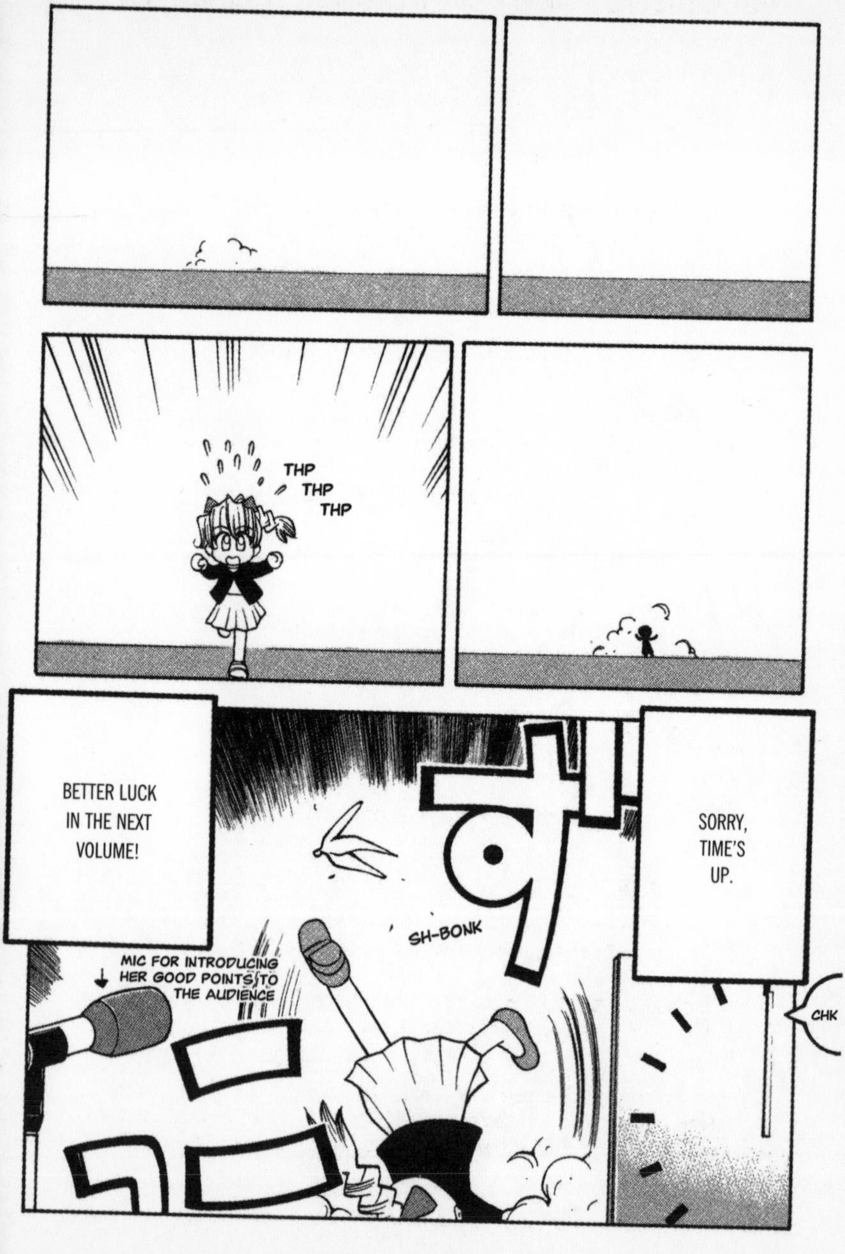
THP
THP
THP
SORRY, TIME'S UP.
CHK
SH-BONK
BETTER LUCK IN THE NEXT VOLUME!
MIC FOR INTRODUCING HER GOOD POINTS TO THE AUDIENCE

FULL METAL PANIC! OVERLOAD! VOLUME TWO

© 2001 Tomohiro NAGAI • Shouji GATOU
© 2001 Shikidouji
Originally published in Japan in 2001 by
KADOKAWA SHOTEN PUBLISHING CO., LTD., Tokyo.
English translation rights arranged with
KADOKAWA SHOTEN PUBLISHING CO., LTD., Tokyo.

Editor **JAVIER LOPEZ**
Translator **AMY FORSYTH**
Graphic Artists **NATALIA REYNOLDS AND MARK MEZA**

Editorial Director **GARY STEINMAN**
Creative Director **JASON BABLER**
Sales and Marketing **CHRIS OARR**
Print Production Manager **BRIDGETT JANOTA**

International Coordinators **TORU IWAKAMI & MIYUKI KAMIYA**

President, CEO & Publisher **JOHN LEDFORD**

Email: editor@adv-manga.com
www.adv-manga.com

www.advfilms.com

For sales and distribution inquiries please call 1.800.282.7202

ADV MANGA™ is a division of A.D. Vision, Inc.
5750 Bintliff Drive, Suite 210, Houston, Texas 77036

English text © 2005 published by A.D. Vision, Inc. under exclusive license.
ADV MANGA is a trademark of A.D. Vision, Inc.

ISBN: 1-4139-0326-6
First printing, September 2005
10 9 8 7 6 5 4 3 2 1
Printed in Canada

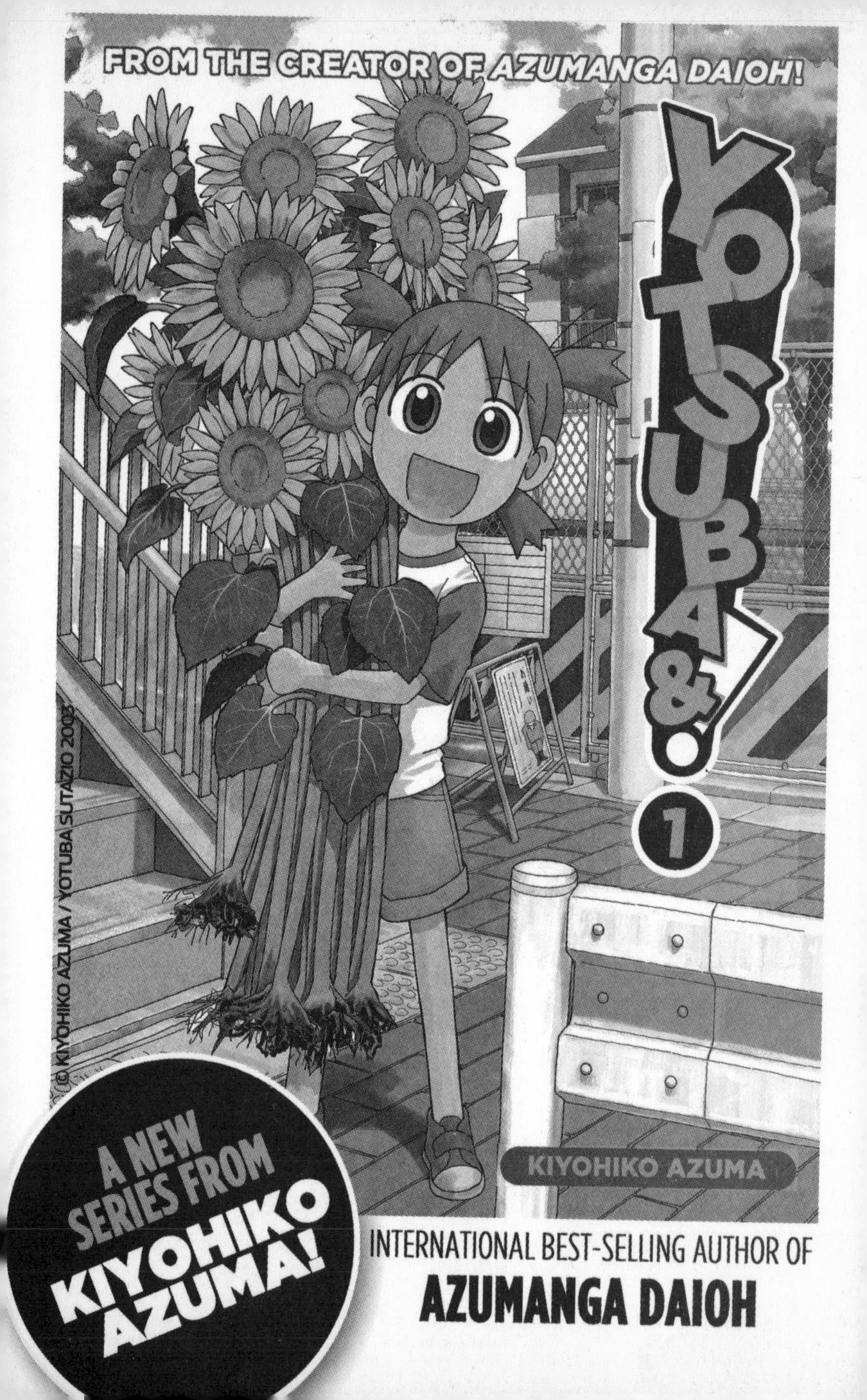
FROM THE CREATOR OF AZUMANGA DAIOH!
YOTSUBA&!
1
KIYOHIKO AZUMA
© KIYOHIKO AZUMA / YOTUBA SUTAZIO 2003
A NEW SERIES FROM KIYOHIKO AZUMA!
INTERNATIONAL BEST-SELLING AUTHOR OF
AZUMANGA DAIOH

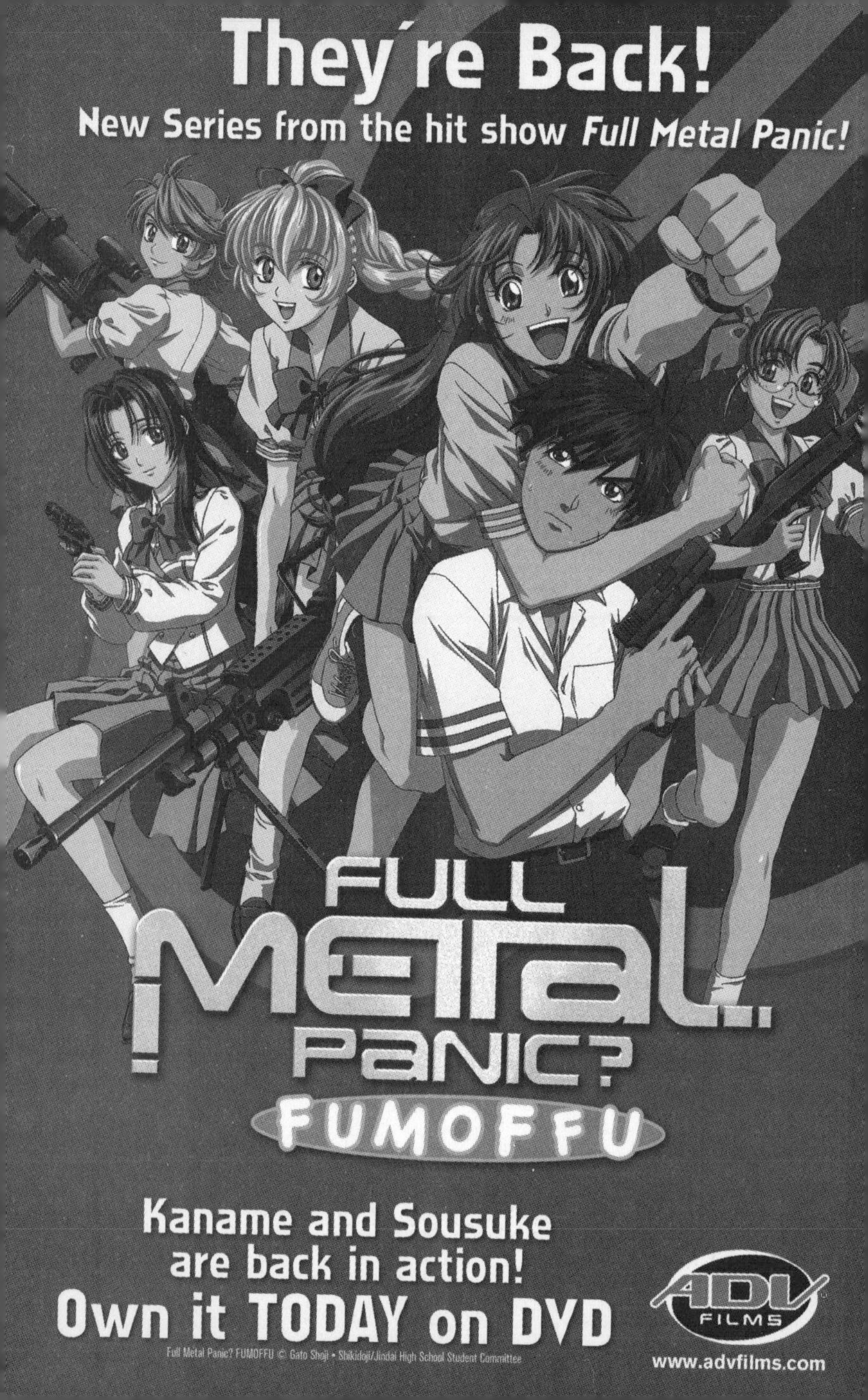
They're Back!
New Series from the hit show Full Metal Panic!
FULL METAL PANIC? FUMOFFU
Kaname and Sousuke are back in action!
Own it TODAY on DVD
Full Metal Panic? FUMOFFU © Gato Shoji • Shikidoji/Jindai High School Student Committee
ADV FILMS
www.advfilms.com

LAGOON ENGINE EINSATZ
A NEW MANGA MASTERPIECE!
FROM THE CREATOR OF D·N·ANGEL

FROM THE PAGES OF
NEWTYPE USA!

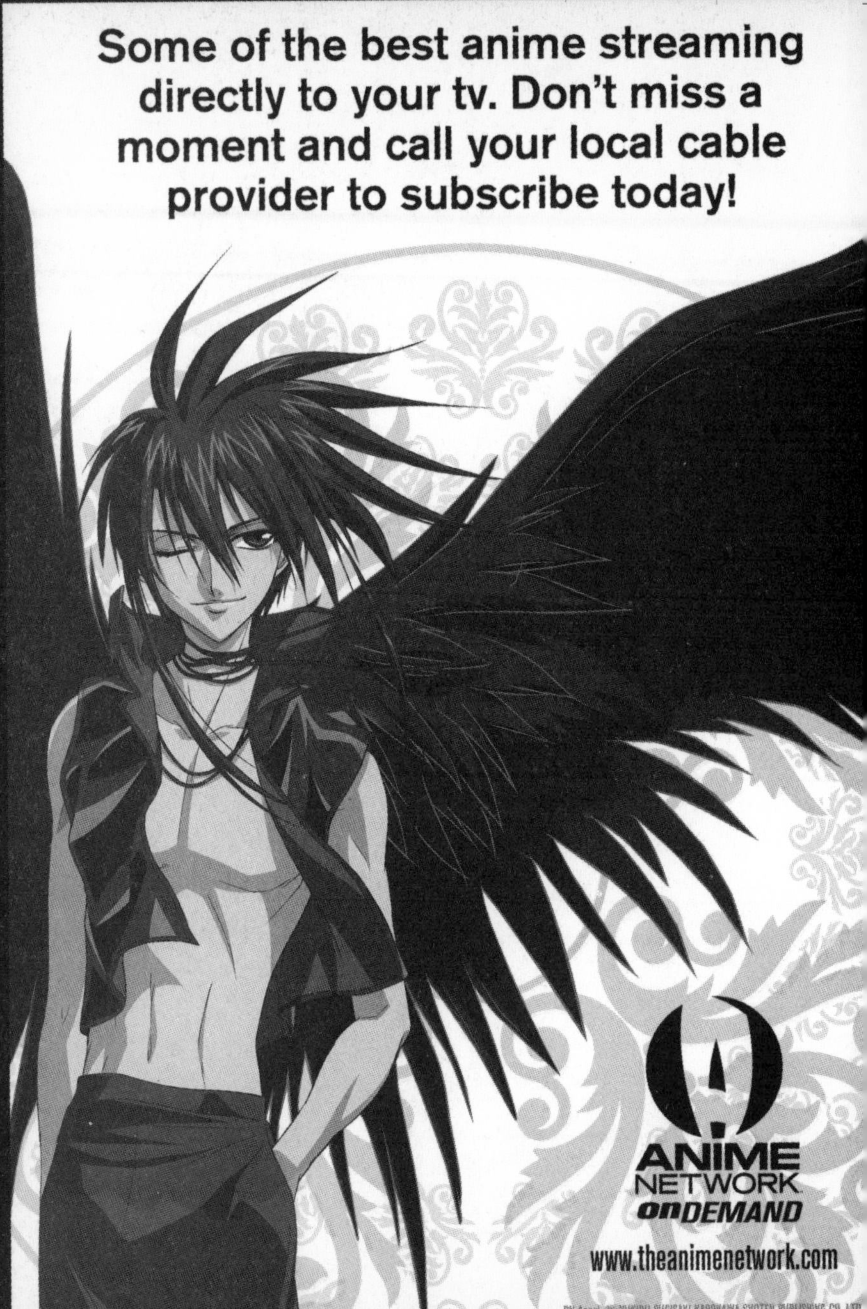
Some of the best anime streaming directly to your tv. Don't miss a moment and call your local cable provider to subscribe today!
ANIME NETWORK onDEMAND
www.theanimenetwork.com
©2005 Anime Network
DN Angel © YUKIRU SUGISAKI-KADOKAWA SHOTEN PUBLISHING CO. LTD
PROJECT DNA TELEVISION TOKYO CHANNEL 12 LTD. All rights reserved.